ARGENTINE DEMOCRACY

THE POLITICS OF INSTITUTIONAL WEAKNESS

ARGENTINE DEMOCRACY

edited by STEVEN LEVITSKY and MARÍA VICTORIA MURILLO

THE PENNSYLVANIA STATE UNIVERSITY PRESS
UNIVERSITY PARK, PENNSYLVANIA

Library of Congress Cataloging-in-Publication Data

Argentine democracy : the politics of institutional weakness /
edited by Steven Levitsky and María Victoria Murillo.
p. cm.
"The book project began with the conference 'Rethinking Dual Transitions:
Argentine Politics in the 1990s in Comparative Perspective,' which was held at
Harvard University's Weatherhead Center for International Affairs in March 2003."
Includes bibliographical references and index.
ISBN 0-271-02715-0 (cloth : alk. paper)
ISBN 0-271-02716-9 (pbk. : alk. paper)
1. Argentina—Politics and government—1983–2002.
2. Argentina—Politics and government—2002- .
3. Argentina—Economic policy.
4. Political culture—Argentina.
5. Democracy—Argentina.
I. Levitsky, Steven.
II. Murillo, María Victoria, 1967- .

JL2031.A745 2005
306.2'0982'09049—dc22
2005019457

The Pennsylvania State University Press is a member of the
Association of American University Presses.

It is the policy of The Pennsylvania State University Press
to use acid-free paper.
Publications on uncoated stock satisfy the minimum requirements of American National Standard
for Information Sciences—Permanence of Paper for
Printed Library
Material, ANSI Z39.48–1992.

To our daughters,
ALEJANDRA SOL MINEO-LEVITSKY *and*
ANAHI CAMILA CABRERA-MURILLO

CONTENTS

ACKNOWLEDGMENTS

Although the idea for this volume was planted before the extraordinary crisis that hit Argentina in December 2001, the project took on greater urgency in its aftermath. There had already existed a need for a good English-language analysis of the political and economic legacies of the 1990s. During that decade, Argentina had combined radical economic reform and democracy in a way that was arguably unparalleled in Latin America. We sought to explain this phenomenon, and to examine the longer-term consequences of the "dual transition." The 2001–2 crisis brought two additional questions to the fore: first, how could a country that had been an international poster child for market-oriented economic reform during the presidency of Carlos Menem (1989–99) suffer such a profound economic collapse—the worst in Argentine history—only a few years after the Menemist decade came to a close? Second, why, in a country that had suffered no fewer than six military coups since 1930, did democracy survive what in many respects was its toughest challenge? As political scientists with both intellectual and personal interest in Argentina, understanding the successes and failures of Argentina's post-1989 democracy was of great importance. Yet the Argentine case also provides an opportunity to draw more general insights about the processes of democratization and market reform that swept across Latin America over the last two decades.

The book project began with the conference "Rethinking Dual Transitions: Argentine Politics in the 1990s in Comparative Perspective," which was held at Harvard University's Weatherhead Center for International Affairs in March 2003. We thank the Weatherhead Center and the David Rockefeller Center for Latin American Studies at Harvard for their generous financial support for the conference. Jeana Flahive of the Weatherhead Center did an extraordinary job running the conference, creating order out of our chaos. All the contributors to this volume presented the initial versions of their chapters in that conference and benefited enormously by the intellectual discussion generated among its participants. We thank the many participants in the conference, including Sergio Berenstein, John Carey, Marcelo Cavarozzi, Javier Corrales, John Coatsworth, Rafael Di

Tella, Rut Diamint, Jorge Domínguez, Jeffry Frieden, Tulio Halperin, Mala Htun, James McGuire, Roberto Saba, Andres Velasco, and Enrique Zuleta Puceiro.

Our three coauthored chapters—the Introduction, Chapter 1, and the Conclusion—were in many respects inspired by the lively discussions that took place during the conference. In writing and revising the chapters, we benefited enormously from conversations with—and comments from—Robert Bates, Ernesto Cabrera, Ernesto Calvo, Javier Corrales, Jorge Domínguez, Sebastian Etchmendy, Peter Hall, Ira Katznelson, Pauline Jones-Luong, Scott Mainwaring, Mario Pecheny, Kenneth Roberts, Juan Carlos Torre, and Kurt Weyland, as well as two anonymous reviewers from Penn State University Press. We also benefited from the editing assistance of Sarah Dix and Maria Koinova.

We also thank the staff at Penn State University Press, and particularly Sanford Thatcher, for their careful assistance in bringing the book to press. Additionally, the project would have not been possible without the support of our home institutions: the Department of Government at Harvard University and the Departments of Political Science and International Affairs at Columbia University.

Finally, for both of us, this project coincided with a long journey to parenthood. Our spouses, Liz Mineo and Ernesto Cabrera, shared with us the immense joy of our daughters' arrivals during 2004. It is to our daughters, Alejandra Sol Mineo-Levitsky and Anahi Camila Cabrera-Murillo, that we dedicate this book.

ACRONYMS

ADEFA	Asociación de Empresarios Fabricantes de Automotores (Automakers' Association)
AOT	Asociación Obreros Textiles (Textile Workers' Association)
APR	Acción por la República (Action for the Republic)
ARI	Argentinos por una República de Iguales (Argentines for a Republic of Equals)
CCC	Corriente Clasista y Combativa (Combative Class Movement)
CEPA	Cámara de Empresarios Petroleros Argentinos (Argentine Chamber of Oil Businessmen)
CGT	Confederación General del Trabajo (General Labor Confederation)
CIS	Centro de Industriales Siderúrgicos (Center for Steel Industrialists)
COFAVI	Coordinadora de Familiares de Víctimas Inocentes (Council of Relatives of Innocent Victims)
CORREPI	Coordinadora contra la Represión Policial e Institucional (Council Against Police and Institutional Repression)
CTA	Congreso de Trabajadores Argentinos (Congress of Argentine Workers)
FATLYF	Federación Argentina de Trabajadores de Luz y Fuerza (Argentine Federation of Light and Power Workers)
FG	Frente Grande (Big Front)
FREPASO	Frente País Solidario (Front for a Country in Solidarity)
ISI	Import Substitution Industrialization
MFR	Movimiento Federal Recrear (Federal Movement for Renewal)
MPN	Movimiento Popular Neuquino (Neuquino Popular Movement)
PANU	Partido Nuevo (New Party)
PI	Partido Intransigente (Intransigent Party)
PJ	Partido Justicialista (Justicialist Party)
SMATA	Sindicato de Mecánicos y Afines del Transporte Automotor (Union of Mechanics and Allied Trades in the Automobile Industry)

SUPE	Sindicato Unico de Petroleros del Estado (Union of State Oil Workers)
TNC	Transnational corporation
UCEDE	Unión del Centro Democrático (Union of the Democratic Center)
UCR	Unión Civica Radical (Radical Civic Union)
UIA	Unión Industrial Argentina (Argentine Industrial Union)
UOCRA	Unión Obreros de la Contrucción de la República Argentina (Union of Construction Workers of the Argentine Republic)
UOM	Unión Obrera Metalúrgica (Metalworkers' Union)
UPCN	Unión Personal Civil de la Nación (Union of Civil Sector Workers)

Introduction

Steven Levitsky and María Victoria Murillo

Between 1989 and 2003, Argentine politics seemed to go full circle: from basket case to international poster child, and back to basket case. During the early 1990s, Argentina was widely hailed as a successful case of market-oriented reform. The far-reaching economic transformation undertaken by President Carlos Menem put an end to a severe hyperinflationary crisis. Unlike other radical reform cases in Latin America, these reforms were undertaken in a context of full-scale democracy. Less than a decade later, however, Argentina plunged into another round of crisis. Massive antigovernment protests, a string of presidential resignations, a debt default, and a collapse into economic depression brought democratic institutions to the brink of rupture. For both Argentines and outside observers, this sudden reversal of fortune seemed eerily familiar: twentieth-century Argentine history was marked by a succession of short-lived miracles followed by extraordinary collapses. Yet the 2001–2 crisis broke with past patterns in an important way. The armed forces, which had toppled six governments between 1930 and 1976, remained on the sidelines, and core democratic institutions remained intact. Amid the worst economic crisis in its history, Argentine democracy proved to be strikingly robust.

This book examines both continuity and change in contemporary Argentine politics. On the one hand, it seeks to explain why Argentina's post-1983 democracy has proven more stable than its predecessors (and many other Latin American democracies). On the other hand, it seeks to explain the country's persistent failure to build enduring political and economic institutions and its continued propensity toward crisis. The chapters in the volume cover a broad range of issues critical to understanding contemporary Argentine politics, including the politics (and legacies) of the Menem government's economic reforms, the evolving role of democratic institutions such as Congress and the judiciary, the transformation (and persistent strength) of Peronism, the crisis of non-Peronist parties, and changing patterns of social and political protest.

From a theoretical standpoint, the chapters focus on five central themes: (1) the causes and consequences of institutional weakness; (2) tensions between radical economic reform and democracy; (3) party system change and the crisis of political representation; (4) the link between subnational- and national-level politics; and (5) the transformation of state-society relations in the postcorporatist era. In this brief introduction, we present an overview of these themes.

THE POLITICS OF INSTITUTIONAL WEAKNESS

The book's central theoretical focus is institutional weakness. By institutions, we mean the humanly devised rules and procedures—both formal and informal—that constrain and enable the behavior of political actors.[1] Following North (1990a, 4–5), we distinguish between institutions (the "rules of the game") and organizations (the "players"). Indeed, few cases illustrate the value of this distinction more clearly than Argentina, where powerful organizations—including trade unions, guerrillas, and the Peronist and Radical parties—have long coexisted with weak rules.[2]

The institutionalist approach that dominated the study of Latin American politics during the 1990s centered primarily on issues of formal institutional design.[3] Given the extensive political and economic reforms undertaken during this period, such a focus is hardly surprising. Yet attention to institutional design has obscured another critical dimension: that of institutional *strength*.[4] Institutional strength may be conceptualized along two dimensions: (1) *enforcement,* or the degree to which the rules that exist on paper are complied with in practice; and (2) *stability,* or the

1. This definition is in line with those of North (1990a, 3–4), O'Donnell (1994, 57–59), and Carey (2000, 735).

2. Indeed, between 1955 and 1983, parties and unions showed extraordinary resilience amid repeated changes in electoral rules and labor legislation.

3. See Shugart and Carey 1992, Linz and Valenzuela 1994, Carey and Shugart 1995 and 1998, Mainwaring and Shugart 1997, Shugart and Haggard 2001, and Morgenstern and Nacif 2002.

4. Exceptions include Mainwaring and Scully 1995, McGuire 1997, and Mainwaring 1999.

degree to which rules survive minor fluctuations in the distribution of power and preferences, such that actors develop shared expectations based on past behavior. Analyses of political institutions often take for granted that rules are routinely enforced and at least minimally stable. Yet in reality, institutions vary considerably on both of these dimensions. Indeed, as Samuel Huntington (1968) argued nearly four decades ago, a major problem in much of the developing world is that institutions of a variety of types have consistently failed to take root. This remains the case in much of Latin America. In the absence of stable and effective rules of the game, both democracy and development are difficult to sustain (O'Donnell 1993, 1994).

Treating enforcement and stability as dimensions along which formal institutions vary—rather than as assumptions—permits us to analyze a broader universe of institutional phenomena. Latin American political institutions, like those throughout the world, are characterized by a mix of stability and fluidity, enforcement and evasion, and formality and informality.

The volume's chapters highlight this variation in Argentina. Some Argentine institutions, including aspects of the federal system, the electoral system, and—since 1983—democracy itself, have proven remarkably robust. Yet Argentina is also plagued by widespread institutional weakness. During the twentieth century, the country experienced a level of institutional instability that was remarkable even for Latin America (Nino 1992). Successive military coups—fourteen military presidents governed the country between 1930 and 1983—repeatedly removed presidents, legislators, and Supreme Court justices before the end of their mandates. Between 1928 and 2003, only two elected presidents—Juan Perón and Carlos Menem—completed their full terms in office, and both Perón and Menem rewrote the constitution to prolong their presidencies. Between 1960 and 1999, notwithstanding a constitutional guarantee of lifetime tenure, Supreme Court justices remained in office, on average, for fewer than four years (Spiller and Tommasi 2000, 22–23). The rules governing executive-legislative relations, elections, and the tax and financial systems were equally fluid. Indeed, in many areas of political and economic life, whenever existing formal rules and procedures were perceived to harm the short-term interests of powerful actors, the rules were circumvented, manipulated, or changed.

The political and economic consequences of institutional weakness were often devastating. In the absence of stable rules of the game, politics became a Hobbesian world of high uncertainty, narrow time horizons, and low trust in which political and economic actors routinely engaged in short-sighted and socially irresponsible behavior (Nino 1992; O'Donnell 1993, 1994). The result was a seemingly endless cycle of political instability and economic failure. Indeed, institutional instability is a major reason why Argentine democracy has consistently underperformed—relative to its level of development—since 1930.[5]

The Argentine case thus points to the importance of moving beyond institutional design to gain a better understanding of the causes and consequences of institutional weakness. Beginning with the historical overview in Chapter 1, several of the contributions to this volume address these questions. The chapter by Mariano Tommasi and Pablo Spiller examines the macroeconomic effects of institutional instability. Tommasi and Spiller argue that the macroeconomic policy instability that plagued Argentina for much of the twentieth century is as important a source of economic underperformance as poor policy design. Policy instability heightens actors' uncertainty and shortens their time horizons, which undermines the cooperation and intertemporal bargains that are so critical to stable growth. Among other factors, the authors locate the cause of Argentine policy fluidity in the instability of the country's overall institutional (regime-level) context between 1930 and 1983.

The chapters by Steven Levitsky and Gretchen Helmke examine the _political_ effects of institutional weakness. Levitsky argues that the absence of stable and binding internal rules frequently creates disorder and conflict within the (Peronist) Partido Justicialista (PJ), but that this internal fluidity also enhances the party's flexibility and adaptive capacity. Indeed, institutional weakness was a major reason why Peronism was able to transform so rapidly from a labor-based party into a vehicle for far-reaching neoliberal reform. Helmke examines the effects of institutional weakness in executive–Supreme Court relations. Argentina's 1853 constitution guarantees Supreme Court justices lifetime tenure, which should permit justices to act with considerable independence of the executive. Yet as Helmke shows, this constitutional guarantee has been routinely violated since the 1940s, as incoming (civilian and military) governments have repeatedly removed unfriendly justices and replaced them with allies. Rather than the independent judiciary prescribed by the Constitution, then, Helmke finds a pattern of "strategic defection," in which justices support the executive while its hold on power is firm but then defect to the opposition when they suspect that the government is on its way out.

The book's conclusion examines the theoretical implications of institu-

5. As Przeworski and Limongi point out, Argentina is the wealthiest country in history (in terms of per capita income) to suffer a democratic breakdown (1997, 170).

tional weakness. It argues that much of the comparative politics literature on institutions is based on the assumption that formal rules are stable and effective—an assumption that does not hold up well in much of Latin America. The conclusion then uses the Argentine case to develop some initial hypotheses about the causes and consequences of institutional weakness.

COMBINING DEMOCRACY AND ECONOMIC REFORM

The book also revisits recent debates about the relationship between democracy and radical market-oriented reform. Much of the early literature on the politics of economic liberalization was pessimistic about the compatibility of democracy and market reform. Because of the status quo bias of voters (Fernández and Rodrik 1991) and the influence of concentrated reform "losers" (Haggard and Kaufman 1992, 1995), reform was said to be more likely to be achieved under nondemocratic regimes. At the very least, it was said to require a substantial concentration of executive power (Przeworski 1991; Haggard and Kaufman 1992, 1995), which, according to several authors, tended to reduce accountability and citizen participation (O'Donnell 1994; Oxhorn and Ducatenzeiler 1998). More recent scholarship has pointed to conditions under which far-reaching liberalizing reforms were possible under democracy. For example, scholars highlighted the role of hyperinflationary crises in generating public support for radical reform (Weyland 2002b), and in encouraging politicians to undertake those reforms (Stokes 2001).[6]

A second strand of scholarship focused on the construction and maintenance of pro-reform coalitions through policy concessions and side payments that compensated potential economic "losers" (Gibson 1997; Murillo 1997, 2001, 2002) and, in some cases, transformed them into winners (Corrales 1998; Etchemendy 2001). A third group of scholars highlighted the role of strong governing parties, legislative coalitions, and unified government in achieving policy reform under democracy (Shugart and Haggard 2001; Corrales 2002). Taken together, this research pointed to the political nature of economic reform processes, and it suggested that political factors such as public opinion, coalition-building, and institutions could facilitate market reforms under democracy.

The Argentine case both confirms and raises questions about these the-

6. Some scholars argued that market reforms can serve democratic goals by breaking ties between economic and political elites, reducing corruption and rent-seeking, and dispersing power. See, for example, Domínguez 1998, 73.

ories. Argentina was arguably the most radical case of economic reform undertaken in Latin America during the 1990s, and it was the only case in which radical reform was successfully implemented under democracy. The Menem government's success in carrying out these reforms offers evidence of how hyperinflation may generate public support for risk-laden policies (Palermo and Torre 1992; Weyland 2002b), and the success of the 1991 Convertibility Law in ending hyperinflation showed how economic stabilization can be used to build electoral support for reform-oriented governments (Etchegaray and Elordi 2001). The Argentine reforms also highlight the crucial role of disciplined governing parties. Peronism not only provided the Menem government with a stable legislative majority (Mustapic 2001; Corrales 2002), but it also played a central role in defusing working- and lower-class protest (Auyero 2000; Levitsky 2003).

Finally, the Argentine case highlights the importance of constructing and maintaining reform coalitions, which often entails political and policy exchanges that compensate potential "losers" under reform. As Sebastian Etchemendy's chapter demonstrates, the Menem government used a series of concessions and side payments to gain or maintain the support of powerful industrialists and trade unions during the early and mid-1990s. Without the cooperation of these potential losers, the Menem reforms would have been extremely difficult to carry out under democracy. Similarly, Kent Eaton's chapter highlights the role of provincial governors in making or breaking reform programs. Thus, the 1992 Coparticipation Agreement between Menem and the governors, which reduced the percentage of federal tax revenues distributed to the provinces but guaranteed the provinces a minimum revenue floor, was critical to the success of the government's fiscal adjustment during the early 1990s.

Yet the Argentine case also raises questions about the longer-term compatibility of democracy and radical market-oriented reform. The Argentine reforms—and the political process that made them possible—were decidedly double-edged. Although convertibility ended hyperinflation, it was a highly rigid policy solution that both eroded export competitiveness and limited the government's capacity to respond to external shocks. Side payments to unions and industrialists helped to limit social protest and distributive conflict, and concessions to Peronist governors helped to ensure legislative discipline and electoral support in the provinces (Jones and Hwang, this volume; Gibson and Calvo 2000; Calvo and Murillo, this volume). Yet these concessions had significant negative effects over the course of the decade. As Etchemendy shows, the very coalition that made the Menem reforms possible also prevented the government from taking steps to enhance Argentina's export competitiveness or attending to the growing pool of unemployed workers. And as Eaton argues, the provincial revenue floor (*piso mínimo*) established by the 1992 Coparticipation Agreement created a devastating fiscal burden after the economy slid into recession in 1998. Each of these consequences contributed in an important way to the 2001 political-economic crisis.

In retrospect, then, the Menem reforms were marked by an important paradox. On the one hand, it can be plausibly argued that the speed and extent of the Menem reforms would not have been possible—at least not under democracy—without convertibility and a series of political and policy deals with governors, unions, and industrialists. On the other hand, these facilitating conditions *were themselves causes of the post-Menemist crisis.* This outcome—together with crises in other "poster child" cases (e.g., Bolivia, Dominican Republic, and Peru) and a troubling decline in public support for democracy in much of the region[7]—raises serious questions about the longer-term sustainability of radical economic reform.

POLITICAL PARTIES, REPRESENTATION, AND DEMOCRACY

A third theme of the volume is that of political parties and contemporary crises of representation in Latin America. Recent literature has pointed to the importance of strong parties and institutionalized party systems in building and maintaining democracy in Latin America (Mainwaring and Scully 1995; Roberts 1998; Mainwaring 1999; Corrales 2001; Levitsky and Cameron 2003). At the same time, however, scholars have pointed to a disturbing regional trend: in many countries, economic crisis and radical market reform generated severe crises of representation, which led, in some cases, to the collapse of established parties and the rise of antisystem or "neopopulist" outsiders (Perelli 1995; Roberts 1995; Weyland 1999; Cavarozzi and Abal Medina 2003). In much of Latin America, party weakness and party system fragmentation were associated with executive-legislative conflict, policy failure, problems of governability, and the crisis or breakdown of democratic regimes (Mainwaring and Scully 1995).

Argentina offers an interesting case with respect to these regional trends. Although the party system's hegemonic tendencies and failure to effectively represent powerful socioeconomic actors undermined regime

7. See the *Economist*, August 14, 2004, p. 35.

stability during much of the twentieth century,[8] the post-1983 party system was more competitive and integrative, and thus was more conducive to regime stability. At the heart of this change was Peronism. As Levitsky's chapter shows, the PJ's transformation from a labor-based party into a patronage-based machine facilitated its survival in the neoliberal era. Because it was the most powerful political force in the country, Peronism's adaptation and survival was critical to democratic governance. The PJ's persistent legislative strength helped prevent the kind of executive-legislative deadlock that undermined governability in Brazil, Ecuador, Guatemala, and Peru in the early 1990s. In addition, the PJ's continued electoral success reduced the space for "neopopulist" outsiders of the kind seen in countries like Peru, Venezuela, and Ecuador (Roberts 1995; Weyland 1999).

After 1999, the party system fell into crisis. As the chapter by Juan Carlos Torre shows, the disastrous performance of the Alianza por el Trabajo, la Educación, y la Justicia—a coalition of the centrist Radical Civic Union (UCR) and the center-left Front for a Country in Solidarity (FREPASO)—government between 1999 and 2001 generated a severe crisis of political representation, which led to the massive protests of December 2001, a large-scale citizen assault on the political class that was crystallized in the widely heard slogan "Throw everyone out!" Yet as Torre notes, antiparty sentiment was not as widespread as the protests seemed to suggest. Rather, it was largely confined to (non-Peronist) urban and educated middle-class Argentines, who had historically backed the UCR and smaller center-left and center-right parties. The failure of the Alianza alienated many of these voters, who expressed their disaffection first by abandoning the UCR and FREPASO (in the October 2001 midterm election) and later through protest against the political establishment. Hence, whereas Peronism's electoral base remained largely intact during and after the 2001–2 crisis, the UCR and FREPASO virtually collapsed.

The post-1999 Argentine party system thus appears to have suffered a *partial* collapse. Peronism's electoral resilience prevented a full-scale party system collapse along the lines of Venezuela and Peru. However, unlike in Chile, Mexico, Uruguay, and even Brazil, no stable partisan alternative emerged to represent disaffected or previously excluded voters in Argentina. The failure of FREPASO, the center-right Action for the Republic, and other new parties to build national organizations and enduring linkages to voters left non-Peronist forces fragmented and disorganized. As a result,

8. See O'Donnell 1973, Cavarozzi 1986, Gibson 1996, and McGuire 1997.

the predominantly middle-class non-Peronist electorate has become increasingly volatile.

FEDERALISM AND THE LINK BETWEEN SUBNATIONAL AND NATIONAL POLITICS

Recent analyses of Latin America politics have pointed to the importance of subnational political processes in shaping national-level political and economic outcomes.[9] Although Latin American politics have traditionally been characterized as highly centralized (Wiarda 1973; Veliz 1980), democratization in federalist countries like Argentina, Brazil, and Mexico, plus far-reaching decentralizing reforms in countries like Bolivia, Colombia, and Venezuela, drew attention to the role of local and provincial politics in the region (Penfold 1999; O'Neill 2003). Subnational politics are increasingly seen as critical to electoral and legislative outcomes (Samuels and Snyder 2001; Samuels 2003), and powerful governors in Brazil, Argentina, and—increasingly—Mexico are said to be important veto players in the policymaking process (Ames 2002; Faletti 2003).

Subnational politics are crucial to understanding national-level politics and policymaking in Argentina.[10] Although Argentina has maintained a federal system since 1853, regime instability and authoritarian rule obscured the importance of the provinces during much of the twentieth century. Yet provincial governors tend to accumulate enormous power under democratic rule. Indeed, as Eaton's chapter demonstrates, the governors proved to be powerful—and at times decisive—players under both Menem and his successors.

The chapters by Jones and Hwang and Calvo and Murillo highlight how the provinces shape national-level democratic politics in Argentina. In their analysis of Argentine legislative politics, Jones and Hwang argue that whereas the most important unit of analysis in studying the U.S. Congress is the individual legislator, the key unit of analysis in Argentina is the provincial party boss (frequently the governor). Individual legislators are elected on provincial party lists, and in most provinces, control over local patronage resources allows governors to control the list-making process. Legislators thus depend heavily on provincial bosses to advance their political careers, which means that governors exert substantial influence over

9. See Gibson 1997 and 2004; Garman, Haggard, and Willis 2001; Snyder 2001a; Eaton 2002; Rodden and Wibbels 2002; and O'Neill 2003.

10. See Calvo and Abal Medina 2001, Saiegh and Tommasi 1999c, Remmer and Wibbels 2001, and Gibson and Calvo 2000.

the legislative process. In effect, the Congress is run by a cartel of provincial bosses. Contrary to analyses that have depicted Argentine presidents as dominating Congress, then, Jones and Hwang argue that executives must negotiate the support of the governors to get bills through the legislature.

Calvo and Murillo examine the link between provincial electoral politics and national-level political outcomes. They argue that the weakness of non-Peronist parties in the peripheral provinces, Peronism's more effective use of patronage resources in the electoral arena, and the overrepresentation of peripheral provinces in Congress gave the PJ a virtual lock over the Senate and a majority of governorships during the post-1983 period. These dynamics effectively ensure divided government when non-Peronist parties capture the presidency, as occurred under both Alfonsín (1983–89) and the Alianza (1999–2001). Calvo and Murillo argue that this inability to build stable subnational (and hence legislative) coalitions was a major reason why both the Alfonsín and Alianza governments fell victim to governability crises.

THE TRANSFORMATION OF STATE-SOCIETY RELATIONS IN THE POSTCORPORATIST ERA

A fifth theme is the transformation of state-society relations in the postcorporatist era. During much of the twentieth century, corporatist institutions served as a primary mechanism of state-society linkage in many Latin American countries (Collier and Collier 1979, 1991). Under the old "state-centric matrix" (Cavarozzi 1994), corporatist labor and peasant organizations emerged as the most important representatives of popular sector interests. In several countries, labor movements became privileged—and powerful—sociopolitical actors. The political and economic liberalization processes of the 1980s and 1990s undermined the state-centric matrix, weakening—and in some cases, destroying—traditional corporatist arrangements linking state and society (Oxhorn 1998). The growth of the urban informal sector and subsequent decline in union memberships reduced once powerful labor movements to increasingly marginal players in the political arena. As unions weakened, many turned inward, protecting their remaining memberships and organizations (Murillo and Schrank, forthcoming), but growing increasingly unrepresentative of the—largely unorganized—urban popular sectors.

The weakening of corporatist institutions gave rise to a variety of new organizations, identities, and forms of social protest (Chalmers, Martin,

and Piester 1997; López Maya 1999). For some scholars, the new postcorporatist scenario opened up promising new avenues for grassroots participation and alternative—and potentially more democratic—patterns of
representation (Fox 1994; Chalmers, Martin, and Piester 1997). In this
scenario, the decline of populism and corporatism paves the way for increased popular sector participation through social movements, identity-
based movements, NGOs, civic associations, and other components of an
emerging civil society. Other scholars have painted a less optimistic picture of postcorporatist Latin America (Oxhorn 1998; Roberts 1998, 2002;
Auyero 2000). These scholars view the decline of organized labor and
traditional left-wing and populist parties as leading to the fragmentation
and demobilization of the popular sectors. They envision not vibrant popular and civic organizations but a scenario in which the poor are increasingly organized along clientelist lines and subject to plebiscitarian and
even authoritarian appeals.

Argentina represents a crucial case of the transformation of state-society linkages. The Peronist labor movement, represented by the General
Labor Confederation (CGT) was one of the most powerful in postwar Latin
America; and Argentina's corporatist institutions were among the most
developed in the region. Beginning in the mid-1970s, however, the industrial unions that had been the core of the Peronist movement were weakened by far-reaching social structural change. The trade opening
undertaken by the 1976–83 military government decimated the industrial
workforce. The number of blue-collar workers declined by more than 10
percent between 1975 and 1985 (Palomino 1987), and many leading industrial unions lost between a third and a half of their memberships (Abós
1986, 189). By the mid-1980s, the largest unions in the CGT were located
in the public and service sectors (Godio, Palomino, and Wachendorfer
1988). Labor was further weakened during the 1990s. The Menem reforms reduced the size of the industrial and public sectors and triggered a
steep increase in unemployment.[11] At the same time, the informal sector
expanded rapidly (CEPAL 1999), as did the percentage of the workforce
working under "precarious" conditions (without contracts and benefits)
(Lindemboim, Cerino, and González 2000).

Although unions preserved their organizational structures during the
1990s (Murillo 1997, 2001), their influence waned considerably. The CGT
ceased to be a major player in the policymaking arena, and powerful

---

11. Public sector employment (as a percentage of total employment) was slashed by
nearly a third during the Menem period (CEPAL 1999) even as provincial-level public sector
employment increased (Orlanski 1994).

unions turned increasingly away from collective demand-making, limiting themselves primarily to the delivery of selective or club goods. Labor's influence in the political arena also declined. As Peronism shifted its urban organization from unions to clientelist networks, union representation in the PJ leadership and in Congress fell precipitously (Levitsky 2003).

The decline of corporatism gave rise to new forms of social organization and protest. Among the middle classes, the post-1983 period saw the unprecedented emergence of civic groups organized around issues of citizen rights and government accountability. As the chapter by Enrique Peruzzotti argues, these new citizen demands were rooted in the "rights-oriented" political culture that emerged in the aftermath of the 1976–83 dictatorship. This cultural shift was manifested in the powerful human rights movement during the 1980s. Although the human rights movement weakened during the Menem years, it engendered a multitude of smaller "rights-oriented" groups aimed at fostering civic participation and government accountability (Peruzzotti 2002a). Buttressed by the rise of watchdog journalism, the new "politics of accountability" played an important role in denouncing and publicizing government abuses during the 1990s.

Among the working and lower classes, several patterns emerged. First, labor protest was increasingly confined to provincial public sector employees (Farinetti 2002). Because public sector employment had such a profound community-wide impact in many peripheral provinces, these protests frequently brought public workers together with pensioners, unemployed workers, and community activists (Auyero 2003; Murillo and Ronconi 2004). Although these protests nourished the provincial branches of the militant Congress of Argentine Workers (CTA), which actively organized unemployed workers (Svampa and Pereyra 2003), they rarely took on a national character.

The post-1989 period also saw the emergence of several new forms of popular sector protest, including provincial "uprisings" (*puebladas*), semi-organized looting, and most notably, blockades of major roads and highways organized by unemployed people (*piqueteros*) seeking public sector jobs or unemployment aid. These emerging patterns of protest are analyzed in the chapter by Javier Auyero. Although the *piqueteros* first emerged in the interior provinces during the 1990s, they spread quickly to the urban regions.[12] By 2002, *piquetero* groups had crystallized into several

---

12. The growth of the movement was assisted by the influx of former union activists and by the De la Rúa government's decision to allow local *piquetero* organizations to distribute unemployment aid (Svampa and Pereyra 2003).

national organizations and had effectively displaced the CGT as the most important channel for popular sector protest. Organized along territorial, rather than sectoral lines, *piquetero* groups used their access to government subsidy programs as selective incentives to build and maintain their organizations. Through 2005, however, the *piqueteros* had not emerged as a coherent national-level actor. Rather, the movement remained fragmented politically, with some groups aligning themselves with militant left-wing parties and others establishing ties to local Peronist machines.

Although *piquetes, puebladas,* and other popular sector protests appear to represent a sharp break with the top-down patterns of popular organization characteristic of corporatism and clientelism, Auyero argues that the break is not as radical or discontinuous as it may appear. The participants in provincial riots and urban lootings are frequently embedded in (and mobilized by) the very clientelist networks that they are said to replace, and the resources for at least some of these new popular protests are often drawn from partisan and other not-so-new channels. Auyero's chapter thus warns against drawing a stark dichotomy between "old" top-down forms of organization and "new" bottom-up forms. Many of the most dynamic social movements in contemporary Argentina combine important elements of new and old.

Indeed, notwithstanding the high-profile nature of *piquetero* protests, much of the urban poor was incorporated into clientelist networks during the 1990s. Widespread unemployment, economic scarcity, and state retrenchment increased the influence of local brokers and party bosses (usually Peronist) who could provide access to public jobs and other state resources (Auyero 2000; Gibson and Calvo 2000; Levitsky 2003). Hence, although clientelism was hardly new in Argentina, particularly in the poor interior provinces, it took on enormous social and political importance— and spread increasingly to urban areas—after 1989.

In sum, as elsewhere in Latin America, Argentina's emerging postcorporatist scenario reveals a trend away from national-level collective organizations and nationally defined class identities toward localized, territorially defined identities. Most of the new social actors—including the CTA, *piqueteros,* and rights-oriented groups based in the middle class—resist close ties to the state. Emerging social organizations have yet to forge strong national collective identities and have increasingly abandoned demands for material public goods. Material demands have largely been reduced to private goods (in the form of clientelism) or club goods (those limited to group members), such as the side payments offered to union members during the 1990s and state subsidies distributed to *piqueteros* after 2001. To the extent that civic and social organizations demand public goods, these demands are limited to nonmaterial issues such as rights, justice, and more recently, public security.

THE ARGENTINE CASE AND THEORY BUILDING IN COMPARATIVE POLITICS

Within the field of comparative politics, Argentina is known—indeed, famous—for its exceptionalism. In both politics and economics, the country's twentieth-century development is said to defy conventional theory (Nun 1967; Huntington 1968; O'Donnell 1973; Mallon and Sourrouille 1975; Waisman 1987; Adelman 1994; Przeworski and Limongi 1997). For example, Argentina has been cast as a case of a wealthy country that experienced a "reversal" of development (Waisman 1987; also Adelman 1994) and military coups despite a comparatively high level of socioeconomic development and a large, educated middle class (Nun 1967; Huntington 1968, 83–84; O'Donnell 1973). In some cases, scholars simply pointed to Argentina as a curious but theoretically unimportant outlier (Przeworski and Limongi 1997). In others, scholars developed specific—idiographic— explanations of Argentine "exceptionalism" (Peralta-Ramos 1978; Waisman 1987). Another group of scholars has used analyses of the Argentine case to both critique existing approaches and develop alternative theories that extend beyond Argentina.[13]

In many respects, this volume follows in the last tradition. It uses the Argentine case to highlight limitations in the existing literature on political institutions and to develop some hypotheses about the causes and consequences of institutional weakness that can help refine that literature. We do not, however, treat Argentina as an exceptional case. Institutional weakness is widespread in much of the developing and postcommunist worlds. Indeed, cases of stable and widely enforced political institutions (such as the United States and other advanced industrialized democracies) are relatively uncommon. Hence, Argentina, with its unstable and weakly enforced institutions, is representative of a much larger universe of cases than the handful of advanced industrialized democracies upon which most of the leading theories of democratic institutions are based.

The Argentine case is thus an excellent one from which to build hypotheses about the causes and effects of institutional weakness. Country studies can (and frequently do) play an important role in building and testing theories in comparative politics (Eckstein 1975; George and Bennett 2004).

---

13. The most influential of these studies is, of course, O'Donnell 1973.

Individual countries do not necessarily represent single cases or observations. Rather, the comparative method may be used within country studies to increase the number of observable implications of hypotheses in a variety of ways (King, Keohane, and Verba 1994). For example, subnational comparisons of provinces or regions, economic sectors, or sector-level organizations (such as unions) allow scholars to engage in systematic comparison while holding historical, cultural, macroeconomic, and national institutional factors constant (Snyder 2001b).[14] Alternatively, studies of national level institutions such as legislatures or Supreme Courts may increase the number of observable implications by comparing those institutions over time, analyzing—usually via quantitative methods—high-frequency events within those institutions (such as legislative votes or Supreme Court rulings), or shifting the level of analysis to individual bureaucrats, legislators, or legislative committees.[15]

A critical advantage of subnational comparison is that it enhances unit homogeneity. Although unit homogeneity is generally a standard assumption in quantitative analysis, these assumptions often do not hold in cross-national comparative research. Political, economic, and cultural differences between countries often ensure that political structures or rules that appear similar on paper function quite differently in practice. By ensuring greater homogeneity along these dimensions, within-country comparisons can enhance our confidence in the validity of our findings.

The value of within-country comparison is clearly seen in the case of the United States. Notwithstanding its single-country status, the United States has been a rich source for theory building in a range of areas, including voting behavior, executive-legislative relations, legislative politics, judicial systems, bureaucracies, and political parties and party systems.[16] Within-country analyses of the United States benefited from the fact that they could hold a number of important variables constant, including the country's extraordinarily stable macroinstitutional context.

The Argentine case may be similarly useful in theory building, in part because it offers such a distinct institutional setting. In contrast to the United States, the Argentine macroinstitutional environment is character-

---

14. For subnational comparisons across a single policy dimension, see Locke 1995 and Snyder 2001a. For cross-sectional comparisons within and across countries, see Vogel 1996 and Murillo 2001.

15. In explaining why his study of Brazilian political institutions and their effect on policymaking is not a case study, Ames (2002, 33) describes how a large number of observations derived from a variety of quantitative and qualitative data provides variation in measures across states, time periods, and levels of government.

16. Weingast (2002) and Orren and Skowronek (2002) provide excellent summaries of these literatures from rational choice and historical institutionalist perspectives, respectively.

ized by pervasive *instability*, which allows scholars to use the comparative method to generate and test theories about how actors and institutions operate in a context of institutional weakness. The chapters in this volume employ within-country comparisons in a variety of ways, including comparisons across subnational territorial units (Calvo and Murillo, Auyero), economic sectors (Etchemendy), and policy areas (Tommasi and Spiller). Others compare national-level institutions over time (Eaton, Helmke, Jones and Hwang). Each of these analyses uses the Argentine case to generate, test, or refine theories whose application extends well beyond Argentina.

ORGANIZATION OF THE BOOK

The book proceeds in the following way. Chapter 1, by Levitsky and Murillo, provides an overview of contemporary Argentine politics. The chapters that follow are organized into four sections. The first section focuses on the politics of economic policymaking and reform. Chapter 2, by Tommasi and Spiller, analyzes the causes and consequences of Argentina's long pattern of policymaking instability. Chapter 3, by Etchemendy, examines the politics of the Menem reforms, showing how the construction of a pro-reform coalition both facilitated radical reform and helped to undermine the longer-term sustainability of the reforms. Chapter 4, by Eaton, analyzes the relationship between the executive branch and the provinces and its fiscal impact during the Menemist and post-Menemist periods.

The second section looks at Argentina's democratic institutions after 1989. Chapter 5, by Jones and Hwang, focuses on Congress, and particularly the crucial link between provincial bosses and the organization of the legislature. Chapter 6, by Helmke, analyzes the behavior of the Supreme Court under Menem and his successors.

The third section examines changes and continuities in the party system. Chapter 7, by Levitsky, examines the post-1983 transformation of Peronism, arguing that the PJ's weakly institutionalized party structure enabled it to adapt and survive in the neoliberal era. Chapter 8, by Torre, looks at the non-Peronist parties, showing how the dramatic failures of the UCR and FREPASO triggered a profound crisis of representation among the Argentine middle classes. Chapter 9, by Calvo and Murillo, shows how the persistent strength of clientelist organization in the peripheral provinces and the overrepresentation of those provinces in Congress have assured the PJ a virtual lock on the Senate, making it extremely difficult for non-Peronist parties to govern.

The final section of the book focuses on new forms of sociopolitical organization and protest. Chapter 10, by Peruzzotti, examines the emergence of new (predominantly middle-class) "rights oriented" civic movements during the post-1983 period. Chapter 11, by Auyero, focuses on working- and lower-class protest, examining the origins of the street blockades, lootings, and other forms of protest seen during the 2001–2 crisis.

The conclusion, by Levitsky and Murillo, examines the origins and consequences of institutional instability in Argentina, as well as its implications for institutionalist theories in comparative politics.

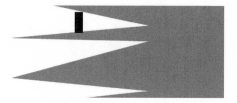

Institutions, Actors, and the Politics of Economic Reform

Building Castles in the Sand?
The Politics of Institutional Weakness in Argentina

Steven Levitsky and María Victoria Murillo

Few countries have puzzled social scientists more than Argentina. Given its level of development, large, educated middle class, and comparatively egalitarian class structure, the country has consistently "underperformed" in terms of both economic growth and democratic stability.[1] Indeed, it is the wealthiest country in history to experience a military coup (Przeworski and Limongi 1997, 170).

The central argument of this book is that a major cause of Argentina's underperformance was persistent and widespread institutional instability. Beginning in 1930, a series of military coups set in motion a self-reinforcing pattern in which periodic crises led to the subversion or collapse of a wide range of political and economic institutions. In the absence of stable and effective rules of the game, political and economic actors operated in a Hobbesian world of extreme uncertainty, short time horizons, and low levels of trust and cooperation (Nino 1992; O'Donnell 1994). As a result, the Argentine polity and economy remained highly vulnerable to crisis, praetorian conflict, and breakdown.

The 1983 democratic transition put an end to the cycle of military coups and ushered in an unprecedented period of democratic rule. The new democratic institutions proved strikingly robust, surviving the hyperinflationary crisis of 1989, the radical economic reforms of the 1990s, and the

---

1. See O'Donnell 1973, Waisman 1987, Adelman 1994, and Przeworski and Limongi 1997.

economic collapse of 2001–2. Many of the core market institutions created after 1989 also proved durable. Yet a variety of other political and economic institutions remained weak, and the political and economic meltdown of 2001–2 suggests that Argentina remains far more vulnerable to severe institutional crisis than neighboring countries such as Brazil, Chile, and Uruguay.

This chapter is divided into three sections. The first section traces the instability of Argentina's political institutions from the early twentieth century through 1989. The second section chronicles the political and economic changes of the Menem period (1989–99), examining both the radical reforms undertaken by the Menem government and the legacies of those changes. The third section analyzes the post-Menemist period (1999–2003), including the rise and fall of the Alianza government, the political-economic crisis of 2001–2, and the first two years of the Kirchner government.

THE ORIGINS OF INSTITUTIONAL INSTABILITY

Argentina's political history is marked by a recurrent pattern of institutional instability. The 1853 constitution, written in the aftermath of nearly half a century of civil war, established a federal and presidential system with a bicameral congress. Limited suffrage and electoral manipulation allowed the emerging political and economic elite to establish a less-than-competitive oligarchic regime—dominated by the agrarian elite–based National Autonomous Party (PAN)—that foreshadowed later periods of majoritarian rule (Botana 1979; Floria and García Belsunce 1992). Middle-class protest spearheaded by the Radical Civic Union (UCR) eventually led to the passage of the 1912 Saenz Pena Law, which established compulsory and secret universal male suffrage (women did not gain the right to vote until 1949). In 1916, democratic elections brought UCR leader Hipólito Yrigoyen to the presidency. The UCR easily retained the presidency in 1922 and 1928.

Although the Radicals established Argentina's first democracy, the new regime failed to consolidate. The rise of the UCR ushered in a new period of one-party dominance (Rock 1975). Conservative forces fragmented after 1912, and in the absence of a large peasantry, they lacked a mass base with which to remain competitive in the national electoral arena. Powerful in the economic realm but unable to win elections, the oligarchic elite never gained a stake in the democratic regime (Di Tella 1968; Gibson 1996). In 1930, soon after the onset of the Great Depression, conservatives backed a military coup that put a premature end to Yrigoyen's second presidency. The coup ushered in a period of authoritarian rule (1930–43) in which conservative elites maintained themselves in power via widespread electoral fraud. It also established a pattern in which electoral losers, facing the prospect of long-term minority status, turned to the barracks as a means of obtaining (or excluding rivals from) power.

Conservative rule was eventually undermined by socioeconomic change. Industrialization and massive urbanization fueled the growth of the urban working classes, and under the conservative post-1930 governments, the demands of these emerging social classes went largely unmet (Matsushita 1988). In 1943, another coup brought to power a group of nationalist military officers that included Colonel Juan Domingo Perón. Using his position in the newly created post of secretary of labor to build working-class support, Perón granted unprecedented political access to union leaders, intervened on the side of unions in labor disputes, and sponsored social legislation that had been long demanded by the labor movement (Murmis and Portantiero 1971; Torre 1990). This populist appeal was extraordinary successful, and when Perón was jailed by fellow officers in October 1945, a massive working-class mobilization forced his release and the calling of elections for early 1946 (Torre 1990, 107–40). The October 17, 1945, mobilization marked the birth of the Peronist movement, and it divided Argentines into Peronist and anti-Peronist camps—a cleavage that would endure for more than half a century.

Perón won the February 1946 presidential election, defeating a broad coalition that included conservative economic elites, the middle-class UCR, and the Socialist and Communist parties. Mobilizing urban workers through unions and the rural poor through clientelist networks (Mora y Araujo and Llorente 1980), Peronism quickly established itself as the most powerful political force in Argentine history. Using a combination of material and symbolic appeals, Perón and his wife Eva effectively incorporated the lower classes into politics (Ostiguy 1998; Navarro 2002). With solid control over Congress, Perón undertook extensive socioeconomic reforms. The new government expanded the state's role in the economy, nationalized key economic sectors such as the railroads and telephones, taxed agricultural exports to promote industrialization, expanded workers' incomes, and introduced reforms that improved working conditions and extended a variety of new social benefits (including social security, health insurance, paid vacations, and mandatory Christmas bonuses) (McGuire 1997). Moreover, the 1945 Labor Law strengthened unions by establishing monopolies of representation for collective bargaining and automatic dues deductions. As a result, the General Labor Confederation (CGT) quickly grew into one of the largest and best organized in Latin America. Yet the corporatist Labor Law also enhanced state control over the unions, which Perón used to purge the CGT of communist, socialist, and even independent Peronist union leaderships (Doyon 1988).

Although he was freely elected in 1946, Perón subsequently assaulted democratic institutions. Government opponents were harassed, jailed, and exiled; public employees were forced to join the Peronist party; press freedom was curtailed; and post-1946 elections were marred by intimidation and abuse of state resources. Moreover, Perón used his majoritarian control to weaken institutions perceived as obstacles to his political goals. Thus, the Peronists packed the Supreme Court, redrew electoral districts to reduce opposition representation in Congress, and in 1949, unilaterally imposed a new constitution that permitted Perón's reelection. Excluded from all centers of political power and facing the prospect of long-term minority status, Radicals and conservatives backed efforts to remove Perón through extraconstitutional means. In 1955, a military coup ousted Perón and forced him into an eighteen-year exile.

The 1955 coup ushered in a period characterized by an "impossible game" (O'Donnell 1973). Unable to defeat Peronism in free elections, military and economic elites opted to ban the movement, effectively disenfranchising a large sector of the electorate. With Perón in exile and the party (renamed the Partido Justicialista, or PJ) banned, Peronism survived within the powerful labor movement (James 1988). Peronism's survival prevented remaining parties from building majority electoral support. The UCR, which was the country's largest legal party, split in 1957. Given the size of the Peronist electorate, the two competing Radical parties were tempted to make deals with Perón, promising legalization in exchange for Peronist votes. But when Peronist candidates were permitted to compete in provincial and legislative elections, as occurred in 1962 and 1965, they won, triggering military intervention. Thus, the presidencies of Arturo Frondizi (Intransigent Radical Civic Union) and Arturo Illia (People's Radical Civic Union) were ended by coups in 1962 and 1966.

Argentine politics was thus deadlocked between 1955 and 1972 (O'Donnell 1973, 166–97). On the one hand, lifting the ban on Peronism would almost certainly result in a Peronist victory, which was unacceptable to key elite sectors. On the other hand, Peronism's exclusion from the electoral arena proved equally destabilizing. Lacking representation in the political arena, the powerful labor movement opted for tactics—such as general strikes, factory occupations, and mass protests—that undermined governability and destabilized regimes (Cavarozzi 1987; McGuire 1997). Peronism's exclusion exacerbated an ongoing conflict between two powerful, but politically unmediated, socioeconomic alliances: a "defensive alliance" of organized labor and domestic industrialists and an outward-oriented alliance of agricultural exporters and international capital (O'Donnell 1978; also Waisman 1987). Because outcomes in this conflict had substantial redistributive consequences, control of the state became a high-stakes game (O'Donnell 1978; Waisman 1987). Yet because Peronism (which represented labor) was banned and conservative parties (which had represented agricultural exporters) were weak, the post-1955 party system failed to mediate this conflict (Cavarozzi 1987; Collier and Collier 1991). As a result, non-Peronist governments—both civilian and military—proved weak and unstable.

By the early 1970s, persistent instability, the proscription of Peronism, and the emergence of urban guerrilla movements (both Peronist and leftist) had given rise to a serious crisis of legitimacy. In 1972, the military government responded to increasing polarization and political violence by calling elections, legalizing Peronism, and permitting Perón's return from exile. The following year, the aging Perón again won the presidency, this time with an unprecedented 62 percent of the vote. However, Perón's return to power failed to stem the rising tide of praetorianism and political violence. Perón's death in 1974 left the presidency in the hands of his widow and vice president, María Estela Martínez de Perón. Amid large-scale labor mobilization and increasing guerrilla and paramilitary violence, Argentina descended into chaos, and in March 1976, Perón's widow was ousted in yet another military coup (De Riz 1981).

The 1976 coup ushered in a period of military rule characterized by unprecedented repression. All political activity was banned, and in what came to be known as the Dirty War, tens of thousands of Argentines were illegally detained, tortured, and "disappeared." At the same time, the military government's economic opening weakened the country's previously protected industrial sector. The reforms failed to produce sustained growth, however, and in the early 1980s, the country fell into a severe economic crisis. In 1982, in an ill-advised bid to win back a minimum of popular support, the military government launched an invasion of the British-controlled Malvinas/Falkland Islands. The Argentine military suffered a devastating defeat at the hands of British forces, which triggered the collapse of the regime and a transition to democracy (Munck 1998).

In October 1983, UCR candidate Raúl Alfonsín won Argentina's first presidential election in more than a decade, handing the Peronists their first-ever defeat. The election inaugurated a democratic period of unprecedented scope and duration. The brutality and dramatic failure of the military regime discredited the armed forces and engendered a broad public consensus around liberal democracy (Catterberg 1991). It also gave rise to a powerful human rights movement, which launched a high-profile civic campaign to bring those responsible for the Dirty War to justice.

The Alfonsín government undertook a series of democratizing initiatives. The most celebrated of these was the prosecution and conviction of military commanders implicated in human rights violations—an initiative that was unparalleled anywhere in Latin America. The human rights trials triggered a backlash among sectors of the armed forces, made manifest by three military rebellions in 1987 and 1988 (Norden 1996; López and Pion-Berlin 1996). The rebellions were met with massive civic mobilizations in defense of democracy, but they nevertheless led the government to limit the scope of the trials to higher-level officers. Still, the government's achievements in the area of civil-military relations were impressive. Unlike post-transition Brazil and Chile, key areas of military decision-making, including the budget, procurement, and national defense strategy, were placed under a civilian-led Defense Ministry. The 1988 Defense Law prohibited the armed forces from intervening in matters of internal security and denied them any role in the policymaking process. Notwithstanding the military rebellions, then, the combination of a military defeat with key institutional and societal changes left the armed forces far weaker than their counterparts in neighboring countries such as Brazil, Chile, and Uruguay.

Alfonsín was less successful on the economic front. The Radical government inherited an economy battered by recession and inflation, which it attempted to combat through a heterodox adjustment program. After some initial success, this program collapsed amid severe distributional conflict among unions, industrialists, and agro-exporters (Smith 1990). Efforts to negotiate a social pact with the Peronist unions failed, and the CGT led an astounding thirteen general strikes between 1984 and 1988 (Gaudio and Thompson 1990). As the specter of a Peronist victory in 1989 elections grew, capital flight and financial speculation soared, culminating in a hyperinflationary burst that brought the economy to the brink of collapse. In May, Peronist candidate Carlos Menem, a populist provincial governor, was elected president. Soon afterward, a wave of mass looting forced Alfonsín to resign the presidency six months before the end of his mandate. Thus, although Menem's inauguration marked the first time in Argentine history that the presidency had changed hands between elected leaders of different parties, it took place in a context of extreme institutional fluidity.

ARGENTINA UNDER MENEM

Carlos Menem's presidency was a critical juncture in Argentine politics. Abandoning Peronism's traditional populist program, the Menem government radically restructured the country's economic institutions, replacing the state-led industrialization model established during the 1940s with a market-oriented model. Menem also oversaw important political changes, including the further erosion of military influence and the drafting of a new constitution in 1994.

In some respects, Argentina was strikingly successful during the 1990s. The country combined economic liberalization and democracy in a way that was unparalleled in Latin America. Virtually none of the most radical economic reforms in post-1973 Latin America were undertaken in a context of full-fledged democracy. In Chile and Mexico, reforms were carried out under authoritarian regimes. In Peru, they were accompanied by an *autogolpe* in which the congress and the judiciary were dissolved and the leading opponent of neoliberalism was forced into exile. Even in Bolivia, orthodox stabilization was implemented via distinctly authoritarian mechanisms, including states of siege and harsh labor repression. By contrast, in democracies such as Costa Rica, Uruguay, Venezuela, and Brazil, economic reform was slower and less extensive. Placed in comparative perspective, then, Argentina's capacity to reconcile radical reform and democracy during the 1990s was extraordinary: among fully democratic cases, Argentina carried out the most rapid and far-reaching economic reforms; among cases of deep crisis and radical reform, Argentina was the most democratic.

Yet there was a dark side to the successes of the Menem period. Many of the policy arrangements and political side payments that made radical reform possible under democracy ultimately proved economically unsustainable. Moreover, Menem did little to strengthen political institutions, and in many important respects, he weakened them. In carrying out radical economic reforms (but also in an effort to concentrate power), the Menem government often circumvented or manipulated institutions of legislative and judicial oversight, which undermined the country's nascent system of democratic checks and balances.

The Politics of Radical Economic Reform

Although he was elected on a populist platform, President Menem responded to the 1989 hyperinflationary crisis with a dramatic policy shift. Filling his cabinet with business leaders, conservative politicians, and market-oriented technocrats to highlight his commitment to free markets, Menem embarked on what was widely viewed as the fastest and most far-reaching economic reform program in Latin America (Gwartney, Lawson, and Block 1996; IDB 1997). The government eliminated price controls, restrictions on foreign capital, and a variety of other regulations; dramatically lowered trade barriers; and sold off virtually all of Argentina's state-owned companies. It also reduced the central government's role in the provision of social welfare by privatizing and decentralizing important responsibilities. For example, it replaced the pay-as-you-go pension system established by Perón with an individualized, privately funded system (Gerchunoff and Torre 1996; Pastor and Wise 1999) and decentralized public education and the provision of health care to the provincial level.

Whereas Alfonsín's mild stabilization and reform efforts were derailed by legislative opposition, popular protest, and distributional conflict, the Menem government implemented its radical neoliberal program with striking success. This success was rooted in several factors. First, the government's ability to end hyperinflation enhanced public support for the overall reform process. Successful stabilization was, in large part, a product of the 1991 Convertibility Law. The brainchild of Minister of the Economy Domingo Cavallo, the Convertibility Law constrained monetary policy through the creation of a currency board. The law established a new currency with a one-to-one parity with the dollar, prohibited the government from printing money not backed by foreign reserves, and permitted contracts in any currency. By tying the government's hands in monetary and exchange rate policy, the convertibility system enhanced the domestic and international credibility of the government's new economic institutions (Acuña 1994; Starr 1997). This credibility was further enhanced by the fact that convertibility was passed into law by Congress, which made it more difficult for governments to change. Convertibility brought inflation down from more than 2300 percent in 1990 to near zero in 1994, triggering—together with privatization—a massive inflow of foreign investment. Between 1991 and 1997, price stability and strong economic growth generated broad public support for the government's reform program (Palermo and Torre 1992; Palermo and Novaro 1996; Etchegaray and Elordi 2001).

A second factor behind the success of the Menem reforms was the strength of the Peronist party. The PJ maintained an extensive grassroots organization, deeply embedded in working- and lower-class society, and a strong subculture and identity, which helped the Menem government maintain a stable support base in a context of crisis and radical reform. The PJ's vast infrastructure of neighborhood branches, soup kitchens, clubs, and clientelist networks played a critical role in dampening popular sector opposition to neoliberalism. In low-income neighborhoods throughout the country, Peronist "problem-solving networks" distributed food, medicine, disability pensions, and odd jobs to people who lacked alternative sources of social assistance (Auyero 2000; Levitsky 2003, 187–91), helping to prevent the kind of urban riots that brought the Alfonsín presidency to an early end. Peronism's continued hegemony among the popular sectors also limited the space for antireform appeals. Because most working- and lower-class Argentines continued to vote Peronist throughout the 1990s, attempts by left-wing and nationalist parties to capture these votes through anti-neoliberals failed repeatedly.

The PJ's electoral strength also provided the Menem government with a majority in the Senate and a near-majority in the Chamber of Deputies, which ensured—with the help of small conservative and provincial parties—the relatively smooth passage of its most important reform measures (Llanos 2001). Although this passage often required arduous negotiation and substantial concessions, unified government was nevertheless critical to avoiding the kind of executive-legislative deadlock that had undermined reform efforts in other Latin American countries. Indeed, Menem's success in pushing neoliberal reforms through the legislature stands in stark contrast to Alfonsín's more modest reform proposals, which were blocked by the Peronist-controlled Congress.

The Menem government also benefited from the PJ's close ties to organized labor. The vast majority of union leaders remained Peronist in the 1990s, and many of them maintained close ties to the party (Levitsky 2003, 130–39). These ties gave union leaders a stake in the government's success and an incentive to limit public opposition to Menem. Union bosses also maintained long-standing personal ties to PJ leaders. By enhancing trust and communication between government and union officials, these ties lengthened the unionists' time horizons and facilitated the negotiation of side payments that were critical to keeping many unions in the pro-government camp. Thus, whereas Alfonsín confronted thirteen general strikes during his presidency, the Menem government gained a remarkable degree of labor acquiescence—and even cooperation—with far more radical reforms.[2] Initially divided into pro- and anti-Menem camps, the CGT did not lead a single general strike during Menem's first three and half years in office and led only one general strike during his entire first term. Although dissident labor organizations such as the Congress of

---

2. It is worth noting that in some unions, there existed substantial rank-and-file support for privatization (Ranis 1992).

Argentine Workers (CTA) and Argentine Workers Movement (MTA) mobilized repeatedly against the Menem reforms during the 1990s, most large unions refused to join them; as a result, these protests failed to mobilize large numbers of workers (Martuccelli and Svampa 1997; Murillo 1997, 2001; Levitsky and Way 1998).

A third factor behind the success of the Menem reforms was the government's use of policy concessions and side payments to construct a stable pro-reform coalition. This coalition included powerful political and economic actors—such as unions, domestic industrialists, and old guard Peronist governors—that might otherwise have opposed neoliberal reforms (Palermo and Novaro 1996; Corrales 1998; Murillo 2001; Etchemendy, this volume). Union support was achieved through agreements not to reform the corporatist labor legislation (which allowed the unions to maintain critical organizational resources) or deregulate labor markets and union-administrated health insurance funds, and by granting unions shares in newly privatized enterprises and participation in the new private pension funds market (Murillo 1997; Etchemendy, this volume). Key domestic industrialists were granted highly favorable conditions for competing in the privatization process, which allowed them to expand their share of critical markets or enter new sectors with protection from foreign competition (Schvartzer 1998; Basualdo 2000; Azpiazu 2002; Etchemendy, this volume). Finally, the support of Peronist governors was assured via the repeated postponement of provincial adjustment and state reform processes (Gibson and Calvo 2000). This last concession was critical to Menem's legislative success, as governors exert substantial influence over their provinces' legislative representatives (Jones and Hwang, this volume). Taken together, these concessions were inefficient and fiscally costly, but they may have been critical to the government's capacity to implement its overall reform program.

Finally, the Menem government's economic reforms were accompanied by a series of executive encroachments on legislative and judicial power. These institutional shenanigans included the widespread use of executive decrees, the 1990 packing of the Supreme Court, and the politicized appointment of federal judges (Verbitsky 1993; Larkins 1998). By creating a loyalist majority on the Court, the government ensured that its reforms would not be blocked on constitutional grounds. Perhaps most notably, in the 1990 Peralta case, the Court upheld the constitutionality of Menem's executive decrees (Helmke, this volume).

Notwithstanding their successful implementation, the Menem reforms left several problematic legacies. One was convertibility. Because it was widely viewed as having ended hyperinflation, and because many middle-class Argentines accumulated debts in dollars, the Convertibility Law enjoyed broad public support throughout the 1990s. Yet by taking monetary and exchange rate policy out of the hands of policymakers, convertibility left them without the tools to respond to either economic shocks or the erosion of Argentina's export competitiveness. A second legacy was a dramatic growth in public debt. Many of the political concessions granted in an effort to accelerate macroeconomic reform—particularly the postponement of adjustment in the provinces—generated substantial fiscal costs. So, too, did the privatization of the pension system.[3] These costs induced both federal and provincial governments to turn to large-scale borrowing. Finally, the Menem reforms generated large-scale social exclusion and growing inequality that shrunk the traditionally large Argentine middle class. The unemployment rate, which had been virtually zero for much of the twentieth century, soared to a record 18.6 percent in 1995 and remained in double digits for the rest of the decade. These legacies left Menem's successors in a difficult bind: future governments would face growing demands to address long unmet social needs, but a massive debt burden and a rigid monetary and exchange rate system would seriously limit their capacity to meet those demands.

Democratic Institutions Under Menem

During the 1990s, Argentine democracy was characterized by both unprecedented stability and persistent institutional fluidity. On the one hand, Argentina remained fully democratic throughout the decade. The fairness of national elections was unquestioned, there were no states of emergency or interruptions of the democratic order, and civil liberties were broadly protected. Moreover, press freedom was extensive: the censorship, co-optation, and bullying of the media found elsewhere in the region was virtually nonexistent.[4] The persistence of full-fledged democracy was particularly striking given the depth of the 1989–90 hyperinflationary crisis and the radical nature of the Menem government's economic reforms.

Democratic institutions were buttressed by an active civil society and a powerful independent media. State encroachments on civil liberties frequently triggered sustained civic protests that imposed heavy political costs

3. Because the state continued to pay out on its obligations to retirees at the same time that contributors moved into the new privately funded system, pension privatization produced a massive fiscal drain.

4. Efforts to limit press freedom (such as a 1992 "Truth in Press" bill and Menem's proposal for a "law of the stick" that would permit citizens to take matters into their own hands when offended by the media) generated massive public opposition, which led the government to abandon them.

on government officials and, in many cases, induced them to undertake serious investigations (Smulovitz and Peruzzotti 2003; Peruzzotti, this volume). For example, in 1990, when the provincial government in Catamarca attempted to cover up the murder of teenager María Soledad Morales (in which members of the governing clan were implicated), civic and church groups organized a series of "marches of silence" that drew national media attention and forced a federal takeover of the case, paving the way for an eventual conviction. Similarly, after the 1997 killing of news photographer José Luis Cabezas (arranged by a mafia boss with close ties to the government), civic and media groups organized a massive and successful campaign—flooding Buenos Aires with "Who killed Cabezas?" posters, fliers, and advertisements—to bring the perpetrators to justice.

The Menem period also saw a dramatic reduction in the military's influence in politics. Weakened and discredited by their defeat in the Falklands/Malvinas War, the armed forces became increasingly marginal players in the political arena. Unlike many other countries in the region, there were no military officers in the cabinet, no independent military political proclamations, and no military shows of force in the streets of the capital. In 1990, the government crushed a rebellion led by Colonel Mohammad Ali Seineldín and issued a controversial pardon of top military officers convicted of human rights violations. After that point, the armed forces stood on the sidelines as the government slashed its budget and overall size, abolished the draft, and privatized military-owned enterprises. By the end of the decade, military spending was under the tight control of the Ministry of the Economy, and responsibility for determining military missions and deployment lay exclusively with the Foreign Ministry. In 1995, Armed Forces Commander Martin Balza issued a stunning apology for the military's behavior during the Dirty War. Although little progress was made in developing civilian oversight capacity in either Congress or the Defense Ministry, the armed forces' subordination to civilian authorities was not seriously questioned during the 1990s. These developments suggest an important lesson for Third Wave democracies in Latin America. In Argentina, a dramatically weakened military, rather than a carefully protected one, appears to have been critical to democratic stability. In this case, then, it was not necessary to spare the military "queen" (O'Donnell and Schmitter 1986, 69) in the name of democratic consolidation.

Notwithstanding these successes, however, many of Argentina's democratic institutions remained fragile during the 1990s. Particularly during his first term in office, President Menem took advantage of his popular support and a weakened opposition to concentrate power and bend a range of political institutions to his advantage. For example, Menem frequently circumvented the legislative process through the use of Necessity and Urgency Decrees. Prior to 1994, decree authority was not explicitly granted by the constitution, and legal experts disagreed over its constitutionality (Ferreira Rubio and Goretti 1998, 285–90). Whereas President Alfonsín issued 10 Necessity and Urgency Decrees between 1983 and 1989, Menem issued 335 of them between 1989 and 1994 (Ferreira Rubio and Goretti 2000, 1, 4).

Menem also showed little respect for judicial independence. In 1990, he pushed through legislation—over the objections of the UCR and with a contested quorum—expanding the size of the Supreme Court from five to nine. He then stacked the Court with loyalists, creating what came to be known as an "automatic majority." The new Supreme Court rarely ruled against Menem on important issues (Helmke, this volume). The appointment of federal judges was also highly politicized.[5] Though hardly new in Argentina, executive intervention in the judiciary was particularly severe during the 1990s, and it seriously eroded the legitimacy of the court system.[6]

Menem's concentration of executive power had several important consequences. For one, the absence of rigorous checks and balances facilitated radical economic reform. Had President Menem been held fully accountable to Congress and the judiciary, the reform process would almost certainly have been slower and less far-reaching. In addition, the deficit of executive accountability permitted a substantial degree of corruption. The economic reform process—including several key privatizations—lacked transparency and was marred by questionable deals, and a series of high-profile corruption scandals involving top government officials created a public perception of widespread and unchecked abuse of power. Indeed, although several ministers and high-level appointees were either directly implicated in scandals or forced to resign amid corruption allegations, none of these officials were brought to justice during the Menem administration.

One of the most striking instances of institutional manipulation during the 1990s was Menem's repeated effort to modify the constitution to enable him to run for reelection. In 1993, Menem took advantage of his broad popular support to bully ex-President Alfonsín into accepting a constitutional reform by threatening to hold a plebiscite on the issue. The

---

5. One of Menem's cabinet ministers is reported to have listed on a napkin all of the federal appeals court justices the government "controlled" (Verbitsky 1997).

6. For example, a 1993 survey found that more than 60 percent of Argentines perceived the judiciary to be in worse shape than it had been at the time of the 1983 democratic transition (*Clarín*, December 7, 2003).

result was the 1993 Olivos Pact, which ensured UCR support for a constitutional reform that included a reelection clause. The pact, which was approved by an elected constituent assembly in 1994, produced a series of institutional reforms, many of which were widely viewed as democratizing. These included a shortening of the presidential mandate from six to four years, the direct election of senators (previously chosen by provincial legislatures), the granting of autonomy to the city of Buenos Aires, and the direct election of the Buenos Aires mayor. The 1994 constitution also created a Magistrates' Council to oversee the selection of federal judges and established clear regulations for executive decrees. Nevertheless, the process that gave rise to the constitutional reforms (a threatened plebiscite, followed by a secret pact between two party *caudillos*), together with the widespread perception that Menem had simply used the reform as a means to gain reelection, deprived the constitutional process of some of its public prestige.[7]

Argentina's democratic institutions survived the Menem government's abuses. As Menem's public support began to wane during his second term, opposition forces gained strength. The legislature became increasingly assertive, and previously deferential justices began to rule against the government (Helmke, this volume). The limits on Menem's power were made particularly manifest in 1998, when he engaged in a blatantly unconstitutional bid for a third term in office. Unlike 1993–94, the "re-reelection" effort generated broad public opposition, was rejected by all major opposition parties, and more crucially, by a large faction of the PJ led by Buenos Aires governor Eduardo Duhalde. When Menem supporters turned to the judiciary, even the famed Supreme Court's "automatic majority" made it clear that it would not rule in the president's favor. As a result, Menem was left with no alternative but to hand over the presidency, as scheduled, in December 1999.

Menem's institutional manipulation had important costs. The government's effort to circumvent, break, or change rules that stood in the way of its political and policy objectives reinforced existing patterns of institutional instability. Thus, even though many of the political and economic reforms undertaken during the 1990s were widely viewed as beneficial,

---

7. It should be noted that the Olivos Pact represented an important bipartisan consensus that was notably lacking in earlier constitutional reform processes (particularly that of 1949). Indeed, a major motivating force behind the pact appears to have been Menem and Alfonsín's belief that a bipartisan consensus was critical to the legitimacy of the new constitution (Smulovitz 1995, 80–81). Nevertheless, the pact had devastating electoral consequences for the UCR, since many Radical voters perceived Alfonsín to have abandoned his opposition to the Menem government's abuses.

abuses committed while carrying out those reforms weakened the legitimacy of the institutions that emerged from the process. Indeed, widespread perceptions of unchecked corruption and abuse eroded the credibility of Argentina's representative institutions, widening the gap between citizens and the political elite (see Torre and Peruzzotti chapters, this volume).

The Party System and Political Representation in the 1990s

The Argentine party system experienced both continuity and change during the 1990s. In contrast to Peru and Venezuela, where the failure of established populist parties contributed to party system collapse and the rise of antisystem outsiders, Argentina's party system proved resilient in the face of economic crisis and radical reform. In large part, this stability was rooted in the PJ's capacity to adapt to the neoliberal challenge while simultaneously maintaining its traditional support base (Levitsky 2003, this volume). As Table 1.1 shows, the PJ won four straight national elections after the Menem government's neoliberal turn. Peronism's decisive victories in the 1991 and 1993 midterm elections were widely interpreted as votes of support for convertibility, and they provided Menem with clear mandates to proceed with economic reforms. The PJ also won the 1994 constituent assembly elections, and in 1995, Menem was overwhelmingly reelected with 50 percent of the vote.

The Radicals, who were discredited by both the failure of the Alfonsín government and the Olivos Pact, fell from 52 percent of the presidential vote in 1983 to an unprecedented low of 17 percent in 1995. UCR candidate Horacio Massaccesi finished third in the 1995 presidential race, behind former Peronist José Octavio Bordón, who ran as the candidate of the newly created Front for a Country in Solidarity (FREPASO). The center-left FREPASO, which campaigned on issues of clean government and institutional integrity, captured much of the UCR's middle-class electorate.

The emergence of FREPASO temporarily divided non-Peronist forces, as both FREPASO and the UCR competed primarily for the middle-class vote. As a result, the PJ, which remained hegemonic among the working and lower classes, dominated electoral politics in the mid-1990s. However, in August 1997, the UCR and FREPASO formed the Alianza por el Trabajo, la Educación, y la Justicia (Alliance for Jobs, Justice, and Education), transforming the previously weak and divided opposition into a viable electoral alternative. The party system remained divided into Peronist and non-Peronist camps, but the latter was now represented by a coalition of the established Radicals and the emerging FREPASO. The Alianza defeated the PJ in

Table 1.1 Argentine electoral results during the 1990s (percentage of valid vote)

Party	1991[a]	1993[a]	1994[b]	1995[c]	1995[a]	1997[a]	1999[c]	1999[a]
Partido Justicialista (PJ)	40.2	42.5	38.5	49.9	43.0	36.3	38.3	33.0
Unión Cívica Radical (UCR)	29.0	30.2	20.5	17.0	21.7	—	—	—
Unión del Centro Democrático (UCEDE)	5.2	2.6	1.5	—	3.2	0.6	—	—
Frente País Solidario (FREPASO)[d]	—	2.5	13.6	29.2	20.7	—	—	—
Movimiento por la Dignidad y la Independencia (MODIN)	—	5.8	9.2	1.7	1.7	0.9	—	—
Alliance for Jobs, Justice, and Education[e]	—	—	—	—	—	45.7[f]	48.4	45.5
Action for the Republic	—	—	—	—	—	3.9	10.2	8.0
Minor and provincial parties	25.6	16.4	16.7	2.2	9.7	2.6	2.8	13.5
Total	100	100	100	100	100	100	100	100

SOURCES: Fraga 1995; McGuire 1995; Gervasoni 1997; *www.mivoto.com.*

[a]Election to the Chamber of Deputies
[b]Election to the Constituent Assembly
[c]Election to the presidency
[d]Frente Grande (FG) in 1993 and 1994.
[e]UCR and FREPASO
[f]Total includes vote for the UCR and FREPASO in districts in which these parties ran separately.

the 1997 legislative elections, breaking a string of six consecutive Peronist victories. In 1999, the Alianza's presidential ticket of Fernando De la Rúa (UCR) and Carlos "Chacho" Álvarez (FREPASO) campaigned on a platform of clean government, institutional integrity, and greater attention to social needs. Taking advantage of increased public dissatisfaction over corruption and increased social exclusion, the Alianza won easily, defeating PJ candidate Eduardo Duhalde by 48 percent to 38 percent.

The rise of the Alianza appeared to stabilize the party system and return it to the competitive parity of the 1980s. However, serious problems lurked beneath the surface. The absence of policymaking transparency and the high-profile corruption scandals of the 1990s had eroded the credibility of Argentina's representative institutions, particularly among middle- and upper middle-class voters. In 1997 and 1999, the Alianza appeared to be a viable alternative for these voters, and the middle-class electorate voted overwhelmingly for De la Rúa. However, middle-class support for the Alianza would prove shallow and short-lived.

THE POST-MENEMIST ERA

The post-Menemist period was marked by an economic collapse and a severe crisis of political representation. Although the crisis again made manifest the resilience of Argentine democracy, it also highlighted both the limitations of the 1990s experiment with democracy and radical market reform and the continued weakness of Argentina's political and economic institutions.

The Unfulfilled Promise of Renovation: The Rise and Fall of the Alianza

Fernando De la Rúa's defeat of Peronist Eduardo Duhalde in the 1999 presidential election brought the Menemist era to a close. Although it accepted the fundamentals of the new economic model, the Alianza promised to combat corruption and address the social costs of neoliberalism, which generated high expectations of the new government. However, De la Rúa failed to deliver on both of these fronts.

On the political front, the Alianza failed to clean up politics. In August 2000, allegations surfaced that government officials had bribed a handful of senators in an effort to pass labor reform legislation. Vice President (and FREPASO leader) Carlos Álvarez, whose party had made anticorruption its central plank, called publicly for a serious investigation, and when De la Rúa balked, Álvarez resigned. Although FREPASO remained in the government, Álvarez's resignation triggered the de facto collapse of both the Alianza and FREPASO. More important, the scandal shattered the Alianza's claim to represent a "new way" of doing politics and convinced many of its erstwhile supporters that none of the major parties effectively represented them (Torre, this volume).

The Alianza fared even worse on the economic front. The De la Rúa government inherited a prolonged recession that was rooted in a series of external shocks, including large-scale capital outflows triggered by the 1997–98 Asian financial crisis, a strengthening U.S. dollar, and Brazil's 1999 devaluation. Yet the Convertibility Law prevented the government from using exchange rate or monetary policy to reactivate the economy. Wedded to convertibility and confronted with a heavy debt burden, fiscal pressure created by declining tax revenues and fixed transfers to the provinces, jittery bond markets, and inflexible IMF demands for fiscal adjustment, the new government opted for a series of pro-cyclical austerity measures that prolonged and deepened the economic downturn. In March 2001, as Argentina entered its fourth consecutive year of recession, a desperate De la Rúa reappointed Domingo Cavallo, the father of convertibility under Menem, as minister of the economy. Yet Cavallo was unable to reverse the situation.

In the midst of a prolonged recession and in the wake of the Senate corruption scandal, Argentine voters vented their frustration in the October 2001 legislative elections. The Alianza was badly defeated by the PJ, and its share of the valid legislative vote was cut nearly in half relative to 1999. More ominous, the percentage of voters who cast blank and spoiled ballots—a protest against the entire political elite—soared to an unprecedented 22 percent of the overall vote. Indeed, the blank and spoiled vote exceeded that of the governing Alianza, and in two of the country's largest districts (the Federal Capital and Santa Fe), it exceeded those of all parties.

Mounting fears of a debt default or currency devaluation, reinforced by the Alianza's devastating electoral defeat, triggered a severe financial crisis. In late November 2001, Cavallo responded to a wave of capital flight by imposing strict limits on bank withdrawals and currency movements. The political consequences of the so-called *corralito* (playpen)—which deprived the middle classes of their savings and starved the cash-dependent informal economy that sustained much of the poor—were devastating. On December 18 and 19, Argentina exploded in a wave of rioting and protest. Confronted with widespread looting, highway blockades, and tens of thousands of middle-class protesters banging pots and pans in downtown Buenos Aires, and after a brutal police repression that resulted in at least two dozen deaths, De la Rúa resigned on December 20. With the vice presidency vacant, Congress elected Peronist governor Adolfo Rodríguez Saá to serve as interim president. Rodríguez Saá immediately declared a default on Argentina's U.S.$132 million debt—the largest default in history. Yet on December 30, after another round of mass rioting and amid severe conflict within his own party, Rodríguez Saá, too, resigned the presidency.

On January 1, 2002, when Congress selected PJ senator Eduardo Duhalde as Argentina's third president in less than two weeks, Argentina stood on the brink of anarchy. Rallying behind the slogan *que se vayan todos* ("throw everyone out"), protesters descended on the three branches of government, demanding the resignation of the Congress and the Supreme Court. At the same time, groups of poor and unemployed people— known as *piqueteros*—blocked major roads and highways throughout the country demanding food and jobs. While new forms of protest seemed to replace partisan channels of representation, citizen anger against politicians reached such heights that Argentines began to physically attack them on the street, in restaurants, and in other public places.

Immediately after his inauguration, Duhalde ended the convertibility system, plunging the economy further into chaos. Within weeks, the value of the peso had fallen by more than 70 percent, triggering fears of hyperinflation.[8] With the banking system paralyzed and no immediate prospect of international assistance, economic activity ground to a halt. Argentina's GDP contracted by 16 percent in the first quarter of 2002, and the unemployment rate climbed to nearly 25 percent. More than five million people fell into poverty between October 2001 and June 2002. By mid-2002, more than half the population was living in poverty, compared to just 22 percent in 1994.

The economic collapse pushed the political system to the breaking point. Widespread public hostility toward the political elite raised the specter of a full-scale party system collapse, and the intensity of social protest and widespread perceptions of chaos triggered talk—for the first time in more than a decade—of military intervention. After police killed two protesters in June 2002, a weakened Duhalde was forced to cut short his own mandate. He announced that he would leave office in May, rather than December, of 2003, and presidential elections were eventually rescheduled for April 2003.

The 2001–2 crisis thus triggered yet another round of institutional collapse. Institutions ranging from the currency board, property rights, and

8. Devaluation generated political pressure from influential dollar-denominated debtors such as provincial governments, business, and much of the middle class. In response, Duhalde subsidized their debts by creating a special exchange rate at great fiscal cost to the state.

central bank autonomy to judicial independence, presidential mandates, and the electoral cycle were dismantled, violated, or seriously threatened. Presidential elections were rescheduled four times. Indeed, throughout 2002, there was little certainty when elections would be held, which offices would be up for election, or how candidates would be selected. Repeated conflict over and manipulation of the electoral rules of the game reinforced the already low levels of public trust in politicians and political institutions.

Political parties also fell into crisis. The parties of the Alianza suffered a meltdown: FREPASO disintegrated, and the UCR fell to less than two percent in opinion polls. As the UCR sank into apparent oblivion, aspiring Radical politicians abandoned the party. Elisa Carrió, a legislator who had emerged as a prominent anticorruption crusader, formed the left-of-center Argentines for a Republic of Equals (ARI), and Ricardo López Murphy, who had briefly served as De la Rúa's minister of the economy, launched the conservative Federal Movement for Renewal (MFR).

Although the PJ remained strong in electoral terms and was widely expected to win the presidency, it was nearly torn apart by internal conflict between Menem, who sought to regain the presidency, and Duhalde. Desperate for a candidate to defeat Menem, Duhalde turned to Nestor Kirchner, the little-known governor of Argentina's least populated province (Santa Cruz). Ex-interim President Adolfo Rodríguez Saá also sought the presidency. The Peronists repeatedly failed to agree on the rules of the game for selecting a candidate, and the nomination process quickly descended into a naked power struggle. Although PJ statutes called for a presidential primary, Duhalde, fearing a Menem victory, used his power in the party to derail such a vote. To avoid a rupture, PJ leaders ultimately opted not to officially nominate a candidate, but rather to allow Menem, Kirchner, and Rodríguez Saá to run outside the party.

The 2003 Election: Democratic Resilience and Partial Party System Collapse

The depth of the 2002 economic crisis and the extent of public hostility toward politicians raised the specter of a party system collapse and a regime-level crisis similar to those of Peru and Venezuela. Nevertheless, Argentina's democratic institutions again remained intact. The role of the armed forces during the crisis was striking. Notwithstanding widespread social protest and an atmosphere of virtual chaos, the military refused to repress protesters, made no attempt to change the government, and abstained from seeking to exert behind-the-scenes influence over political events (as occurred in Bolivia, Ecuador, Peru, and Venezuela). Given the depth of the crisis and Argentina's history of military intervention, this was an extraordinary outcome.

As the 2003 election approached, the political and economic crises began to ease. Buoyed by an incipient economic recovery, the Duhalde government used a combination of old-school clientelism and effective social policies—including the distribution of low-cost medicine and monthly subsidies to nearly two million unemployed heads of households—to restore a minimum of social peace. Levels of protest declined, and political activity was increasingly channeled into the electoral arena.

The May 2003 presidential election was the most fragmented in modern Argentine history. Peronism (unofficially) ran three candidates: Rodríguez Saá, who campaigned as a populist outsider; Menem, who ran as a law-and-order conservative; and Kirchner, who adopted a progressive center-left platform. The leading non-Peronist candidates were ex-Radicals who had formed their own parties: Carrió, who adopted a left-of-center, anticorruption platform, and López Murphy, who combined a clean government appeal with a conservative and market-oriented platform.

The election marked a departure from the protest politics of 2001–2. Notwithstanding widespread public anger and the political elite, no anti-establishment outsider received even two percent of the vote, and the blank and spoiled vote, which had surpassed 20 percent in 2001, fell to just 2.5 percent. Menem, who enjoyed the strong support of a minority of voters but was intensely *disliked* by a majority, finished first with 24.5 percent of the vote. Kirchner, who was backed by Duhalde's powerful Peronist machine in the province of Buenos Aires, finished second with 22.4 percent.[9] Because no candidate secured 45 percent of the vote, Menem and Kirchner, two Peronists, qualified for a runoff election. In the second round, the anti-Menemist vote coalesced behind Kirchner.[10] Facing the prospect of overwhelming defeat, Menem abandoned the race, handing the presidency to Kirchner.

The 2001–2 crisis thus had an uneven impact on the party system. On the one hand, the established non-Peronist parties were virtually wiped out. FREPASO and Domingo Cavallo's Action for the Republic disintegrated, and UCR, which had been the country's leading middle-class party for more than a century, suffered an unprecedented decline. Radical candidate Leopoldo Moreau's 2.3 percent of the vote was easily the worst performance in party history. On the other hand, Peronism proved remarkably resilient. Peronist presidential candidates won a combined 61 percent of the vote, and the PJ eventually secured a majority of seats in the

9. López Murphy finished third with 16.4 percent of the vote, followed by Rodríguez Saá and Carrió, each with 14.1 percent.

10. Almost immediately after the first-round vote was counted, surveys showed Kirchner winning the second-round election with more than 70 percent of the vote.

Chamber of Deputies, retained control of the Senate, and won the vast bulk of the country's governorships.

The PJ's electoral resilience was critical to preventing a full-scale party system meltdown and the rise of an anti–political establishment outsider. In Peru and Venezuela, the success of outsider candidates was rooted in the collapse of established populist parties, which left a large number of low-income voters available for "neopopulist" appeals (Roberts 1995; Weyland 1999). In Argentina, by contrast, working- and lower-class voters remained solidly in the Peronist camp, confining the "throw everyone out" vote to the non-Peronist electorate (Escolar et al. 2002; Torre, this volume).

Non-Peronist forces remain unstable. The two "post-Alianza" parties with the strongest claim to middle-class votes, Carrió's center-left ARI and López Murphy's center-right MFR, are little more than personal vehicles for their respective founders. They lack national organizations, and their support bases were concentrated largely in the major metropolitan centers. Since the emergence of Peronism in the 1940s, national-level party building has proven exceedingly difficult in Argentina. Indeed, of the many parties that competed in national elections between 1983 and 2003, only the PJ and the UCR succeeded in penetrating the entire national territory. Alternative political forces, such as the Intransigent Party and FREPASO (on the center-left) and the Center Democratic Union and Action for the Republic (on the center-right), were weakly organized, Buenos Aires–based parties, and all of them virtually disappeared within a decade. If the ARI and the MFR do not extend their influence into the peripheral provinces, they will almost certainly suffer a similar fate.

Argentina's post-1999 party system thus appears to have suffered a *partial collapse*. On the one hand, Peronism's electoral resilience prevented a full-scale party system collapse along the lines of Venezuela and Peru. On the other hand, unlike party systems in Chile, Mexico, Uruguay, and even Brazil, no stable partisan alternative emerged to represent disaffected or previously excluded voters. In contrast to the National Action Party (PAN) and Party of the Democratic Revolution (PRD) in Mexico, the Broad Front in Uruguay, the Workers Party (PT) in Brazil, and the Independent Democratic Union (UDI) in Chile, Argentina's emerging partisan alternatives (FREPASO, Action for the Republic) never developed national structures during the 1990s and quickly collapsed, leaving non-Peronist forces fragmented and disorganized.

The Kirchner Presidency: A New Round of Institutional Change

Following an election in which he won only 22 percent of the vote, President Kirchner quickly established his authority by launching a set of bold reform initiatives. The new government restructured the military and police hierarchies, shook up several state agencies long linked to corruption, pushed successfully for the removal—via impeachment and resignation—of leading Menemist-era Supreme Court justices, and established mechanisms to ensure a more transparent and consensual judicial nomination process.[11] The new government also solidified its support among middle-class progressives by launching a campaign to reopen judicial proceedings against military officials implicated in human rights violations. Finally, Kirchner distanced his government from the economic policies of the 1990s. The new government adopted a harder line in negotiations with international creditors and began to revise several post-privatization concessions and regulatory arrangements that were deemed harmful to consumers. In many respects, these moves went beyond the progressive-reformist platform that had been charted but abandoned by the Alianza. Public opinion surveys showed broad support for the new government and a striking degree of optimism about Argentina's future, at least until the third quarter of 2005.[12]

The longer-term impact of Kirchner's reforms remains uncertain. In at least some respects, the early Kirchner presidency resembled that of Menem. The new president concentrated power in the executive, demonstrated an unusual degree of political initiative and energy, and undertook a series of bold initiatives from above that shook up or undid institutional and policy arrangements associated with discredited past governments. Similar to the early Menem years, these rapid-fire initiatives won broad public support and helped to restore public confidence in the political process. However, Kirchner's initiatives were more transparent and more oriented toward institutional integrity than those of early 1990s—perhaps because the primary crisis he faced was one of public confidence, not hyperinflation. Thus, whereas Menem routinely sacrificed institutional integrity in the pursuit of short-term political and economic goals, the Kirchner government faced an important dilemma between process and outcomes. On the one hand, facing a skeptical and highly mobilized public, Kirchner needed to achieve certain institutional outcomes—such as a reshuffling of the Supreme Court and other discredited state agencies—quickly to avoid the fate of his immediate predecessors. On the other hand, simply stacking the Court, as Menem did, would reinforce existing patterns of institutional instability. In some areas, including the Supreme Court, Kirchner was able

11. As of late 2005, the Senate had approved four of Kirchner's proposed appointees to the Supreme Court following the new open debate process.

12. Kirchner's public approval rating reached 80 percent soon after his inauguration in May 2003 and remained above 70 percent through early 2005.

to achieve his goals while taking issues of process seriously, which could enhance the long-term credibility of those institutions. In other areas, such as regulatory agencies that were stacked by the executive in order to protect consumers from rate hikes, outcomes won out over process. Hence, whether the Kirchner round of reforms will break or reinforce preexisting patterns of institutional instability remains to be seen.

If institutional instability remains a central feature of contemporary Argentine politics, however, the scope of that instability may be narrowing. Although the political-economic crises of 1989–90 and 2001–2 resembled earlier ones in that they were accompanied by widespread contestation, subversion, and alteration of the rules, they differed in that certain core political and economic institutions survived. The democratic institutions established in 1983 endured the collapse of the Alfonsín government (and later, that of the Alianza government), and notwithstanding the profound socioeconomic crisis of 2001–2 and the election of a critic of neoliberalism in 2003, the primary free market institutions created during the 1990s remained largely intact. This core institutional stability constitutes a significant break with earlier patterns, and it permits a measure of optimism about Argentina's political future, even as the country struggles to recover from the devastating crises of the not-too-distant past.

2

The Institutional Foundations of Public Policy: A Transaction Cost Approach and Its Application to Argentina

Pablo T. Spiller and Mariano Tommasi

In the 1990s, Argentina underwent a broad and profound process of market-oriented reform. With its ambitious program of macroeconomic stabilization, liberalization, privatization, and deregulation, Argentina became the poster child of the Washington establishment. After decades of inward-looking policies, stagnation, and fiscal crises that produced hyperinflation in 1989, Argentina seemed to have found its way at last. For a good part of the 1990s, Argentina's macroeconomic performance was extremely strong. From negative growth in the 1980s, its GDP grew over 50 percent in the 1991–97 period, and inflation fell from 23,104 percent in 1990 to around zero in 1997.

Unfortunately, in 1998 the Argentine economy entered into a long, drawn-out recession that exploded into one of the deepest crises in modern economic history in December 2001. In the end, the 1990s turned out to be just one more cycle in Argentina's history of hope and despair. Evaluating Argentina's dismal performance, most economists have blamed poor economic policies for these sad outcomes. We tend to agree with this perspective, but instead of emphasizing the "content" of economic policies (for example, how market-friendly they are), we focus on general policy "characteristics." Argentine policies are unstable in ways that weaken their

This chapter draws extensively from our article in the *Journal of Law, Economics, and Organization* (fall 2003), and from our forthcoming book. We thank Jeff Frieden, Steve Levitsky, Bob Barros, and especially Vicky Murillo for their insightful comments and criticism.

credibility in the eyes of economic actors. This weakened credibility renders them far less effective in bringing about the desired sustainable economic behavior (investment, saving, job creation, and the like) and the associated desired economic outcomes (growth, employment, and so on). Argentine policies are not only unstable, but they are also poorly coordinated among the different tiers of its federal structure, even among national government ministries, secretariats and programs. In many instances, Argentina lacks the investments in capacity that would be needed to produce effective policies. Furthermore, the Argentine state is quite ineffective in enforcing its policies.

We argue in this chapter that these undesirable properties of Argentine public policies are the result of a noncooperative policymaking process. Historical legacies and the constitutional context make the Argentine Congress a weak policymaking arena that lacks professionalization. Legislators respond to provincial party elites who care little about the quality of national policies. Furthermore, presidential proactive powers are too extensive in practice. As a result, the relevant policymaking actors, such as the president, the provincial governors, and interest groups, lack an institutionalized arena in which they can make intertemporal policy agreements. Additionally, they cannot delegate the implementation of potential policy agreements to a professional bureaucracy, because there is none. Nor can they rely on enforcement of contracts by the judiciary, because it is weak and politicized. Therefore, policymaking becomes the outcome of a noncooperative game that results in each actor behaving myopically and opportunistically. This causes policy volatility, poor coordination, and poor enforcement. Political and economic actors (domestic and foreign) distrust the Argentine polity's ability to deliver credible policies. In order to overcome this credibility problem, policymakers occasionally resort to very rigid mechanisms, such as the convertibility regime. Under adverse economic shocks, these approaches often turn out to be excessively costly.

In the first section below, we present our argument. The next section describes the features of Argentine policies. We then summarize the policymaking process. This is followed by an examination of the "archeology" of the workings of the Argentine political system, which explains the policymaking process.

THE ARGUMENT

Public policies are the outcomes of political decisions and exchanges among political actors over time. We argue that the policymaking process in Argentina is characterized by both a lack of cooperation and volatility over time, which results in low-quality policies. Two sets of variables shape this policymaking process: (1) high democratic instability from 1930 to 1983, and (2) constitutional structure and electoral rules. Together, these factors have brought about short time horizons for key policymakers and an inability to make and enforce intertemporal political and policy agreements.

A crucial component for the self-enforcement of intertemporal political and policy deals is that political actors have long horizons in their interactions. This is missing in Argentina, in part because of democratic instability. Between 1930 and 1983, twelve executives (both elected presidents and heads of de facto regimes) were removed from office by force. This history of instability has left an imprint on how political and institutional actors operate. For instance, the tendency of military governments and civilian regimes to remove Supreme Court justices has weakened the judiciary over the last half of the twentieth century, affecting its current functioning and reputation. It has transformed the Court into an institution with limited ability to restrain any excesses of the incumbent president. Also, high turnover in the executive has translated into even higher turnover in the upper echelons of the bureaucracy. This has hindered the development of cooperation across government agencies and has made it difficult to build a strong civil service.

Electoral mechanisms also contribute to the myopia of key political actors and to the weakening of arenas for intertemporal political compromise. Electoral rules in Argentina transfer power away from national legislators and national parties toward provincial party bosses. This leads to transient and "amateur" legislators, as party bosses have incentives to rotate them. These amateur legislators lack the incentives to undertake congressional activities, including supervising the bureaucracy or implementing the budget. This in turn gives the executive ample discretion in budget design and implementation. The executive's ability to make policy with little congressional intervention is an additional source of policy instability. And alternative institutions that could enforce intertemporal agreements, such as a well-functioning judiciary or an independent bureaucracy (to which policy implementation could be delegated), are absent.

All these factors lead to a policymaking process that lacks the institutional mechanisms for intertemporal agreements. Furthermore, the process fosters distrust among crucial actors (legislators, president, governors, and interest groups). It also encourages a lack of cooperation and vertical coordination across federal units and weak horizontal coordination across ministries. Actors work with short time horizons, and with each turn of

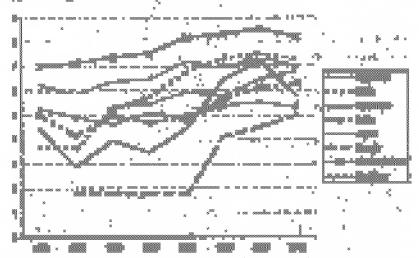

Figure 2.1   Volatility of economic policies. The vertical axis indicates the index of economic freedom (according to Gwartney, Lawson,and Block 1996)

the political wheel, policies tend to be changed. Citizens and investors distrust policies, and to bridge this credibility gap, governments have imposed awkward and rigid mechanisms in an attempt to build credibility. But these rigid mechanisms are unable to respond to the economy's changing states and in the end, they turn out to be very costly.

PUBLIC POLICIES IN ARGENTINA

The most noticeable characteristic of public policy in Argentina is its instability.[1] To illustrate the extent of this instability, we construct an aggregate indicator of policy stability using international indexes such as the Fraser Index of Economic Freedom, which grade the overall economic policy stance of a country according to its market-friendliness. In Figure 2.1, we plot the value of this variable from 1970 until 2002 for a small number of countries. During this period, Argentina swung from being one of the most market-friendly countries in a small sample of countries, to being the second least friendly country, surpassed only by the Soviet Union. It then rose in "friendliness" during the reform process of the 1990s. In terms of the complete sample of 106 countries, Argentina ranks as the

1. This section is based on Spiller and Tommasi, forthcoming, which presents evidence on Argentine public policies in international perspective, as well as a number of case studies of specific policy areas.

seventh most volatile country as measured by the coefficient of variation of the Fraser index over time. Argentina ranks as the fourth most unstable, if we consider only countries that oscillate in both directions (toward and away from market-friendliness), and exclude countries such as Chile or Russia that experienced changes in just one direction (market liberalization) (See Spiller and Tommasi, forthcoming).

Argentina displays policy instability not only at this very aggregate level but also at the level of more specific policies. For instance, in Spiller and Tommasi (forthcoming) we document the volatility of antipoverty programs in the 1990s. During these years, antipoverty programs underwent large changes, although congressional mandates stayed the same. Each time a new cabinet minister or secretary took office—a frequent event in Argentina—the incoming minister or secretary felt compelled to discontinue preexisting programs and to create his or her own policy, often with a substantial amount of tinkering with the geographical distribution of program funds.[2]

This volatility of policies shortens the time horizons of the economic and social actors that are supposed to respond to the policies, and hence reduces their effectiveness, inducing poor economic and social outcomes. For instance, in international surveys of businesspersons, corporate officers express the view that this policy volatility in Argentina is quite costly for the operation of their businesses (Spiller and Tommasi, forthcoming). On the other hand, other research suggests that Argentine businesses are reluctant to respond to export-promotion policies, because of uncertainty about their durability (Acuña 1991), and because trade policy uncertainty has had a substantial negative impact on Argentina's macroeconomic performance (Hopenhayn and Neumeyer 2003).

The Argentine state is also a weak enforcer of its policies. International evidence shows Argentina at the bottom of the list in terms of its ability to enforce tax collection, social security contributions, and the payment of minimum wages (Kay 2003; Spiller and Tommasi, forthcoming). This inadequate enforcement also weakens the credibility of Argentine economic policies.

The lack of credibility leads, at times, to the adoption of highly rigid policies. A notable example was the 1991 adoption of the straitjacket monetary mechanism of convertibility, which prevented the government from undertaking any macroeconomic policies in response to very adverse

---

2. The average tenure of a department head at the National Secretariat for Social Development is less than a year. Furthermore, the agency has been a secretariat, an undersecretariat, and a ministry and headed by, variously, highly qualified technocrats, high-profile politicians, the spouse of one president, and the sister of another.

shocks throughout the 1990s.[3] Another example of the inability to undertake efficient and flexible policies is found in the history of Argentina's fiscal federalism. Attempting to protect themselves from the opportunistic behavior of other actors down the road, national and provincial authorities have introduced all kinds of rigidities into the Federal Tax Sharing Agreement. These rigidities, such as tying specific tax revenues to specific geographical distributions, created all sorts of microeconomic inefficiencies during the 1980s and 1990s. An example of this was the national government agreement to transfer fixed nominal amounts to the provinces. In the great downturn of 2001, it was impossible for the national government to fulfill that promise. The conflict over its commitment and the inability to adjust the treasury to the adverse circumstances have been credited as the immediate causes of the Argentine default and the 2001–2 crisis (Tommasi 2002).

In sum, Argentine public policies are quite volatile, oftentimes too rigid, poorly coordinated among different policymaking actors, and plagued by the state's failure to invest in policymaking capabilities.

THE POLICYMAKING PROCESS

A federal republic consisting of twenty-three provinces and a semi-autonomous federal capital, the Argentine state is a presidential system with a bicameral legislature. In view of its similarities to the United States in terms of the basic constitutional structure, we begin by contrasting the role of the Argentine Congress with that of the U.S. Congress. The voluminous literature on the U.S. Congress provides a set of widely accepted characteristics: (1) members of the U.S. Congress exhibit remarkable longevity in their tenures in the legislative body; (2) members of the U.S. Congress tend to specialize in committees; (3) the U.S. Congress plays an active role in policymaking; and (4) the U.S. Congress engages in considerable oversight of the public bureaucracy.[4]

None of those characteristics is true of the Argentine Congress. Legislators are transient and do not specialize or acquire much policy expertise; Congress does not play an active role in the policymaking process (at most, it plays the role of a blunt veto player); Congress pays little attention to

---

3. The convertibility regime fixed the exchange rate of pesos to dollars at 1:1. The law made it difficult to change the nominal exchange rate. For details on the adoption of the convertibility regime and the subsequent dynamics that exploded into the 2001–2 economic, social, and political crisis, see Galiani, Heymann, and Tommasi 2003.

4. References for these assertions are provided in Jones et al. 2002.

oversight activities; and crucial political and policy bargains are struck in a less institutionalized manner, outside the national legislature.

There are several reasons why the Argentine Congress is not the center of policymaking. Most important is that existing electoral mechanisms make national legislators dependent upon provincial party leaders, while the executive avails itself of several instruments that amount to "making policy without Congress." Legislators depend most on provincial party bosses when they are also governors of the province, as often is the case. Although the president has many instruments to "undo" laws, it is Congress that has the constitutional power to legislate. In order to produce laws, the president is forced into exchanges with the "masters of the legislators," the governors, in order to assure approval of the president's legislative agenda. Governors, in turn, are not interested in national policies in general, but are especially interested in particular policies that have substantial impact in their provinces. It turns out that the foremost interest of provincial governors is the distribution of funds from the Federal Tax Sharing Agreement in order to finance their provinces as well as their political machines. This leads to continuous exchanges of votes in Congress, whereby the presidential agenda gains support in exchange for favors in the federal distribution of funds (a point further explained in the next section).

One of the consequences of amateur legislators, who spend short periods in Congress and who depend on provincial leaders who are not primarily interested in the quality of national policy, is that there is little or no investment in building legislative capacities or institutions. This neglect reinforces the centrality of the executive in policymaking. When specific policy issues are on the table, affected social and corporative actors focus their lobbying energies on the executive. Since executives are transient by definition, the result is that any possible policy deals are defined by short time horizons. This shortness of horizons, in turn, induces noncooperative behavior among the relevant actors. (From a game-theoretical perspective, especially the theory of repeated games, the possibility of cooperation depends crucially on the players' horizons.)[5]

Self-enforcement through the expectation of repeated interactions in the future is one way of inducing cooperative behavior over time. Cooperative agreements might be sustained through alternative enforcement mechanisms. One such mechanism would be the presence of a strong and independent judiciary that might enforce previous political bargains over

5. See Spiller and Tommasi 2003 and Spiller, Stein, and Tommasi 2003 for a more formal treatment of these issues.

time. Unfortunately, Argentina's judiciary, especially the Supreme Court, has not been a good enforcer either, as it has tended to be "too aligned" with the president (see below; also see Helmke, this volume).

Delegating the implementation of policy agreements over time to an independent and technically qualified bureaucracy would be another way of enforcing cooperation. A professional bureaucracy, well supervised by Congress, could be a channel for enforcing intertemporal political agreements. As we explain in more detail later in this chapter, Argentina does not have such a bureaucracy, the top echelons of the bureaucracy are very unstable, and the quality of policy implementation (including enforcement) is quite poor.

All these factors combine to produce a policymaking process that lacks the institutional means for well-informed debate, negotiation, and implementation of policy agreements. This inability to sustain and enforce policies over time leads to the deep lack of credibility that characterizes Argentine policies. Attempts to overcome these credibility problems are usually rigid policy mechanisms that prevent future policy changes. Unfortunately, these mechanisms, which are designed to avoid political opportunism, are hard to adjust when economic and social circumstances change. This leads to very large costs in the end, as is sadly illustrated by the history of Argentina's convertibility regime.

THE WORKINGS OF POLITICAL INSTITUTIONS IN ARGENTINA

Congress Is Not Too Important in Policymaking

Legislators in Argentina have high turnover and low tenure rates. Part of that high turnover has come from Argentina's great political instability in the second half of the twentieth century. High turnover, however, is not just the result of past democratic instability. High turnover still characterizes the Argentine Congress twenty years after the return to democratic rule in 1983. Since 1983, turnover rates have always exceeded 40 percent, with very low reelection rates—only 20 percent of incumbents return to their seats. Of all the members of the lower house elected from 1983 to 2001, 85 percent served only one term, 11 percent two terms, and only 4 percent three or more terms.[6] These figures are similar to those of countries with term limits, like Costa Rica (Jones et al. 2001).

---

6. Furthermore, Jones et al. (2001) show that the probability of reelection *declines* with tenure.

Looking at the determinants of high turnover, one discovers that it is not the result of voters' rejection. Most legislators simply do not show up in the provincial party list for the next election. Those who do have a two-thirds probability of being reelected. That conditional reelection rate is lower than the 94 percent of the United States, but comparable to that of many other countries that have, nonetheless, much higher unconditional reelection rates. In Brazil, for instance, 70 percent of legislators seek reelection, and 62 percent of them obtain it, leading to a total reelection rate of 43 percent. Comparable figures for Chile are 76 percent, 78 percent, and 59 percent (Spiller and Tommasi, forthcoming).

Argentine legislators have short tenures because those in charge of compiling the list of candidates (the "selectorate") do not reappoint them. Given that electoral districts coincide with provinces, and given the mechanisms of internal candidate selection, this *selectorate* is made up of provincial party elites.

The 257 members of the Argentine lower house are elected from twenty-four multimember districts, the twenty-three provinces, and the Federal Capital, for four-year terms. One-half of the lower house is renewed every two years, with every district renewing one half of its legislators. Members are elected from closed party lists. A major difference from the United States is that intraparty and general electoral rules have made provincial party leaders powerful actors in national politics.

De Luca, Jones, and Tula (2002) show in detail that provincial-level party leaders are the key players in the nomination process, with both national party leaderships and rank-and-file members playing a decidedly secondary role. Jones et al. (2001), analyzing the incentives of local party leaders and legislators, show that in equilibrium, no one has an incentive to build a long-term career in Congress.[7]

All of this limits the incentives of legislators to invest in policymaking capacities. Legislators have little incentive to specialize, to acquire policy expertise, or to develop strong congressional institutions. As a consequence, Congress is not a source of strong oversight of the executive or the bureaucracy. Jones et al. (2002) provide evidence on the patterns of legislative committee organization and membership: legislators tend to belong to a large number of committees, and they remain less than one legislative period on each committee, even on the important ones. This is

7. These amateur legislators are nonetheless *professional* politicians. After serving a term in Congress, they are shifted to other political activities in the party, province, or federal government. Jones et al. (2001) show that of the 108 lower-house members in the 1991–95 cohort, as of mid-1998, 83 percent were in other positions strongly influenced by party ties. Congress is just a temporary stop in their political careers.

a sharp contrast with the situation in the U.S. Congress, where legislators are selected by constituencies, have long careers, specialize in powerful committees, and acquire substantial policy expertise.[8]

We have noted that national legislators owe allegiance to provincial party leaders. This dependence is strengthened when the leadership in question coincides with provincial government. This heightened dependence occurs because provincial executives both have more currency with which to reward and punish their representatives in the national congress, and more need to occasionally pull legislative strings to obtain benefits for their provinces. The strength of provincial governors has been reinforced by electoral outcomes. During 1983–2001, the legislative contingent of the president's party has oscillated between 45.1 percent and 51.6 percent (Molinelli, Palanza, and Sin 1999, Table 2.121; Calvo and Murillo, this volume, Table 9.1), automatically granting veto power over the president's agenda to any unified block of votes from a few provinces.

Governors, then, are extremely important players even for *national* politics and policies. A crucial question then is what do governors care about? The next section analyzes the arena in which provincial governors' main concern, the distribution of tax revenues, is determined.

The Federal Game

In Argentina, national and subnational politics and policies are intertwined to a much larger (and more convoluted) extent than in other federal polities. The main "linkages" are (1) from the subnational to the national political arena, through the electoral mechanisms described in the previous section, and (2) from "central" decision-making to provincial politics and policies, through the channel of federal fiscal arrangements.

Provinces undertake a large fraction of total spending, yet collect only a small fraction of taxes. Provincial spending amounts to 50 percent of the total consolidated public sector spending. This figure rises to close to 70 percent if we exclude the pension system and focus on "more discretionary" spending. Furthermore, the type of spending in the hands of provincial governments, such as public employment and social programs, tend to be the most politically attractive, and much closer to territorially based

---

8. Several comparative indicators place the quality of Argentine legislators and the policy-making capacity of the Argentine Congress below that of some comparable Latin American countries, such as Chile or Brazil. For instance, Argentine legislators are less educated than those in Chile or Colombia, have lower reelection rates than all the countries in Latin America except those with term limits, and are less focused on substantive policy issues than their Chilean or Brazilian counterparts (see Jones et al., forthcoming, and references there).

constituencies. Yet, on average, provinces finance only 35 percent of that spending with their own revenues. The rest of their spending is financed out of a common pool of resources, the "Federal Tax Sharing Agreement." In a large number of small provinces the proportion of funds coming from this common pool constitutes over 80 percent of their funding. Local politicians, then, enjoy a large share of the political benefits of spending and pay only a small fraction of the political costs of taxation.[9]

This fiscal structure at the provincial level is one reason why many professional politicians are more interested in pursuing a career through appointment at the provincial government or even party level, than in the national Congress. At the same time, the powerful provincial brokers, namely, the governors, depend heavily on the allocation of "central" monies to their provinces to run both their political and their policy businesses. That is, they need central money to deliver particularistic political goods, as well as to provide general public goods in their province. There are several channels for funneling central funds to the provinces, with the main mechanisms being the geographical allocation of the national budget and the Federal Tax-Sharing Agreement.

The game in which these allocations are determined is the source of many political and policy distortions, at both the national and the provincial levels. The game even affects the quality of democracy at the local level. The Argentine voter at the provincial level tends to reward the politicians who are most effective at extracting resources from the center, and who are not necessarily the most competent or honest administrators.[10] Given the political mechanisms by which funds are allocated, this also adds uncertainty to provincial public finances, because it is not easy to project future allocations.

The history and evolution of the Tax-Sharing Agreement (narrated in detail in Tommasi 2002) is fraught with examples of opportunistic manipulation, occasionally curtailed by fairly rigid and inefficient mechanisms. Unilateral, bilateral, and coalitional opportunism (by the national government, a province, or a set of provinces that turn out to be pivotal for an important vote in Congress) has been common in the allocation of central government monies to the provinces. The national executive has enjoyed substantial discretion in the geographical allocation of items in the federal budget. In an attempt to prevent adverse changes in the future (such as a

9. Calvo and Murillo (in this volume) address the details of these mechanisms, their geography, and the comparative advantages of different parties in reaching different constituencies.

10. Jones, Sanguinetti, and Tommasi (2002) show that voters in Argentina, unlike those in the United States, reward provincial spending at gubernatorial elections.

reduction in the amount going to any specific province), political actors have tended to impose increased rigidity on the Tax-Sharing Agreement, reducing government capacity to adjust fiscal policy to changed economic circumstances. An example of such rigidities was the earmarking of taxes for specific programs with clear regional distributional effects. This earmarking led to a rigid and convoluted system of federal tax collection and tax distribution, which became known as the "Argentine Fiscal Labyrinth."

Recent attempts at simplifying that labyrinth, which also reflect the inability to strike efficient intertemporal agreements, led to the 1999 and 2000 "Fiscal Pacts" between the national and provincial governments. As explained in Eaton (in this volume) and Tommasi 2002, the central government's rigid guarantee of a minimum revenue for the provinces became a very costly straitjacket for the De la Rúa government in the weeks that led to the 2001 crisis. Similarly, the provinces' lack of cooperation has been cited as on immediate cause of the country's move to default (Eaton, this volume).[11]

The last episode of the Argentine federal fiscal drama, leading to the largest default in modern world economic history, was a clear manifestation of one of the central points in our argument. Provincial governors are crucial players in national politics and policymaking, but have only a secondary interest in national public goods (such as macroeconomic stability), in the quality of national policies, and in investing in institutions (such as a professional Congress, or a stronger civil service) that might improve the quality of polices.

Weak Judicial Enforcement

The workings of judicial institutions have direct implications for the feasibility of private contracting, of contracting among private and public actors, and of arrangements among political agents.[12] We focus here on the latter, emphasizing the role of the Supreme Court as potential enforcer of constitutional and legislative contracts. In the last several decades, the Argentine Supreme Court has not been a strong and impartial enforcer of political agreements. The reasons for weak judicial enforcement lie more in politics than in the lack of jurisprudence. Indeed, Iaryczower, Spiller, and Tommasi (2002) show that a strategic behavioral model similar to the one used to explain the U.S. Supreme Court explains the behavior of

11. Tommasi (2002) also describes how the build-up of a very dangerous aggregate fiscal position in the late 1990s was related to national-provincial political bargaining.

12. All claims in this subsection are substantiated in Iaryczower, Spiller, and Tommasi 2002.

Argentine Supreme Court justices quite well. Furthermore, the fragmentation of the Argentine polity would suggest that the Argentine Court should
be rather strong and independent. History, however, has intervened to
give key explanatory variables of the behavior of Argentine Supreme Court
justices very different values from those observed in the United States.
These characteristics have resulted in a substantially diminished role for
the Argentine Supreme Court.

In particular, since the mid-1940s, Argentine Supreme Court justices
have had very short tenures. Indeed, it is one of the supreme courts with
the shortest average tenure in the world. From 1960 until the mid 1990s,
the average Argentine justice served less than five years. This low average
tenure of Argentine justices puts the country at the bottom of the rankings,
along with countries not usually associated with long-term stability and
the rule of law, such as Lesotho and Rwanda. Argentina ranks far below
the United States, where tenures average over twenty-two years, and Chile
and Norway, where tenures average over fifteen years (Iaryczower, Spiller,
and Tommasi, forthcoming).

Short tenures were not always the norm in Argentina. After World War
I, the Argentine Court was on a path of convergence with the U.S. Supreme Court. From the creation of the Argentine Court in 1863 until the
mid 1920s, the average tenure of Supreme Court justices increased systematically, reaching the same level as in the United States during the
1920s (Iaryczower, Spiller, and Tommasi 2002). Subsequent political instability drastically reduced the tenure of justices on the bench. During his
first administration, Perón impeached the sitting Supreme Court justices,
an act which had a lasting impact. At that point, the norm of not manipu-
lating Supreme Court membership disappeared. Subsequent military and
civilian executives who alternated in power appointed their own Courts. In
1991, the first time since 1946 that a president might have faced an opposition Court, President Carlos Menem expanded the size of the Court from
five to nine members, thereby granting himself a "working" judicial majority. Indeed, control over the Court was such that from the mid-1940s
until Fernando De la Rúa's inauguration in 1999, no president faced a
Court with a majority appointed by a political adversary.

Courts whose justices' tenures are very short naturally tend to be
aligned with the sitting government and, hence, are unlikely to wield their
power of judicial review with any force. During a large part of the twentieth
century—mostly because of the de facto nature of the governments, but
also because of the political alignments that occurred during the interim
spells with democratic rule—executives often enjoyed a high level of political support in the legislature. This alignment is also a variable that discour-

ages the Supreme Court from challenging the government (Iaryczower, Spiller, and Tommasi 2002).[13]

The dynamics of a Court without much clout and respect are fairly perverse and self-reinforcing, to the point that several recent presidential candidates have promised to remove sitting justices, and the current president Nestor Kirchner is successfully altering the composition of the Court.

A Bureaucracy Without Long-Term Principals

One possible mechanism for the enforcement of intertemporal political agreements is delegation to a relatively independent, yet accountable, bureaucracy. Argentina, however, has not developed such a bureaucracy. Rauch and Evans (1999) rank Argentina in the bottom five among thirty-five developing countries in terms of bureaucratic quality. As argued by Spiller and Urbiztondo (1994), the absence of long-term principals conspires against the buildup of a professional bureaucracy. Executives in almost all presidential systems are transient. Likewise, in Argentina, the Congress is a not long-term principal, as legislators rotate rapidly and are not particularly motivated to control the administration.[14]

The bureaucracy, as a consequence, faces weak long-term incentives, facilitating shirking and requiring intrusive administrative controls to avoid corruption. This further reduces the ability to generate timely and effective policies. Each new executive, unable to motivate or fire the permanent bureaucracy, nominates large numbers of political appointees. This is usually done under flexible labor agreements; they can be easily fired, something that often happens when their direct superiors change. This practice creates a transient parallel bureaucracy. The parallel bureaucracy undertakes the same actions that the normal bureaucracy is designed to effect, but is unable or unwilling to undertake. The turnover at the ministerial and secretarial levels also implies turnover in the "parallel bureaucracy." This turnover limits the extent of institutional knowledge and the

---

13. Helmke (this volume) points out that justices start tilting their rulings *against* the executive when he becomes less likely to stay much longer, in what she calls "strategic defection." But both strategic accommodation and strategic defection reflect some deviation from impartial rulings only on the merits of the case, something that we conjecture would be more likely if the Supreme Court were stronger. See also Miller 1997.

14. As Krehbiel (1991) argues, legislators everywhere tend to undersupply a kind of public good such as controlling the administration. That effect is magnified in Argentina, since legislators only attend to the interests of provincial party leaders, who are not particularly interested in the quality of national policymaking.

development of cooperation across ministries and secretariats, deepening both the heterogeneity in policy quality and the lack of policy coherence.

The parallel bureaucracy is widespread, but its extent is difficult to measure. Bambaci, Spiller, and Tommasi (2001) report information for one agency. In that case, the parallel bureaucracy represented well above 50 percent of total employment in the agency studied and a larger fraction of the wage bill, as those employees in the parallel bureaucracy tended to be better paid (but more transient) than permanent civil servants at similar levels.[15]

The Executive in a Noncooperative Policymaking Equilibrium

The policymaking environment in Argentina is one in which institutions like Congress that are designed to facilitate political debate, bargaining, and the intertemporal enforcement of agreements are quite weak; in which key political players (the governors) care little about national policy; and in which complementary enforcement mechanisms such as a strong judiciary or a strong bureaucracy are also lacking. These factors are reinforced by, and in turn reinforce, the capacity and tendency of the executive to act unilaterally.

The reasons behind the executive's ability to act without constraint and undo previous (say, legislative) agreements are varied. Factors include the Supreme Court's tendency to be politically aligned with the president, the lack of a strong and independent bureaucracy, and the "general equilibrium" result that Congress has not built strong technical capacities. The budget process manifests this feature. Congress's inability to monitor and control the budget has given the administration substantial budgetary discretion. Since the beginning of the twentieth century, Congress has often failed to approve in time the budget sent by the executive, which in practice has meant that the administration has functioned independently of Congress. In high inflation years the executive often did not bother to submit a budget. Even in the low inflation period of the 1990s, although ex ante budgets began to be approved on time, ex post control was not exercised. The ex post budget verification process ("Cuenta de Inversión") was not

---

15. Although in principle, national parties could develop a cadre of potential bureaucrats, the fragmentation of national parties into provincial parties makes such cadre development ineffective as compared to the practice of a parallel bureaucracy composed of individuals highly aligned to the secretary or minister of the moment. A current example of this fragmentation is the composition of the top echelons of the administration of President Kirchner, crowded with people from his home province.

initiated promptly enough for Congress to use it as an operational instrument to verify the fulfillment of the budget "contract" by the executive.[16] Current budget practice has tended to overestimate revenues, and the (nonlegislative) ex post adjustment mechanism has given substantial leeway to the secretary of the treasury to allocate scarce funds. Secretaries of the treasury have exercised this prerogative according to a mix of their own whims and pressure from line ministries, occasionally arbitrated by the president.[17]

The executive's unilateral power has also been based on constitutional capacities and practices that amount to granting proactive legislative powers to the president. These practices have evolved partly because political instability tended to focus processes in the executive that in a more stable environment would have drifted toward the legislature. They also result from explicit constitutional capacities and constitutional lacunae (and their interpretation by a weak Supreme Court). These include the fact that the president is endowed with the capacity to "regulate" the laws from Congress, and has taken up the practice of issuing Decrees of Urgency and Necessity (Carey and Shugart 1998; Molinelli, Palanza, and Sin 1999).

Some authors, such as Magar (2001a) and Jones (2001), have argued against the oversimplified "hyperpresidential" views of Argentine politics, indicating that policies in Argentina are not the outcome of an all-powerful executive interacting with a totally irrelevant Congress. We have no quarrel with this assertion. As Jones's (2001) account of the budget process makes clear, the distribution of seats in Congress does matter, for instance, for the geographical distribution of the budget. However, it is remarkable that these "deals" are not cut in Congress, but in executive chambers. Further evidence of extralegislative exchanges with the executive is presented in Murillo (2001), with regards to many of the market-oriented measures of the 1990s.[18]

16. Jones (2001) indicates that almost all of the substantial budget activity happens in executive quarters, not in Congress: "Relatively little modification of the budget proposed by the executive branch occurs at any time during the treatment of the budget bill in Congress" (161). Furthermore, Jones indicates that while ministries and other entities submit detailed disaggregated budget plans to the (executive) National Budget Office, the draft finally sent to Congress contains expenditure only at a very macro level (160).

17. Based on a personal interview in 1999 with the then secretary of the treasury, Pablo Guidotti, as well as on a recent presentation by Jorge Baldrich (2003), who was secretary of the treasury in 2001.

18. Pion-Berlin (1997) also provides an excellent example of the different loci for lobbying activities in the United States (Congress-centered) and in Argentina (executive-centered), for defense budgeting.

QUO VADIMUS?

We return now to some of the issues raised at the beginning of this chapter. In the 1990s Argentina undertook a rather surprising, sharp turn toward market-oriented policies. According to the logic of policymaking described here, that turn was not the outcome of a reasoned public debate in which most relevant political actors considered whether this policy shift was the most desirable course of action. It was a decision of the executive of the day, approved by Congress through "votes" that were largely purchased through the federal fiscal system and related mechanisms.[19]

The implementation of these reforms carried the imprint of the noncooperative policymaking process described here. This was reflected in several peculiar characteristics of the policies of the 1990s, such as the rigidity of the convertibility regime, the inefficiencies of federal fiscal arrangements, the lack of enforcement of some policies, and the incoherence of privatization and regulatory policies across sectors. The overall experiment, including the convertibility regime, did not end well, at least as evaluated by the Argentine public at the time of this writing. The current Kirchner administration is fairly outspoken in its opposition to several aspects of the reform process of the 1990s. It seems clear that unless some fundamental changes in the rules of the political game take place, we will continue to observe low-quality policies, independent of their political orientation.

19. See Tommasi 2002, Etchemendy (in this volume), and references there.

Old Actors in New Markets:
Transforming the Populist/Industrial Coalition
in Argentina, 1989–2001

Sebastián Etchemendy

INTRODUCTION: RECASTING THE POPULIST/INDUSTRIAL COALITION

Dominant approaches to the study of the political economy of marketization have to a great extent overlooked the role that traditionally protected actors in industry and labor have played in shaping emerging market economies. Indeed, we know little about the transformation of the old populist/ industrial coalition in cases of sweeping economic liberalization such as Argentina during the 1990s. Why were the "insiders," that is to say, union leadership and workers who remained in the formal sector, rather than laid-off workers or the rising mass of unemployed, the most privileged by governmental attempts to lessen the costs of reform? Why were some industrial interests, and not others, able to gain crucial government concessions? Even a government that has forsaken traditional macroeconomic tools for favoring domestic actors in industry and labor can still resort to a variety of compensatory policies, such as the awarding of state assets, tariff regimes, direct subsidies, or the granting of specific protections in future markets. Thus, rather than being unambiguous losers from market re-

The author thanks David Collier, Ruth Berins Collier, Candelaria Garay, Steven Levitsky, Victoria Murillo, and the members of the Latin American Politics Group at Berkeley.

form, some key industrial and labor actors within the old ısı coalition[1] can and do preserve their existing market power in the new "liberal" order.

Moreover, a salient, though often neglected, aspect of Argentina's marketization is that main actors of the "old order"—such as powerful industry-based groups and mainstream union leadership—were favored by the government and brought into the liberalization coalition. This pattern of compensations bestowed on old powerful ısı actors was not replicated in other experiences of sweeping market reform such as Chile from 1973 to 1989, Spain from 1982 to 1995, Peru in the 1990s, or Brazil under President Fernando Henrique Cardoso. In Argentina, I argue, dominant unions and certain established industrial players were part of the *reform coalition*. Not only were they favored by government policies, they were actively involved in the drafting of the deregulatory frameworks that affected their business and sectors. Crucially, the alliance with protected actors of the old order, based on compensations such as the partial deregulation of specific markets and targeted privatizations, facilitated rather than obstructed the general process of market restructuring in Argentina.

Toward the late 1980s, Argentina appeared to be an unlikely case for radical and sustainable neoliberal reform. Traditional Peronist unions and powerful and protected industry-based conglomerates had thwarted liberalization attempts by the democratic administration of President Raúl Alfonsín (1983–89). Indeed, the political viability of the market reforms that President Carlos Menem carried out in the 1990s cannot be understood without focusing on the politics of compensations to these traditional actors. However, this chapter will argue that the political deals built around compensatory policies in the early 1990s had a double-edged nature: they made sweeping economic liberalization politically feasible in a context of a democratic regime and powerful antireform actors, yet at the same time they undermined the governance and economic sustainability of the neoliberal model in the long run.

This chapter has two main goals: first, to explain why the Menem government chose to compensate some specific labor and industrial interests, and not others, in crafting its coalition for reform; and second, to assess the consequences of this pattern of transformation of the populist/industrial coalition in Argentina for the eventual crisis of the neoliberal order in late 2001. The first part of the chapter explains what interests in the domain of business and labor were brought into the reform coalition in Ar-

1. By ısı (import substitution industrialization), I refer to the semi-closed economy in place before the sweeping liberalization of the 1990s. The old coalition consisted of unions and the manufacturing industry, which were the main beneficiaries of the protection of domestic markets and of the inward-oriented pattern of development.

gentina, and in what way. In the case of business, firms in four of the formerly protected industrial sectors—oil, autos, steel, and petrochemicals—can be defined as *political* winners. These firms were deliberately favored by some kind of governmental compensatory policy—a targeted privatization, a special tariff regime, or some other form of subsidy—in the face of tariff deregulation.

This handful of firms and industrial groups shared some fundamental traits. First, they operated in mixed (namely, public and private) sectors of production, which had historically wielded a high lobbying power because of their constant accommodation with the state. Second, these firms were the most powerful in economic and political terms at the outset of reform. Therefore, they had resources to invest in exchange for compensatory policies, and they could ensure the acquiescence of major sectoral and national industrial associations to general market restructuring. Finally, the fact that these companies were mostly locally owned and hegemonic in their sectors increased the pressure for compensations. They were not like foreign companies that could resort to external networks to attenuate the costs of reform in tariff liberalization. Nor were they like state industrial companies, whose managers respond to reformers and can get payoffs in alternative arenas. In contrast, the viability of these private domestic firms based in heavy industries in which Argentina did not have any particular comparative advantages depended heavily on state compensatory measures. In short, unlike other semi-closed economies, Argentina's postwar development had generated *very strong* potential losers of marketization, a fact that subsequently shaped the bargains around compensations.

In the case of labor, I contend that the Argentine corporatist institutional structure strongly biased the compensatory policies toward union leaders and insiders (workers who remained in the formal sector). As this chapter argues, the negotiation between corporatist unions and governments over market reforms is likely to turn into a positive-sum game. Once the course of market restructuring seemed unavoidable, mainstream unions in Argentina had a major goal concerning the liberalized economy: the preservation of noncompetitive corporatist institutions in the new order. By contrast, in noncorporatist settings—such as, for example, Spain or Bolivia—unions have much to lose and little to gain from marketization. Moreover, as I show below, central features of corporatist labor institutions in Argentina turned side payments such as the union administration of pension funds or ownership programs in privatized companies into rational options for union leaders.

In the final part of the chapter I argue that the way in which a coalition with powerful ISI actors was crafted in the early 1990s contributed to the economic and political crisis that has subsequently destabilized the Argentine neoliberal experiment. Compensations had two main consequences for businesses. First, by buying off the losers from an increasingly overvalued exchange rate for labor and industry in the tradable sector, compensations supported an exchange rate policy that would eventually undermine Argentina's economic performance. Second, no governmental strategy of industrial policy for global competition beyond side payments—such as targeted privatization or the granting of market reserves—was developed. In these times of international liberalization, the compensations found in the Argentine case were, paradoxically, based on control of *domestic* markets. Consequently, when those payoffs were "consumed" in the boom of the first half of the decade (that is to say, when no more domestic market share could be gained and the privatization process was over), and in view of the continuous overvaluation of the Argentine currency, even the most powerful players in the business industrial sector were caught with very disadvantageous relative prices and very low export capacity.

In the case of labor, compensatory policies biased toward the unions and workers who remained in the formal sector cemented a strong insider/outsider divide within the working class. The unions' concentration on bureaucratic and regulatory benefits obtained in the 1990s, and their lack of incentives to build any bridge toward the unemployed, paved the way for the surge of autonomous and rebellious organizations of the unemployed. Abandoned by national compensatory programs and mainstream unionism, the unemployed were ready to be mobilized and to engage in direct action in the streets. The rapid spread of a variety of these organizations, the majority of which lacked any connection with the traditional system of representation, fueled the governability crises that eventually resulted in the collapse of Menem's successor government led by the UCR-FREPASO coalition in December 2001.

WHO WAS COMPENSATED AND WHY

Industry: Political Winners

President Menem took office in July 1989 in the midst of a hyperinflationary spurt, which significantly reduced his room for maneuver. To curb spending and restrain public sector wages, the administration launched a harsh stabilization plan. In a context of initial macroeconomic instability the government did not hesitate to deepen the liberalization trend by lifting capital controls and liberalizing the exchange rate and the current account. In March 1991, the recently appointed minister of the economy Domingo Cavallo launched the "Convertibility Plan." At Cavallo's request, Congress fixed the exchange rate at one to one in relation to the dollar. The Convertibility Law also required the monetary base to match the amount of foreign reserves in the Central Bank and, therefore, precluded financing the fiscal deficit by means of Central Bank monetary emission. Along with the fixed exchange rate, tariff reform became a crucial tool to anchor the price of tradable goods. The process of economic integration with Brazil, Uruguay, and Paraguay in the context of Mercosur, formalized in the Ouro Preto Agreement of 1994, deepened the liberalization trend. After successful stabilization, Argentina experienced a period of sustained growth: GDP grew at an average rate of 7.6 percent per year between 1991 and 1994. Following the Mexican crisis of 1995, the country resumed growth during 1996 and 1997, albeit at a slower pace. In addition, by 1996 the vast majority of Argentine public enterprises had been transferred to private hands in one of the largest privatizations in the region.[2]

Analyses of manufacturing industry during the liberalization period have pointed out the difficulties for domestic production that result from the trimming of tariffs and exchange rate appreciation. However, even within a process of "disarticulated restructuring" (Kosacoff 1993), some sectors were able to profit from the higher domestic and foreign investment and by the stability in relative prices set off by the Convertibility Plan. Yet my measure of what constitutes a winner in the industrial domain is *political*. It is political in that the government implemented a public policy—a privatization, a specific tariff regime or moderation of the liberalization pace, or a direct subsidy—the goal of which was to benefit a specific group of firms within a sector.

In a context of exchange rate appreciation and general tariff deregulation, the government compensated groups of firms in four tradable sectors—oil extraction, petrochemicals, autos, and steel—through two basic means. In the first place, industrial privatization in these sectors consisted of a more or less direct awarding of state assets. Second, especially in autos, steel, and oil, the pace of deregulation was consistently slowed down, and businesspersons in these sectors were actively involved in formulating the deregulation polices that affected their business. For example, the regime for motor vehicles was drafted at the bargaining table with ADEFA, the association of local automakers. The decrees that established the (partial) deregulation of the oil sector were pushed through in constant

---

2. For a general analysis on the political economy of neoliberal reform in Argentina during the first part of the 1990s, see Gerchunoff and Torre 1996 and Acuña 1994.

consultation with the affected domestic companies.[3] The leverage of the local steelmakers in the organization of the bidding for the privatization of SOMISA also appears to have been quite high.

Let me briefly address the dynamics of deregulation and industrial reform in these four sectors. In the case of petroleum production, most private capital was integrated in the industry through service contracts of oil extraction with the state, which were signed in different periods since the 1950s. Prior to the 1990s, private contractors at the level of extraction did not own the oil but had to deliver it to the oil state monopoly YPF for a fixed price. As a result, deregulation posed severe threats to upstream private producers: their old contracts of extraction could become uncertain in a general restructuring of the sector, and refiners would enjoy a greater ability to buy crude oil in the international market. Yet, in the privatization of oil fields the state consistently favored domestic producers over foreign companies such as Shell or Amoco.[4] Moreover, the pre-reform contracts of extraction were transformed into private concessions under which domestic producers would actually own the oil and would be free to sell it in the domestic market or abroad. In other words, deregulation of the old regimes of oil extraction was limited to the areas run by the former state monopoly and not by the domestic producers. As a result of these compensatory policies, former YPF contractors were able to expand their share of production in the post-reform period. For example, the national producer Pérez Companc went from 8 percent of the market share in 1988 to 15 percent in 1995. Astra, another traditional contractor, expanded its market share from 1.2 percent in 1988 to around 8 percent in 1997.

A second group of private firms favored by governmental policies in the midst of liberalization is found in the steel industry. In this case, industrial adjustment was also tempered by a combination of awarding of state assets and a consistent moderation in the opening of the sector. National holdings Acindar and Techint (through its controlled firms Siderca and Pro-

3. As a top official at the Department of Energy during the deregulation asserted, "The lawyers of the involved oil companies actively participated in the drafting of the decrees that established the oil sector deregulation. In fact it could be said that the lawyers of ASTRA and the other companies wrote those decrees" (personal interview, Buenos Aires, November 2000).

4. As a top executive of Amoco Argentina, one of the losers in the liberalization of the oil sector, put it: "We presented a bid just formally, to stay on good terms with the government, but everyone knew who the winners would be" (personal interview, Buenos Aires, January 15, 2001). Of the four oil fields with greatest productivity, three were awarded to national producers Astra, Pérez Companc, and TecPetrol, and only the fourth went to foreign producer Total. Shell Argentina criticized the privatization of one of the central areas—the "Puesto Hernandez" oilfield, awarded to Pérez Companc—as not very transparent (see Gadano and Stuzenegger 1998).

pulsora Siderúrgica) were the only private companies integrated in the three main segments of the production chain: reduction of iron, production of crude steel, and hot/cold steel rolling. Any assessment of liberalization of the steel sector in Argentina should take into account the privatization of the state giant SOMISA in 1992. The government sold the state mill to Techint, the only holding company to participate in the bidding. The German firm Thyssen and the Italian firm Iretecnia pulled out of the privatization bidding, denouncing a bias in favor of domestic producers (Lozano 1992, 11; see also Bisang and Chidiak 1995, 17). The sector was also advantaged through a series of antidumping measures that seriously undermined the opening of the steel market (Gerchunoff, Bozzalla, and Sanguinetti 1994). Besides, the nominal tariff, even if lowered, was set well above the national average and also above international averages for steel products (M&S Consulting 2002, 31). As a result of these measures, the position of the traditional private producers of steel in the domestic market was notably strengthened.[5]

Finally, the automobile and petrochemical industries were also brought into the coalition with local industrial sectors. In the case of autos, although the sector was gradually opened, foreign competition was initially eschewed in favor of established producers. Local producers CIADEA (Renault license), Sevel (Fiat and Peugeot licenses), and Iveco (trucks), as well as the foreign group Autolatina (a product of the merger of Volkswagen and Ford in Argentina), obtained a special regime that set the tariff at 30 percent—well above the nominal general average—both for Mercosur and world imports. Likewise, it regulated import quotas of 10 percent of local production. Local petrochemicals industries Ipako and Indupa were awarded full control of their joint ventures with the state in the initial privatization round in the sector. No competitive bidding was undertaken in the awarding of these assets. Most crucially, these companies obtained a favorable renegotiation of their debts with the National Development Bank, BANADE, the state bank that had subsidized credit for domestic industry before 1989 (see Chudnovsky and López 1997).

At this point the question becomes: why were firms within these four sectors able to get to the bargaining table and obtain important payoffs, while firms in other sectors, such as the parts and components car industry, textiles, paper, and machine tools, had to face unfettered liberalization? Moreover, why would a government generally friendly to international investors initially privilege local production over foreign competition in these

---

5. See Etchemendy 2001, 18, for details of market share before and after reform.

Table 3.1 Leading thirty nonfinancial firms in sales and profits at the outset of reform (1988)

	In the top thirty in sales		In the top thirty in profits	
	Number	Percentage	Number	Percentage
Compensated Firms 1989–99 (autos, oil, steel, petrochemicals)	9	23%	11	52%
Foreign Firms	8	22%	10	24%
Local, Non-Compensated	5	11%	7	17%
State*	8	44%	2	7%
Total	30	100%	30	100%

SOURCE: Mercado Review Ranking, August 31, 1989.

*Because of the unreliability of the data, state utility and service firms with high volatility in their balances are excluded from the assessment of profits. The only two state firms included are Aerolíneas Argentinas and PBB. State companies in the utility and service sectors were unlikely to be among the top thirty most profitable firms.

sectors? The answer lies in a series of structural and political characteristics of dominant firms in these sectors

In the first place, these are firms that operate in mixed sectors, that is, sectors with state and private production. In cases of ISI models that have undergone some deepening, firms in mixed sectors hold, all else being equal, a greater lobbying capacity when compared to firms in entirely private sectors: companies in mixed sectors have been establishing oligopolies with the state for years, alternating disputes with accommodation. As classic political economy perspectives assert, these heavy industries with sunk costs have traditionally exerted great pressure on the state, especially in Latin America (Frieden 1991a, 35). The lobbying experience that mixed sectors had developed because they were core ISI sectors with high levels of state intervention constituted a good asset for the future negotiation over liberalization. In addition, firms in mixed sectors obviously had greater chances to concentrate their market share through privatization in the post-reform period as compared to sectors where production was already entirely private.

Second, firms in these four sectors were the largest and most powerful in economic terms at the outset of reform. This power can be assessed on three levels: volumes of sales, volumes of profits, and what I call structural power: the value that the sectors generate in relation to their level of concentration. Table 3.1 summarizes data on sales and profits.

These firms—Pérez Companc, Bridas, and Astra (oil); Sevel and Autolatina (autos); and Techint and Acindar (steel), plus the chemical-based Indupa and Ipako—were among Argentina's largest companies in terms of sales and profits. They poured the highest level of sales into the economy after the state-run firms (mostly public services), albeit on similar levels as foreign world players such as IBM, Shell, Esso, and Unilever. More impressively, however, they supplied 52 percent of the total profits among the country's top thirty companies at the outset of reform, more than twice that of foreign firms. Such high earnings were the result of their degree of protection, their frequent role as state contractors, and industrial promotion policies based on tax exceptions and subsidized credits implemented by both the military and Alfonsín governments. Of the top thirty Argentine firms that were not compensated, on the other hand, such as Molinos, Mastellone, Sancor, and Arcor, most were in the food sector, where Argentina enjoyed greater comparative advantages.

In addition to sales and profits, the level of concentration relative to economic power provides a third indicator of structural power. Sectors that not only generate more value, but also are more concentrated (with fewer firms in the sector) would in principle have more lobbying capacity vis-à-vis the state. Indeed, classical theories of collective action would predict that the fewer players in a sector, the more likely that organized business pressure would arise.[6] An estimate of the level of concentration across all the industrial sectors can be measured through the number of "productive establishments" found in the last Industrial Census before reform (1985).[7] Thus, an "index of structural power" can be constructed as the ratio between value generated by the sector and its level of concentration.

The table excludes the food industry, where top Argentine firms argua-

6. Horacio Losoviz, former CEO of Iveco (one of the national compensated firm in autos) and president of ADEFA (the automakers' association) from 1992 to 1998 puts it this way: "The auto sector had advantages over the other sectors. One was that there were few people, few actors. When the motor-vehicle regime was drafted, we were six actors, Ciadea, Sevel, Scania, Iveco, Autolatina, and Mercedes Benz. That was a big advantage; six people can get to an agreement very easily" (personal interview, Buenos Aires, January 29, 2001).

7. Although this number is not a perfect measure, as it counts the number of plants rather than of firms, it is a good proxy for the level of concentration of each sector. More concentrated sectors (i.e., with fewer firms) tend to have, overall, fewer plants or "productive establishments." The International Standard Industrial Classification (ISIC), on which the Argentine 1985 Economic Census is based, defines the productive establishment as "the economic unit that dedicates, under the same owner or control, to a single or predominant form of economic activity in a unique physical location, or in very proximate ones" (ISIC, 2d ed., UN, 1974). Therefore, by 1985 the Argentine motor vehicle industry had six firms and eleven productive establishments, whereas the textile industry, with many more firms, had 1,610 productive establishments. A better measure for the level of concentration of each sector, is, of course, the Hirschman-Herfindhal Index typically used in the industrial organization literature. However, it would be very difficult to get the data (exact number of firms, market share, and so on) to construct that index for the approximately eighty industrial subsectors in Argentina given by the ISIC four digits.

Table 3.2 Index of structural power (1985): Manufacturing sector excluding food industry (leading fifteen sectors)*

Code	ISIC second revision	Gross production value (in 1985 pesos)	Concentration (prod. establishments)	Production value/ concentration
3530	*Petroleum industry*	527,331,376	12	43,944,281
38431	*Automobiles (assembly plants)*	162,431,037	11	14,766,458
3710	*Steel*	160,418,504	270	594,143
3140	Tobacco	60,770,657	127	478,509
3411	Pulp for paper	69,493,118	155	448,343
3311/13	*Basic chemicals*	183,219,181	589	311,068
3842	Railway material	12,696,410	45	282,142
3821	Construction of engines	21,836,892	83	263,095
3522	Pharmaceutical products	102,255,010	485	210,835
3692	Cement and lime	29,233,479	145	201,610
3512	Fertilizers	14,803,717	83	178,358
3720	Nonferrous Metals	47,422,523	266	178,280
3551	Tires	33,445,950	200	167,230
3211	Textile (textures and yarns)	228,621,776	1610	142,001
3832	Radio, TV, and communications	45,111,010	372	121,266

*Compensated sectors in italics.

bly enjoy comparative advantages. It concentrates on the quintessential "potential losers" from market reform, sectors where Argentina has, in principle, less comparative advantage. If we were to predict lobbying capacity as a function of the level of concentration and the resources generated by each sector, the auto, oil, and steel sectors in Argentina are in by far the best position to exert pressure on the state. Besides, domestic firms in these sectors had been displacing both state firms and foreign companies in their markets in the years prior to reform. Transnational corporations (TNCs) in the automobile sector, such as Chrysler, Fiat, and Renault, had withdrawn from Argentina in the decade or so prior to full-scale liberalization. By the early 1990s two firms of domestic capital, CIADEA and Sevel, were dominant in the subsector of commercial vehicles. Foreign capital had never made inroads in the steel sector. The local oil companies had greatly expanded after the military dictatorship (1976–83) and favored domestic companies in awarding service contracts for oil production. Finally, the local petrochemical sector had boomed during the 1980s, underpinned by protection, very high international prices, and lucrative joint ventures with the state.

The fact that locally owned firms were dominant in these sectors arguably increased the pressure for compensation. While TNCs could resort to external networks and state managers could lobby for subsidies or get payoffs in alternative arenas of the administration, local manufacturing capitalists, particularly those based in heavy industries, had little to win and much to lose from unfettered liberalization in their markets. Indeed, other sectors that ranked at the top of the index shown in Table 3.2 were either dominated by TNCs—as in the tobacco industry—or relatively competitive due to natural endowments, as in the pulp industry. In contrast, the powerful and locally owned protected companies in the sectors that ranked at the top in Table 3.2 strongly depended on the state to become viable in more open markets.

Finally, the manufacturing firms that were brought into the reform coalition also belonged to the country's most powerful industrial-sector associations, especially in the case of autos, oil, and steel. All of these sectors had developed monopolistic business associations that brought together all the major firms in the sector or subsector. ADEFA and the CEPA, the association of Argentine domestic oil producers, have been traditional players in the Argentine political economy for years. The CIS (Center for Steel Industrialists) was the most powerful single sectoral association within the Argentine Industrial Union (UIA).[8] Moreover, beginning in the 1990s, the major industrial groups based in the compensated sectors began to colonize the UIA. During the 1980s, the main local industrial groups had taken advantage of their direct relationship with the administration, sidelining the UIA on many occasions. Yet by 1991, in view of the government's increasingly liberal economic stand, the "big groups," including the main "compensated" companies based in chemicals, autos, and steel, attempted a comeback and supported the candidacy of the more protectionist Israel Mahler as president in lieu of a liberal candidate linked to the food industry. By 1993 the big groups succeeded in appointing José Blanco Villegas, from SOCMA—one of the main local players in the auto sector—president of the UIA. Blanco Villegas would remain president of the UIA until 1997, representing essentially the same coalition of big firms from the sectors favored by compensatory policies. The fact that compensated companies, particularly in the steel and auto sectors, held dominant

8. The steelmaker Techint played a prominent role in the UIA, especially in its institute for economic studies, the Institute for Industrial Development, whose authorities were controlled by the Techint group (see Sidicaro 2002, 205–11).

positions in the UIA helped moderate the industrial peak association's position in relation to the government.[9] This did not imply, however, that the UIA was a crucial institutional locus for the implementation of compensatory policies. It meant that officials knew that buying off the big local industrial groups would bring sufficient support from the UIA in the midst of a liberalization process that strongly affected the industrial sector.

It is of course difficult to disentangle structural and political variables when examining the power of these industrial groups under the semi-closed economy. These firms and their sectoral associations enjoyed a great capacity for lobbying the state during the ISI period, in part because of their structural endowments: they were in mixed sectors, they were very concentrated (had fewer players in the sector), and they were the most economically powerful. Their *political* predominance, in turn, historically helped to reinforce their position in the market. In any case, both the structural and political levels of power were intertwined and were crucial in their ability to influence the liberalization path after 1989.

In sum, some traditional industrial players of the old semi-closed or "populist" model did get to the bargaining table, even in the context of the initial blitzkrieg for market reform. Many of these traditional industrial groups obtained not only minor participation in the privatization of public services and utilities, as has been emphasized by other authors (for example, Azpiazu and Notcheff 1994 and Arceo and Basualdo 2002), but the restraint of liberalization *in their own base of tradable industrial production*. Although some of these groups had diversified into nonindustrial sectors, particularly during the 1980s, their main business was still based in the manufacturing sector (Bisang 1996, 426–27). Indeed, Argentina's ISI model had produced relatively strong domestic players in manufacturing, in relation to both state industrial companies and TNCs. These groups had economic resources to invest and could use their institutional power to undermine liberalization by putting on pressure through the sectoral associations and the UIA. They could even sue the government, as the domestic oil producers threatened to do in the event of the deregulation of their service contracts. Therefore, it did not make sense for the government to confront them. As Mario Dasso, former executive director of ADEFA stated, Minister of the Economy "Cavallo did not have a general theory, he was

9. The landing of the big industrial groups in the command position of the UIA is well described in Viguera 2000, 183–87. He writes that "the explicit support of the UIA for the economic policy of the Menem government is explained by the predominance of the big groups in its leadership" (186). An interesting and suggestive analysis of the relation between the UIA and the Menem government in the context of the Convertibility Plan is also found in Sidicaro 2002, 205–13.

not a classical liberal, he was ready to bargain with industry sector by sector. And he picked those which he believed could give something to the economy and invest in the country."[10]

Of course this willingness to negotiate with certain sectors that could "invest in the country" could be more properly translated as those that had enough political and economic power to constitute a threat. In a different liberalizing context, for example, one in which the polity was more authoritarian and the main producers were not local private groups based in the industrial sector but state firms or foreign TNCs, this type of strategy based on compensations to domestic actors would arguably have been much less likely.

The Working Class: Compensating Union Leaders and Insiders in the Formal Sector

In some cases of sweeping neoliberal reform, such as Bolivia (1985–90), Chile (1973–89), and Peru (1990–99), organized labor was repressed, while governments focused their compensatory policies on the poor workers of the informal sector. In other cases, such as Spain, the government confronted the union leadership while targeting its compensatory measures at the laid-off workers hit by industrial adjustment. In Argentina, by contrast, the mainstream labor movement was brought into the reform coalition. The politics of compensations concentrated first and foremost on the union leadership. As with the major ISI industrial players, all these compensatory policies were implemented through more or less formal conciliatory mechanisms involving officials and union representatives. In addition, those workers in the formal sector who kept their jobs could reap some of the benefits that their leaders were able to negotiate. Unemployed and laid-off workers were for the most part left to their fate by the national government.

The government administered four kinds of payoffs in order to obtain the acquiescence of the Peronist unions: (1) maintenance of the corporatist labor structure; (2) preserving labor's role in administering the health-care system; (3) granting unions a privileged position in the private pension funds market; and (4) granting unions a share of privatization.

MAINTENANCE OF THE CORPORATIST LABOR STRUCTURE

In neoliberal Argentina, labor reform advanced at a notoriously slow pace. Three features of the corporatist labor structure were a major concern for

10. Personal interview, Buenos Aires, March 7, 2001.

the unionist old guard. First, unions sought to maintain the union monopoly at the firm level; in other words, they sought a ban on forming multiple unions. Second, they aimed at preserving a centralized framework for collective bargaining. Although some decentralization of collective bargaining took place under Menem, it occurred mainly on the side of business negotiators. National union leaderships continued to be present in most of the new collective bargaining rounds, even those that took place at the level of firms.[11] The government did achieve some progress in increasing the flexibility of individual labor contracts. An example was regulations governing layoffs, which not surprisingly were the aspect of labor reform that implied the least damage to the union structure. A variety of fixed-term contracts were approved in 1994, yet most of them were outlawed by the 1998 labor reform. Finally, in spite of general marketization, the government maintained the automatic renovation of the pre-reform collective agreements in many sectors, which generally conferred more advantages on union leaders.[12] In the privatized firms however, the government repealed the old collective agreements in response to business demands, which resulted in more flexible conditions of work in the involved sectors. Yet the government addressed a major concern of the unions facing privatization: that their monopoly and scope of representation would be maintained in the newly private sector, even if the privatized company was divided into more than one firm.

THE UNION-RUN HEALTH-CARE SYSTEM

The trade-union control of the health-care system for workers (*obras sociales*) has been a crucial source of union power in Argentina. It was achieved through union appropriation of the social security taxes paid by both business and workers. In light of pressure from private HMOs to enter the business, the government threatened to deregulate the union monopoly in the health market for workers. However, health deregulation was finally restricted to competition *within* the union-run system.[13] Moreover, the labor movement controlled a key governmental agency during the entire Menem period: the National Administration of the Health Sys-

11. In Etchemendy 2004 I compare alternative patterns of labor reform in cases of sweeping neoliberal marketization, including Argentina.

12. In 1997, after seven years of pro-market reforms, 88 percent of the workers in the formal sector were still covered by centralized, prereform agreements and only 12 percent were covered by new company-level agreements (Ministry of Labor and Social Security 2002).

13. Private HMOs were allowed to enter the market, however, if they reached an agreement with a union. This fact triggered a complex dynamic in the health market by which small unions formed joint ventures with powerful private HMOs with the goal of recruiting workers affiliated to other welfare funds run by bigger unions.

tem. This agency was in charge of managing the workings of the union-run health-care system and of channeling state subsidies to the unions.

PENSION FUNDS

In 1993 the government partially privatized the pension system. A capitalization market was created in which private pension funds could freely compete with the state for a worker's affiliation. In the course of privatization, the government amended the bill and accepted some union demands. The unions were allowed to create their own pension funds to compete in the market. Many union leaders hoped that their experience in administrating workers' welfare funds would enable them to successfully participate in the newly created market. When the system was launched, sixteen unions controlled or were participating in three pension funds. These were Claridad, in which the construction workers' (UOCRA) and health workers' unions held 30 percent of the fund; Futura, in which the electric power company workers' (FATLYF), insurance workers', and autoworkers' (SMATA) unions held 80 percent of ownership; and San José, in which the restaurant workers' union held 30 percent in addition to the minor participation of eight smaller unions such as chemical workers and glass industry workers. These three pension funds initially shared about 10 percent of the market. By 2000 most unions had sold their stakes in the system, and only one union-run pension fund was left—Futura—holding less than 2 percent of the market and managing $292 million in assets.[14]

EMPLOYEE SHARE OWNERSHIP PROGRAM (ESOP) AND OTHER STATE ASSETS

As in the case of the powerful ISI industrial players, compensation included the sale of state assets. The government pushed forward one of the most ambitious privatization processes in the region, which resulted in huge downsizings and the decimation of industrial communities around the country.[15] However, as Murillo (1997) has shown, the direct distribution of specific state assets to unions in the privatization rounds was an important feature of the Argentine reform process. A handful of unions participated in some of the privatization rounds: for example, FATLYF (Argentine Federation of Light and Power Workers) bought stakes in a number of electricity generators, and SUPE (Union of State Oil Workers) bought YPF's fleet of ships (Murillo 1997, 86). In addition to the direct awarding of assets, the Employee Share Ownership Program (ESOP) also became a

14. Data from the Regulatory Office for Pensions (SJP), Buenos Aires.
15. Duarte (2002, 39) estimates a 70 percent degree of downsizing in the public service sector companies.

vital side payment targeted at the union structure. The State Reform Law, which structured the legislative framework that governed the privatization, granted a percentage of the stock share of each privatized company to the workers. The stocks reserved for sale to the workers would be paid for by the profits that those same shares would yield after privatization. In practice, the price of the stocks targeted at workers was negligible.

Two aspects of the ESOP should be emphasized: first, the law and the series of decrees that regulated the ESOP established that only the workers remaining in the company after privatization were eligible to enroll in the program. In other words, the program was targeted at the insiders. Second, although there is no mention of the unions in the legislative framework that governs the ESOP, in all the cases the program ended up being managed by the monopolistic union in each company. In fact, the government negotiated the percentage of stocks to include in the ESOP with each sectoral union. The government permitted the unions to take over the program in almost every company to be privatized.

As stated above, the price that the workers had to pay for the shares distributed to them was almost token. Workers could subsequently sell the shares or keep them and collect future dividends. Both options involved important benefits: most of the state companies were sold after the state had acquired their debt, in markets that remained uncompetitive and weakly regulated. Thus, the value of these stocks generally soared, underpinned by the economic boom of the early 1990s. The value of the ESOP can be measured by the market value of the shares reserved for the workers on the first day they were listed on the Buenos Aires Stock Exchange. Measured in this way, the ESOP market value was, for example, $757 million in the case of YPF (oil), $426 million for Telecom (telecom), $338 million for Telefónica (telecom), and $134 million for Siderar (steel).[16]

This matrix of payoffs was first and foremost geared to protect the interests of the old Peronist union leadership in the hostile environment of market reforms. As Murillo (1997) has argued, the unions sought to protect their organizations when their resources to fight in the industrial and political arena were shrinking. It could be argued, though, that some of these benefits also accrued to the workers who were not fired during adjustment and remained in the formal sector. For example, the dividends that the ESOP distributed ended up in the hands of the workers who kept their jobs. Likewise, the partial deregulation of the labor code and the relatively higher protection from layoffs, as compared to other cases of exten-

---

16. Data from the Stock Exchange, Buenos Aires.

sive neoliberal reform such as Peru, Spain, or Chile, also prioritized the interests of the mass of workers remaining in the formal sector.

Finally, a sweeping deregulation of the health sector would probably have hurt low-salaried workers, who would be much less appealing to private HMOS. Rather, the measures taken by the government could be considered as favoring formal sector workers. Of course, not all of the traditional unions could reap the benefits entailed by compensations in the same way. The ESOP was obviously available to unions in public companies that were privatized. Some unions, particular those in the tradable sector such as the metalworkers (UOM) or the textile workers (AOT), were decimated by job losses, compensations notwithstanding. By contrast, some other unions in nontradable and less adjusted sectors, such as the autoworkers (SMATA), the civil sector workers (UPCN), truck drivers, and commerce employees, which suffered less of a drain of workers and resources, were in a better position to enter some of the businesses opened by marketization.[17]

Why were union leaders and (to a lesser extent) formal sector workers the main winners among the potential losers in the working class? This chapter argues that a pattern of side payments was essentially made possible by the corporatist labor structure set forth in the labor law. In the first place, the *mere existence* of a system of corporatist inducements[18] brings to the table an issue about which labor leaders can bargain. Relatively strong labor movements in semiclosed economies have much to lose from neoliberal reform: their access to economic policymaking would be curtailed, and rising levels of unemployment would hamper strike activity. Yet once the general course of market reforms seems unavoidable, corporatist unions may have something to win: the preservation of at least some aspects of their monopolies in the labor market. Moreover, unlike labor negotiations over adjustment in more pluralist settings, bargaining with reformers over corporatist institutions can be more easily turned into a positive-sum game. In other words, some features can be modified (frequently individual labor law, in which unions are hurt less) and the collective labor law framework can remain largely untouched.[19]

17. The question of which unions were more prepared to profit from compensatory policies targeted at unions in the formal sector in general is a crucial issue for future research, but it exceeds the goals of this chapter.

18. The classic account on how corporatism in Latin America can induce union power or enforce labor control from above is Collier and Collier 1979.

19. The fact that both the reforming government and the unions belonged to the Peronist party also facilitated compensations targeted at labor leaders. Yet the "party affiliation" variable should not be overstated. Reforming governments such as those in Bolivia or Spain crushed unions affiliated with the party in power.

Two more decisive features of the Argentine corporatist labor legislation make it ideal for the negotiation over bureaucratic payoffs:[20] the monopolies enjoyed by unions in their sectors and the weakness of union work councils on the shop floor. Compensations such as the partial deregulation of the health-care market, the competition for pension funds, and the administration of the ESOP depend on unions' future ability to control and encourage workforce participation in those businesses. Union leaders need to assume that the possibilities for individuals or groups of workers to channel these resources outside the sectoral union—stock options in the case of the ESOP, social security taxes in the case of health system and pension funds—would remain low. If alternative unions at the firm were able to challenge, for example, the recruitment of workers to join the pension or welfare funds, or the union administration of the ESOP, those payoffs would be much less appealing to the unionists.

By the same token, if work councils were in a position to question upper-level decisions concerning the administration of these new (and reformed) businesses, the union leadership's role in future markets would also be threatened. Yet unlike other cases of corporatism—such as Germany—in Argentina, work councils are weak and strongly controlled from above. In other words, the corporatist institutional framework granted the union leadership a certain reassurance that their future control of resources in a variety of markets would not be challenged either by alternative unions or by their own rank and file.

Consider the case of the ESOP. For the program to be carried out, workers needed information about the functioning of the program, stocks had to be distributed among the workers according to certain criteria, and assemblies had to be held in order to elect representatives in the company board of shareholders. Crucially, the workers' assemblies of stockholders to elect the ESOP management were controlled by the established unions. The union was the organization that was already there, was hegemonic in the plant, and had maintained the monopoly of representation after privatization.[21] In summary, unions can be bought off by bureaucratic payoffs when the institutional structure makes those payoffs a rational alternative for labor leaders.

20. I prefer the term "bureaucratic" to "organizational" payoffs, given that these are policies geared to benefit the union leaders/bureaucrats more than the "organization" as such.

21. My assessment of the ESOP is based on interviews with Carlos Lefort, manager of the National Bank Department in charge of the administration of the ESOP; Carlos Urtasum, director of the ESOP Executive Committee managed by the water utilities union FNOS; and Carlos Herrera from the Regional Board of UOM-San Nicolás, which managed the ESOP for steelworkers.

THE CONSEQUENCES

The organized system of compensations to the losers of the exchange rate level was the complementary side of macroeconomic policy in Argentina during the 1990s. The fixed exchange rate tied to the dollar[22] and the subsequent currency appreciation benefited nontradables (privatized companies) and financial sectors while undermining labor and industrial firms in the tradable sectors (see Frieden 1991b). Protected industry and the major unions had been the traditional beneficiaries of the stop-go cycles triggered by periodical devaluations in pre-reform Argentina. Industrial firms would benefit via improvement of their relative prices, and the largest unions would profit from inflationary expansion and their privileged role in the centralized wage bargaining that followed devaluations. When the government abandoned those macroeconomic strategies, the compensatory policies became the main arena of coalition building involving traditional ISI actors.

Yet the system of compensations and the way a reforming coalition was put together in the early 1990s contributed to the general crises that erupted in the late 1990s. The coalitional arrangements forged in the first part of the 1990s carried the seeds of economic and political instability for three reasons. First, they helped to prolong a fixed exchange rate that proved to be a liability in a world of unstable financial markets. Second, compensatory policies targeted at industrial actors were essentially based on the control of domestic markets, disregarding any strategy for export competition in an age of increasing economic internationalization. Finally, labor compensation that largely focused on the formal sector workers and their unions, or insiders, paved the way for the militant reaction of the outsiders excluded from the labor market.

Compensatory Policies and the Endurance of Convertibility

In the October 1999 presidential elections, the Alianza coalition, formed by the UCR and FREPASO (a center-left splinter of the Peronist party back in the early 1990s), defeated Peronist Eduardo Duhalde and elected the Radical Party candidate Fernando De la Rúa. The Alianza government would soon be undermined by two legacies of the Menem administration: a rising fiscal deficit and a fixed exchange rate tied to the dollar, which became a burden when the dollar rose against most West European cur-

22. On the politics underpinning the implementation of the Convertibility Plan in Argentina, see Palermo 1997 and Starr 1997.

rencies, Russia defaulted on its foreign debt in 1998, and Brazil devalued its currency in 1999. By mid-2001, and despite a previous IMF bailout in December 2000, Argentina was experiencing major liquidity and financial crises: government-bonds yields had tripled, dollar-denominated and local currency deposits were draining away from commercial banks, and the government was powerless to avert a third consecutive year of recession. Meanwhile, amid increasing political tension between the two main coalition partners, Peronist unions had returned to the streets to protest a proposed labor reform, and new organizations of the unemployed had launched a massive series of road blockades and street demonstrations that seriously challenged governmental authority. In December 2001, De la Rúa resigned in the midst of riots and looting that had spread throughout the city of Buenos Aires and its suburbs. In January 2002, Senator Eduardo Duhalde, the most powerful politician in the Peronist party, was elected president by the Congress. One of his first economic measures was to float the peso, which then devalued 300 percent with respect to the dollar.

The endurance of the convertibility system, which helped spark the 2001 crises, cannot be understood without considering this matrix of payoffs that set aside the most powerful sectors in labor and industry affected by the exchange rate level. True, in contexts of inflationary economies, many reforming governments—including those in Chile, Brazil, and Mexico—resorted to fixed exchange rates. A question, though, remains unsettled. Why could a fixed and increasingly appreciated exchange rate last much longer in Argentina than in other neoliberal experiments? While many economists suggest that the main reason for the economic collapse was Argentina's staunch maintenance of a fixed exchange rate in an unstable financial world (see Pastor and Wise 2001, Krugman 2001, and Lucangeli 2001), few have looked at the coalitional basis that helped the system remain in place for so long. Analogous experiences of fixed exchange rates in contexts of extensive marketization in Latin America—for example, Chile between 1975 and 1982—had not replicated similar systems of compensation for the losers. In such cases pressure stemming from affected social actors for more competitive exchange rates was arguably greater.[23] In Argentina, the largest conglomerates based in the tradable sector only started to lobby against convertibility when the costs of deflation were too high and had begun to undermine the gains of the early

23. For example, Silva (1996) explains how in Chile during the early 1980s the pressure of the domestic bourgeoisie in the tradable sector was important to overhaul the fixed exchange rate and initiate a policy of competitive devaluations.

1990s. By that time it was too late to find an ordered transition out of the fixed exchange rate scheme.

The Paradox of Argentina's Industrial Adjustment: Adapting to Globalization Through Control of Domestic Markets

Compensation to industrial actors amid market reforms in Argentina was based on the control of domestic markets and disregarded any strategy for future competition in the global marketplace. Many neoliberal governments had defined a certain industrial strategy in the wake of economic liberalization. The Chilean neoliberal government, for example, targeted some firms in sectors endowed with comparative advantages during the period 1983–89 through a variety of microeconomic incentives (Kurtz 2001). The Mexican government developed a broad system of export promotion in the process of integration into NAFTA (see, for example, Weiss 1999). In Argentina, in times of economic internationalization, the main domestic industrial groups, paradoxically, adapted to the new conditions by expanding in the domestic market. The largest groups based in the steel, auto, and oil sectors are paradigmatic examples in this respect. In brief, unlike other cases of thorough market reform, the government did not develop any significant or sustainable industrial policy for the open economy and limited itself to appeasing the powerful.

However, adaptation to globalization through payoffs based on the concentration of domestic markets proved to be a very short-term strategy. The trajectory of the main Argentine industrial group, the conglomerate Techint, in the 1990s is illuminating in this respect. Largely concentrated in the steel sector, Techint was one the main groups favored by compensatory policies. The "targeted" privatization of the state mill SOMISA and the restraint of the liberalization in the steel market helped the group minimize the perils that marketization entailed. After privatization, Techint concentrated its export activities on Siderca, the traditional exporter of rolled steel, and oriented the former SOMISA to regain the domestic market share of flat steel, which the state firm had been losing to imports in the years before reform. Whereas in 1988, SOMISA was selling only 40 percent of its production in the domestic market and exporting the remaining 60 percent, by 1994, a privatized Siderar was selling 90 percent of its production in the domestic market and only 10 percent abroad.[24] Yet even if Siderar's control of the domestic market was assured, the peso became

---

24. Data from Siderar's annual report published in *La Bolsa*, no. 10.312, Buenos Aires Stock Exchange, April 1996.

increasingly overvalued, undermining the competitiveness of Argentine steel and industrial products in the world. The January 1999 currency devaluation in Brazil (Argentina's main commercial partner in the Mercosur) only made things worse. Of note, Roberto Rocca, head of the Techint conglomerate, was the first significant businessperson to publicly criticize convertibility in August 1999, provoking a big commotion in Argentine financial and political circles.[25]

Thus, after the compensation period in the first half of the 1990s, and in the absence of any form of state support for global competition, the main industry-based groups were essentially left with only two options: to sell their assets in the tradable sector (whose value had significantly increased as a result of compensatory measures)[26] or lobby against convertibility in order to improve their relative prices. By mid-2000, the UIA formed the Grupo Productivo, in a process led by the largest compensated industrial group, Techint, in conjunction with construction and rural interests. Voices within the Grupo Productivo started to question and lobby against the convertibility scheme more and more. In short, the consensus around the fixed exchange rate, built to a great extent on compensations targeted at tradable industrial (and labor) interests during the 1990s, proved to rest on weak foundations once those compensations were "consumed" in the boom of the first part of the decade. The breakup of the consensus within the capitalist class over the exchange rate system arguably undermined its credibility and contributed to its traumatic demise in late 2001.[27]

Compensating Working-Class Insiders: Paving the Way for the Rebellion of Outsiders

The Alianza period saw a massive upsurge in popular protests led by unemployed workers. Relatively isolated episodes of popular uprisings in peripheral communities decimated by the privatizations of state industries (see Auyero, this volume) were eventually followed by a wave of organized

---

25. *Página/12*, August 19, 1999.

26. Many compensated groups would follow this course, especially in the petrochemical, auto, and oil sectors. Among others, Astra, Sevel, Ciadea, Ipako, and Indupa were sold to foreign investors. Pérez Companc oil division was sold to the Brazilian state giant Petrobras in 2001. Yet in this case, the sale was triggered more by the 2001 crises and the firm's large dollar-denominated debt than by the recession and currency appreciation after 1997.

27. Moreover, Ignacio De Mendiguren, president of the UIA (1999–2001) and one of the heads of the Productive Group, became minister of production in the Duhalde administration, under which the Convertibility Law was repealed and the peso was devalued in January 2002.

road blockades and street demonstrations in the urban areas of greater Buenos Aires during 2000 and 2001. A new actor, *los piqueteros,* community-based organizations of the unemployed, appeared as the main opposing force to the deflationary policies pursued by Alianza. The unemployed, the main group excluded from the compensatory deals of the 1990s, had emerged as the most militant actor within the working class.

This new type of working-class protest can be traced back to the compensatory policies of the early 1990s in two respects. On the one hand, the government's focus on bureaucratic payoffs during the 1990s paralled the absence of any nationally organized system of compensations to the informal sector or the unemployed in the heydays of neoliberal reform. In 1994, unemployment in the industrial suburbs of Buenos Aires was already over 22 percent. Of course, the clientelistic networks that the Peronist party expanded during the 1990s served in part to cushion the costs of neoliberal reform for parts of the lower classes, especially in the formerly industrialized suburbs of Buenos Aires.[28] Yet, unlike Chile or Mexico's neoliberal experiences, no significant *national policy* was developed in order to attenuate the costs of adjustment for the unemployed and the informal sector. The extent of unemployment compensations remained marginal in Argentina until recently.

The reductions in social security taxes are a good example of the way in which the government privileged traditional unions over other actors in the working class. After 1992, the government implemented a series of reductions in businesses' social security taxes in order to boost competitiveness in the tradable sector. These taxes help finance a series of social expenditures: family allowances, the pension system, the fund for the unemployed, the state-run health-care system for seniors, and finally, the union-run health-care system. Yet while some social security taxes were reduced by more than 70 percent after 1992—40 percent in the case of the unemployment fund—the reduction in the tax that went to the union's coffers *was much lower* than in the other cases—only around 16 percent. In short, the government was choosing to support the unions over the unemployed.

On the other hand, bureaucratic compensations resulted in a labor movement as dependent as ever on regulatory state decisions. Organized labor's stake in the health-care system, in the monopolistic and centralized system of collective bargaining, and in the boards of the privatized companies shaped a union movement deeply entrenched in the formal sector.

---

28. The best study on the transformation of the Peronist party from a labor-based to a patronage-based party in reaction to neoliberal reforms is Levitsky 2003.

The unions' focus on bureaucratic and regulatory benefits obtained in the 1990s and their lack of incentives to build any bridge toward the unemployed also paved the way for the surge of autonomous and rebellious organizations of the jobless. Only the new national confederation, the CTA (Congress of Argentine Workers), which split from the CGT in 1992, sought to mobilize the unemployed. Indeed, CTA unions did not depend on any state compensation in terms of labor regulations or payoffs in the health, pensions, or equity markets. Therefore, following the logic of my argument, the CTA had greater incentives to seek a new constituency and organize the mass of workers being thrown out by adjustment policies. Yet the CTA was a minor confederation within organized labor and had considerably fewer resources than its counterparts in the traditional CGT. The CTA encompassed only two national federations, the largest union of teachers and one of the state workers' unions. In 2000 the CTA formally joined forces with some of the growing organizations of the unemployed. Yet the CTA did more than organizing the atomized jobless; it also allied with some of the already existing moderate groups, such as the FTV (Federation of Land and Housing) and the CCC (Combative Class Movement), which had emerged out of grassroots organizations in the shantytowns of greater Buenos Aires.

In sum, abandoned as a constituency by national policies during the 1990s, and with no connection whatsoever to the more traditional channels of labor representation, the unemployed were left with few options but to resort to direct action in the streets. Of course the lack of attention from the government and the largest unions to the growing masses of the jobless is not the only explanation for the rise of the organizations of the unemployed in the late 1990s. As classical theories of social movements indicate, grievances do not always result in mobilization. Yet this chapter argues that the government's *political* choices of the first part of the 1990s in terms of who would bear the costs of radical adjustment—union leaders and formal sector workers or the unemployed and the informal sector—set the stage for an upsurge in alternative forms of labor contestation.[29]

CONCLUSIONS

Traditional approaches to the politics of marketization would expect potential losers in protected industry and labor to either block reform or be

---

29. For the surge of organizations of the unemployed in Argentina, see Delamata 2003, Garay 2003, Lodola 2003, and Svampa and Pereyra 2003.

ignored and fundamentally undermined.[30] Recently, however, comparative perspectives on marketization in developing economies have moved beyond classic institutional, public-choice, and structural/class-based perspectives. First, the new emphasis is on how officials may buy off protected interests in their attempt to build a constituency for reform. In this light, alliances with established actors facilitate rather than obstruct the liberalization process. Second, recent studies tend to explicitly or implicitly stress the multidimensional logic of market reform. Moreover, they point out that in order to make reform politically viable, economic liberalization may often occur with the preservation of pockets of protection or spending.[31]

However, in examining countries that abandon closed or semiclosed economies, we lack a systematic theory of which interests tend to be bought off, and under what circumstances. This chapter has advanced some ideas in that direction. A more complete explanatory framework of which interests are compensated should avoid the excessive focus on state elites or, conversely, the economic/social determinism of traditional approaches. It should focus, instead, on state-society interactions. In other words, it should acknowledge that society is organized in a certain way, providing opportunities and constraints on what strategies are available for the reformer to craft a national policy coalition. In Argentina, the configuration of industrial and labor interests at the outset of reform ultimately determined the patterns of compensations. In the case of the sheltered manufacturing industry, the government could not avoid bringing into the reform coalition a certain group of largely local firms that happened to be the most powerful in economic and political terms. In the case of labor, a corporatist institutional structure strongly biased the compensatory policies toward union leaders and insiders. An explanation of compensatory policies that takes into consideration the economic and institutional configuration of social groups does not rule out politician's roles and skills. In fact, compensatory policies were the result of complicated bargains and political crafting, whose final outcome was determined by more than the shape of actors. Yet this chapter argues that the type of actors that unfolded under the ISI model—a corporatist union movement and a local industrial bourgeoisie powerful in relation to both state and foreign TNCs—strongly conditioned the government's coalition crafting in the domain of labor and business.

Furthermore, the compensatory policies analyzed in this chapter re-

---

30. See, for example, Krueger 1993, Haggard and Kaufman 1995, and Frieden 1991a.

31. See, for example, Kessler 1998, Etchemendy 2001, Murillo 2001, Shleifer and Treissman 2000, Hellman 1998, and Gibson 1997.

vealed a double edge. On the one hand, they made adjustment politically feasible in the context of democratic rule and powerful actors anchored in the old model. On the other hand, those same compensations carried the seeds of political and economic instability. In an era of internationalization, compensatory policies targeted at a handful of industrial groups were based on the control of domestic markets. This fact, coupled with the absence of any state strategy for global competition, affected Argentina's industrial performance in the long run and hindered the consensus around exchange rate policy within the capitalist class. In addition, bureaucratic payoffs to labor leaders resulted in a union movement as dependent as ever on state regulatory protections. The disregard for workers expelled by the adjustment process created a profound division in the working class, one that helped give rise to a new type of labor unrest.

Notwithstanding the sweeping market policies of the 1990s, old protected actors such as industrial groups and traditional unions reappeared as major supporters of the post-convertibility economic policy. The support of the mostly domestic-oriented industrial sector for the administrations of Duhalde (2001–3) and his Peronist successor Nestor Kirchner (2003–present) is founded on a thoroughly depreciated exchange rate that has made tradables more competitive and has hampered imports. Moreover, the abandonment of any idea of further "labor reform" and the appointment of labor ministers with links to the traditional union movement during these two Peronist administrations[32] has assured union loyalty—even in a context of a phenomenal devaluation that has reduced considerably the real value of wages. It remains to be seen if actors within industry and organized labor become further involved in a broader economic policy coalition. However, the recent return of traditional union and industrial interests to political prominence shows that in Argentina, market reforms have blended elements from the old order and the new in a way that is probably unmatched in the rest of Latin America.

---

32. Graciela Camano, minister of labor during the Duhalde administration, was a staunch defender of traditional union's right in Congress and is married to Luis Barrionuevo, one of the most notorious unionists from the old guard. Carlos Tomada, first minister of labor in the Kirchner administration, is a labor law expert and academic, and has been the attorney for the main CGT unions in Argentina.

Menem and the Governors:
Intergovernmental Relations in the 1990s

Kent Eaton

For much of the twentieth century, Argentina was a federal country in name only. By centralizing power in the hands of the national government, most of the leading political and economic developments in that century were unkind to federalism. In the political realm, chronic coup making by the armed forces weakened the country's federal identity by replacing democratically elected provincial officials with military appointees and by closing the most important arena for the expression of provincial interests: the federal legislature. Meanwhile, in democratic and semidemocratic periods alike, charismatic leaders like Hipólito Yrigoyen and Juan Perón built political parties that forced rank-and-file politicians to privilege the national party line over the concerns of their home provinces. In the economic realm, Argentina's particularly radical version of state-led industrialization, together with a crisis-management style of policymaking necessitated by the country's repeated stop-and-go cycles, served over time to strengthen the center at the expense of provincial governments. Thus, at the time of Argentina's most recent transition to democracy, in 1983, the provinces had been at the receiving end of decades of political and economic change, all of which tended to undermine provincial leverage in the national political system.

The return to democracy in 1983, however, marked a sea change in the relationship between the provincial and federal governments. In the past two decades, governors have wrested substantial political and fiscal authority from the center, a complex process that culminated in the profound fiscal crisis of 2001–2. Gone are the days when students of Argentine politics can attempt to make sense of the country's political life without paying serious attention to the provinces and to the governors who control them. The importance of the roles now played by governors can best be demonstrated by examining the economic reforms that dominated the policy agenda in the 1990s.

According to a growing body of research, provincial governors directly influenced reform outcomes in a variety of dimensions over the course of the 1990s. Gibson and Calvo, for example, argue that the interior provinces constituting Peronism's "peripheral coalition" were able to secure advantageous fiscal transfers in exchange for supporting Carlos Menem's market-oriented policies (Gibson 1997; Gibson and Calvo 2000). Remmer and Wibbels (2000) show that federal transfers emboldened provincial officials to flout the preferences of national politicians and to expand dramatically the size of provincial public sector payrolls. In their survey of policy change during Menem's two terms as president, Tommasi and Spiller (2000, 136–40) document the governors' ability to veto the market-oriented economic reforms that Menem wanted them to adopt at the provincial level. Jones, Sanguinetti, and Tommasi (2000) find that opposition governors posed particularly acute problems for the president's fiscal adjustment drive, and Eaton (2002) argues that provincial officials used the legislators representing their districts in Congress to acquire preferential policy treatment from the center.[1]

I contend that the provinces are critical in seeking to explain *both* Argentina's economic successes in the first half of the 1990s and its spectacular failures later in the decade. To illustrate this argument, I focus on the institution of federal revenue sharing. Given the time and energy that politicians in Argentina devote to securing access to revenues, this institutional arena is a particularly useful window onto the balance of power between the federal and provincial governments. In the early 1990s, President Menem introduced major changes in the rules governing revenue sharing with the provinces through the negotiation of two distinct fiscal pacts. According to the logic of each pact, the federal government was authorized to remove tax revenues from the revenue-sharing pool and to

---

1. The 1990s proved to be a fruitful time for research into provincial actors and institutions more broadly. On the incidence of provincial factors in privatization, see Llanos 1998 and 2001. On the importance of provincial parties, see Palanza and Sin 1997. For a study of attempts to strengthen the rule of law in the provinces, see Bill Chávez 2003. On the provincial incentives facing legislators, see Jones et al. 2002. On the role of provincial party leaders relative to both national and grassroots Peronist actors, see Levitsky 2001. For a study of the transfer of education to the provinces, see Murillo 1999.

devote these revenues exclusively to national government expenditures in exchange for guaranteeing that provincial transfers would not drop below a minimum floor (*piso mínimo*). In other words, provinces were compensated for the percentage reduction in revenue sharing with a new set of property rights vis-à-vis federal tax revenues. Compensation strategies proved to be especially important in Argentina, Latin America's most striking case of market-based reform under democratic auspices, and intergovernmental relations offer yet another example of how compensation was deployed as a reform tool (Etchemendy, this volume; Murillo 2001; Torre 1998).

In the 1990s, these two fiscal pacts proved to be as momentous for Argentina's political economy as the 1991 Convertibility Law, which to date has received more attention from scholars and policymakers alike. Indeed, as new institutional rules, the fiscal pacts and the Convertibility Law share several features. Just as convertibility served to bind the hands of politicians by tying the peso to the dollar at parity, the pacts instituted a rigid system of minimum revenue guarantees to replace the traditional method of percentage-based revenue sharing. Like convertibility, the two fiscal pacts were expressly designed to bolster Menem's attempt to achieve and defend macroeconomic stability at the center, an achievement that led to his reelection in 1995. The new revenue-sharing rules contributed directly to the ability of the federal government to control federal budget deficits, fight inflation, and meet the rigors of a new fiscal paradigm in which money printing was no longer an option. By surrendering their full legal shares of federally collected tax revenues, the provinces contributed to the historic stabilization of the macroeconomy in Menem's first term.

Also like convertibility, however, the revenue floor proved to be double-edged. Undoubtedly, with the surge in tax collection in the first half of the 1990s, the fiscal pacts delivered important gains to the federal government by no longer requiring it to share with the provinces a set percentage of a dramatically expanding pie. Yet once revenues declined at the end of the 1990s, institutional innovation in the guise of minimum revenue guarantees came back to bite the federal government, now obliged by the pacts to share a set amount with the provinces regardless of actual tax revenues. Rule changes that had represented a revenue grab by the federal government and a sacrifice on the part of the provinces in 1992 and 1993 were transformed into a major boon to the provinces and a serious problem for the center after 1996. Though economic decline seriously compromised the tax collection of the federal government during the two years that Fernando De la Rúa governed Argentina, he was powerless to remove the *piso mínimo* and experienced as a result a real loss of maneuverability in his attempt to forestall the country's catastrophic default on its external debt. The behavior of the governors in defense of the revenue guarantee was thus directly implicated in the fiscal crisis that erupted in 2001 and which led to De la Rúa's resignation at the end of that year.

This chapter is organized in the following manner. In the next section I discuss the sources of gubernatorial power that, in periods of democratic rule, have enabled governors to project a considerable amount of authority into national-level debates and decisions. In order to set the stage for the struggles over revenue that took place in the 1990s, the second section returns to the decision of the provinces in the 1930s to delegate taxing powers to the federal government in exchange for a share of the proceeds. All subsequent changes have essentially been reforms of this earlier arrangement, and the depth of the current crisis suggests the need to return to the logic of this initial act of delegation. Considering the significant leverage that governors enjoy under democracy, the decision by the provinces to depend on fiscal transfers rather than collect their own taxes has emerged as an important source of fiscal strain. The third section focuses on Menem's unique opportunity to restructure intergovernmental relations through the fiscal pacts of the early 1990s. Initially these pacts delivered short-term gains to the federal government, but as the fourth section shows, over the course of Menem's second administration they generated unanticipated benefits for the provinces. Furthermore, governors successfully increased the level of the *piso mínimo*, demonstrating the weakening of Menem's political authority within the Peronist party. The fifth section reviews the content and outcome of reform attempts under the aborted De la Rúa administration and closes with a discussion of how Duhalde built political support for the revoking of revenue guarantees in early 2002. The final section concludes by mining this case for insights into the larger questions of institutional design and strength that are at the center of this volume.

THE SOURCES OF GUBERNATORIAL POWER IN ARGENTINA

How did Argentine governors in the last two decades of the twentieth century achieve greater political prominence? One answer to this question lies in a process of redemocratization initiated in 1983, which for all its problems and limitations, has been far more successful than the country's five prior attempts at democratization. In the past, transitions from military government that reinstated provincial elections temporarily raised the governors' visibility and enabled them to secure gains for their provinces (Eaton 2001). Sooner or later, however, democracy collapsed in the aftermath of these earlier transitions, and the reversal to nondemocratic forms of government denied provinces the types of channels they could use to defend and build on these gains. It is important to remember that military coups interrupted democracy not just at the national level but at the subnational level as well, and that their frequency in the twentieth century hindered the development of stable democratic institutions at both the national and provincial levels. Thanks to the failure of coup attempts after 1983, Argentine provinces have now accumulated over two decades of uninterrupted experience with the holding of regularly scheduled elections. These elections endow governors with a degree of democratic legitimacy that has strengthened them in their negotiations with the center.

In combination with the longevity of Argentina's current experience with democracy, a number of other factors help explain the newfound importance of the provinces and their governors. One is the decreased use of a constitutional prerogative that enables the federal government to dismiss the elected government of a given province. Though President Menem used this power of intervention more than President Alfonsín, who declined to intervene in a single province, the post-1983 period stands in sharp contrast to the second-longest period of democratic rule (1916–30), during which President Yrigoyen intervened in no fewer than twenty provinces. Second, not only have federal authorities refrained from using their full powers over provincial elected officials, but the use of nonconcurrent elections has increased the influence of provincial electoral outcomes on a range of political phenomena at the national level (Jones 1997a). Specifically, the holding of provincial elections in the months leading up to national elections has generated a great deal of national leverage for victorious governors. Third, many provinces rewrote their own constitutions in the 1980s and 1990s to allow the reelection of the governor, similar in spirit to the reform of the federal constitution in 1994 that paved the way for Menem's reelection as president the following year. In many provinces, successful reelection campaigns following the removal of term limits have made it easier for governors to dominate politics within their provinces and to translate this dominance into increased influence in national decision-making arenas.[2] Partially as a result, the same imbalance

2. Eduardo Duhalde, former governor of Buenos Aires province and president of Argentina from January 2002 to May 2003, and Néstor Kirchner, former governor of Santa Cruz and president of Argentina since May 2003, are the two most important examples of this

that favors the executive branch relative to the legislature at the national level is replicated at the provincial level, to the great benefit of the governors.

The structure of political parties and the content of electoral rules are the final and perhaps most important present-day sources of gubernatorial power. As Jones and Hwang show in their contribution to this volume, partisan and electoral incentives endow governors with significant leverage over the legislators who belong to their parties and who represent provincial electoral districts in the federal legislature. With respect to the Senate, governors wield considerable influence over the selection of the candidate who will represent his or her party in the general election. In the Chamber of Deputies, representatives are elected according to closed lists written by three sets of actors: national party organizations, provincial party organizations, and less often, rank-and-file party members. Despite cross-provincial variation in the relative importance of these three actors in writing party lists, provincial party leaders often negotiate a single list among themselves and avoid primary elections entirely (Jones 1997b, 9–13). In practice, when the leader of the provincial party is also governor, that individual retains significant power over the voting behavior of federal representatives. However, as Jones notes, when the president of the national party organization is also the president of the nation, his or her influence over the composition of provincial candidate lists tends to increase relative to provincial authorities.

In the struggle between national and provincial party leaders for influence over legislators, much depends on the career prospects of the national party leadership. Menem's successful bid to change the Constitution and run for reelection enabled him to exert tight control over Peronist legislators in his first administration. Menem used this power to force the revenue-sharing pacts upon the provinces, the majority of which were governed by fellow Peronists. This type of power was unavailable to Menem once he became a lame duck with his reelection in 1995, which reduced his powers over Peronist legislators relative to Peronist governors and ensured that he would have a much more difficult time imposing losses on the provinces. Thus, while the continued playing of the democratic game has certainly strengthened governors since 1983, the degree of their influence over legislators still fluctuates in response to national phenomena, including the strength of presidential leadership and the national electoral calendar.

---

dynamic, but there are other examples as well, including former interim president Adolfo Rodríguez Saá of San Luis, Juan Carlos Romero of Salta, and Ruben Marín of La Pampa.

INSTITUTIONAL INNOVATION: THE CREATION OF
CO-PARTICIPACIÓN

Understanding the significance of how intergovernmental relations changed in the 1990s requires some background. Conflict over revenue between the federal and provincial governments has been at the heart of Argentine political history from the very beginning. Nominally a federal regime but in practice one that brutally repressed the interior, the government of Juan Manuel de Rosas (1829–53) crystallized support among the interior provinces for a national government that would be strong enough to constrain the province of Buenos Aires and to check its abuses of the port.[3] Consequently, one of the core features of the 1853 constitution that provincial representatives wrote was the exclusive assignment of taxes on external trade to the federal government.[4] While the federal government was endowed with exclusive control over the most important tax base, the 1853 constitution reserved for the provinces exclusive authority over direct taxes and stipulated that *both* levels of government could raise domestic consumption taxes (Pírez 1986, 11).[5] Before the 1930s, a pronounced degree of separation characterized revenue collection in Argentina: the federal government collected most of its revenues from trade taxes, and the provincial governments collected most of their revenues from domestic consumption taxes (Macón 1985; Randall 1978).

Just as the international economic crisis of 1930 set in motion deep changes in the country's economic policy orientation (Díaz Alejandro 1970), this same exogenous shock proved to be a critical juncture for intergovernmental relations. The decline in external trade seriously compromised the federal government's fiscal strength at the very moment it was seeking to expand infrastructure projects to keep unemployment rates from skyrocketing. In this context, the government of Agustín Justo proposed two important measures. First was the introduction of a direct tax on incomes, formally the exclusive prerogative of the provinces, though

3. For a discussion of regional conflicts in the formation of Argentine federalism, see Gibson and Falleti 2003.

4. In a response that reflected the interior's overarching goal of restraining the most important province, Buenos Aires refused to sign the 1853 constitution, blockaded the Paraná River in an attempt to bring the interior to heel, and subsequently defeated the interior in the 1861 battle of Pavón. Subsequent to its military victory, Buenos Aires agreed to ratify the 1853 constitution, but only after insisting on key amendments, including suppressing language that would transform the city of Buenos Aires into a national capital and force it to share its trade revenues. Only in 1880, with the federalization of the port city, was the centralization of trade taxation actually achieved (Ruiz Moreno 1980).

5. The Constitution also stipulated that every power not expressly delegated to the federal government would remain with the provinces.

the 1853 constitution allowed federal collection of direct taxes in emergencies and for limited periods. Second was the passage of new federal sales and excise taxes that required the provinces to cease collecting similar taxes in exchange for a share of federal revenues from these tax bases.

Several aspects of this new institutional arrangement, henceforth referred to as coparticipation, deserve emphasis. One is the extent to which revenue sharing initially favored the federal government, which would receive 82.5 percent of the proceeds from the new taxes. Over time, the distribution of revenues between the two levels of government would increasingly favor the provinces relative to the federal government. The apparently disadvantageous terms for the provinces in the 1934 legislation raise the question of why provincial authorities agreed to this new arrangement. According to Pírez (1986) and FIEL (1993), the federal government offered debt forgiveness as a means of encouraging governors to agree to the coparticipation scheme, essentially playing to the vulnerabilities of provincial authorities. It is also the case that revenue sharing appealed to governors, despite the small share of revenues that would come back to the provinces in the form of transfers, because it enabled them in a period of economic turbulence to shift the political and administrative costs of tax collection onto the federal government. Focused on the short term, provincial authorities agreed to changes that in effect reduced the institutional capacity of the provinces as separate units of government.

The introduction of revenue sharing in 1934 proved to be a watershed event for the subsequent development of intergovernmental relations in Argentina. Even though the 1934 laws were of limited duration, when the provinces agreed to surrender responsibility for these tax bases, their decision had powerful and highly negative consequences for the integrity of provincial governments for years to come. Technically, the provinces in subsequent decades were free to revoke the right of the federal government to collect their taxes each time they negotiated extensions of the coparticipation regulation.[6] In his time as governor of La Rioja in the 1980s, for example, Carlos Menem threatened to do just that by calling on his counterparts in other provinces to declare a state of rebellion in the interior, cutting the supply of energy to the capital, blocking provincial ports, and taking back all powers delegated to the federal government (Pírez 1986, 68). But such threats were less than credible. Once the provinces delegated taxing authority in the 1930s, provincial tax-raising capacity atrophied in a way that foreclosed this option. In effect, the 1934 decision shifted the terms of the debate over subnational institutions from a discus-

---

6. New coparticipation laws were legislated in 1947, 1959, 1964, 1973, and 1988.

Table 4.1   Vertical fiscal imbalance in Argentina, 1997

	Taxes			
	(excluding social security contributions)		(including social security contributions)	
	Where the taxes are collected (*recaudación*)	Where the revenues are spent (*recursos*)	Where the taxes are collected (*recaudación*)	Where the revenues are spent (*recursos*)
Federal Government	77.3%	45.4%	81.6%	55%
Provinces	22.7%	54.6%	18.4%	44%

SOURCE: Piffano 1998.

sion over the appropriate division of governing responsibilities to nearly constant political battles over the division of revenues collected by the federal government. In this sense, the events of 1934 mark a critical juncture in the relationship between the provinces and the federal government.

Due to the stickiness of the decision to delegate provincial taxing authority to the federal government, coupled with the transfer of responsibilities to the provinces in the early 1980s and again in the early 1990s, Argentina experienced increasing vertical fiscal imbalance. By 1997, as seen in Table 4.1, the country's fiscal structure reflected a serious disparity between the level of government where taxes are collected and the level of government where tax revenues are spent.

In order to appreciate the significance of how Menem altered the system in the early 1990s, we should also note what did *not* change in the nearly six decades between 1934 and 1992. In these years, the exact size of provincial revenue transfers was determined by applying a fixed percentage to a pool of revenues that changed with actual tax collection in any given year (Nuñez Miñana and Porto 1982; Porto 1990). Taxes were taken in and out of the revenue pool, and provinces experienced increases and decreases in the share they received, but the sharing was consistently percentage based, and therefore highly pro-cyclical (IDB 1997). In good years, the increase in federal tax collection could translate into sharp real increases in the amount of revenues provinces would receive from the federal government. In bad years, provinces could likewise experience debilitating declines in actual revenue transfers. Nothing was guaranteed in this period other than the application of an exact percentage to a changing pool.

Because coparticipation asks the provinces to forgo collecting some of the taxes that the Constitution assigns to them in exchange for receiving federal transfers, it raises important and difficult questions about their rights to these transfers and the status of these revenues as either provincial or federal in origin. On the one hand, the claim by provincial authorities that they have legal rights to the transfers seems justifiable, particularly in the case of the direct taxes that the Constitution reserves for the provinces alone. This view of transfers is clearly reflected in the recalcitrance of demands by Peronist governors in 2001 that the De la Rúa administration make good on its past revenue-sharing obligations before they would contemplate any changes in the system. Though the press typically understood these transfers as handouts,[7] they were essentially revenues that came to the federal government at least in part because of the ongoing provincial delegation of taxing authority. On the other hand, it was the federal government that had long paid the administrative and political costs of collecting taxes that the provinces stopped collecting decades ago.

INSTITUTIONAL REDESIGN IN THE FIRST MENEM ADMINISTRATION: *LOS PACTOS FISCALES*

After two harrowing years, President Menem's attempts at macroeconomic stabilization finally succeeded in 1991 with the adoption of the Convertibility Law. Success immediately posed serious problems for the president, including the reality that stabilization and the consequent strengthening of tax collection would automatically generate a sharp increase in provincial transfers. Ironically, the chief problem for the president was a 1987 coparticipation law pushed by the Peronists themselves that reserved 57 percent of federal tax revenues for the provinces. For Menem's purposes, the defense of macroeconomic stability would require a revision in the rules governing revenue sharing to benefit the federal government so that it could meet its obligations and eschew its former reliance on the inflation tax. Accordingly, in 1992 and 1993, he proposed two fiscal pacts that would reduce provincial revenue shares by reserving 15 percent of the revenues subject to provincial sharing and dedicating these revenues to a key expenditure of the federal government: social security.

The effect was to reduce the percentage share of the provinces, which was not a new phenomena in Argentina, since similar centralizing

7. See "Argentina Says It Will Restructure Debt: Government Hopes to Avoid Defaulting on Loans as Economic Crisis Deepens," *Washington Post*, October 29, 2001, p. A14, and "Argentine Leader in Talks to Avoid Default on $132 Billion Debt," *New York Times*, November 1, 2001, p. 6.

changes had occurred in the wake of military coups in 1966 and 1976 (Eaton 2004). What was new, however, was that Menem agreed in exchange to the introduction of a minimum floor for revenue transfers below which transfers would not dip, regardless of actual revenue collection. Thus in the first fiscal pact of August 1992, the federal government committed itself to transfer no less than U.S.$720 million to the provinces every month, which it raised to $740 million in the second pact one year later. Neither pact was designed to be permanent; indeed, the terms of the second pact were binding only until July 1, 1995. Whereas all governors signed onto the first pact before it was approved by the legislature, only sixteen out of twenty-three governors agreed to the second pact before its implementation, which reflects the fact that the second pact made additional transfers contingent on a series of federally mandated provincial reforms.[8]

Significantly, the logic behind these changes was not to benefit the provinces in an attempt to thereby build support for Menem's market reforms.[9] Though the revenue guarantee would later prove to be a godsend for the provinces, in 1992 and 1993 the pacts demanded that the governors give up their legal shares of tax revenues at a time when these revenues were finally becoming more substantial. Percentage cuts for provincial transfers were difficult for the governors to swallow given the growth in tax revenues and the symbolic quality of the 1987 legislation, which had sought to reverse the prejudicial treatment suffered by the provinces under the preceding military dictatorship. Several opposition legislators warned in Congress that governors who signed these pacts and thereby agreed to accept less than their provinces' full percentage shares of revenue might very well find themselves subject to legal action.[10]

Support for my argument that provincial authorities considered the fiscal pacts to be first and foremost a loss for them can be seen in the months that preceded the signing of the pacts, during which Menem depended

8. Ultimately, afraid that they would be penalized for not signing the pact, all governors who did not originally agree to the terms of the second pact eventually signed it.

9. See Gibson and Calvo 2000 for the argument that Menem made federal transfers to Argentina's less developed provinces conditional on their support for federal economic reforms. As Gibson and Calvo argue, the increase in *discretionary* transfers can be attributed to Menem's attempt to court the "peripheral coalition" of interior provinces. The story is different, however, for those tax revenues subject to automatic sharing (coparticipation) as opposed to discretionary disbursement. In the area of automatic revenue sharing, the increase in transfers in the 1990–95 period was not the result of political manipulation by Menem and would have been even *greater* if Menem had not acted to limit the transfers through the two fiscal pacts. Thus we need to distinguish the centralizing logic of the fiscal pacts from the important argument that discretionary transfers were manipulated to favor peripheral provinces in the interests of economic reform.

10. *Diario de Sesiones de la Cámara de Diputados de la Nación*, August 19–20, 1992.

heavily on the use of selective incentives to get a sufficient number of governors on board. For example, his minister of the economy increased the pressure on provincial governments to sign by pledging to lift certain taxes on companies located in provinces that had signed the pact. Menem also pledged help in a variety of forms for provinces that were inclined not to sign (CGE 1993). Governors in Chaco and Formosa, for example, reversed their initially hostile stances after Menem pledged federal help with provincial debts (Chaco) and the establishment of a special free-trade zone (Formosa). In other words, that the *piso mínimo* turned out to be such a boon for the provinces should not blind us to fact that the pacts were inspired by the central government and, in the flush times of 1992 and 1993, represented an immediate and huge loss in revenue to the provinces. According to Cetrángolo and Jiménez, the provinces lost approximately US$13 billion between 1992 and 1996 because of the pacts (Fundación CECE 1997, 43). Nor should the problems later created by revenue guarantees prevent us from appreciating the extent to which the fiscal pacts helped Menem defend macrostability at the center in the first half of the 1990s.

In addition to financing the generous use of side payments, Argentina's economic successes in the early 1990s facilitated the negotiation of the fiscal pacts in another way as well. The increase in tax revenues that followed from economic stabilization and tax reform made it possible for governors to accept cuts in revenue sharing and still receive more from the federal government in transfers than they had received during the chaotic years of the late 1980s. Later, when the economy stalled and tax revenues declined, governors were not nearly as willing to consider requests for cuts in transfers, though these continued to emanate from the executive branch. The increase in tax revenues in the early 1990s, together with the general euphoria surrounding the end of hyperinflation and renewed economic growth, also mattered because they gave the federal government less pause about the wisdom of extending a fixed revenue guarantee to the provinces. Not expecting revenue to decline and convinced of the need to cut revenue transfers as quickly as possible to produce federal savings, representatives of the federal government agreed to bind it in a way that had long-lasting and negative consequences. As for the governors, although they were unable to defend the advantageous terms of the 1987 revenue-sharing law, they were quite savvy in their insistence on a revenue floor that looked low in 1992–93 but much higher later in the decade.[11]

---

11. Apart from the question of where the revenue floor was set, governors liked knowing exactly how much revenue they would receive each month, which reduced uncertainties in the provincial budgeting process.

Ultimately, however, side payments and differing estimates of revenue collection in the future cannot explain Menem's ability to secure the fiscal pacts politically. Critical is the degree of authority Menem enjoyed over the Peronist governors with whom he negotiated the pacts and over the Peronists in Congress who provided final legislative support. This authority resulted directly from Menem's successful stabilization in 1991, an achievement that had proved elusive in the years since the onset of the debt crisis in 1982 and the return to democracy in 1983. Menem's economic successes led to convincing Peronist victories in the midterm elections of 1991 and 1993, which further bolstered his influence within the Peronist party. In these years, for a Peronist governor to defy Menem's reform of revenue-sharing institutions would have entailed high political costs. A less risky and more effective response for the governors was to sign onto the pacts while simultaneously lobbying for side payments to the provinces they governed.

INTERGOVERNMENTAL RELATIONS IN MENEM'S SECOND TERM: POWER TO THE PROVINCES

This section describes and explains the shift in the balance of power back to the provinces and away from the federal government during Menem's second administration (1995–99). While the complexity of the policies proposed and outcomes legislated make it somewhat difficult to determine the net effect of relevant changes, it is clear that the federal government was less able to impose losses on the provinces in this period and, in fact, that the provinces were increasingly able to impose losses on the center. In these years, faced with gubernatorial recalcitrance in defense of revenue guarantees the federal government was forced to overadjust at the national level (Remmer and Wibbels 2000), a solution that ultimately proved to be unsustainable.

In the wake of the economic turmoil provoked by the Mexican "tequila crisis" in 1995 and 1996, the first signs that Menem was losing the political initiative relative to the governors can be seen in congressional attempts to extend the federal government's minimum revenue guarantee over the objections of the federal executive branch. Just as the poor economic performance of these years depressed tax collection and began to render the revenue floor increasingly attractive to all governors, Peronist governors came to enjoy greater leverage over Peronist legislators relative to a president who had just begun his second term. The effect of the crisis on tax receipts checked the earlier optimism of the federal government about its ability to afford revenue guarantees and led its representatives to favor their abandonment. When the second fiscal pact expired in July 1995, however, the Senate proposed making this extension indefinite "until such time as representatives of the federal and provincial governments can definitively agree on the way to implement the terms of the second fiscal pact."[12] Governors and the legislators over whom they held sway were increasingly focused on ensuring the continuity of the *piso mínimo*. In demanding the extension of the revenue guarantee, legislators even proposed giving the president additional discretion over the budget in order to make the necessary cuts that would enable the federal government to continue to meet its obligations to the provinces.

In response to legislators' efforts on behalf of the revenue guarantee, the minister of the economy argued that the federal government was not legally bound (*no existía disposición legal*) to honor the guarantee beyond July 1, 1995. Senators responded that the federal government then had no legal right to continue deducting the 15 percent amount from the revenue pool for social security.[13] As the conflict between defenders of provincial and federal interests escalated, Peronist and Radical senators proposed extending the federal government's obligations to honor revenue guarantees, while simultaneously eliminating from the second fiscal pact the obligation that provinces would have to reform their own tax systems.[14] Though Peronist party discipline prevented this proposal from succeeding, with the result that both federal and provincial obligations were formally carried over, in practice the provincial implementation of the tax and other reforms called for in the 1993 pact proved to be very spotty. Among other things, the difficult economic situation of the provinces in the 1995/96 period bolstered the claims of the governors that they could not afford to do away with taxes simply because they were deemed to be inefficient by the minister of the economy. According to Tommasi and Spiller (2000, 140), while provinces made significant headway in the reform of specific taxes on gas and electricity, they introduced far fewer changes in the turnover tax (*ingresos brutos*) that had been at the core of the second fiscal pact. In effect, the provinces were the victors in this important showdown with the federal government.

In his second administration, Menem also failed to advance two new reforms to the revenue-sharing system. First, the Ministry of the Economy proposed changing the criteria governing the distribution of automatic rev-

---

12. *Diario de Sesiones de la Cámara de Senadores de la Nación*, July 3, 1996, p. 3376.

13. Ibid., pp. 3377 and 3380.

14. See the speeches of Senators Cristina Fernández de Kirchner (PJ, Santa Cruz) and Luis León (UCR, Chaco) on pages 3378 and 3379.

enue transfers to incorporate rewards for provincial tax effort. Such a change would represent a major departure for the system of coparticipation. Although the criteria used to alloocate revenues have changed significantly over the years, from the initial use of criteria that favored productive capacity and population size toward increasingly redistributive criteria that favored poor and sparsely populated provinces (Nunez Minana and Porto 1983), the effort exerted by provincial authorities has never been explicitly considered. Indeed, the fact that governors would not have to expend political capital and energy on local tax collection was one of the key factors that encouraged them to delegate taxing authority in the 1930s. While governors signed onto the most important institutional innovation of Menem's first term—the two fiscal pacts—they simply refused to consider rewards for provincial tax effort, which was the most important institutional reform proposal of his second term. When the federal government's proposal went nowhere in Congress, Menem proposed the more limited use of provincial tax effort to distribute funds in excess of the *piso mínimo,* but this more circumscribed proposal also failed.[15]

In addition to proposing new criteria, Menem also floated the idea of direct revenue sharing with the municipalities. Municipal revenue sharing was attractive to the president both as a threat that would force the governors to contemplate cuts in provincial revenue sharing and as a sop to the country's numerous Peronist mayors who could help Menem in his attempt to run for a third term in 1999. Despite its appeal to the president, governors successfully rejected this proposal.

Not only did the governors defeat these attempts to discipline the provinces and control provincial spending, they were also able to increase the federal government's minimum revenue guarantees to U.S.$850 million per month in 1998.[16] The ability to raise the revenue floor, even as Menem was trying to move in the opposite direction by introducing greater flexibility into revenue sharing, demonstrates the governors' growing power in the president's penultimate year in office. But the increase in revenue guarantees is also significant because of how the guarantees were used by the governors. In the late 1990s, rather than attempt to control spending, governors sought to maintain or expand spending by borrowing from private sector banks and by using revenue guarantees as collateral in securing these loans. Since most provincial banks had been privatized in the wake of the 1995 crisis, the ability to contract loans from private banks was

15. See "La reforma fiscal entra en la etapa del realismo político," *El Economista,* February 6, 1998.

16. See "Gobernadores se aseguran $850 milliones cada mes," *Ambito Financiero,* October 10, 1998.

crucial in enabling governors to resist adjustment pressures. This option would not have been nearly so available to governors in the absence of guaranteed revenue transfers. Though private banks started refusing to issue new debt to the provinces in 1999 (even loans that would be guaranteed with federal revenue guarantees), in the years leading up to this decision the provinces incurred significant debts. According to the Economist Intelligence Unit, provincial debt rose to U.S.$18 billion or 7 percent of GDP by 1999, the year private banks cut off further loans (EIU 1999). In some provinces, debt service payments amounted to nearly half of all revenue transfers from the federal government.

How were the provinces able to frustrate the reform proposals coming out of the federal executive in the second half of the 1990s? I emphasize a mix of economic, institutional, and partisan factors. With respect to economic factors, the country's declining economic situation toward the end of the 1990s gave the governors additional reasons to defend the *piso mínimo*. Thanks to the decline in federal tax revenues, rules that favored the federal government in 1992 increasingly came to favor the provinces, especially after 1998. Declining revenues from provincial taxes and licensing fees, combined with surging unemployment rates throughout Argentina, transformed these revenue guarantees into a vital lifeline for many provincial governors. In some provinces, between 80 and 90 percent of the workforce was employed by provincial governments that were able to meet their payrolls only because of transfers from the Federal Capital. In this context, the loss of certain institutional power resources caused by such changes as the privatization of provincially owned banks in the second half of the 1990s encouraged governors to redouble their energies in defense of the *piso mínimo*.

With respect to institutional rules, governors were abetted in their attempt to deflect reform initiatives in Menem's second term by changes in the federal constitution that had been introduced in 1994. Specifically, the new constitution called for the negotiation of a new revenue-sharing law to replace the 1987 legislation, and stipulated that as a result of this new law, no province could receive less in revenue than it had received in 1994.[17] The Constitution also determined that all legislation affecting the revenue-sharing system had to originate in the Senate. Though both chambers are characterized by malapportionment in Argentina, the poorer and

17. Initially, the agreement between Menem and former president Alfonsín that gave rise to the constitutional reform (the so-called *núcleo de coincidencias básicas*) included no mention of provincial or revenue-sharing issues. A provincial coalition among the members of the constitutional convention, however, managed to insert language on revenue sharing into the new constitution.

less populated provinces that depend so heavily on revenue transfers are much better represented in the Senate and better able to use their foothold in that body to veto the types of reforms that Menem proposed after 1995. In practice, over the course of Menem's second administration, these constitutional rules prevented the negotiation of a new revenue-sharing law that might have introduced greater flexibility into the transfer system or revoked the rigid guarantees that had been introduced earlier in the decade.[18]

With respect to partisan dynamics, growing factionalism within the PJ over the course of the president's second term made it harder for Menem to control the governors within his party. Controlling the governors and forcing Peronist legislators to follow the national party line had never been easy. As Levitsky shows, few provincial leaders belonged to the president's Menemista faction (Levitsky 2001). But the struggles to succeed Menem as the party leader that emerged immediately after his reelection in 1995 complicated his attempts to achieve further policy changes. That Menem could not necessarily count on the support of Peronist governors for such measures as criteria that would reward provincial tax effort illustrates one of the main findings in Remmer and Wibbels's (2000) study, which is that partisan ties do not explain variation in provincial adjustment in Argentina in the expected direction. In other words, in his second term Menem had as much difficulty bringing Peronist governors to heel as he did in controlling governors from opposition parties.[19]

The combined effect of these stalled revenue-sharing reforms is interesting given the argument of Gibson and Calvo about the sequence of economic reform "events" in Argentina (Gibson and Calvo 2000). As they argue, it was the country's metropolitan provinces that bore the brunt of the market reforms that Menem was able to adopt in his first administration with the support of the peripheral provinces: "Only after 1994, once the major adjustments in the metropolitan economies had been made, and once the local political dividends of these adjustments began to be collected, did the national government turn its attention to reform of the

18. To date, no new coparticipation law has been legislated by Congress, and revenue sharing in Argentina continues to be governed by a confusing mix of distinct and heavily amended laws (Saiegh and Tommasi 1999a).

19. The economic, institutional, and partisan factors highlighted in this chapter explain why the governors were able to defend the revenue guarantee past its usefulness to the federal government, but it is important to also note that Menem's own interest in revenue reform certainly waned with the waxing of his drive to win a second reelection in 1999. Trying to remove the revenue floor was a sure way of antagonizing the very governors whose support Menem would have needed to make this second reelection a reality. I am grateful to an anonymous reviewer for this point.

provinces" (40). Thus, when the center finally did shift its focus onto the peripheral provinces, there were sharp limits on how much provincial reform it was able to impose. Ironically, these limits were in large part determined by the very instrument—revenue guarantees—that Menem had used to build support for his centralizing reforms of coparticipation in his early years as president.

RETURN TO CRISIS: PROVINCIAL-FEDERAL RELATIONS
AFTER MENEM

Conflict between the federal and provincial governments over revenue sharing and provincial debt used up a great deal of Fernando De la Rúa's political capital in his two difficult years as president (December 1999–December 2001). Although De la Rúa's alliance of FREPASO and the Radicals won both presidential and congressional elections in 1999, it was much less successful in provincial elections. As in the Alfonsín administration of the 1980s, under De la Rúa most provinces were governed by the Peronists. In both periods, this political reality infused center-provincial relations with a much greater degree of partisanship that had been the case under Menem. One salient example is the 2000 attempt by the new minister of social development Graciela Fernández Mejide to increase federal control over the implementation of provincial social programs. Designed as a measure that would reduce clientelism, the proposal provoked strong opposition in Peronist-controlled provinces.

It is also the case, however, that governors from the governing Alianza—including Roberto Iglesias in Mendoza, Angel Rozas in Chaco, Alfredo Avelín in San Juan, and Sergio Montiel in Entre Rios—often sided with Peronist governors against De la Rúa. Thus, in contrast to Menem in his first administration, not only did De la Rúa face a majority of provinces that were governed by the opposition, but he enjoyed much less leverage over those governors who in fact belonged to one of the two governing parties. As a result, governors emerged victorious from most of the negotiations that took place with the federal government in this period (see the time line in Table 4.2).

One of De la Rúa's first attempts to deal with the significant federal budget deficit he had inherited from the outgoing Menem administration was to propose the creation of new taxes, the proceeds of which would not be shared with the provinces (EIU 1999). On the one hand, by excusing the federal government from sharing additional revenues with the provinces, De la Rúa's ability to get this proposal through Congress can be

Table 4.2 Time line of events affecting the provinces from 1999 to 2002

Event	Date	Description
Fiscal Convertibility Law	August 1999	Limited 2000 deficit to 1.5% of GDP and called for a balanced budget by 2003
Revenue-sharing agreement between De la Rúa and the governors	December 1999	US$1.35 billion monthly transfers in 2000 and US$1.36 billion in 2001 in exchange for tax increases that would not be shared with the provinces
Federal Pact for Growth and Fiscal Discipline	November 2000	Stipulated that revenue transfers in 2003–2005 would be a moving average of the previous three years, with a floor of US$1.45 billion
Zero Deficit Law	July 2001	13% cut in revenue transfers and public sector wages and pensions
Creation of *lecops* and *bono interprovincial*	August 2001	*Lecops* are federally issued bonds meant to substitute for provincial script, which can be used to pay federal taxes, and *bonos* compensate the provinces for shortfalls in revenue-sharing obligations
Negotiations break down b/w Peronist governors and De la Rúa	October 25, 2001	Peronists insist that De la Rúa honor minimum revenue obligations before considering a broader set of reforms
Chaco defaults	October 26, 2001	
La Rioja defaults	November 6, 2001	
S&P lowers Argentina's credit rating to selective default	November 6, 2001	
Peronist governors agree to reductions in transfers	November 2001	
Elimination of the minimum revenue guarantee (*piso mínimo*)	February 2002	Duhalde convinces governors to relinquish the guarantee by agreeing to share proceeds of a new tax on checks and to convert dollar-denominated provincial debts at a rate of 1.4 pesos to the dollar

contrasted with Menem's failure to amend the criteria used to distribute excess tax revenue in his second administration (Bertea and Iturre 2000, 24). On the other hand, De la Rúa paid handsomely for this proposal in the form of a commitment to increase the revenue guarantee to $1.35 billion per month in 2000 and $1.36 billion in 2001. Given the low rate of inflation in these years, the increase from a revenue floor of $850 million in 1998 to $1.35 billion two years later was indeed a considerable victory for the provinces.

According to De la Rúa's gamble, if the tax increases succeeded in generating substantial new revenues, which was unlikely given the state of the economy, the federal government would enhance its stature relative to the provinces. But if tax revenues did not increase as the president had hoped, then revenue guarantees would enable the provinces to gain at the expense of the center. In the end, increases in tax revenues never materialized, and the increase in revenue obligations served to hamstring the federal government precisely as it was grappling for solutions to the deepening economic crisis. Despite the worsening situation over the course of 2000, the governors were able to increase the revenue floor still further in the so-called Federal Pact for Growth and Discipline of November 2000. According to this pact, transfers in the 2003–5 period would be a moving average of the previous three years, with a minimum floor of $1.45 billion per month. As a result of this pact, De la Rúa's commitments to the provinces between 2000 and 2001 experienced an increase despite the fact that total federal government revenue declined in this period by 3.5 percent (EIU 2001).

The year 2001 marked the beginning of the end for the rigid system of federal revenue guarantees initiated in 1992. In the middle of the year, after continued declines in tax revenues, De la Rúa managed to push through Congress the Zero Deficit Law, which included a 13 percent cut in public sector wages and revenue transfers. Despite growing evidence of the crisis in public revenues, the provincial governors agreed to lower the revenue quota, but not to abandon it altogether. Though it is significant that governors agreed to this reduction, one should not lose sight of the fact that the 13 percent reduction only lowered the monthly revenue guarantee in 2001 to $1.19 billion, still considerably above the 1998 floor. Furthermore, in exchange for agreeing to the cut, the federal government was forced to renegotiate provincial liabilities with private banks at interest rates no higher than 7 percent (EIU 2001).

In the end, the federal government failed to meet its revenue obligations with the provinces even after the July cut, and arrears began to accumulate. In August 2001, the De la Rúa government created a new interprovincial bond (*bono interprovincial*) to be issued by a provincial development fund (Fondo Fiduciario para el Desarrollo Provincial), which it sent to the provinces to pay revenue-sharing arrears. It was conflict over these arrears, and demands by the Peronists that De la Rúa release $250 million in overdue transfers, that triggered the breakdown of dialogue between the president and the governors and the acknowledgement on October 28, 2001, by the federal government that it would have to restructure its $132 billion debt. De la Rúa's inability to reach a deal with Peronist governors over the obligations of the federal government was a key sign of his inability to govern the country.

It would certainly be a mistake to overstate the importance of the *piso mínimo* in the collapse of the Argentine economy; a more complete explanation would no doubt pay attention to such factors as the fixed exchange rate, corruption, and an unfavorable external environment. But the unintended consequences of the fixed revenue guarantee are crucial, and the easiest way of appreciating the importance of the *piso mínimo* comes from the relevant counterfactual. Had Menem not agreed to demands for a *piso mínimo* in 1992 and 1993 in order to grab more revenues for the federal government, revenue transfers to the provinces later in the decade would have declined in step with the country's faltering tax collection. Instead, as it happened, fixed revenue transfers proved to be increasingly expensive for De la Rúa, generating a constraint on his government that was as intractable as the fixed exchange rate system.

When Congress selected Eduardo Duhalde as the country's new president on January 1, 2002, he targeted for elimination both of the institutions—convertibility and the revenue floor—that had so constrained his predecessor. Duhalde declared a formal end to the first institution—convertibility—in less than a week, in effect providing formal recognition of the fact that convertibility had really come to an end in November 2001 with the debt default and with the imposition of limits on bank account withdrawals (e.g., the so-called *corralito*). Removing the revenue floor took more political skill in that it was not a foregone conclusion and instead was to require direct and prolonged negotiations with the governors. Ultimately, however, Duhalde prevailed and successfully put an end to a decade of fixed revenue transfers through the negotiation of a new pact with governors signed on February 27, 2002. As Duhalde declared at the signing ceremony for this pact, "We shall distribute only what we actually collect" (vamos a repartir lo que ingresa).[20] Thus, on March 20, the federal

20. "Las claves de un acuerdo que todavía guarda algunas dudas," *Clarín*, February 26, 2002.

government paid to the provinces for the very last time the monthly guaranteed revenue transfer of $1.185 billion.[21]

How was Duhalde able to eliminate the *piso mínimo* when this same institutional change had proved so elusive to his predecessors? First, no actual revenues had been transferred to the provinces since August 2001, which certainly may have complicated the efforts of those who wished to defend the continued use of a *piso mínimo*. The reliance on arrears and bonds demonstrated to all concerned that the federal government could not guarantee to send revenues it simply did not have. In this sense, one could argue that the revenue floor had ended months before its formal removal on February 27, 2002, just as the convertibility era had come to a close before its official end on January 6, 2002. Second, Duhalde's negotiating position as president was clearly enhanced by his prior and continuing position as the leader of the Peronist party in the province of Buenos Aires. This position gave him extensive control over the largest provincial bloc of legislators in Congress, a tremendously useful asset that Menem could not necessarily rely on in his second term and which De la Rúa never enjoyed.

It would be a mistake, however, to conclude that Duhalde's influence in Congress enabled him to formally withdraw the revenue floor without making other concessions to the provinces. In fact, considering the concessions he had to make and the damage they did to the economy of Argentina, the end of the governors' beloved *piso mínimo* did not come cheap to the president. Duhalde sought to bolster the support of the governors in three ways. First, he agreed to share with the provinces the proceeds of a new tax on checks, a grossly distorsionary but productive generator of revenues. Initially the federal government offered 20 percent of this tax to the provinces, but it was subsequently forced by the governors to increase this percentage to 25 percent and finally to 30 percent.[22] Second, although the federal government wanted no further provincial bonds to be issued, it was forced to let the provinces issue bonds to cover current costs (though not to pay debts with the federal government). Third, Duhalde agreed to a deal according to which dollar-denominated provincial debts would be converted to pesos (*pesificada*) at a rate (1.4 pesos to the dollar) that was advantageous to the provinces. What is striking is that, even after De la Rúa's fall, the default on the external debt, and the worst economic crisis in Argentine history, governors were still strong enough to demand significant compensation for the withdrawal of the revenue floor.

---

21. "Negociación con el FMI: Aval y reclamos de las provincias," *Clarín*, April 12, 2002.
22. *Clarín*, February 26, 2000.

CONCLUSION: INTERGOVERNMENTAL RELATIONS AND
INSTITUTIONAL DESIGN

As this discussion of the establishment, maintenance, and eventual
abandonment of the revenue guarantee rule demonstrates, questions of
institutional volatility and stickiness are central to the study of intergovernmental relations in Argentina. On the one hand, those who wish to
draw attention to institutional uncertainty as an underlying cause of Argentina's difficulties can find substantial support in the area of revenue
sharing. There has been a great deal of volatility in revenue-sharing rules,
with nearly constant political conflict and negotiations between governors
and representatives of the federal government since the creation of coparticipation in the 1930s. Intergovernmental relations in the last three decades have been subject to a dizzying number of changes, including
revenue decentralization in 1973, revenue centralization after the 1976
coup, the devolution of some education and health-care responsibilities
in the early 1980s, an ad hoc system of revenue transfers in the mid-
1980s, and the passage of further revenue decentralization in 1987.
Though the use of the *piso mínimo* remained constant in the 1992–2002
period and was its defining feature, disagreements over where the floor
should be set occasioned significant conflicts between the federal and the
provincial governments on a yearly (and sometimes even more frequent)
basis. Opposition governors throughout the 1990s complained of lags in
the distribution of guaranteed transfers from the center, and the lack of
respect for formal institutional rules was certainly the hallmark of Menem's governing style (De Riz 1996; Ferreira Rubio and Goretti 1998).

On the other hand, my analysis demonstrates that some Argentine institutions have been too rigid. Attention should be paid to the deeper
causes of institutional volatility as an apparently constant feature of the
country's political economy, but this attention does not mean that we
should ignore questions of institutional design. Despite the general picture of volatility, one particular institutional rule—the extension of the
revenue floor or *piso mínimo*—generated significant staying power. Once
granted, the minimum revenue guarantee proved to be quite difficult to
rescind as governors rallied repeatedly and aggressively in its defense.
Governors were successful in these efforts thanks to the considerable authority they have come to enjoy in Argentina's current democratic period.
As I have argued, this authority results both from the structure of Argentine political parties, which gives governors considerable leverage over federal legislators, and from the content of the country's electoral rules,
including the holding of nonconcurrent national and provincial elections.

After 1992, governors no longer had cause to worry about sudden decreases in transfers caused by a drop in federal tax collection. Consequently, the minimum revenue guarantee enabled them to reduce provincial tax effort, expand the size of provincial payrolls, and slough off demands from the center for provincial adjustment. Furthermore, subsequent to the shift from percentage-based sharing to an actual revenue guarantee, provincial authorities used these guarantees as collateral that enabled them to run up significant debts with private sector banks. In other words, the *piso mínimo* let governors partially circumvent the privatization of provincial public banks that the federal government had achieved at such great effort in the mid-1990s. The revenue floor can thus be understood as an institutional rule that directly shaped the behavior of provincial officials and generated negative consequences at both the provincial and federal levels. While flexibility in the past often opened up room for the highly political use of revenue transfers, the experience of the 1990s suggests that the federal government needs more flexibility than revenue guarantees allowed. However one comes down on this question, the last decade clearly suggests that design considerations, including the appropriate balance between rigidity and flexibility, are hardly superfluous.[23]

Beyond the fixed nature of the *piso mínimo* in the 1990s, I argue that intergovernmental relations in Argentina have been characterized by a deeper form of institutional rigidity. For all the conflict over the size of revenue transfers and the timing of disbursements, the underlying norm of revenue sharing from the federal to the provincial governments has proved to be remarkably sticky. Given some of the pathologies associated with automatic revenue sharing, one could argue that Argentina would have benefited from more rather than less institutional change in this arena. Revenue sharing was initiated in the 1930s when the fallout from the Great Depression encouraged the provinces to delegate responsibility for the collection of key provincial taxes to the federal government. In the decades that followed, politicians debated which tax bases should be shared and what the provinces' shares should be, but not the more fundamental rule according to which the federal government continues to collect provincial taxes. The severing of the connection between tax collection and expenditure has profoundly compromised the integrity of provincial governments. Thus, while governors enjoy considerable strength as political actors, the provinces they govern are relatively weak as units of government. The combination of gubernatorial strength and provincial weakness

---

23. For more on the trade-off between rules and flexibility in the Argentine context, see Saiegh and Tommasi 1999b.

was disastrous for Argentina in the 1990s in that it led to guaranteed revenue transfers of a magnitude that were neither realistic nor sustainable. One can hope that the depth of the recent crisis will generate a substantive debate that revisits the provinces' fateful decision in the 1930s to forgo a more meaningful role in tax collection.[24]

---

24. For specific reform proposals, see the excellent working papers on coparticipation by scholars at the Centro de Estudios para el Desarrollo Institucional at the Fundación Gobierno y Sociedad, available at http://www.fgys.org/cedi.

Rethinking Democratic Institutions

5

Provincial Party Bosses:
Keystone of the Argentine Congress

Mark P. Jones and Wonjae Hwang

INTRODUCTION

Between 1989 and 2003, in regard to the major policy issues of the day,
legislative politics in Argentina was often very adversarial with a relatively
homogenous legislative majority party (which was also the party of the
president) employing its majority status to pass legislation that was
strongly opposed by an equally homogenous principal minority party. The
consequences of this dynamic were numerous legislative victories for the
majority party and numerous legislative defeats for the principal minority
party (as well as for most other opposition parties).

The success of the majority party in the Argentine Congress stems from
its functioning as an effective cartel. The origins of these cartels are, however, distinct from those in the U.S. Congress (Cox and McCubbins 1993).
In the United States, the members of Congress are the crucial actors who
delegate power to the party leadership, while in Argentina provincial-level

Research for this project was supported by the National Science Foundation (SBR
9709695), the Centro de Estudios para el Desarrollo Institucional (CEDI) de la Fundación
Gobierno y Sociedad, and the Political Institutions and Public Choice (PIPC) Program at
Michigan State University. We thank Gerardo Adrogué, Rubén Bambaci, Paloma Bauer de la
Isla, Silvina Danesi, Alberto DiPeco, Marcela Durrieu, Alberto Föhrig, Sebastián Galmarini,
Ariel Godoy, Steven Levitsky, Sergio Massa, Victoria Murillo, Baldomero Rodríguez, David
Rohde, and Rossana Surballe for answering questions and providing helpful assistance, sug-
gestions, and comments. This chapter benefited from the ongoing collaborative study of the
Argentine Congress by Jones with Sebastián Saiegh, Pablo Spiller, and Mariano Tommasi.

party bosses are the key players who engage in this delegation, but the end effect on the functioning of the national legislature is quite similar. The majority party leadership uses its majority status (especially agenda control) to dominate the legislative process, excluding legislation it believes may pass despite its objection (negative agenda control), as well as implementing legislation it desires (positive agenda control). The opposition, lacking both negative and positive agenda control, is left in a very reactive position.

The portrayal of Argentine politics during the 1990s presented in this chapter is at odds with studies that have attempted to explain the recent functioning of the country's political system by focusing on the ambition, strategies, and behavior of one man: Carlos Saúl Menem (president from 1989 to 1999). Contrary to the underlying argument in these studies, the ability of President Menem to implement many (though not all) of his desired policy reforms in the 1990s was not due primarily to Argentina being a "delegative democracy," Menem's status as a "neopopulist president," or Menem's "abuse" of constitutional decree authority. President Menem's policy success was due much more to his ability to maintain the support of the provincial party bosses, support that was manifested in many respects by their delegation to the party leadership in Congress (and indirectly to President Menem).[1] This delegation came at a price, however, and that price was the continued flow of resources to the provinces. To keep the resources flowing, President Menem increasingly was forced to contract debt in the international and, to a lesser extent, domestic capital markets. This growing debt burden was unsustainable and eventually contributed to the country's economic and political collapse in December 2001.

POLITICAL INSTITUTIONS AND PARTY POLITICS IN ARGENTINA

This chapter focuses on the years 1989 (July 8) to 2003 (May 24), a period of profound economic and social transformation in Argentina (Corrales 2002; Etchemendy, this volume; Murillo 2001). This section provides a series of general conclusions that can be drawn from the recent literature on the Argentine political system.[2]

1. President Menem's frequent use of executive decrees to bypass the Congress (Ferreira Rubio and Goretti 1998) is merely the logical extreme of this delegation of power by the provincial party bosses (via the Congress) to the president.

2. This section draws heavily on De Luca, Jones, and Tula 2002; Jones 2002 and 1997a; Jones and Hwang 2005; and Jones et al. 2002.

The Political Institutions

Argentina is a presidential republic. The president is constitutionally quite powerful, possessing both a strong veto and executive decree authority (Magar 2001b; Negretto 2001). Argentina has a bicameral national legislature (Senate and Chamber of Deputies) as well as a federal system of government in which provincial governors exercise substantial autonomy (Eaton, this volume; Sawers 1996; Tommasi 2002). Every one of the twenty-four provinces (twenty-three provinces and an autonomous federal capital) possesses three senators (two prior to 1995) and a number of deputies proportional to its population in 1980, with every province receiving a minimum of five deputies. The Argentine Congress, while certainly much more of a reactive blunt veto player than a proactive agenda setter, is nevertheless an important actor in the policy process (Corrales 2002; Eaton 2002; Jones et al. 2002; Llanos 2002; Mustapic 2002; Spiller and Tommasi, this volume).

The Party System: 1989–2003

During the 1989–2003 period two political parties dominated Argentine politics, the Partido Justicialista (PJ, Peronists) and the Unión Cívica Radical (UCR, Radicals). From time to time a "third party" achieved a modest degree of national prominence.[3] However, to date every single one of these parties has seen its electoral support evaporate after only a few elections. In contrast to the PJ and UCR, these national third parties never established an effective party organization and overly depended on the popularity of a single leader (or small group of leaders). Furthermore, these national third parties have consistently failed to extend their influence beyond their initial core geographic area of support, the Federal Capital and the portion of the province of Buenos Aires adjacent to the Federal Capital (Greater Buenos Aires) (De Luca, Jones, and Tula 2002).

This PJ-UCR dominance can be seen in the substantial control exercised by these two parties (especially the PJ) over the most important political posts in the country: the presidency, the Congress, the governorships, and the mayoralties. The period July 8, 1989, to May 24, 2003, encompasses the presidency of Carlos Saúl Menem (1989–95, 1995–99) of the PJ, the

3. Third parties that achieved this ephemeral national prominence include the Partido Intransigente (PI), Unión del Centro Democrático (UCEDE), Movimiento por la Dignidad y la Independencia (MODIN), Frente País Solidario (FREPASO), Acción por la República (AR), and Argentinos por una República de Iguales (ARI).

abbreviated tenure of Fernando de la Rúa (1999–2001) of the UCR, and
the term of interim president Eduardo Duhalde (2002–3) of the PJ.[4]

During this period the PJ held an average of 55.2 percent of the seats in
the Senate and 45.4 percent of the seats in the Chamber of Deputies, while
the UCR accounted for an average of 30.3 percent of the seats in the Senate
and 31.9 percent of the seats in the Chamber of Deputies (see Tables 5.1
and 5.2).[5] The most successful third party in the Senate during this period
was the Movimiento Popular Neuquino (MPN), which averaged 3.6 percent
of the seats (no party other than the PJ or UCR ever held more than two
senate seats during any legislative period).[6] In the Chamber, the most successful third party (FREPASO) reached a zenith of 14.8 percent of the seats,
with the largest third party in the eight (1987–2003) two-year legislative
periods (a status held by four different parties) occupying an average of
only 7.2 percent of the seats. Suffering the fate of all national third parties
in Argentina, by the 2001–3 period FREPASO's Chamber contingent had
been reduced to a mere 2.7 percent of the seats, a number that dropped
even further (to 1.2 percent) following the December 2003 elections.

This PJ and UCR dominance extends to the governorships. As Table 5.3
details, the PJ controlled an average of 63.7 percent of the governorships
between 1989 and 2003, with the UCR placing second with an average of
20.2 percent. In contrast, no other party ever possessed more than one
governorship at any one time during this period, with the highest average
for a third party (the MPN) only 4.3 percent.

Finally, the important post of mayor was generally occupied either by a
Peronist (PJ) or a Radical (UCR) between 1989 and 2003 (see Table 5.4).[7]
Among municipalities with four thousand or more inhabitants (based on
the 1991 census), during this period an average of 55.4 percent of the municipalities were controlled by PJ mayors and an average of 32.1 percent by

4. Raúl Alfonsín of the UCR was president from December 1983, when Argentina returned to democracy, to July 1989.

5. Since Menem's presidency included the final five months of the 1986–89 (Senate)
and 1987–89 (Chamber) legislative periods, all analysis includes these periods in the calcula-
tion of the averages and ranges.

6. Argentina has a large number of parties that successfully compete either solely (or
effectively) in only one province (De Luca, Jones, and Tula 2002; Palanza and Sin 1997).
This diverse group is collectively referred to as the "provincial parties." With one exception,
all of the governorships held by parties other than the PJ or UCR have been held by provincial
parties. During the past twenty years, the MPN has been the country's most successful provincial party.

7. For a detailed analysis of the dominance, at the provincial and municipal level, of the
PJ and UCR in the all-important province of Buenos Aires (where 38 percent of the Argentine
population resides), see Galmarini 2004.

Table 5.1 The Composition of the Argentine Senate, 1983–2003 (percentages)

Political party	1983–86	1986–89	1989–92	1992–95	1995–1998	1998–2001	2001–3
Partido Justicialista	45.7	45.7	54.4 / 54.2	62.5	55.7	55.7	57.1
Unión Cívica Radical	39.1	39.1	30.4 / 29.2	22.9	28.6	30.0	31.4
Others	15.2	15.2	15.2 / 16.7	14.6	15.7	14.3	11.4
Total number of seats	46	46	46 / 48	48	70	70	70

NOTE: The parties listed held three or more seats in at least one legislative period. In 1995–2001, two seats from the province of Catamarca were never occupied because of a political dispute. Because of similar political conflicts in 2001–3, a seat from the Capital Federal and a seat from the province of Corrientes were never occupied. In early 1992, the Senate grew from forty-six to forty-eight members with the creation of the province of Tierra del Fuego. Beginning in 2001, the Senate partial renovation period (previously triennial) became biennial.

Table 5.2 The composition of the Argentine Chamber of Deputies, 1983–2003 (percentages)

Political party	1983–1985	1985–1987	1987–1989	1989–1991	1991–1993	1993–1995	1995–1997	1997–1999	1999–2001
PJ	43.7	37.8	38.6	47.2	45.1	49.4	51.0	46.3	38.5
UCR	50.8	50.8	44.9	35.4	32.7	32.7	26.5	25.7	31.9
FREPASO	—	—	—	—	—	—	8.6	14.8	14.4
ARI	—	—	—	—	—	—	—	—	—
Others	5.5	11.4	16.5	17.3	22.2	17.9	14.0	13.2	15.2
Total number of seats in the Chamber	254	254	254	254	257	257	257	257	257

NOTE: All parties that in at least one two-year legislative period held 5 percent or more of the seats are listed separately. Also, the total number of seats in the Chamber of Deputies rose from 254 to 257 in late 1992 when Tierra del Fuego became a province.

Table 5.3   Partisan control of the provinces (governorships), 1983–2003

Political party	1983–1987	1987–1991	1991–1995	1995–1999	1999–2003
Partido Justicialista	54.6	77.3	60.9	58.3	58.3
Unión Cívica Radical	31.8	9.1	17.4	25.0	29.2
Others	13.6	13.6	21.7	16.7	12.5
Total number of governorships	22	22	23	24	24

NOTE: All parties that held more than one governorship in a province during at least one gubernatorial period are listed separately. The 1993–97, 1997–2001, and 2001–03 gubernatorial periods for Corrientes are included with the data for 1991–95, 1995–99, and 2001–2003 given in the table. The 1996–2000 and 2000–3 gubernatorial periods for Capital Federal are included with the 1995–99 and 2001–3 data given in the table.

UCR mayors.[8] In municipalities that possessed populations of a hundred thousand or more (based on the 1991 census), the PJ on average held 61.7 percent and the UCR 23.5 percent of the mayoralities; in provincial capitals the corresponding figures for the PJ and the UCR were 48.5 percent and 31.8 percent (Myers and Dietz 2002). The average percentage of municipalities held by the most successful provincial party during each of the four mayoral periods was a mere 1.6 percent. Even more striking is the almost complete failure of any national third party to win more than a handful of municipalities during this period, an indication of the universal inability of these parties to establish any significant type of party organization and to institutionalize. The average percentage of mayoralties occupied by the most successful national third party during each of the four mayoral periods (a status held by four different parties) is a scant 0.7 percent.

Intraparty Politics

The locus of partisan politics in Argentina is the province (Benton 2002; De Luca, Jones, and Tula 2002; Gibson and Calvo 2000; Jones 1997b; Levitsky 2003; Remmer and Wibbels 2000). Political careers are generally based at the provincial level (with even positions in the national government often a consequence of provincial factors), and the base of political support for politicians and parties is concentrated at the provincial level.

A single person or small group of politicians generally dominates political parties at the provincial level (De Luca, Jones, and Tula 2002; Jones et al. 2002). In provinces where the party controls the governorship, with

8. The four thousand inhabitants threshold was employed in order to insure a more accurate comparison across the provinces, among which the legislation regulating the creation of self-governing municipalities in less populous localities varies.

Table 5.4 Partisan control of mayoralties for municipalities with more than four thousand inhabitants (percentages)

Political party	Categories	1983–87[a]	1987–91	1991–95	1995–99	1999–2003
Partido Justicialista	All municipalities	43.3	55.9	55.7	58.6	51.5
	4000–24,999	45.7	55.0	53.8	56.2	52.2
	25,000–99,999	36.9	54.5	60.5	62.7	50.4
	Over 100,000	36.5	67.3	61.5	69.6	48.2
	Provincial capitals	36.4	59.1	39.1	47.8	47.8
Unión Cívica Radical	All municipalities	45.8	32.8	30.4	28.8	36.2
	4000–24,999	43.8	33.9	33.1	31.0	36.8
	25,000–99,999	48.4	31.7	25.0	24.6	36.0
	Over 100,000	57.7	25.0	17.3	19.6	32.1
	Provincial capitals	45.5	27.3	30.4	34.8	34.8
Most successful[b] provincial party[c]	All municipalities	2.6	1.8	1.7	1.7	1.3
	4000–24,999	3.0	1.7	2.1	1.9	1.2
	25,000–99,999	1.6	2.4	0.0	0.8	1.6
	Over 100,000	1.9	1.9	1.9	1.8	1.8
	Provincial capitals	4.6	4.64	.4	4.4	4.4
Most successful national (third) party[d]	All municipalities	0.6	0.5	0.8	0.5	0.9
	4000–24,999	0.4	0.2	0.6	0.6	0.0
	25,000–99,999	1.6	1.6	0.8	0.0	1.6
	Over 100,000	0.0	0.0	1.9	0.0	7.1
	Provincial capitals	0.0	0.0	0.0	0.0	0.0
Total number of municipalities with populations greater than four thousand		644	653	659	666	687

[a]Control of the mayoralty is measured as of January of the even-numbered year following normal municipal elections.

[b]"Successful" is defined as holding the highest percentage of mayoralties among municipalities with four thousand or more inhabitants (1991 Census) during that period.

[c]The most successful provincial parties were as follows: in 1983–87, the Partido Autonomista (PA) in Corrientes; in 1987–91, the Partido Liberal (PL), in Corrientes; the PA again for 1991–95 and 1995–99; and in 1999–2003, the Fuerza Republicana, in Tucumán.

[d]The most successful national parties were as follows: in 1983–87 and 1987–91, the Partido Intransigente; in 1991–95, the Unidad Socialista; in 1995–99, the UCEDE; and in 1999–2003, FREPASO.

rare exceptions the governor is the undisputed (or at least dominant) boss of the provincial-level party. In many other provinces where the governorship is not held by the party, the party is nonetheless dominated in a comparable manner (with a greater amount of space for intraparty opponents) by a single individual. Finally, in the remaining provinces where the party does not control the governorship and there is no single dominant leader, there is generally a small group of influential party leaders who predominate in party life.[9] In these latter two instances (where the party does not control the governorship) the single dominant party boss or small group of leaders commonly occupy the most prominent post or posts held by the party in the province (e.g., national senator, national deputy, mayor of the capital city).

Most PJ deputies have come from provinces with PJ governors, who in all but a few instances are the undisputed party bosses. Between 1989 and 2003 a median of 73 percent of the PJ delegation came from provinces with PJ governors. In contrast, only a median of 24 percent of the UCR delegation came from provinces where the UCR held the governorship.

This dominance by provincial party leaders is based principally on patronage, pork barrel politics, and clientelism. Patronage positions are particularly important for maintaining the support of second- and third-tier party leaders, who in turn possess the ability to mobilize voters, especially for party primaries. The ability to engage in pork barrel politics improves the party's reputation with key constituents and aids clientelistic practices through the provision of jobs to party supporters as well as the infusion of money into the party coffers, which in turn is employed to maintain clientelistic networks. Clientelism, that is, the direct exchange of selective material incentives (Kitschelt 2000), assists party leaders at all levels in maintaining a solid base of supporters.

The provincial-level party has a large number of positions at its disposal, with the exact portfolio depending on the party's control of national, provincial, and municipal governments (De Luca, Jones, and Tula 2002). All parties control positions (of varying number) in the national, provincial, and municipal legislatures. If the party controls the provincial government, it has further access to positions in the provincial executive branch, and likewise, where it controls municipal governments (the degree of this control varies depending on the province's province-municipality revenue-sharing system), it also has access to positions in the municipal executive

9. In provinces where the party leadership is fragmented, the role of the national party (especially if it is the party of the president) in provincial-level politics is often more pronounced than is the case where the provincial-level party is united under a single leader (Jones 1997a).

branch.[10] Finally, if the party controls the national government, provincial party leaders have access to a host of positions in the national government, both in the Federal Capital and in the provincial offices of the national executive branch.

The provincial party also controls the distribution of national-, provincial-, and municipal-level expenditures, with this control varying depending on the party's control over the national, provincial, and municipal governments.[11] These expenditures provide the resources needed by party leaders to engage in clientelistic activities. Argentina's federal revenue-sharing system automatically transfers funds to the provinces, which are then mostly utilized at the province's discretion. During the past dozen years the distribution of expenditures in Argentina has been roughly equal between the national government and the provinces (Saiegh and Tommasi 1998; Tommasi 2002) with, for instance, in 2000 52 percent of expenditures being carried out by the national government, 40 percent by the provincial governments, and 8 percent by the municipal governments (Tommasi 2002).[12]

Governors (and to a lesser extent mayors) exercise considerable influence over the execution of public policy (either through their direct control of the provincial budget or their discretionary control over the execution of programs funded by the national government) (De Luca, Jones, and Tula 2002). This influence allows them to obtain and maintain the loyalty of their supporters through the granting of privileges in the distribution of material and economic subsidies, low-interest loans, scholarships, and so on.[13] It also allows them to construct a relationship with a wide variety

10. The size of the provincial public sector is quite large in most provinces. For example, in 2000 the ratio of private to provincial employees was above ten in only three provinces (Buenos Aires, Federal Capital, and Córdoba), and as low as three in four provinces (Catamarca, Formosa, La Rioja, and Santa Cruz), with a median value of six (Guido and Lazzari 2001). If one includes all public employees (national, provincial, municipal), public employees account for over 25 percent of the work force in six provinces, with a median percentage among the twenty-four provinces of 19 percent (Guido 2002). Finally, all but one province spends over 50 percent of its total revenue on provincial public employee salaries, and over half spend more than 67 percent.

11. The control of the government also opens up other potential sources of funding for some, unscrupulous, politicians, such as payments received to pass certain legislation or to turn a blind eye to, or protect, illicit activity.

12. Operational control over a significant component of national government expenditures is actually delegated to provincial and municipal-level officials. An excellent recent example is the Plan Jefas y Jefes de Hogar Desocupados, which delegates most of the decisions regarding beneficiaries (1,903,855 as of January 2003 according to the Argentine Ministerio de Trabajo) to provincial and municipal-level officials.

13. For detailed discussions of the practice of clientelism in Argentina, see Auyero, this volume; Brusco, Nazareno, and Stokes 2004; Calvo and Murillo, this volume; and Levitsky 2003.

of other organized groups. These benefits also accrue in a more limited manner to legislators (at the national, provincial, and municipal levels) who are able to allocate funds and resources given to them by the legislature or are able to directly allocate national-, provincial-, or municipal-level funds and resources working in concert with the respective executive branch.

The fruit of these patronage, pork barrel, and clientelistic activities is the dominance of the provincial-level political party. First and foremost, dominance of the provincial-level party requires that a party leader be able to defeat any rival in an intraparty primary (either to choose candidates for elective office or to elect the provincial-level party leadership).[14] Patronage, pork barrel activities, and clientelism are important for success in general elections, but they are indispensable for success in party primary elections. In a related manner, patronage, pork barrel, and clientelistic-based support often has the same anticipated reaction effect on potential intraparty challengers that a large campaign war chest has in U.S. politics; it causes potential challengers to desist from any attempt to defeat the party leader.[15]

Political parties, not the government, run party primaries (for both party leadership positions and candidacies for national, provincial, and municipal office) (De Luca, Jones, and Tula 2002). Primaries involve a considerable amount of mobilization (get out the vote, GOTV) efforts by the competing intraparty lists. The electorate for these contests is either party members (elections for party leadership positions are restricted to party members) alone or party members and those not affiliated with any party (i.e., independents).[16]

Vital to these GOTV efforts is the support of three groups (De Luca, Jones, and Tula 2002). First, every list needs the support of its own machine—the regional and neighborhood-level leaders (*punteros*) who have established ties (normally fostered and maintained via patronage) with the leader or leaders supporting the list. Second, lists seek the support of *punteros* not initially aligned with any of the competing lists. Third, lists seek

14. The party leader, through his or her control of the provincial-level party organization, has a great deal of latitude regarding when and under what conditions the primaries are held; thereby providing incumbent party leaders with an additional advantage vis-à-vis challengers.

15. Challenging the party boss is always an option for intraparty opponents. It is, however, a decision that is taken with great care, since a failed challenge often entails serious negative consequences for the challenger.

16. During the 1989–2001 period, in PJ provincial-level national deputy primaries restricted to party members and open to independents, respectively, the median percentage of registered voters who participated was 7 percent and 13 percent. The comparable figures for the UCR were 3 percent and 5 percent. These estimates are based on partial data, and thus should be treated with some caution. All the same, what is clear is that a relatively small percentage of the overall electorate participates in most primaries.

the support of other organized groups with a strong ability to mobilize large numbers of people. In addition to obtaining the support of these groups, to be competitive a list must be able to carry out the following tasks (De Luca, Jones, and Tula 2002): engage in campaign advertising, hire a large number of taxis and buses to transport voters to the polls, purchase the votes of the more instrumental voters, and deploy several election monitors to every precinct (*mesa*) to prevent the list from being the victim of electoral fraud.

In sum, when a primary is held, success thus depends almost entirely on financial and material resources. As then (1999–2003) Chubut governor José Lizurume aptly stated, "La interna es aparato puro" (The primary is pure machine) (*Diario El Chubut*, July 18, 2003).

The Chamber Electoral System, Political Careers, and Internal Rules

Members of the Argentine Chamber of Deputies are elected from closed party lists in multimember districts (with a median district magnitude of three and a mean of five), lists that are created at the provincial level through elite arrangement or party primary (De Luca, Jones, and Tula 2002).[17] In closed-list systems, voters cast a single ballot for a party's rank-ordered list of candidates. Voters cannot modify the order of the candidates on the list. Under a closed-list rule, if a party wins, for example, five seats in an election for the Chamber of Deputies, then the first five people on its rank-ordered candidate list take the seats.

As this would suggest, in most instances, it is the provincial-level party boss, not the individual deputy, who decides whether a member of the Argentine Chamber of Deputies will stand for reelection. These party bosses tend to rotate their representatives (Jones et al. 2002), with the consequence being very low reelection rates for Chamber deputies. Between 1989 and 2003 only 19 percent of Chamber deputies achieved immediate reelection (the lowest reelection rate we are aware of in a presidential democracy that does not prohibit immediate reelection), with an overwhelming majority of deputies returning home to political posts in their provinces, or going to national-level posts, often "representing" their province. For instance, as of mid-1998 85 percent of the PJ and UCR members of the legislative class of 1991 occupied partisan or governmental posts (2 percent were deceased, and 2 percent were in prison or fugitives from justice). Furthermore, a large majority (69 percent) of these deputies

17. One-half (127 and 130) of the Argentine Chamber of Deputies is renewed every two years, with each of the twenty-four electoral districts (provinces) renewing one-half (or the closest approximation) of its delegation.

either held posts at the provincial level (44 percent) or continued to represent the province in the national congress (25 percent).

As documented in Jones 2002 and Jones et al. 2002, Argentine deputies are amateur legislators, but professional politicians.[18] Virtually all national deputies occupy elective, appointive, or party positions prior to election as deputy, and an overwhelming majority continue to occupy elective, appointive, or party positions following their tenure in the Chamber of Deputies.

The internal rules of the Argentine Chamber of Deputies (and Senate) provide the party leadership with a great deal of power, and in addition endow the majority party with a high level of control over the legislative agenda. The principal organizing unit in the Chamber and Senate is the party delegation. When discussing the majority and minority party delegations, it is important to place this discussion within the political context of the 1989–2003 period. First, between 1989 and 1999 and 2001 and 2003, the PJ was the dominant force in the Chamber, and between 1989 and 2003 was also the dominant force in the Senate, enjoying either an absolute majority or near-majority of the legislative seats (see Tables 5.1 and 5.2).[19] The UCR-FREPASO Alianza occupied a similar position in the Chamber (but not the Senate) from 1999 to 2001. While an absolute majority was rarely achieved in the Chamber, throughout most of this period the majority party had enough seats to exercise majority control of the Chamber, either alone or through the tacit support of a subset of the numerous minor parties. This latter ability was enhanced by the fact that throughout this period the majority party in the Chamber was also the party of the president (except for December 10–20, 2001), who was in the unique position of possessing resources with which to influence the behavior of nonmajority party legislators. In Argentina the majority party leadership in the Chamber and Senate is in most instances a faithful servant of the presi-

18. As a consequence, the behavior of deputies is best explained by a modified version of progressive ambition theory (where progressive is interpreted in a more flexible manner), with static ambition (where the deputy pursues a career in the Chamber), and especially, discrete ambition (where the deputy withdraws from politics after serving his or her term in office) being uncommon (Jones 2002; Morgenstern 2002; Samuels 2003). Most deputies serve only one term in the Argentine Chamber. Nonetheless, following their tenure in the Chamber, most deputies do not withdraw from politics, but rather occupy a political position at the national, provincial, or municipal level (a modified form of progressive ambition).

19. An exception to this statement is the period from July 8 to December 9, 1989. As part of the general agreement between then president Raúl Alfonsín (UCR) and president-elect Carlos Menem (PJ), in order to obtain the latter's early assumption of office on July 8 (under the Constitution Menem was not due to assume office until December 10), the UCR ceded control of the presidency of the Chamber of Deputies to the PJ as well as agreed to assist in providing a quorum until December 10 (Jones 1997a; Llanos 2002).

dent (e.g., during this period the majority party leadership in both the Chamber was always held by individuals considered loyal to the president; this was also the case in the Senate, except for the 1999–2001 period). Furthermore, the Argentine president plays an active and influential role (either personally or through members of his cabinet and close advisers) in the activities of the majority party (i.e., his party) in the Congress.[20]

When in the majority the PJ and Alianza tended to operate in a hegemonic manner, both in the allocation of the most coveted committee presidencies and in the determination of the partisan composition of the key committees as well as in the construction of the legislative agenda in the Chamber Rules Committee (Alemán 2003; Danesi 2003; Jones and Hwang 2005). While the Rules Committee operates in part based on consensus, when a disagreement occurs, the majority party's position prevails.

CARTEL THEORY, CPG THEORY, AND THE ARGENTINE CONGRESS

The two most prominent theories of congressional organization in the United States are cartel theory and conditional party government theory (Cox and McCubbins 1993; Rohde 1991).[21] Under these theories members of the U.S. House are considered to be relatively autonomous actors, exercising a great deal of independent control over their political careers. Cox and McCubbins (1993), Finocchiaro and Rohde (2002), and Rohde (1991) have highlighted the manner in which individual legislators in the U.S. House of Representatives delegate power to the House party leadership in order to further their own reelection efforts both generally (party reputation) and specifically (pork, perks of office) as well as to achieve policy goals (passage of legislation, especially distributive policy that benefits their district). This delegation to the party leadership helps the legislators achieve their collective goals.

Argentine deputies do not possess a level of autonomy comparable to that of U.S. House members, but most Argentine provincial-level party bosses do. Hence, in both legislatures delegation occurs. But whereas delegation is by the legislators to the party leadership in the United States, in Argentina delegation is by the provincial-level party bosses to the party leadership.

In Argentina the electoral goals of the provincial party bosses are best served by distributive policy (since their hold on power is based primarily

---

20. For an excellent review of President Menem's proactive role in the enactment of privatization legislation, see Llanos 2002.

21. This section draws heavily from Jones and Hwang 2005.

on patronage, pork, and clientelism). In Argentina there is thus a greater interest in the passage of distributive policy than there is in the United States (where reputational and ideological factors tend to predominate), although distributive policy is relevant in the United States and Argentine provincial party bosses are concerned with the national reputation of their party (Jones and Hwang 2005). Argentine provincial party bosses also tend to actively parlay their legislative support (i.e., the votes of their legislators) in exchange for financial benefits from the national executive branch in the form of transfers, subsidies, government posts, and pork.

In sum, the normal operating procedure in the Argentine Congress is for the majority party leadership (normally following presidential directives) to manage the functioning of the Congress, leaving the governors and other provincial party bosses to concentrate on provincial politics. The actions of the majority party leadership are, however, constantly influenced by the preferences of the provincial party bosses, both in terms of what they place on the legislative agenda (negative agenda control) and in terms of the drafting of the legislation they want to pass (positive agenda control). In equilibrium, however, the majority party leadership, not the provincial party bosses, exercises the principal direct influence over legislator voting behavior. Of course, provincial bosses reserve the right to dissent (via their legislators), and at other times they must be called upon by the party leadership to "control" their legislators. It is in these out of equilibrium moments that we most commonly observe the direct influence of governors, and the other provincial party bosses, on legislative politics. Absent these relatively rare instances, provincial bosses focus on provincial politics, and the majority party leadership in the Chamber (most commonly following the directives of the president) runs congressional politics.

INTERPARTY HETEROGENEITY

This section examines roll call voting in the Argentine Chamber of Deputies. Consistent with cartel theory, in Argentina the majority party leadership uses its majority status (especially agenda control) to dominate the legislative process, excluding legislation it believes may pass despite its objection (negative agenda control), as well as implementing legislation it desires (positive agenda control). The opposition, lacking both negative and positive agenda control, is left in a very reactive position.

Jones and Hwang (2005) employ a Bayesian estimation procedure to uncover the number of dimensions present in Argentine roll call vote behavior (they find a single dimension underlies this voting behavior), and then to identify Argentine Chamber deputies' median ideal points (i.e., each deputy's preferred location on this single dimension).[22] The use of legislator ideal points to study congressional behavior is the norm in U.S. legislative studies (e.g., Aldrich, Berger, and Rohde 2002; Clinton, Jackman, and Rivers 2004; Poole and Rosenthal 1997) and is increasingly popular for the study of legislatures in other countries (e.g., Alemán and Saiegh 2004; Londregan 2000; Poole and Rosenthal 2001). Each deputy's ideal point (ranging from –1.0 to 1.0) represents the median of ten thousand (or five thousand) draws from the deputy's posterior distribution of ideal points. In this section, we use these ideal points to examine the evolution of interparty heterogeneity in the Argentine Chamber between 1989 and 2003.[23]

This section examines the evolution of interparty heterogeneity in the four Argentine parties that occupied at least 5 percent of the seats in the Chamber from 1989 to 2003: PJ, UCR, FREPASO (1995–2001), and ARI (2001–3). Figure 5.1 provides information on the evolution of interparty heterogeneity, measured using the respective party delegation's median ideal point (i.e., the median ideal point of the ideal points of the deputies belonging to the party's delegation), for the PJ, UCR, FREPASO (1995–2001), and ARI (2001–3) (Aldrich, Berger, and Rohde 2002). Two principal conclusions can be drawn from this figure.

First, if we focus on the two dominant parties during this period (the PJ and UCR), we see that Figure 5.1 indicates that the level of interparty heterogeneity has remained both high and relatively constant (with the exception of the 2001–3 period). With the exception of the 2001–3 period, the difference in the two parties' median ideal points ranged from 0.95 (1993–95) to 1.32 (1989), with a median of 1.07. During this entire period the PJ's median ideal point ranged between 0.47 and 0.64, while the UCR's

22. This single dimension is not primarily ideological, as is the case in the United States and Western Europe (Poole and Rosenthal 2001). Instead, it reflects the government or opposition status of the political parties, with the governing party on one side of the dimension and the opposition parties (to varying extents) on the other. For a complete discussion of this government versus opposition dimension, see Jones and Hwang 2004.

23. These data represent five full two-year legislative periods, corresponding to the biannual partial renovations of the Chamber (1989–91, 1991–93, 1993–95, 1995–97, 1997–99), and four partial periods (July 8, 1989, to December 9, 1989; December 10, 1999, to October 6, 2000; October 7, 2000, to December 9, 2001; December 10, 2001, to May 24, 2003). The former period represents the first five months of Carlos Menem's presidency (following then president Raúl Alfonsín's resignation five months prior to the end of his constitutionally mandated six-year term). The middle two periods respectively represent the Alianza government before and after the resignation of Vice President (and FREPASO leader) Carlos "Chacho" Álvarez in 2000. The final period represents the complete presidency of interim president Eduardo Duhalde.

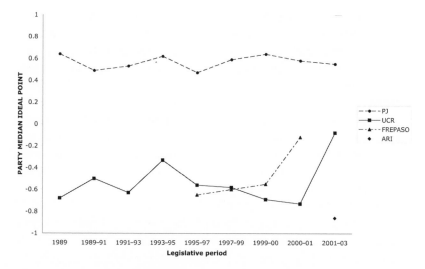

Figure 5.1   Interparty heterogeneity

(excluding 2001–3) ranged from –0.33 to –0.73. Except for the 2001–3 period, there was little variation in the interparty differences, with the consistent large gap between the two parties suggesting that members of the majority party would want to endow their party's leadership with substantial powers (thereby allowing it to function as an effective cartel) in order to achieve their distributive goals (Aldrich, Berger, and Rohde 2002).

The 2001–3 period marked a significant shift in the role of the UCR within the Argentine political arena. During this period numerous UCR leaders were co-opted by the administration of President Eduardo Duhalde, and in many instances the UCR ceased to represent a significant source of opposition to the PJ in the Chamber of Deputies. This change in UCR behavior is reflected in the massive shift in the party's median ideal point to –0.08 for the 2001–3 period.[24] As the UCR relinquished its role as the most prominent opposition check on the PJ, this space within the Chamber was filled by ARI, which registered a median ideal point of –0.86, extremely distant from that of the governing PJ (which in 2001–3 remained proximate to its historic median at 0.55).

Second, FREPASO was a relevant actor in the Chamber of Deputies between 1995 and 2001, occupying between 8.6 percent (1995–97) and 14.8 percent (1997–99) of the seats. FREPASO formed an electoral (but not leg-

24. By 2004 the UCR had returned to its traditional opposition position on this dimension, with a median ideal point (–.64) that was comparable to that found prior to 2001–3 (Jones and Hwang 2004).

islative) alliance with the UCR for the 1997–99 period, and finally established an electoral, legislative, and governmental alliance with the UCR for the 1999–2001 period, during which time the UCR-FREPASO Alianza was the majority "party" in the Chamber, and De la Rúa of the UCR occupied the presidency. During the 1995–99 period, when the UCR and FREPASO were both opposition parties, the UCR and FREPASO had virtually identical median ideal points (see Fig. 5.1). However, when the UCR and FREPASO were at last in government during the 1999–2001 period, we find that, after less than one year in office, FREPASO had moved significantly away from the UCR (its coalition partner) toward the center of the single dimension underlying Chamber voting behavior.

In 1999 the Alianza took control of the presidency and the Chamber of Deputies. It thus faced many of the dilemmas that the PJ had faced during the previous ten and a half years: the need to pass legislation that was not always popular with the public as well as with many of its governors, senators, and deputies. Confronted with a UCR president who seldom consulted with FREPASO leaders regarding major policy decisions, and generally more comfortable playing the much easier role of the opposition (rather that of responsible political leaders) in Argentina's adversarial government versus opposition legislative environment, a majority of the FREPASO deputies quickly adopted policy positions that placed the FREPASO delegation significantly more toward the positive side of the legislative policy continuum than the UCR. While the parties' respective ideal points remained close during the first eleven months of the Alianza government (i.e., prior to FREPASO leader, and vice president, Carlos "Chacho" Álvarez's resignation), during the Alianza government's final thirteen months FREPASO deputies moved toward the center of the government versus opposition dimension, assuming a median ideal point position (−0.12) that placed them closer to the opposition PJ (0.58) than to their coalition partner (UCR, −0.73) (see Fig. 5.1). Despite growing internal unrest over the direction of President De la Rúa's government, the UCR deputies remained relatively homogenous as well as generally supportive (at least on those issues that made it to the Chamber floor) of the government until the final two months of the De la Rúa administration.

In sum, the Alianza worked very well when the two parties were in the opposition and united in their aversion to the PJ government of President Menem. When, however, the Alianza became responsible for actually governing (through its control of the presidency and the Chamber), it (particularly the FREPASO politicians) was not up to the task. While the UCR remained united (albeit increasingly grudgingly so in 2001), only a minority of FREPASO deputies maintained ideal points close to the UCR median

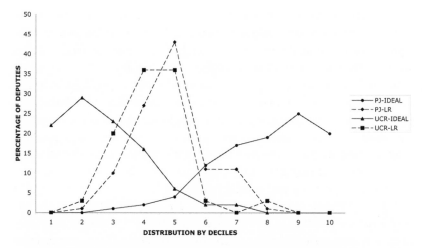

Figure 5.2   Distribution of deputy ideal point and left-right self-placement, 1995–99

following Vice President Álvarez's resignation in October 2000. The consequence for the final thirteen months of the Alianza government was a
gap of 0.61 between the two parties' respective median ideal points, when
the difference during the 1997–99 legislative period had been a mere 0.02
(the gap for the 1999–2000 period was 0.14). This profound difference
for the 2000–2001 period was in spite of the fact that, in contrast to the
1997–99 period, when the UCR and FREPASO maintained completely separate delegations in the Chamber (with no institutionalized mechanisms of
joint consultation), there existed a joint UCR-FREPASO Chamber delegation
(as well as separate UCR and FREPASO subdelegations). The defeat suffered
by the Alianza in the 2001 congressional elections resulted in its loss of
majority status in the Chamber on December 10 of that year, and ten days
later the governmental option represented by the Alianza ended in failure
with President De la Rúa's resignation from office.

LEFT-RIGHT SELF-PLACEMENT VERSUS IDEAL POINT LOCATION

Figure 5.2 provides additional evidence of the cartel nature of Argentine
legislative politics. It demonstrates the important effect that the party leadership has on deputy voting behavior. While the deputies in the major
parties (PJ and UCR) are in many instances indistinguishable in terms of
their ideological self-placement, their voting behavior on the Chamber
floor is quite distinct and polarized.

Figure 5.2 displays the distribution (on a ten-point scale) of the PJ and

UCR deputies along two dimensions. PJ-LR and UCR-LR provide the distribution of the ideological self-placement, on a ten-point traditional Left-Right Scale (1 being the extreme left and 10 the extreme right), of the individual PJ and UCR deputies included in two sample surveys of deputies conducted during the 1995–97 and 1997–99 legislative periods (Alcántara 2004). PJ-IDEAL and UCR-IDEAL provide the distribution of the individual PJ and UCR deputies along the single policy dimension that underlay voting behavior in the Chamber of Deputies during the 1995–97 and 1997–99 periods (the –1.0 to 1.0 ideal point scale was converted to a 1 to 10 scale, with, for instance –1 to –.81 equal to 1, –.80 to –.61 equal to 2, –.60 to –.41 equal to 3, and so on).

The two LR distributions demonstrate that there exists little aggregate ideological differentiation between the PJ and the UCR deputies, with substantial overlap existing among the members of the two parties' respective congressional delegations. In contrast, the two IDEAL distributions reflect a highly polarized legislative body, with sharp differentiation between the PJ and the UCR deputies, and very little overlap between the two parties' respective congressional delegations. While several factors account for these profound differences between the LR and IDEAL distributions, the most prominent is the substantial role played by the Chamber party leadership through its control of the legislative agenda (for the majority party) and the influence it exercises over the behavior of its deputies (both parties).

MAJORITY PARTY CONTROL OVER THE LEGISLATIVE PROCESS

Table 5.5 provides information on the origin (i.e., primary sponsor/author) of all laws enacted during 1996 and highlights how the PJ dominated the legislative agenda during the 1989–99 and 2001–3 periods, when it occupied the presidency as well as possessed working majorities in the Chamber of Deputies and Senate. The PJ executive branch was the primary sponsor of 47.3 percent of the 129 laws enacted in 1996, while PJ members in the Senate and Chamber respectively sponsored 15.5 percent and 17.8 percent of these laws. Combined, the PJ authored 80.6 percent of the laws enacted in 1996, followed by the UCR (11.6 percent), and numerous minor parties that authored one or two laws each. Furthermore, of the legislation authored by the UCR and minor parties, nearly one-half dealt with relatively inconsequential topics such as the transfer of a parcel of government-owned land to a soccer club, the expropriation of a building,

Table 5.5   The sponsorship of laws enacted in 1996 by institution and party

Institution	Party	Number of laws	Percent of laws
Executive branch	Total	[61]	
	Partido Justicialista	61	47.3
Senate	Total	[27]	
	Partido Justicialista	20	15.5
	Unión Cívica Radical	3	2.3
	Cruzada Renovadora	1	0.8
	Movimiento Popular Fueguino	1	0.8
	Movimiento Popular Neuquino	1	0.8
	Partido Liberal (Corrientes)	1	0.8
Chamber of Deputies	Total	[41]	
	Partido Justicialista	23	17.8
	Unión Cívica Radical	12	9.3
	Frente País Solidario	1	0.8
	Movimiento de Integración y Desarrollo	1	0.8
	Movimiento Popular Fueguino	1	0.8
	Partido Demócrata (Mendoza)	1	0.8
	Partido Liberal (Corrientes)	1	0.8
	Unidad Socialista	1	0.8
Total by party	Total	[129]	
	Partido Justicialista	104	80.6
	Unión Cívica Radical	15	11.6
	Movimiento Popular Fueguino	2	1.6
	Partido Liberal (Corrientes)	2	1.6
	Cruzada Renovadora	1	0.8
	Frente País Solidario	1	0.8
	Movimiento de Integración y Desarrollo	1	0.8
	Movimiento Popular Neuquino	1	0.8
	Partido Demócrata (Mendoza)	1	0.8
	Unidad Socialista	1	0.8

the construction of a small monument honoring Jonas Salk, and the establishment of a congressional prize for young artists.

In sum, the PJ dominated the legislative agenda throughout the 1990s in Argentina. It is, however, important to note that the PJ's domination of the legislative agenda is not synonymous either with President Menem's domination of the legislative agenda or with Menem possessing the ability to implement his "ideal" policy agenda unfettered by institutional or political checks. Throughout this period this PJ dominance was the consequence of the strategic use of positive and negative agenda control by the PJ (under the leadership of Menem) in which the preferences of the PJ provincial party bosses were always of paramount importance.

President Menem vetoed twenty-one (thirteen full vetoes and eight partial vetoes) bills passed by Congress in 1996. This percentage of approved
bills vetoed (14.8 percent) is comparable to that during the entire Menem
presidency (14.1 percent) (Molinelli, Palanza, and Sin 1999).[25] Of these
twenty-one vetoed bills, only two (a full veto and a partial veto) were overridden by the Congress. Both bills provided enhanced pension benefits for
veterans (and their survivors) of the 1982 Malvinas (Falklands) War. The
vetoes were overridden in the Chamber by votes of 170 to 0 and 163 to 0.
The override rate for 1996 (9.5 percent) is somewhat less than that experienced by Menem during his ten and a half years in office (16.1 percent).[26]

This agenda control exercised by the majority party also indicates we
should be cautious in using presidential vetoes as a measure of serious
indiscipline, vis-à-vis the president's policy preferences, by the PJ legislative bloc (Jones 2002). Between 1989 and 1999 no legislation was passed
without the majority support of the PJ in the Chamber and Senate. Given
this majority support (as well as the near-universal willingness of the UCR,
FREPASO, and a few minor parties to override Menem's vetoes), it is note-
worthy that between 1989 and 1999 only 18 of 88 full and 13 of 105 partial
vetoes were overridden. While the legislative coalition that passed the vetoed legislation initially could easily have overridden all of the vetoes, only
20.5 percent and 12.4 percent of the respective full and partial vetoes were
overridden (Molinelli, Palanza, and Sin 1999). There are certainly multiple
explanations for this failure to override (particularly for some, though not
all, of the partial vetoes). However, the most salient is that the PJ congressional leadership did not wish to override the veto. While they were willing
to pass legislation that Menem opposed (a mild form of protest), they were
unwilling to override his veto. In the end Menem most commonly obtained his desired legislation while the PJ legislators (and their bosses back
in the provinces) in some instances avoided responsibility for its unpopular content (or used the threat of an override to extract additional resources). When, however, the PJ legislators decided to override a
presidential veto, they did so in a near unanimous manner. In fact, of all
Chamber overrides of Menem's vetoes between July 1989 and December
1999, in only two instances did the percentage of PJ deputies opposing
the override surpass 5 percent (13 percent and 20 percent), with the mean
and median percentage of PJ deputies voting to override 97 percent and
98 percent respectively.

25. Presidents De la Rúa and Duhalde respectively vetoed 11.8 percent and 18.9 percent
of the bills passed by Congress.

26. President De la Rúa's override rate was 16.7 percent while President Duhalde's was
8.8 percent.

CONCLUSION

Between 1989 and 2003, when it came to many of the most salient public policy/legislative initiatives of the day, the majority party in Argentina tended to govern alone, with the president's party's (which was always the majority party in the Chamber of Deputies) median ideal points significantly distinct from those of virtually all other parties (Jones and Hwang 2004). Even Argentina's only experience with a coalition government (1999–2001) revealed the system's inherent majoritarian tendency. With a few exceptions, most of the members of the Alianza, except those from the president's party (UCR), moved toward the opposition end of the policy continuum within a year of the life of the coalition.

Consistent with cartel theory, in Argentina the majority party legislators (acting based on instructions received from the provincial party bosses) delegate a considerable amount of power to the congressional party leadership (and indirectly to the president). This leadership in turns uses its majority power to obtain policy and electoral benefits for its members. Given the highly distributive nature of most of these benefits, the opposition parties often have little incentive to support the majority party's agenda, and strong incentives to oppose it (given the general lack of distributive benefits for them as well as the reputational benefits that can be achieved through opposing some policies).

During the 1990s Argentina was characterized by strong majority party dominance of the legislative agenda. The PJ, which controlled the presidency as well as working majorities in the Chamber of Deputies and Senate throughout this period, was able to use its negative agenda control to ensure that legislation it opposed would not be passed, and at the same time employ positive agenda control to draft legislation such that it would obtain passage. In this latter case, the individuals that the PJ party leadership in the Congress (and most important, President Menem) had to satisfy most were the provincial party bosses. These bosses could be satisfied in many ways, but since the most relevant (with relevance based on the number of deputies and senators who responded to their directives) of them were governors, the key to their support was generally the transfer of funds or other resources by the national government to their respective provinces (often these "transfers" took the form of allowing the provinces to avoid the implementation of fiscal and administrative reforms). A significant portion of these transfers was initially funded by the national government with the revenue obtained from the privatization of state-owned companies (e.g., electricity, natural gas, telephone) and the tax revenue obtained from the considerable investment by foreign companies in the initial renovation and expansion of these companies. Later, when there was little left to privatize, the national government financed a significant portion of these transfers by going into debt with foreign and domestic creditors through the sale of government bonds and related securities. This mounting debt burden was unsustainable and would contribute to the country's economic and political meltdown in 2001.

This chapter underscores the prominent role played by the provincial party bosses (especially governors) and, in turn, the legislative branch in the Argentine political system. In doing so it suggests that explanations of important developments in recent Argentine history, such as the implementation of neoliberal policies in the 1990s and the political meltdown of 2001, that ignore the incentives facing, and influence exercised by, the provincial party bosses and the legislative branch are incomplete, and quite possibly inaccurate. There has, for instance, been an erroneous tendency to explain policy in the 1990s by overly focusing on the incentives and strategy of one man, Carlos Menem, ignoring the powerful effect that the design of Argentina's political institutions has on the functioning of its political system (Spiller and Tommasi, this volume).

Throughout his tenure in office, President Menem had to maintain the support of his party's provincial party bosses (and, at times, those from other parties) in order to achieve the passage and implementation of his policy agenda. These party bosses faced their own set of incentives, which often differed from those of Menem, and in turn these provincial party bosses exercised a profound effect on the types of policies passed into law during the 1990s, the price that had to be paid to obtain the passage of these laws, and the manner in which these laws were implemented. In sum, to adequately understand partisan politics and the policy process in Argentina during the 1990s, one must possess an adequate understanding of the prominent role played by the provincial party bosses and their followers in the Congress during that era.

Enduring Uncertainty:
Court-Executive Relations in Argentina During the 1990s and Beyond

Gretchen Helmke

There is no major political issue in the country that does not end up as a legal issue.
—Julio Nazareno, Chief Justice of the Argentine Supreme Court, 1990–2003

On February 1, 2002, at the height of one of Argentina's worst financial crises in history, the Supreme Court struck down a government freeze on bank deposits. Signed by six of the nine justices, the *Smith* decision stood in sharp contrast to the Argentine Supreme Court's notorious pattern of favoring the government. Indeed, many of the same members of the Court who signed the decision against Duhalde's government had freely granted similar powers to the Menem government during an economic crisis just a decade earlier.[1] Now, in a move that pushed Argentina's economic and

This chapter contains material previously published in *Courts Under Constraints: Judges, Generals, and Presidents in Argentina* (Cambridge: Cambridge University Press, 2004) and in "Checks and Balances By Other Means: The Argentine Supreme Court in the 1990s," *Comparative Politics*, 2003.

1. Most notably, in the case of *Peralta* (1990) the Court upheld an executive decree (36/90) freezing bank accounts and issuing government bonds in exchange. The Court justified its ruling on the basis that "individual rights and guarantees can be protected only to the extent that the country's overall well-being is ensured" (cited in Rogers and Wright-Carozza 1995, 57).

political stability to the brink, the Court's majority took a very different stance.[2]

The Argentine justices' contrariness in *Smith* challenges what many scholars have long assumed was a thoroughly entrenched pattern in Argentine politics: unremitting judicial subservience to the executive branch. Within Latin America, the Argentine Supreme Court is seen as a quintessential example of the problems associated with delegative democracy and weak horizontal accountability (O'Donnell 1998a, 1998b; Larkins 1998). Yet despite its profound lack of political independence, the Court has not always given the government of the day what it wanted. The Argentine case, therefore, poses a series of intriguing questions about the emergence and consequences of interbranch conflict in new democracies.

In seeking to understand the interaction between Argentina's judges and politicians, this chapter provides a systematic framework for understanding the broader dynamics of Court-executive relations in contexts marked by high stakes and political uncertainty. Whereas standard accounts of interbranch relations have automatically linked politicians' control over selection and sanctioning to judicial subservience (Dahl 1957), this chapter challenges that assumption. Rather, the argument developed here is that sometimes the very lack of independence can induce judges to rule against the government. I refer to this phenomenon as strategic defection (Helmke 2002, 2003, 2004). In this chapter, I briefly summarize the logic underlying the theory of strategic defection and explore its applicability to Argentina during the decade of the 1990s. I then conclude with a preliminary analysis of changes in Court-executive relations in the post-Menem era.

THE SEPARATION-OF-POWERS THEORY AND THE LOGIC OF STRATEGIC DEFECTION

Within the growing judicial politics literature, the separation-of-powers approach has gained widespread prominence. At the most basic level, this approach considers how the institutional constraints judges face shape the

2. Moreover, the Court had also ruled just weeks earlier against the depositor in *Kipper.* The policies in question in that case, however, referred to temporary exchange controls taken in the final days by De la Rúa's government (Cavallo 2002). The issue at stake in *Smith* dealt instead with the government's right to permanently convert savers' U.S. dollars into pesos at an arbitrary rate. In the latter case, some observers noted the Court argued that the government had gone much further, and thus the Court was acting as a legitimate check on excessive governmental power. In short, the Court's apparent inconsistency between the two cases rests on a misunderstanding of the issues involved in different government policies (ibid.).

choices that they make (Epstein and Knight 1996, 1998). In the United States, for example, Congress has the ability to overturn judicial decisions on statutory matters with a simple majority vote (Ferejohn and Weingast 1992; Spiller and Gely 1990). Thus, judges whose preferences diverge sufficiently from Congress's face incentives to strategically adjust their decisions to bring them more in line with what the current legislative majority wants. Assuming a stable institutional context marked by secure tenure and complete information, proponents of the theory argue that judges tend to support the current government not because they necessarily share its views, but because they want to avoid a worse outcome in which Congress overrides their decision (see Helmke 2004).

Now shift the theoretical approach to a different type of institutional environment, one which more closely matches the Argentine experience. Despite obvious formal constitutional similarities with the United States,[3] in Argentina judges routinely face far greater threats than simply having their decisions overturned. Since Perón, justices have been removed with every change in regime (Helmke 2004). Sanctions have ranged from suspension and forced resignation under military dictatorships to Court-packing plans and impeachment resolutions under democracy. In most instances, the motivating force carrying out these sanctions against the Court has been the executive branch, which has long been recognized as the most powerful institutional actor in Argentine politics (Shugart and Carey 1992; O'Donnell 1994). In contrast to the United States, the de facto influence of the executive in Argentina limits substantially the transaction costs associated with punishing the Court (cf. Segal 1997). Put differently, compared to their North American counterparts, judges in Argentina face both more intense and more credible threats for failing to act strategically.

In this scenario, however, the crucial lesson is that supporting the government of the day may not always be the best strategy for judges seeking to escape punishment. Of course, if the president is strong and has already appointed judges who share his or her views, the Court will have little reason to rule against the government (see Iaryczower, Spiller, and Tommasi 2002). But if the current government begins to lose power, judges confront a very different situation in which an incoming opposition government gains increasing sway over their fates. Instead of being free to

3. The Argentine Supreme Court (Corte Suprema de Justicia de la Nación) stands at the head of a federal judiciary established by the Constitution of 1853, modeled on the United States Constitution, and recently reformed in 1994. The Argentine Supreme Court is the highest court in the country, with original and appellate jurisdiction over all federal questions. In 1887, the Court established through its own jurisprudence the power of judicial review. It cannot exercise abstract review.

support the government that appointed them, they face pressure to curry favor with the opposition by ruling against the incumbent.[4] This is the logic of strategic defection.

In addition to offering a systematic explanation of why institutionally insecure judges rule in favor of the government in one instance, and against it in another, strategic defection incorporates the intuition that Latin American politics is fraught with uncertainty and institutional instability. In fact, as I elaborate elsewhere (Helmke 2004), strategic defection only makes sense in a world where judges both believe that they face a threat and that changing their behavior can have some positive impact on the incoming government's decision to punish them. Mutual uncertainty between judges and incoming politicians is precisely what makes defection a rational response for judges who lack secure tenure and suspect that the current government's days are numbered. Put differently, strategic defection does not impute to judges perfect foresight, it merely assumes that judges are able to place sufficiently high probabilities on the current government losing power and on the new government conditioning its treatment of the judges based on their behavior. Thus, the theory of strategic defection escapes the standard criticism (Weyland 2002a) that rational choice models fail to capture adequately problems of institutional instability and incomplete and imperfect information that plague Latin American politics.

Taken together, the foregoing discussion leads to three testable hypotheses about judicial behavior. To capture the notion that judges' evolving beliefs about the ability of the current government to stay in power and the capacity of the incoming government to punish them shape judges' behavior, each hypothesis predicts a relationship between the number of months left in a government's term and the judges' willingness to support it. Specifically, the first hypothesis (H1) predicts that antigovernmental decisions will increase once the incumbent government begins to lose power. The corollary to this (H2) is that support will increase once judges grow confident that the incumbent government is likely to remain in office. The third hypothesis (H3) takes into account the fact that, because incoming government is likely to be focused on cases that deal with salient political issues, strategic behavior (either support or defection) will be concentrated in the most important cases coming before the Court.

Note, however, that the true underlying functional form of strategic behavior is always an empirical question. Each of these hypotheses is funda-

---

4. For a formal signaling model of Court-executive relations under incomplete information, see Helmke 2004.

mentally about judges' changing beliefs, not the passage of time per se. For example, only if we assume that judges' insecurity about their fates grows monotonically over the course of the government, would we expect a negative perfectly linear relationship between the amount of time remaining in a government's term and the proportion of antigovernmental decisions. It may be the case, however, that insecurity instead peaks in the middle of the campaign before the intentions or the capacity of the opposition to punish the justices are entirely clear. Thus, rather than assume either scenario ex ante, I employ below a series of separate logit regressions that breaks the final two years of both Menem governments down into three-month increments. Although in general I expect to find a significant relationship between judicial decision-making and the political cycle, this modeling choice provides enough flexibility to capture the possibility that the relationship may not be strictly linear. To lay the groundwork for this empirical analysis, the following section summarizes the varying degrees of insecurity that the Argentine Supreme Court faced throughout the decade of the 1990s.

JUSTICES UNDER ATTACK: COURT-EXECUTIVE RELATIONS ARGENTINA IN THE 1990s

During the 1990s, the Argentine judiciary was frequently criticized as a mere appendage of the executive branch. Despite its increasingly prominent role as protector of human and civil rights in the wake of the country's transition to democracy in 1983, the judiciary's image suffered a dramatic blow under Carlos Menem's two-term presidency (1989–99). Public opinion surveys indicate that the positive image of the judiciary fell from approximately 27 percent in 1990 to 20 percent in 1993 (Baglini, D'Ambrosio, and Orlandi 1993, 86) to only 13 percent in 1995.[5]

Beginning in 1990, the Argentine Supreme Court, in particular, became a target for the new administration's heavy-handed tactics. Most notably, Menem began his first term by sending to Congress a Court-packing plan that increased the number of justices on the Supreme Court from five to nine (Verbitsky 1993; Baglini, D'Ambrosio, and Orlandi 1993; Smulovitz 1995; Larkins 1998). Although changing the size of the Court did not violate the letter of the law, it destroyed any the illusion that the Supreme Court was above political manipulation. Despite the new government's claims that adding more justices would help to improve the Court's

---

5. Instituto de Gallup de la Argentina, cited in Dakolias 1996, 168.

efficiency, few doubted that Menem's aims were political. Members of Menem's own cabinet proclaimed that, in the midst of an economic crisis, the country could not afford a Court "out of step" with the administration (Larkins 1998, 428). While the administration drew frequent comparisons with Franklin Delano Roosevelt's Court-packing proposal during the New Deal Era in the United States (see, for example, Rogers and Wright-Carozza 1995), Menem did little to hide his motives. In an interview with one of Argentina's most popular television newscasters, Mario Grondona, Menem simply proclaimed, "Why should I be the only Argentine President not to have my own Court?" (cited in Larkins 1998).

Despite opposition from the sitting justices, the legal community, and the opposition Radicals, the Peronist-dominated Senate easily passed the Court-packing bill. In the Chamber of Deputies, however, the bill passed under a shroud of controversy involving allegations that the Peronists had not had a true quorum (Ferreira Rubio and Gorretti 1998).[6] When all was said and done, the new law, combined with the resignations of Justice José Severo Caballero and Chief Justice Jorge Bacqué, gave the administration six vacancies to fill on the Court.

The government did not waste any time seeking to appoint judges with close personal or political connections to the new government (Verbitsky 1993; Baglini, D'Ambrosio, and Orlandi 1993; Larkins 1998; Dakolias 1996). Many of the appointees were members of Menem's inner political and social circle. Julio Nazareno was a former law partner of Menem's brother, Eduardo (a Peronist senator); Eduardo Moliné O'Connor was the brother-in-law of Menem's then-chief of state intelligence, Hugo Anzorreguy. Mariano Cavagna Martínez, Rodolfo Barra, and Antonio Boggiano were well-known Peronist supporters (Verbitsky 1993). Together, these judges formed what became known as the "mayoría automática" (automatic majority), which validated Menem's policies unconditionally.

In 1993, the issue of Menem's reelection came to the forefront. In exchange for consenting to a constitutional reform that would allow Menem to run for a second term, the leader of the UCR, Raul Alfonsín, demanded various reforms, including strengthening the independence of the judiciary (see Acuña 1995). A key condition for the "Pacto de Olivos" was the resignation of three of Menem's appointees to the Supreme Court. In

---

6. According to a report by Poder Ciudadano, opposition deputies charged that, in order to form a quorum, the Peronists had called a special emergency session in the middle of the night and filled the upper banks with people who were not even legislators. The bill was then passed in approximately seven minutes (see http://www.poderciudadano.org/relaciones/ 394_highton.doc).

1994, Justices Barra and Martínez Cavagna tendered their resignations[7] and were replaced by Guillermo López and Gustavo Bossert. In 1995, a third Menem appointee, Ricardo Levene, retired and was replaced by Adolfo Vázquez. Of the new appointees, only Bossert could be considered independent of Menem. Thus, the overall impact of the "Pacto de Olivos" on Court-executive relations was relatively insignificant: Menem's loyal majority remained intact and was entirely insulated from the political opposition.[8]

A very different scenario emerged during Menem's second term. Although Menem had been reelected in 1995 with over 50 percent of the popular vote, his popularity waned over the latter part of the decade. In 1997, for the first time in more than a decade, the Peronists lost the midterm legislative elections. According to exit polls, almost 40 percent of those who changed their vote to support the opposition in 1997 did so because of dissatisfaction with the administration's handling of unemployment.[9] Despite outspending the opposition more than sevenfold, the PJ lost its majority in the Congress, giving up fourteen seats in the lower house.[10] Almost immediately after the votes for the midterm elections were counted, the race for the presidency in 1999 began.

Reluctant to challenge Menem's economic model, presidential candidates across the political spectrum sought to distance themselves from him by capitalizing on the public's disgust with the judiciary, promising sweeping changes if elected. On the right, Domingo Cavallo, Menem's former economic minister and now leader of a new center-right party, Action for the Republic, repeatedly criticized the lack of independence in the Argentine judicial system. One well-known anecdote told by Cavallo was that the former minister of the interior Carlos Corach had written a list of the justices controlled by the government on a napkin.[11] In 1995 Cavallo was sued by Justice Belluscio for libel after Cavallo publicly declared him to be a "corrupt thief."[12] Cavallo, who was subsequently found guilty in a separate criminal case dealing with customs officials during

7. Subsequently, Cavagna Martínez was appointed ambassador to Italy and later served as Menem's attorney in the Ecuadorian-Croation arms scandal. Barra was appointed minister of justice and later served as the main proponent of Menem's bid for a third presidential term.

8. Of the thirty-one requests to impeach either individual Supreme Court justices or the entire Supreme Court made between August 1990 and March 1993, not a single one made it out of committee (Poder Ciudadano 1997).

9. *Clarín*, November 2, 1997

10. *Tres Puntos*, December 3, 1997; *Clarín*, October 28, 1997,

11. *Clarín*, July 11, 1997.

12. *Buenos Aires Herald*, August 14, 1997.

his campaign, claimed that the Menem government trumped up charges against its political opponents and then left the judges to do its dirty work.[13] Playing into citizen's concerns about corruption and lawlessness, he used his own experience with the courts to make more general claims against the Menem government. According to Cavallo, Menem's corruption of the judiciary not only put at risk the country's economic security by scaring away investors but also endangered "the rights of the innocent, of the honest, and of the average citizen."[14]

From the center-left coalition forged between the Radical Civic Union and FREPASO—the Alianza por el Trabajo, la Educación, y la Justicia— came equally strident demands to remove the justices on the Supreme Court. In 1996 Radicals in the Chamber of Deputies had published a book titled *Juicio a la Corte* (Impeach the Supreme Court) (Baglini, D'Ambrosio, and Orlandi 1993), in which they chronicled in over two hundred pages the abuses committed by the Court. Among the charges made in the report the authors included evidence on the suspect procedures used by the Peronists in the Senate to approve the Court-packing plan, the political ties of the members to the executive branch, and the specific decisions made by the Court. As the authors of the report themselves put it, "We do not consider the current justices guilty of misconduct in one, two, or even ten cases; we consider them worthy of impeachment for their total submission [in all cases] to the politicians in power" (Baglini, D'Ambrosio, and Orlandi 1993, 36–37). Unlike the United States, Argentina never developed the norm against impeaching justices for the content of their decisions.

Finally, some of the harshest demands for reforming the Court came from within the PJ. Duhalde, who had deep personal antipathy for Menem, promised that if he were to win the presidency in 1999, he would convoke a constituent assembly to suspend the constitutional clause prohibiting the justices' removal, declare Menem's justices "en comisión" (suspended), and use the Magistrates Council to select new justices.[15] The Alianza immediately echoed this proposal, asserting that "we would not have put the denunciation of the judiciary at the center of our political discourse if we intended to afterwards continue with the same judges."[16]

In sum, throughout Menem's decade in power, the Court was strongly challenged by the political opposition. Yet, during Menem's first term (1989–95), there were relatively few sanctions that the opposition could

13. *Clarín*, July 11, 1997; July 30, 1997; July 31, 1997; August 24, 1997; August 26, 1997; September 30, 1997; October 1, 1997; *Página/12*, July 30, 1997.

14. *Clarín*, August 24, 1997.

15. *La Nación*, September 25, 1997.

16. Ibid.

deploy against the justices. Aside from the Radicals' attempt to weaken Menem's majority on the Court in the notorious "Pacto de Olivos," Menem's own popularity, combined with the Peronists' domination of both houses of Congress, effectively meant that the opposition had no ability to sanction judges. Thus, out of the hundreds of requests made to impeach judges during Menem's first term, not a single petition resulted in the removal of a judge. In sharp contrast, by the end of Menem's second term, the threat against the judges began to look far more credible. Given this context, then, we should expect a pattern of strategic defection only at the end of Menem's second administration.

FROM SUPPORT TO DEFECTION: PATTERNS IN JUDICIAL DECISION-MAKING DURING THE 1990s

To begin to evaluate whether the patterns in judicial decision-making conform to the expectations generated by the theory of strategic defection, I begin with an overview of some of the better-known decisions handed down by the Supreme Court during the 1990s. In accordance with what one would expect, during Menem's first administration the Court rarely challenged the government's most controversial policies. Under the second administration, however, the situation began to change.

To protect Menem's interests, the Court was often willing to bend blatantly the rule of law. For example, in the case of *Corrientes,* the majority opinion overturned the Court's own jurisprudence regarding the autonomy of provincial elections, thus paving the way for federal intervention in the gubernatorial election in the province of Corrientes (Baglini, D'Ambrosio, and Orlandi 1993). In the case of *Fiscal Molinas,* the majority opinion overruled the trial and appeals courts to allow Menem to dismiss without impeachment the prosecutor in charge of investigating administrative affairs (Verbitsky 1993). Perhaps the most egregious violation of judicial neutrality came in the case of *Banco Patagónico* (1993). According to various sources, the justices mysteriously "lost" the Court's first opinion, in order to hand down a new decision that was more in line with what the government wanted (Verbitsky 1993; Larkins 1998). Although the holdover justices refused to join the majority in these cases, in other, arguably more important cases, even they supported the government.

Among the Court's various decisions handed down in Menem's first term, *Aerolineas Argentinas* (1990) is among the best known. *Aerolineas* involved a dispute between the ministry of Menem's new government in charge of privatization of the national airlines and members of the opposition in Congress, who were seeking to halt the sale. A trial court granted the opposition an injunction (*recurso de amparo*) against the executive decree 1024/90. Rather than risk another hostile decision in the lower courts, the administration went directly to the newly packed Supreme Court. In its arguments, the government encouraged the Court to adopt a judicial doctrine known as *per saltum*, which would allow the Court to seize cases directly from first-instance courts (Carrió and Garay 1991; Carrió 1996). While it is hardly surprising that Menem's hand-picked justices supported him, under the first administration it was Justice Petracchi, who had been appointed under the previous government, who wrote the opinion giving the government what it wanted.

In the case of *Peralta* (1990) a similar situation occurred. Here, the majority opinion upheld the administration's highly controversial Plan Bonex, which was based on presidential decree 36/90 freezing private savings accounts. Moreover, by legitimizing the power of the executive to legislate in times of crisis, the decision was also widely seen as endangering the separation of powers on which the Argentine Constitution rests (Baglini, D'Ambrosio, and Orlandi 1993). In their analysis, Ferreira Rubio and Gorretti point out that the opinion was based on a legally tenuous thesis of "presumed consent." From the Court's viewpoint, because Congress had not overturned the decree, it was as though the legislature had passed a statute (Ferreira Rubio and Gorretti 1998, 55). In this case, it was Justice Fayt, another holdover judge, who is supposed to have written the majority opinion favoring the government.

In Menem's second term, however, a very different picture began to emerge. Most notable was the Court's stance in the so-called re-reelection controversy. The problem began in early 1998, when Menem announced his intention to run for a third term.[17] Opposition leaders immediately denounced the decision as unconstitutional.[18] Within the Congress, the anti-Menem Peronists, most of whom backed Duhalde, promised to thwart Menem's efforts. Around the same time, the Menem administration also approached the Court, asking the justices to issue a resolution that proclaimed unconstitutional the ban on Menem's running for a third term.

Around this time, Menem supporters began presenting writs of *amparo*[19] before the lower tribunals, arguing that the grandfather clause in-

17. Ibid., February 16, 1998.
18. Ibid.
19. The *recurso de amparo* was introduced into Argentine jurisprudence by the Court in the mid 1950s and was formally added to the Constitution as part of the 1994 reforms. Essentially, the writ of *amparo* is an injunction granted by the Court to stop the state from

cluded in the 1994 constitution that effectively barred Menem from a third term in office constituted unfair discrimination. The clause in question had been included at the behest of the Radicals in the Pacto de Olivos specifically to prevent Menem from running for a third term and stated: "The mandate of the current president at the moment of the sanctioning of the reform shall be considered as his first term."

In the midst of the growing controversy over Menem's re-reelection bid, the justices and their futures stood at the center of the political battle. The Court faced an impossible choice. On the one hand, deciding against the government would mean that the justices were foreclosing Menem's only chance to serve another term and thus to keep themselves protected from future sanctions. As one local newspaper report put it, the administration made this clear to the justices by warning them, "If you do not sign the resolution [permitting the reelection], you are signing your own death warrant[s]."[20] Although such a warning was only figurative, it drove home the idea that the justices' protection depended on the Menem government remaining in power. On the other hand, if the Court allowed Menem to stand for a third term and he lost, the consequences for them would be even more disastrous. One of the justices on the Court observed, "If we vote for a third term, we had better hope that [Menem] wins next year, because if we allow him to run and he does not win, I can already imagine the hordes on the Plaza Lavalle and in the entrance of Tribunales who will be demanding our heads."[21]

Given the declining probability that Menem would actually win a third term, the Court's best option ultimately would lie in refusing to support Menem. Even among the most loyal justices (Nazareno, Moliné O'Connor, Vázquez, López, and Boggiano) support for issuing a ruling declaring the ban unconstitutional rapidly evaporated. In stark contrast to their usual support for the government, Justices Nazareno and Moliné O'Connor leaked to the press that they would not back the government unless some popular support for the reelection emerged.[22]

Meanwhile, a coalition between the Alianza and Duhalde's supporters in the Senate emerged over the question of impeachment proceedings. In particular, the anti-Menem coalition threatened to impeach Justice Vázquez immediately if he supported the re-reelection bid. At the very least, the opposition could ask that Vázquez, who had publicly proclaimed his

---

violating basic constitutional rights and guarantees (interview with Justice Moliné O'Connor, Buenos Aires, May 1998).

20. *La Nación*, 1998.
21. *Clarín*, May 17, 1998.
22. Ibid., March 28, 1998.

personal loyalty to Menem, recuse himself from the case. Given the reluctance of Nazareno, Moliné O'Connor, and Boggiano to handle the case, the loss of Vázquez meant that Menem's so-called automatic majority had all but vanished. As one justice put it, "This Court often votes 5–4 in cases that involve the interests of the government. The only issue on which the Court will vote 9 to 0, you can be sure, is to avoid resolving the [re-reelection] case."[23]

Ultimately, the Court's strategy—to avoid deciding the case—worked, and Menem dropped his bid for a third term. As the elections approached, the Court defected in several other cases as well. In 1999 the Court voted to limit the discretion of the executive to rule by decree.[24] It curried favor with state employees by ruling against the state to increase the pensions to military officers in retirement. And it declared the Menem administration's decree unconstitutional in the IVA case.[25] Less than two months before the election the Court unanimously rejected the government's appeal that it hear three cases involving key members of the administration in an alleged Croatian-Ecuadorian illegal arms deal. As *Clarín* remarked, "The Court's stock of good will toward the government, clearly shown by several justices in the last years, seems to be coming to an end. After having let Menem know this past February that the political climate would not permit a third term, the Court refuses to venture into a case like the arms deal."[26]

While the Court's behavior in several of its most important and politically charged cases suggests strong support for the hypotheses associated with the theory of strategic defection, the next question is whether we can observe the same patterns of behavior more systematically by looking at trends in judicial decision-making over time. To this end, I draw on original individual-level data on the Argentine Supreme Court justices' decisions between 1989 and 1999, contained in the Argentine Supreme Court Decisions Database (ASCD), which I constructed.[27] Inferences about strate-

23. Ibid., May 1998.
24. It should be noted, however, that the Court's ruling would end up affecting the next president, Fernando de la Rúa, far more than Menem.
25. *Clarín*, September 15, 1999.
26. Ibid., August 20, 1999.
27. The indexes contained in the back of each volume of Argentine Supreme Court decisions (Fallos de la Corte Suprema de Justicia de la Nación) allowed me to select all cases that met one or both of the following criteria: (1) the case named the state as a party, or (2) the case named a decree passed by the current executive, thus providing a systematic way of identifying cases in which the government had an interest. Additional information on case type and types of issues involved help to address the concern that the government may not care equally about winning all of the cases in which it is a party or in which the legality of a particular decree is at stake. Each decision is coded dichotomously according to whether the

gic behavior are based not simply on the total percentage of pro- or antigovernment decisions, which may be affected by any number of factors, but on whether the willingness of judges' behavior *changes* relative to changes in their political environment.

Table 6.1 presents the results for the entire Court and for different subsets of justices for the two Menem administrations.[28] Consistent with the strategic support hypothesis (H2) under the first Menem government, the evidence shows either no effect of timing or a positive effect on the willingness of judges to decide against the government. Coinciding with the signing of the Pacto de Olivos in late 1993, for example, Models 3 and 4 show support among the entire Court increasing in the last year and six months prior to Menem's reelection in 1995. Among the subset of holdover judges, Models 9 and 10 show a similar pattern. Calculating the marginal effects, the likelihood of all judges supporting Menem increased by 10 percentage points, and by 16 to 18 percentage points among the subset of holdover justices, who would have been most at risk as Menem's power grew.

If we move to the lower half of Table 6.1, we see that the evidence is even stronger in favor of the strategic defection hypothesis. Models 13–16 show the probability of judges handing down an antigovernment decision increasing among the entire Court in the last two years of Menem's second government. If we recalculate these coefficients as marginal effects, then the likelihood that a judge would hand down an antigovernmental decision grew 17 percentage points in the last two years and 8 percentage points in the final six months. The lack of a statistically significant effect during Menem's last three months (Models 17–18, 23–24) reflect the aforementioned point that strategic defection may not be strictly linear with respect to the passage of time. Empirically, these findings most likely reflect the fact that De la Rúa, who was less threatening to the Court than the other candidates, was leading in the polls in the last three months. Among Menem's so-called automatic majority, defection against the Menem government occurred at roughly the same rate (Models 19–24), with the

---

justice voted in favor of or against the government, abstained, or issued a separate concurrence or dissent.

28. To capture the effect of changes in the political environment on changes in judicial behavior, I employ a series of logit models using dummy variables with adjusted cut-points at twenty-four, eighteen, twelve, six, and three months prior to the change in government. These different cut-points allow me to assess how judges' behavior changes as an election approaches and a renewal or change of the government becomes increasingly likely. I assign a value of 1 to all decisions falling within the periods of the transitions. All other decisions take on a value of 0.

Table 6.1 Individual Supreme Court justices' antigovernment votes by time to transition

	Final 24 months	Final 18 months	Final 12 months	Final 6 months	Final 3 months	Final 3 months vs. before final 24 months
	First Menem government, 1989–1995					
	Model 1	Model 2	Model 3	Model 4	Model 5	Model 6
Constant	0.45***	0.44***	0.40***	0.44***	0.46***	0.42***
	(0.09)	(0.09)	(0.08)	(0.08)	(0.08)	(0.09)
Transition	0.09	0.10	0.48**	0.49*	0.13	0.28
	(0.13)	(0.13)	(0.17)	(0.23)	(0.24)	(0.26)
N	1640	1613	1640	1640	1640	1272
Sig of X^2	.001	.001	.001	.001	.001	.001
	First Menem government (holdover justices), 1989–1995					
	Model 7	Model 8	Model 9	Model 10	Model 11	Model 12
Constant	0.25	0.24	0.21	0.27	0.29	0.19
	(0.16)	(0.16)	(0.16)	(0.16)	(0.16)	(0.17)
Transition	0.26	0.26	0.75**	0.91*	0.64	0.67
	(0.20)	(0.20)	(0.26)	(0.41)	(0.42)	(0.42)
N	574	565	574	574	574	448
Sig of X^2	.301	.301	.012	.055	.222	.140

Second Menem government, 1995–1999

	Model 13	Model 14	Model 15	Model 16	Model 17	Model 18
Constant	0.41**	0.31*	0.21	0.15	0.10	0.48
	(0.16)	(0.16)	(0.16)	(0.16)	(0.15)	(0.20)**
Transition	−0.74***	−0.66***	−0.43***	−0.36**	0.06	−0.34
	(0.10)	(0.10)	(0.11)	(0.14)	(0.17)	(0.18)
N	1807	1807	1807	1807	1807	1023
Sig of X^2	.001	.001	.001	.001	.013	.103

Second Menem government ("automatic majority"), 1995–1999

	Model 19	Model 20	Model 21	Model 22	Model 23	Model 24
Constant	1.20***	1.06***	0.97***	0.94***	0.88***	1.27***
	(0.17)	(0.16)	(0.16)	(0.16)	(0.15)	(0.22)
Transition	−0.61***	−0.56***	−0.33*	−0.40*	0.04	−0.31
	(0.13)	(0.13)	(0.15)	(0.18)	(0.23)	(0.24)
N	1056	1056	1056	1056	1056	592
Sig of X^2	.000	.000	.046	.055	.287	.279

NOTE: The unit of analysis is a justice's vote in a (full opinion) decision, coded 0 = against the government, 1 = for the government. Transition is measured as described in column headings. Cell entries are logistic regression coefficients. Dummy variables for each justice are included in each model, but the results are not presented here. Standard errors are in parentheses. $*p < .05$; $**\ p < .01$; $***\ p < .001$, two-tailed test.

Table 6.2 Antigovernment votes by time to transition among decree cases and salient decree cases

	Decree subset	Salient decree subset
	First Menem government (holdover justices), 1989–1995	
	Model 25	Model 26
Constant	−0.01	−0.07
	(0.27)	(0.27)
Last 12 Months	0.72*	0.74*
	(0.32)	(0.33)
N	219	205
Sig of X^2	.123	.119
	Second Menem government ("automatic majority"), 1995–1999	
	Model 27	Model 28
Constant	1.03***	1.20***
	(0.20)	(0.23)
Last 12 Months	−0.21	−0.52*
	(0.20)	(0.23)
N	657	490
Sig of X^2	.377	.099

NOTE: The unit of analysis is a justice's vote in a (full opinion) decision, coded 0 = against the government, 1 = for the government. Transition is measured as described in column headings. Cell entries are logistic regression coefficients. Dummy variables for each justice are included in each model, but the results are not presented here. Standard errors are in parentheses. *$p < .05$; ** $p < .01$; *** $p < .001$, two-tailed test.

likelihood of handing down an antigovernment decision increasing up to 14 percentage points in this period.[29]

To examine whether the predicted changes in judicial behavior occur in the most important cases coming before the Court (H3), Table 6.2 shows the effect of being in the last year of both governments in two subsets of important decisions, decree cases and salient decree cases. Decree cases provide a rough measure of importance based on political rather than legal criteria. Because these cases involve only decrees passed by the sitting government, this group represents decisions that deal with timely political issues as opposed to those decisions involving the government as a litigant, which as result of case backlog, may be less important by the time

29. Interestingly, for both administrations it appears that there are no significant changes in judicial behavior in the three-month period prior to the change in government (even excluding the prior twenty-one month period). While this could cast suspicion on the strategic view, it could also indicate that judges think of strategic behavior as effective, but only up to a certain point. If true, then the effect of timing on changes in judicial behavior would be consistent with a reverse u-shape pattern suggested by the data, rather than purely linear.

the cases reach the Supreme Court. The second variable, *salient decree*, takes account of the fact that not all decrees are of equal importance (see, for example, Ferreira Rubio and Gorretti 1998). To deal with this concern, I selected a subset of the decree cases that dealt with issues considered to be especially relevant under each of the three governments, including cases involving issues of constitutional interpretation and *amparo* cases.

Overall, the evidence accords well with what we would expect for both periods if judges behave strategically. For the first period, among the hold-over justices (Models 25–26) there is a significant increase in decisions in favor of the government in the last year of Menem's first term, with the likelihood of handing down pro-government decisions increasing by approximately 17 percentage points for both subsets of cases. The results for the automatic majority in the second administration are also encouraging. Although there does not seem to be a significant change in the broader category of decree cases (Model 27), there is a clear effect of Menem's last year on the judges' willingness to decide against the government in the most politically sensitive decree cases (Model 28). Among the most politically sensitive cases, the chances of a decision in favor of the government declined by 12 percentage points among Menem's own appointees.

THE COURT'S SURVIVAL IN THE POST-MENEM ERA

Despite his harsh criticism of the justices and his campaign promises to "purify" the Supreme Court, Fernando De la Rúa was the first Argentine president in over fifty years to maintain a Court composed entirely of justices appointed by his predecessors. From the very beginning of his term, the new administration sent signals to the Court that it wanted a harmonious relationship.[30] In his opening address to Congress, for example, De la Rúa did not mention a single word about "renovating" the Court.[31] In the words of the Ministry of Justice, the government was committed to an approach based on "de equilibrios" (counterbalances) that relied on conciliation and persuasion.[32]

Exactly why De la Rúa took this tack is unclear. One possibility is that, despite his dislike of Menem's justices, De la Rúa's overarching desire to build respect for democratic institutions trumped his desire to replace individual justices. A more cynical possibility is that De la Rúa realized that it might be in his best interests to try to work with the Court, particularly in

30. *La Nación*, December 20, 1999.
31. Ibid., March 18, 2000.
32. Ibid., December 20, 1999.

the realm of economic reforms.[33] Along these lines, the justices' behavior at the end of Menem's term undoubtedly improved their fates under De la Rúa. The fact that the justices refused to support Menem in the higher-profile cases certainly reduced De la Rúa's incentive to sack them. Moreover, particularly in the months just prior to De la Rúa's inauguration, observers noted that "the Court was extremely careful not to make 'irritating' decisions, and did not appear poised to do in the future."[34]

In sum, even if the justices' sudden defection at the end of Menem's term did not fully convince De la Rúa that the Court was an unconditional ally, it may have been sufficient for convincing the new government that the Court would not openly thwart its policies.[35] For the most part, the relationship between De la Rúa and the Court remained mutually supportive. For just as the president wanted approval for his policies, so the justices wanted a stamp of legitimacy. Thus, in the middle of 2000, the Court validated decree 290/95, which imposed salary cuts on public employees. Although the decree had been passed under Menem, De la Rúa, who had recently issued similar decrees, viewed it as a signal of support for his economic policies.[36] Moreover, even as De la Rúa's government began to run into trouble, the Court hardly engaged in wholesale defection. For example, at the height of the government scandal leading to Vice President Carlos Álvarez's resignation and the collapse of the coalition government, the Court simply delayed approving another important economic decree regarding public salaries, rather than striking it down.

Two factors likely contributed to the relative absence of strategic defection in this period. First, despite the government's unpopularity, none of the justices could have predicted that the president would suddenly resign, let alone who would take his place. Thus, in contrast to the end of the Menem government, this time around the judges did not have sufficient information to engage in this type of strategic behavior. Second, and perhaps more important, is the fact that, because the Court was composed entirely of holdover justices, none of its members necessarily needed to prove their independence from De la Rúa per se. Indeed, most of the criticism during this period continued to center on the fact that the Court was still too loyal to Menem, who was seen by some as having master-minded the financial crisis in order to pave the way for his own return.

Along these lines, the Supreme Court's controversial decision in November 2001 to free Menem from house arrest for his role in the Ecuador-

33. Ibid., March 18, 2000.
34. Ibid., December 20, 1999.
35. Ibid., February 3, 2002.
36. Ibid., June 1, 2000.

ian-Croation arms scandal unleashed a storm of protest. Alluding to Menem's ties with the Chief Justice, graffiti "Nazareno + Menem = Asociación ilícita" was painted on the two columns of the Supreme Court building. The day after the Court's decision, Menem announced his intention to run for president again. Before a crowd in his home province of La Rioja, Menem proclaimed, "I am going to be president in 2003, today I am launching my candidacy. . . . To tell the truth, I feel like I have the same force that I did in 1988 to defeat any other Peronist candidate and lift Argentina back up again."[37] Although Menem would ultimately not succeed,[38] at that point in time it seems entirely likely that the justices saw Menem as potentially able to fill the growing vacuum of power surrounding De la Rúa's presidency.[39]

Shortly thereafter the Alianza government collapsed. In the midst of massive social protests and violence, on December 20, 2001, De la Rúa resigned. Over the next few weeks, as Argentina plunged further into economic disaster, culminating in the largest debt default in history, the country experienced a rapid succession of presidents. On January 1, 2002, Eduardo Duhalde, who had lost to De la Rúa in 1999, was appointed by Congress to lead the country as the second interim president. As the new government fought to regain control over the economy, the people took to the streets in massive pot-banging demonstrations, known as *cacerolazos*.

Among the most visible targets of these demonstrations were the members of the Supreme Court. It is hard to overstate the people's anger at the Court during this period. Almost immediately upon taking office, Duhalde began to move against the Supreme Court. Two days after being sworn in, the headlines reported that the new administration was studying plans to renovate the Court. According to government sources, the administration initially considered reducing the Court from nine justices to five and calling for individual justices to resign.[40] Leading the list were Julio Nazareno and Adolfo Vázquez, who had recently signed the *Yoma* (2001) majority opinion freeing Menem from corruption charges, despite their well-known

37. Ibid., November 22, 2001.

38. According to a poll taken in early 2003, 54.9 percent said they "would never vote for Mr. Menem, but he was also considered a "very good" presidential candidate by public opinion." He also had the best scores on "credibility" (7.1 percent); "social sensitivity" (8.7 percent); "capacity to generate consensus" (18.4 percent); "capacity to rule" (8.9 percent); "government team" (5.5 percent); "adapting Argentina to the new international context" (15.6 percent); and "own criteria" (16.4 percent) (see http://www.mercopress.com/Detalle.asp?NUM=1864).

39. In addition, there was also considerable speculation that De la Rúa had pressured the Court to release Menem in order to further divide and weaken the Peronist party (*La Nación*, November 21, 2001).

40. Ibid., January 3, 2002.

personal ties to the former president. Meanwhile, the minister of welfare called on the Court to help with the national economic crisis by slashing its budget by 13 percent.[41] Normally exempt from paying taxes, the justices were also asked to give up this privilege.

When it became clear that none of the justices was willing to bend to these pressures, Congress began to move forward with the impeachment of the entire Court. Among the several charges that would be leveled at the judges included allegations of misconduct in several of the Court's highest-profile cases dealt with during the last decade, including the Israeli Embassy investigation, the "re-balancing" of the telephone rates, the decision to free Menem, and the Court's decision to use the doctrine of per saltum to validate the highly unpopular banking freeze, known as the *Corallito*.[42]

On February 1, 2002, one day after the impeachment process began, the Court handed down a second decision on the banking restrictions in the case of *Smith*. While President Duhalde quickly dismissed the decision as politicized and proclaimed the Court "thoroughly discredited," the head of the impeachment committee, Sergio Acevedo, vowed to work, "morning, noon, and night, to prepare the charges against the Court before the month's end."[43] The attempt to impeach the justices, however, would ultimately prove one of the biggest failures of Duhalde's presidency. Nine months after the process began, Congress voted to drop all charges, and the Court remained intact.

Several factors played a role in the Court's ability to weather the crisis. Despite the huge public outcry to remove the justices, the IMF had made it known relatively early on that it disapproved of Duhalde's efforts to do away with the Court. As it turned out, the congressional strategy of getting rid of all of the justices at the same time also resulted in enormous delays and sloppiness. For example, Justice Bossert complained that the committee did not understand the reach of many of the Court's decisions or the norm of recusal, and misrepresented the individual actions of the justices.[44] As a result of these and other errors, elite opinion gradually turned against the process.[45]

Yet, to fully understand why the justices stayed, we must also consider

41. Ibid., January 21, 2002.

42. A complete list of the charges against the Supreme Court justices and the justices' defenses are posted on the website of Lower House at http://www.diputados.gov.ar/.

43. *La Nación*, February 2, 2002.

44. For example, in *Fayt* (1997), Bossert had issued a dissent from the majority opinion declaring mandatory retirement for judges at age seventy-five unconstitutional (*La Nación*, October 15, 2002).

45. Ibid., September 18, 2002.

the Court's own actions throughout this period. Starting with the *Smith* decision, the majority of justices made it clear that they would do everything within their power to stay on the Court. As several commentators were quick to point out, the fact that Court's decision came once the impeachment process had already begun suggests a highly calculated move by the justices to blackmail the government into dropping the impeachment charges. In the words of FREPASO legislator Nilda Garre: "The Court's decision was not made to protect those with savings, but to extort the powers of the state, especially the Congress, that initiated the proceedings against several members of the Court. Surely, Menem's famous automatic majority, which recently allowed him to go free for having put into place the economic policies under which we all now suffer, is again functioning in the service of their boss (Menem) and his project of destabilizing institutions."[46]

As thousands of *amparos* against the banking freeze and pesification were making their way to the Supreme Court, it soon became very clear that the Court would have the last word on Duhalde's plans for economic recovery. Although one of the justices complained that "everything is subject to appeal, thus everything is subject to impeachment,"[47] from the government's perspective, the situation seemed just the opposite. The Court was using the mounting number of cases against the government as a Sword of Damocles over Duhalde's head. Thus, almost as soon as the impeachment proceedings began, the government began a series of backroom negotiations with the justices. By mid-July, Duhalde had fired his minister of justice and called for the end to the impeachment proceedings. Chief Justice Nazareno responded to this positive gesture by simply saying, "This Court has lived with various presidents. It is not a hostile Court."[48] Although it would take another several months to get the quorum needed to dismiss the charges, the judges had clearly won.

Stepping back from this narrative, the strategic situation that the judges faced during this period was both more exaggerated and different than it had been in the past. Although the Court had long been unpopular, never before had there been such public demand to remove the Court. Surveys showed that 90 percent of the population was in favor of getting rid of the justices. Clearly, *not* remaking the Court carried enormous political costs. Indeed, this was one of the key reasons why the Radicals were so reluctant to provide a quorum to dismiss the charges. In the Court's favor, however,

46. Ibid., February 3, 2002.
47. Ibid., June 12, 2002.
48. Ibid., July 20, 2002.

few presidents had been as weak as Duhalde. One consequence was that, as the impeachment process dragged on, it became increasingly clear that even if the judges were removed, Duhalde would have a difficult time getting the opposition to allow him to construct the Court he wanted.[49] Put it terms of the theory of strategic defection, while the political costs of removing the Court were thus probably lower than they had ever been, the costs of replacing it were far higher (Helmke 2004). In this sense, Duhalde's presidency exemplifies the lame-duck dynamic of incumbent presidents who are unable to punish judges once they defect.

The situation that the Court faced, however, was more than simply an exaggerated version of the past. It was also fundamentally different in several important respects. Most notably, in the original theory of strategic defection judges appointed by one government anticipate political changes driven by exogenous events and seek to use their decisions to appeal to the incoming government. In the post-Menem era, by contrast, judges had no particular allegiance to the outgoing government. Nor, given the events of the time, could they have had any prior beliefs who the next president would be. They were reacting to events as they unfolded. That said, once the new government was in power, the judges faced a clear choice of whether to support the new president, or not. That in *Smith* the judges declared the outgoing government's decree unconstitutional is incidental. The real loser was clearly the new government.

One interpretation of the justices' strategy is that once Duhalde came to power, they saw no chance of being able to convince the new government that the Court would be compatible. Given the long-standing enmity between Duhalde and Menem, they knew that their fates were sealed, so they simply faced no incentives to support Duhalde. In support of this interpretation is the fact that the Court handed down *Smith* once the impeachment proceedings had already begun. Cast in theoretical terms, this interpretation fits with the idea that if the justices know that they are going to be punished, they face no incentives to switch their votes.

Yet, what is far more striking about the story is their clear commitment to staying on the Court. Not supporting the government was thus not acceptance of the inevitable, but an active attempt to change the outcome. As a spokesman for the Court bluntly put it at the time, "Kill or be killed: that was the situation. And they decided to shoot first."[50] Although cer-

---

49. Moreover, given the Court's severe legitimacy problems, the pool of available judges was also far shallower than it had been in the past. For example, as Carlos Arslanian's refusal to accept Duhalde's subsequent attempt to appoint him to the bench shows, few respected jurists wanted to be associated with the Court (*La Nación*, October 23, 2002).

50. Ibid., February 2, 2002.

tainly in the past defection did not help incumbent presidents, in each of the previous periods exogenous events were far more important. Defection began only after the presidents grew weak. In this period, by contrast, weakness did not trigger defection; it was the justices' goal. As the press put it, the *Smith* decision represented an attempted judicial coup against the government. Political change was thus not merely an external factor shaping judges decisions, it was endogenous to the judges' decisions.

AN EPILOGUE: THE COURT UNDER KIRCHNER

By the end of Duhalde's presidency, the Court seemed unstoppable. In response to the Court's split decision to overturn the government's "pesification" plan converting dollars into pesos, the first lady, Chiche Duhalde, bitterly complained, "Our country is governed by the judiciary, the only branch that is not chosen by the people, that is lamentable."[51] Yet, with the inauguration of a new popularly elected president in May 2003, Nestor Kirchner, the situation again changed for the Court. Within a month of being sworn in, Kirchner appeared on public television demanding that Congress reopen the impeachment proceedings.

Having apparently learned from Duhalde's experience, this time around, the Impeachment Committee decided to proceed one justice at a time. Kirchner's first target was the symbol of the Menem era, Chief Justice Julio Nazareno. Of all of the justices facing multiple allegations in the previous trials, at a total of forty-four charges, Nazareno had the highest number.

Facing inevitable impeachment, the threat of additional criminal charges, and the possibility of losing his pension, Nazareno resigned. In the months that followed, the Senate voted to remove the Supreme Court's vice president, Moliné O'Connor, Menemist justice Guillermo López resigned, and Carlos Fayt announced his retirement. With the earlier appointment of Justice Juan Carlos Maqueda,[52] and the subsequent resignation of Justice Vázquez in 2004,[53] the era of the automatic majority was over.

51. Ibid., March 6, 2003.
52. Once the impeachment charges under Duhalde were dropped, the least compromised justice, Gustavo Bossert, tendered his resignation, claiming "moral exhaustion." To replace him, Duhlde appointed Juan Carlos Maqueda. Although the choice was broadly criticized as purely political, Maqueda's position as the provisional Peronist leader of the Senate meant that his confirmation was virtually guaranteed. Maqueda was sworn in on December 30, 2002.
53. In September 2004, Vazquez resigned in the face of impeachment charges. Two months earlier, Uruguay refused to grant Vazquez asylum after gunmen shot at his car on a highway in Buenos Aires.

Kirchner's relative success in remaking the Court was due to a number of factors. Unlike Duhalde, Kirchner was popularly elected, which gave him a much clearer mandate to make changes on the bench. In addition to gaining the support of the IMF for remaking the Court, the fact that the economic situation had also relatively improved also made his government less vulnerable to the vicissitudes of the Court's decisions. Perhaps most important of all, however, was the new president's decision to limit his discretion in appointing new judges. In a highly publicized move, Kirchner thus issued Decree 222, which mandated public transparency and participation in the judicial candidate selection process. The degree of public debate and participation over the subsequent appointments of Justices Eugenio Zaffaroni, Elena Highton, and Carmen Arbigay suggests a qualitative difference with past attempts to remake the Court.

In sum, the Argentine Supreme Court was at the forefront of politics between 1989 and 2003. Beginning with Menem's court-packing scheme in 1990s, the general impression of the Court throughout much of the last decade—further verified in this chapter—is that the judges were subservient to the government of the day. A decade later, this situation was profoundly reversed. Using a modified separation-of-powers approach, this chapter reconciled these two different snapshots of Court-executive relations during this period by arguing that, under certain conditions, judges face incentives to engage in strategic decision-making in order to maximize their chances of remaining on the bench. Depending on the relative strength of the incumbent government and the justices' beliefs about the threat they face, strategic support and defection alike constitute logical responses for judges whose fates are not automatically guaranteed. Although recent efforts to reform the judicial nomination process are ostensibly aimed at creating a more consistently independent court, whether or not the incentives leading judges to engage in the cycle of strategic behavior will be truly eliminated remains to be seen.

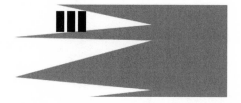

Change and Continuity in the Argentine Party System

7

Citizens Versus Political Class:
The Crisis of Partisan Representation

Juan Carlos Torre

With the end of the authoritarian regime in 1983, Argentine political parties came to play a central role in the nation's political life and were welcomed by citizens with fervor and confidence. Evidence of this was the impressive boost in party membership, which officially numbered 2.97 million in March 1983. Twenty years later, those feelings of fervor and confidence had been replaced by a widespread feeling of rage and mistrust, epitomized by the slogan "Throw Everyone Out!" which significant groups among the citizenry hailed in their mobilizations. This hostile reaction was not directed toward democracy as a political system in and of itself, which continues to enjoy majority public support, but rather toward the overall performance of political parties.

This chapter on the crisis of party representation examines two questions. First, what is the nature of the crisis? Second, what is its scope—has it affected all political parties equally? Regarding its nature, I believe that the crisis of party representation is the counterpoint of one of the main developments of twenty years of democracy: the gradual consolidation of a critical mass of citizens with high expectations of democracy. More specifically, the hostile atmosphere that currently haunts political parties reveals the discrepancy between their behavior and the more qualitative

Translated by Kathryn Auffinger. The author appreciates the comments and suggestions received from Ana María Mustapic, Carla Carrizo, Vicente Palermo, and Luis Alberto Romero.

demands of this critical mass of citizens, which is typically recruited from urban middle-class (primarily non-Peronist) sectors of society, and which tends to support center-right and center-left forces. Concerning the scope of the crisis, it should be noted that its impact has differed among Argentine parties. It affected non-Peronist parties significantly more than Peronism. The problems that the Peronist party confronted after 2001 were mainly due to its lack of internal cohesion as a political organization, rather than to its relationship with its core supporters. Instead, in recent years non-Peronist parties have experienced a veritable hemorrhage of supporters.

In order to examine these questions, we will broadly outline the trajectory of political parties in democratic Argentina, from their auspicious beginning in 1983 to the current crisis of party representation. First, we will look into the parties' electoral behavior; then, we will tackle the changes that took place in Argentine political culture. The purpose of this historical reconstruction is to trace the political role that center-right and center-left voters have come to play, as well as the sources of their new and greater demands they make on political parties.

THE ELECTORAL DYNAMICS OF PARTY-CENTERED DEMOCRACY

In the first elections after authoritarianism collapsed in 1983, the two major national parties, the (Peronist) Partido Justicialista (PJ) and the Radical Civic Union (UCR), set aside their historical antagonisms and competed for power within shared rules of the game. In this changed political climate, the two-party format of the electoral contest reactivated the main cleavage that since 1945 had split Argentina's political map into two poles, the Peronist and the non-Peronist. When the political movement led by Juan Perón emerged in the mid-1940s, it restructured the social bases of party identification in a way that had a lasting effect on Argentine electoral politics. Created in a short period of time from the apex of state power, the electoral coalition that brought Perón to the presidency in 1946 drew support from the entire political spectrum, capturing socialist, Radical, and conservative votes. What was distinctive about the outpouring of votes for Perón was that his support came mainly from the popular sectors of society. For example, Perón won support from unionized and nonunionized urban workers, some of whom had previously voted for socialism or Radicalism. In the provinces outside Buenos Aires, Perón also gained votes from the lower- and lower middle-class sectors, which had previously supported conservatives and Radicals. In effect, Peronism took working-class supporters away from the other parties. In turn, the non-Peronist pole mostly relied upon the middle and upper classes, whose allegiance was distributed among the UCR and small center-right and center-left parties.

According to Mora y Araujo (1991), Argentina's social pyramid exhibits an electoral dividing line separating those below it who voted Peronist from those above it who voted for a variety of non-Peronist parties. In this scenario, the equilibrium of electoral politics rested on two factors. The first was the difficulty for non-Peronist parties to move below the dividing line and gain working- and lower-class support. The second factor was the obstacles that these parties faced in forming electoral coalitions above the dividing line, to bring non-Peronist voters together. Under these conditions, the Peronist movement dominated any election it was permitted to participate in freely.

The 1983 elections overturned the "iron-clad rule" of Argentine politics that Peronism was unassailable in free elections. Under Raúl Alfonsín's leadership, the UCR won the presidential election with 51.7 percent of the vote, defeating Peronist candidate Italo Luder, who received 40.1 percent. The UCR's victory was primarily due to a small but decisive number of votes from a traditionally Peronist constituency—the upper stratum of the wage-earning population, skilled workers, and white-collar employees. This electoral shift occurred in conjunction with a second phenomenon: the UCR's victory put an end to the lack of cohesion that had been characteristic of the non-Peronist vote. In effect, Alfonsín's candidacy received the support of a majority of the middle and upper classes, including those with both center-right and left-of-center orientations.

However, the pattern of two-party competition displayed in the 1983 elections did not persist over time. The concentration of the vote in the UCR and the PJ gradually decreased. By analyzing legislative elections, which more faithfully reflect political preferences because of their proportional electoral system, we see that the combined vote for the UCR and the PJ declined from 86 percent in 1983 to 73 percent in 1989, to only 65 percent in 1995. The weakening tendency in two-party politics did not affect both parties equally. As shown in Table 7.1, this change was driven largely by a significant decline in support for the UCR.

The loyalty of the PJ's electorate contrasts with the UCR's progressive loss of votes. Electoral analyses have shown that since 1983, after having defeated Peronism, the UCR lost votes to the center-right and the center-left of the electoral spectrum, thus favoring the growth of third parties (Adrogué 1995; De Riz 1998; De Riz and Adrogué 1991). The right-of-center parties initially included the Center Democratic Union (UCEDE), founded by the patriarch of Argentine neoliberalism, Alvaro Alsogaray,

Table 7.1 Variation in PJ and UCR electoral performance, 1983–1995 (legislative elections)

| Year | UCR | | PJ | |
	Percentage of vote	Performance relative to 1983 (%)	Percentage of vote	Performance relative to 1983 (%)
1983	48.0	—	38.5	—
1985	43.2	90.1	34.3	89.2
1987	37.2	77.6	41.5	107.8
1989	28.7	59.9	44.7	116.1
1991	29.0	60.5	40.2	104.5
1993	30.2	63.0	42.5	110.4
1995	21.7	45.3	43.1	111.9

SOURCE: Ministry of the Interior.

as well as various provincial parties. Among the left-of-center parties, the Intransigent Party (PI), which maintained close ties to the human rights movement, was initially the strongest. After lending their support to Alfonsín's presidential candidacy, center-right and center-left voters regained their autonomy and made their own choices, which—through the fluctuation of their vote—produced a highly competitive political environment.

If we analyze the trajectory of the two most dynamic groups—the center-left PI and the center-right UCEDE—we find that the PI received 2.8 percent of the legislative vote in 1983, and later gained support from former Alfonsín voters and won 7.7 percent of the vote in the midterm legislative election of 1985. Two years later, the PI's electoral support fell back to 2 percent. This decline coincided with the reemergence of the PJ as a competitive force after the internal crisis triggered by its defeat in 1983. With a new leadership and more pluralist credentials, Peronism recovered its traditional voters and was able to attract a segment of the PI's progressive middle-class vote to win the 1987 legislative elections. Later on, in 1989, the confluence of the PI with Peronism became explicit, when its leadership called for its supporters to vote for PJ presidential candidate Carlos Menem; subsequently, it lost its electoral presence.

The UCEDE also experienced a positive evolution in the beginning: it received 3.2 percent of vote in 1985 and climbed to 5.8 percent in 1987 with a platform that attracted the politically conservative and pro-market electorate. In 1989, conservative provincial parties backed UCR presidential candidate Eduardo Angeloz in an effort to prevent a victory by the (then) populist Menem, but the UCEDE opted to run its own ticket, thereby dividing the center-right's vote. UCEDE presidential candidate Alvaro Alsogaray won 7.2 percent of the vote, while the UCEDE-led legislative list received 9.9 percent, its best-ever electoral performance.

Menem's victory in 1989 did not come as a surprise, considering the Radical administration's troubles with the two main problems in the first stage of transition to democracy: dealing with past human rights violations and managing the economic emergency that followed the external debt crisis. However, his postelection ideological and political about-turn—toward market reform, pacification of the military, and alignment with the United States—was a major surprise. Predictably, Menem's shift brought about another restructuring in center-left and center-right alignments. Among the right-of-center parties, Menem's move to the right prompted an alliance with the PJ. For example, Alsogaray joined the new administration as a top presidential adviser, alongside other party officials. Subsequently, the UCEDE's electorate followed suit. This shift in voting patterns crossed the horizontal dividing line of electoral politics, in this case from above to below. The effects of this electoral shift were made especially evident by the steep decline in support for the UCEDE in its major electoral stronghold, the capital city of Buenos Aires. After receiving 22 percent of the vote in the capital in 1989, the UCEDE fell to 8.6 percent in 1991 and just 3 percent in 1993.

While conservative voters migrated to Peronism, left-of-center voters moved in the opposite direction. In 1991, a small number of PJ representatives who disagreed with Menem's political and ideological shifts left the party to form the Frente Grande (FG), which started by gaining 1.5 percent of the vote in that year's legislative election. The FG leaders' expectation that the PJ's popular bases would desert it never materialized. Instead, the FG's dissident center-left platform gained more support among middle-class voters who were generically identified with the democratic left and in the process of leaving behind their recent flirtation with Peronism. With this support, the FG received 2.5 percent of the national vote and 13 percent in the capital in the 1993 legislative elections. Less than a year later, the FG broke through when Menem and Alfonsín signed the Pacto de Olivos (Olivos Pact), establishing the constitutional reform that paved the way for Menem's reelection. The discontent among UCR sympathizers for the party's abdication of its role as the main opposition produced a large-scale transfer of the Radical vote to the FG in the 1994 constituent assembly elections: the new party received 12.7 percent of the national vote and became the largest political force in the Federal Capital with 37.6 percent of the vote. The growth of the left-of-center parties reached a peak in the 1995 presidential election, by which point the FG had evolved into the FREPASO coalition through the recruitment of other minor forces. Menem won the election with 47.7 percent of the overall vote. But the outstanding fact was that running a campaign with a strong moral and institutional slant gave Jose Octavio Bordón and Carlos "Chacho" Álvarez 28.2 percent of the vote, relegating UCR candidates to a poor third place with 16.4 percent.

Two corollaries can be drawn from the electoral realignments recounted above. The first was a change in the composition of the electoral coalition that made Menem's reelection possible (Gervasoni 1998a). Between 1989 and 1995, he managed to maintain the majority of Peronist core supporters, while at the same time making up for the loss of support among center-left voters with gains in the center-right electorate. The second corollary was the transformation of the FG/FREPASO into a rising opposition force.

In 1997, two years into Menem's second term, a party system dynamic that had been characterized by a divided opposition and PJ predominance abruptly changed. Shortly before that year's legislative election, the UCR and FREPASO joined forces to form the Alianza por el Trabajo, la Educación, y la Justicia (Alliance for Jobs, Justice, and Education). Facing an administration that was losing support after eight years in power, and taking advantage of a climate in which rising unemployment, growing inequality, and corruption overshadowed the government's previous achievements of economic stability and modernization, the Alianza made its competitive potential clear. The new coalition received 45.6 percent of the vote, finishing almost nine and a half points ahead of the PJ.

The unification of the opposition parties into the Alianza was not the only factor that contributed to ending the string of five consecutive Peronist victories between 1987 and 1995. The Menemist electoral coalition also suffered attrition on the center-right. In 1996, Minister of the Economy Domingo Cavallo, author of the highly popular convertibility plan, left the government because of conflicting political interests. Shortly afterward, he filled the center-right electoral space vacant since the UCEDE's decline by creating a new political party, Acción por la República (Action for the Republic). In 1997, the APR made its electoral debut as an opposition party and obtained 3.9 percent of the vote by channeling the discontent of a fraction of center-right voters toward Menem's government's political habits, rather than its economic orientation.

In sum, the dynamics of national-level electoral competition between 1983 and 1997 can be largely explained by the behavior of the non-Peronist pole and the electoral decisions made by center-right and center-left voters within this camp. This electorate has been the primary source of electoral volatility in Argentina, as well as changes in electoral coalitions. As I will show, this electorate was also the site of important changes in Argentine political culture during the post-1983 period.

CHANGES IN POLITICAL CULTURE

At the beginning of this chapter, I argued that the crisis of party representation was a result of society's high expectations of democracy. More generally, discontent with representation is a symptom of changes in the political culture of significant segments of the electorate (Miranda 2002). These changes brought about a new understanding of the relationship between representatives and constituents and led to a redefinition as immoral and unjust of political practices that were previously considered to be natural and tolerable. To trace its genealogy, I will turn now to the transformations undergone by Argentine political culture.

The catalyst for change has been appropriately located in the human rights movement that emerged during the last dictatorship and gained strength with the transition to democracy (Peruzzotti 2002a). Apart from its effectiveness against the consequences of state terrorism, the human rights movement is also important for the cultural innovation it helped forge. Its criticism of an extreme version of state arbitrariness provided the foundation for the symbolic construction of a more general criticism of all forms of abuse of state power. The human rights movement thus inspired and paved the way for a second wave of movements that framed demands in terms of rights and sought to defend those rights through the judicial system (Smulovitz 1997). Several incidents of police violence prompted the first mobilizations of citizens groups demanding justice, using methods aimed at attracting media attention. The success of these initiatives encouraged the emergence of others, which in turn promoted the formation of organizations against police repression. Over time, the repertoire of civil rights whose transgression or lack of acknowledgment triggered civic organization and protest movements expanded to include consumers' rights, environmental protection, gender rights, and others.

These citizens' movements, carried out independently of partisan structures, challenged conventional political practices through the creation of nongovernmental organizations (such as Poder Ciudadano, Conciencia, and Ciudadanos en Acción) primarily oriented to the promotion of civic participation and the control of government action. Their campaigns for the protection of rights and greater transparency and legality on the part of the authorities found an important ally in investigative journalism, as reporters increasingly revealed flagrant abuses of power and political corruption. The mobilization of these "active minorities"—particularly during Menem's administration, whose scandals and the constant manipulation of the law provided more than adequate motive for this mobilization—eventually resulted in a political agenda that moved beyond traditionally distributive matters toward the enforcement of the rule of law and public ethics (Peruzzotti 2002b, this volume).

These changes in political culture led to changes in discursive logics and practices, which in turn raised questions about the traditional political parties' representative link. In opposition to a vision of this link as mere authorization, grounded in strong identification linkages between the representatives and the represented, the citizen movements created the conditions for a new vision, based upon the representatives' accountability for their actions and promises. As public scrutiny became more important in the relationship between citizens and parties, confidence in the political arena was replaced by vigilant mistrust. Thus change in political culture consolidated a more demanding electorate—one that was better informed and more aware of partisan alternatives. It was ultimately in this electorate that civic associations dedicated to supervising elected officials and journalistic denunciations of misconduct found their natural audience.

While this mutation in the representative link was taking place among significant numbers of the citizenry, the main political parties were experiencing a parallel development: a decline in their ability to influence public policy. Since the mid-1980s, public policy decisions were in large part the result of responses to extragovernmental pressures, not of the platforms with which parties presented themselves before the voters. The denouement of the policies to make amends for past violations of human rights, and the initially moderate and then radicalized shift toward market reform—the two main chapters in the history of the established parties' management of Argentine democracy—showed the difficulties of the UCR and the PJ to sustain coherent public policies. However, the UCR and the PJ's ability to use public office to generate patronage resources was virtually unrestricted. Indeed, this power was increasingly used to maintain party structures and to offer leaders opportunities to finance their political careers and their personal advancement. Under these conditions, when the inquisitive "active minorities" and the media looked at party organizations and wondered what purpose they served, the reply they gave themselves was that parties only served their own corporate interests.

It should not, therefore, be surprising that in a country with solid partisan cleavages, these divisions faded, and the term *political class*, used without much discrimination to designate professional politicians, would gain prominence in public discourse toward the end of the 1990s. Generally, both Peronist and Radical politicians were leading members of this category. They were included in this category, not only because the PJ and the UCR were the two largest parties, but also because new challenges actively exploited their inability to adapt to the new political culture, which further discredited them both. Their reluctance to renovate their leadership in the face of corruption charges, their practice of financing their cadres with public funds, and their concentrated efforts toward self-interested political reproduction within their organizations all increased the gap between the parties and the new citizen demands. In fact, both while in power and as part of the opposition, Peronists and Radicals continued to do what they had always done. But now they were doing it in an environment where changes in political culture were transforming what had long been considered the normal functioning of party-centered democracy into intolerable transgressions against decent political life.

Having examined these transformations in political culture, as well as the changes in electoral behavior dynamics, it is possible to identify and assess the impact of the critical mass of citizens located in the center-left and center-right "areas." These political categories are referred to as "areas" in order to emphasize the space of dominant values, rather than a stable partisan alignment. In both areas, political parties have succeeded each other over time and have not always been the medium to aggregate political preferences. The individuals occupying these areas are independent middle- and upper-class urban voters with a relatively high level of education and political information, as well as easy access to the media. They fit the profile of independent voters: they believe in a set of values that guides their voting and their choice of which party organization would best uphold and defend them.

The clout of this critical mass of citizens on Argentine politics has rested on their electoral influence and on their agenda-setting power. As far as their electoral influence is concerned, I have already indicated that independent center-right and center-left electoral volatility alone defined electoral outcomes for the two main parties. To appreciate this influence, we should underscore that until recently the party system's stability rested on the PJ's solid base of support, and to a lesser degree, that of the UCR. Peronism maintained an average of 37 percent of the valid vote; the party's switch from economic distributionism and nationalism to neoliberalism has not substantially altered these loyalties. For their part, the Radicals have assembled around 18 percent, although this has been declining since their victory in 1983. Leaving aside small provincial parties (about 10 percent) and the radical left (3 percent) because of their low electoral significance, the election scale is clearly tipped toward the center-right and center-left areas. Tallying the number of votes obtained by the political groups representing each area in legislative elections where they ran their own tickets, we see that the center-right attracts 10–12 percent of the vote and the center-left attracts 22 percent.[1] Between 1983 and 1997, fluctuations within this portion of the electorate, whether in the same or in opposite directions, determined the fate of the UCR and the PJ in presidential elections.

Concerning its agenda-setting power, the human rights movement emerged in the center-left and played a major role in defining priorities during the initial stage of democratic transition. After the relative demise of this movement, the center-left area found new reasons to mobilize against corruption and the abuse of power and for transparency and the rule of law. In turn, the center-right placed fiscal problems, monetary stability, market reform, private property, and economic freedom on the political agenda. These issues and others framed public debate and influenced the course of action followed by the UCR and PJ administrations. The political fate of these parties rested on leaders who, acting as "outsiders" to their traditions, embraced the dominant new ideas, reinventing their parties' identities and, through this, their administrations' strategic orientation. That was the experience of Raul Alfonsín's 1983 presidential campaign, which emphasized the rule of law and making amends with the past, and also of Carlos Menem's shift toward neoliberalism after taking office in 1989. In both cases, as I have noted, the source of the ideas that nourished these political innovations was alien to the leaders that promoted them.

Notwithstanding the party leaders' programmatic flexibility, the credibility of the political class came under increasing attack during the 1990s. The politics of discredit of the political class was encouraged by forces on both the center-left and the center-right. The former denounced the collusive relations between the main parties (e.g., the Olivos Pact) as undermining democratic principles. The latter questioned the lack of attunement of the political class with the existing consensus over efficiency in public administration and modernization of the economy. This cultural atmosphere created the conditions for the emergence of new political parties, such as FREPASO and the APR, and made them vehicles for the promise of political renewal. Their subsequent poor performance, during the Alianza

---

1. The percentages attributed to the center-right are based on the performance of the UCEDE and the APR in the 1989 and 1999 legislative elections, respectively. Percentages for the center-left are based on FREPASO's performance in the 1995 legislative election.

government of 1999–2001, extended the moral condemnation of traditional parties to the new political forces as well. In the next section, I examine the immediate political context that surrounded the crisis of party
representation.

THE EXTENT OF POLITICAL DISAFFECTION

The constitutional calendar stipulated that presidential elections should be
held in 1999 to elect Menem's successor. The PJ headed into the election
suffering an internal crisis. Eduardo Duhalde, governor of the province
of Buenos Aires, where the Peronist party has its most powerful party
machine, announced his candidacy, only to clash with Menem, who—
constitutional prohibition notwithstanding—sought a third term. Although Duhalde ultimately won out and obtained his party's nomination,
he never enjoyed the Menem government's full support. Although less
visible, political tension also existed within the opposition Alianza. Militant sectors of FREPASO still had not fully digested the idea of a coalition
with the UCR, which they viewed as weakly committed to changes in traditional politics. However, these reservations were silenced in the face of a
certain victory, which would put an end to a decade of Menemism. Additionally, FREPASO lacked the Radicals' strong national organization, which
was needed to compete successfully against the vast Peronist movement.

The Alianza's candidates were Fernando De la Rúa, leader of the UCR's
conservative wing, for president and FREPASO leader Carlos "Chacho" Álvarez for vice president. In addition to the PJ, the Alianza faced the center-
right APR, which nominated Domingo Cavallo as its presidential candidate. The 1999 electoral results maintained the distribution of preferences
emergent in 1997. The Alianza won handsomely with 48.4 percent of the
vote, while the PJ earned 38.3 percent, its worst performance in a presidential election since 1983. Cavallo finished third with 10.2 percent of the vote.

Two years later, this scene would be dramatically altered. In the October
2001 legislative election, a strong sentiment of political alienation became
evident as the percentages of blank votes, spoiled ballots, and abstentions
reached unprecedented levels. This election served as an ominous pro-
logue to the abrupt conclusion of De la Rúa's presidency two months later,
in the midst of greater political isolation and a wave of protests.

Looking back at events leading up to this explosion of party disaffection,
we should note that the Alianza platform that brought De la Rúa to the
presidency focused on correcting the legacies of Menem's ten-year rule:
the social costs of market reforms, widespread corruption, countless

Table 7.2   A Comparison of the 1999 and 2001 legislative election results

	1999	2001	Variation
PJ	6,605,318	4,809,495	−1,795,823
Alianza	7,998,504	3,058,569	−4,939,935
Action for the Republic	1,427,056	174,068	−1,252,988
ARI and Social Pole	—	1,616,104	+1,616,104
Left-wing parties	531,488	1,499,293	+967,805
Provincial parties	1,310,395	1,200,118	−110,277
Others	644,101	1,737,549	+1,093,448
Blank votes	1,092,901	1,704,514	+611,613
Spoiled ballots	190,896	2,261,332	+2,070,436
Abstentions	4,398,543	6,777,624	+2,379,081

SOURCE: Ministry of the Interior.

abuses of power, and during its final two years, economic stagnation. Measured against the expectations it had generated, the Alianza's performance during its two years in office could not have been more unsatisfactory. Poverty and unemployment levels remained high, there was no economic recovery, and attempts to overcome the economic crisis had brought unpopular austerity measures. Finally, the government was shaken by another major episode of corruption: the August 2000 allegations of bribery in the Senate by the executive. The scandal was never cleared up, bringing the Alianza's ethical credentials into question (Novaro 2002). This state of affairs exacerbated internal conflicts within the Alianza, which resulted in Vice President Álvarez's resignation and President De la Rúa's distancing from his own party, the UCR. The Alianza's first electoral test was complicated by the presence of center-right leader Cavallo, in whose hands De la Rúa had placed the Ministry of the Economy after the initial failures of the economic policymakers from the 1999 electoral coalition. Table 7.2 below shows the electoral impact of the Alianza administration's performance.

A comparison of the 1999 and 2001 legislative elections shows, first of all, the considerable electoral about-face suffered by the political groups involved in the De la Rúa administration. Compared to the votes obtained two years earlier, the UCR-FREPASO alliance lost 4.94 million votes, or 61 percent, whereas Minister Cavallo's party, the APR, lost 1.25, or 87 percent. Second, electoral figures indicate that the PJ lost 1.8 million votes, a 27 percent decline relative to 1999. Taking both observations into consideration, it is clear that public discontent with party representation had an impact on all the major parties, but in an uneven manner. The generalized climate of citizen protest practically eliminated center-right party options and dealt a lethal blow to the governing coalition; with respect to the loyalty of the Peronist electorate, the data show that the PJ was also affected but to a lesser degree, which allowed it to emerge victorious amid a deep crisis of party democracy.

Using available data, it is possible to reconstruct the social and political profile of the movement of party disaffection that marked the October 2001 elections. First, we observe that while the abstention rate was relatively homogeneous throughout the country, blank and spoiled ballots were concentrated in the most urban and developed metropolitan districts. These ballots exceeded 20 percent in the city of Buenos Aires, the provinces of Buenos Aires, Santa Fe, Córdoba, and Entre Ríos, and the southern provinces, all of which have substantial middle-class populations. On the other hand, the sum of blank and spoiled ballots fluctuated between 4 percent and 9 percent, with few exceptions, in poorer northern provinces such as Catamarca, Chaco, Corrientes, Formosa, and Santiago del Estero. Negative votes also appear to have been more frequent in more affluent social sectors. In the city of Buenos Aires, these votes reached more than 30 percent in the upper- and upper-middle-class neighborhoods of Palermo, Saavedra, Socorro, Belgrano, and Pilar, while they were below 24 percent in more working-class neighborhoods such as Villa Lugano, Balvanera Oeste, and Concepción. A similar tendency was observed in the districts of Greater Buenos Aires, where negative votes were above 31 percent in the suburbs of San Isidro and Vicente López, and below 18 percent in low-income neighborhoods such as Almirante Brown, Esteban Echeverria, Malvinas Argentinas, Merlo, and Moreno (Cheresky 2003).

Analyses of the party affiliation and the destination of vote transfers between the 1999 and 2001 elections reveal the profile of the realignment that occurred in 2001 (Escolar et al. 2002). It can be inferred that APR voters decided en masse to cast blank or spoiled ballots, as this was the choice of 74 percent of those who had voted for Cavallo's party in 1999. Ex-Alianza voters also contributed heavily to the exceptional growth of negative votes. The sum of blank and spoiled ballots (almost four million) exceeded the Alianza's share of the vote, and was surpassed only by the number of PJ votes.[2] However, voters who deserted the governing Alianza also channeled their discontent in two other directions: small leftist parties (such as Trotskyites, revolutionary socialists, and communists), which doubled their levels of prior support, and Argentines for a Republic of Equals (ARI), a new left-of-center party that was created shortly before the

2. Between 1983 and 1999, spoiled votes had fluctuated between 0.5 percent and 1.5 percent of votes cast, and blank votes varied between 2 percent and 4 percent. In 2001, the former reached 12.5 percent and the latter 9.4 percent. Meanwhile, the abstention rate, which had averaged between 15 percent and 20 percent during the 1983–99 period, reached 27 percent in 2001.

election, to morally condemn traditional political leaders. Many ARI voters were probably former FREPASO supporters.

To sum up, electoral dissent was common in more urban and prosperous areas, among the middle class, and in political terms, among non-Peronist voters, particularly APR and FREPASO supporters. This enables us to question a rapidly popularized explanation of the outcome of the October 2001 elections, which held that it demonstrated a general lack of confidence in political parties. Indeed, the leading proponents of this interpretation came from the center-right electorate and center-left circles. By means of their highly defiant electoral choices and their agenda-setting ability, these groups converted their respective dissatisfaction with the existing partisan alternatives into a crisis of party representation in Argentina. We know, however, that despite its importance, the crisis was far from a generalized phenomenon in the party system. Against the backdrop of a drastic shrinkage in party identification, the PJ was able to survive the avalanche of negative votes.

The 2001 electoral results showed the paradoxical nature of the transformations of party democracy in Argentina. Indeed, changes in the electorate's political culture eventually punished the very parties that initially epitomized those changes: the APR and FREPASO. These parties were more vulnerable because they did not possess a reserve of loyal voters to shield them from the consequences of their performance in government. The APR and FREPASO were examples of a distinct form of representation that might be called political opinion movements. In these movements, the bonds of trust that support the representatives are both fragile and demanding, because they depend on the accomplishment of short-term results for voters who evaluate their performance independently and without restraint. Prevailing ties within the PJ are different. The greater degree of loyalty of the Peronist electorate throughout the years has rested on two pillars. The first is a party identification grounded in a dense web of historically grounded ties of solidarity. Second, this party identification is cemented by clientelistic political machines that gave the PJ a significant advantage in maintaining territorial control (Calvo and Murillo, this volume). Under such circumstances, the growing wave of protest voting that brought about the virtual disappearance of FREPASO and the APR, and dealt a hard blow to the UCR, did not severely damage the PJ.

CONCLUSION: AN UNBALANCED PARTY SYSTEM

After twenty years of existence, Argentine democracy has produced two divergent phenomena. On the one hand, it has generated a mass of critical citizens and civic activism that maintains a state of high alert toward the behavior and performance of politicians. On the other hand, the political dynamics generated by greater expectations from democracy have contributed to a crisis of party representation. The country thus faces an ironic disjuncture: the positive aspects of the crisis for the improvement of the quality of democracy are also the cause of a negative institutional impact, such as an unbalanced party system. In order to appreciate the magnitude of this crisis, it is necessary to consider an additional aspect of the present situation. In contrast with Peru and Venezuela, the crisis of party representation in Argentina did not bring about the collapse of the party system in its entirety (Levitsky and Murillo 2003). Rather, the crisis has resulted in an unbalanced party system with one relatively well-established pole, the PJ, and another pole in a state of flux, the non-Peronist parties.

Examining the asymmetries between these two poles, we see that the UCR's decline has resulted in the loss of the only other major force with a strong national presence besides the PJ. Although it is premature to claim that the UCR has disappeared altogether, the party's capacity to offer a viable electoral alternative appears to have been substantially diminished. Many Radicals have returned to local bastions in the provinces and the municipalities. Others have left the party in search of other vehicles through which continue to their political careers. In the wake of the collapse of the APR and FREPASO, ex-Radical politicians have sought to occupy the areas available in the center-right and the center-left. Such is the case of Ricardo López Murphy, an orthodox economist whose brief stint as De la Rúa's minister of the economy was cut short by widespread opposition to his austerity measures. López Murphy left the UCR and formed the Federal Movement for Renewal (MFR). Another Radical, Elisa Carrió, a member of the legislature who gained notoriety for her anticorruption crusade during the Alianza administration, founded ARI, which occupied the center-left space in the political spectrum.

However, these party endeavors, which appeared to restore a kind of equilibrium to the party system, face two problems that have hindered development and stability of similar political initiatives in the past. First, such initiatives are above all expressions of opinion movements, rather than party organizations. As such, they still lack structure and embeddedness in the electoral arena. At their inception, they depended heavily on the support of well-known political figures that have gained visibility through media coverage. Thus, these new parties are at the mercy of their leaders' moods and decisions, as well as the volatility of their highly independent electorates. Second, Argentina's federal and electoral systems present obstacles to new party initiatives. The parties that have previously aspired to represent the center-right and center-left voters, like the UCEDE, PI, FREPASO, and the APR, have shared a similar challenge. All of these parties emerged in more populated and developed provinces but failed to gain a foothold in peripheral regions. In part, this is because these new parties lacked national organizations and thus never established a real presence in the interior. Yet their failure was also a product of highly disproportional electoral systems at the national and provincial levels (Calvo et al. 2001), which heavily favor larger parties. These institutional arrangements have helped consolidate PJ control in most of the poorer provinces in the country.

Beyond the institutional obstacles to the growth and consolidation of new non-Peronist parties, the precariousness of their organizational structures and their limited territorial presence, there is an additional problem that creates a serious party imbalance: fragmentation. The capacity of non-Peronist parties to compete in the electoral arena hinges on their ability to form coalitions that bind the non-Peronist electorate together, as happened with Alfonsín in 1983 and the Alianza in 1999. At present, ideological cleavages have fractured the non-Peronist pole at the national level. The contrast to the PJ is, in this respect, striking. Within the PJ, one can identify different ideological orientations, as might be expected given the scope and heterogeneity of its constituencies. However, largely thanks to Peronism's organizational structure, this has not seriously affected the party's unity (Mustapic 2002). The PJ's territorial decentralization into autonomous (usually provincial) power centers, its low levels of institutionalization, and arrangements that facilitate the coexistence of leaders and cadre maintaining conflicting positions have worked to avoid lasting political schisms.

Given the current weakness and fragmentation of non-Peronist parties, it is foreseeable that in the new political cycle that began with the 2003 presidential election, the PJ will once again be the dominant political party. If this is indeed the case, what remains to be seen is how and in what ways the critical mass of alert and demanding citizens that emerged over the past twenty years—and its claims for a more transparent and accountable party-centered democracy—will make its political presence felt.

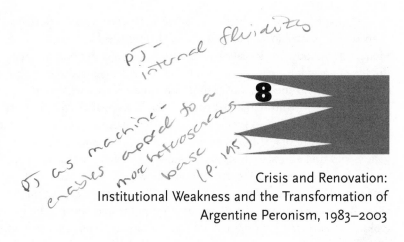

PJ – internal fluidity

PJ as machine – appeal to a class not because (p. 195)
enables

8

Crisis and Renovation: Institutional Weakness and the Transformation of Argentine Peronism, 1983–2003

Steven Levitsky

Few political parties have confounded conventional analysis as repeatedly as the Peronist Partido Justicialista (PJ) of Argentina. On the one hand, the PJ has been characterized by an extraordinary degree of internal conflict and disorder. Throughout its history, Peronism has suffered severe institutional crises, frequent schisms, and occasional descents into chaos. At times, these internal conflicts have spilled over into the larger polity, with grave consequences for democratic institutions. On the other hand, the PJ has demonstrated an extraordinary capacity to adapt and survive during periods of crisis. Peronism survived Perón's overthrow in 1955, nearly two decades of proscription (1955–72), and the death of its founder in 1974. Under the presidency of Carlos Menem (1989–99), the traditionally statist PJ survived a profound socioeconomic crisis by transforming itself—virtually overnight—into a politically successful vehicle for carrying out radical market-oriented reforms.

This chapter examines the causes and consequences of the PJ's striking flexibility. It focuses on Peronism's distinctive organizational structure. Although the PJ is a well-organized party with deep roots in working- and lower-class society, its internal structure is weakly institutionalized.[1] Unlike most established labor-based parties, it lacks stable internal rules and even a minimal bureaucracy. This internal fluidity is simultaneously a

1. McGuire (1997) has made a similar argument.

cause of the PJ's propensity for internal crisis and a source of its extraordinary flexibility.

The chapter shows how the PJ's weakly institutionalized structure shaped its capacity to respond to crises during the Menemist and post-Menemist periods. In the late 1980s and the 1990s, Peronism's internal fluidity enabled it to adapt successfully to the challenges posed by working-class decline and the crisis of import substitution industrialization (ISI). The PJ's weakly institutionalized party-union linkage allowed reformers to dismantle traditional mechanisms of labor participation, which enabled the party to both appeal to a new constituency (independent middle-class voters) and find a new basis—clientelism—with which to maintain an old one (the urban poor). At the same time, the weakness of party leadership organs and the absence of stable norms of intraparty accountability provided President Menem with substantial room for maneuver as he undertook a radical market-oriented reform program. The post-Menemist period, and particularly the crisis triggered by President Fernando De la Rúa's resignation in December 2001, revealed the costs of the PJ's weak institutionalization. Lacking an effective authority structure and binding internal rules of the game, Peronism fell into a severe internal conflict that exacerbated the crisis and further weakened Argentina's democratic institutions. Yet internal fluidity also helped the PJ survive the 2001–2 crisis, for it facilitated another far-reaching renovation of the party leadership and platform.

INSTITUTIONALIZATION AND PARTY ADAPTATION

Institutionalization is a process by which rules and procedures come to be widely known, accepted, complied with, and expected to endure, often to the point of being "taken-for-granted" (Jepperson 1991). It allows individual actors to "go about the everyday process of making exchanges without having to think out exactly the terms of an exchange at each point and in each instance" (North 1990a, 83). Thus, actors often comply with institutionalized rules without evaluating the immediate costs and benefits of such compliance (Zucker 1977, 728). Institutionalization is critical to the efficient functioning of complex organizations (Nelson and Winter 1982, 74–110; March and Olsen 1989, 24). In an institutionalized context, actors develop stable expectations about how others will behave, which lengthens their time horizons, enhances mutual trust, and facilitates cooperation (O'Donnell 1994, 57–59). By contrast, when organizational rules are ambiguous, contested, or constantly changing, actors cannot form stable expectations. Consequently, time horizons tend to be shorter, mutual trust lower, and cooperation more difficult to sustain. In such a context, actors must invest substantial time and energy into resolving internal conflicts, settling procedural disputes, coordinating activities, and monitoring others' behavior. The result is often inefficiency, disorder, and even chaos.

Yet institutionalization also inhibits organizational change (Zucker 1977). It narrows the options considered by actors and raises the social, psychic, and material costs of departing from established patterns (March and Olsen 1984, 740). In such a context, sudden or far-reaching change tends to be widely resisted (Zucker 1977, 729), and organizational change tends to take place "slowly and laboriously" (Panebianco 1988, 58). Institutionalized organizations thus tend to be "sticky," in that they do not change as quickly as underlying preferences and power distributions. During periods of crisis, such "stickiness" may severely handicap organizations. Decision makers tend to consider a narrower range of alternatives (Nelson and Winter 1982, 74–83), none of which may be appropriate in a context of crisis or rapid change. Even when leaders manage to devise new strategies, established routines and decision rules may limit their capacity to implement them. By contrast, weakly institutionalized organizations may be better equipped to respond to environmental shocks. Because more is "up for grabs" in the short run, actors have greater room for maneuver in searching for and carrying out adaptive strategies, and because rules and procedures are not buttressed by vested interests or taken-for-grantedness, they have less difficulty modifying them when it serves their short-term goals. Hence, lags between institutional outcomes and underlying distributions of power and preferences can be closed with relative ease.

Institutionalization limits political parties' adaptive capacity in at least two ways. First, it inhibits leadership turnover, which is widely associated with party adaptation (Panebianco 1988, 242–44; Harmel and Janda 1994, 266–67). Where party hierarchies are institutionalized, usually in the form of bureaucracies, leadership renovation tends to be slow. Old guard leaders become entrenched in the party hierarchy, and internal recruitment filters and established career paths ward off reformist movements (Kitschelt 1994b, 17–21). Bureaucratic hierarchies thus tend to take the form of oligarchies, in which leadership turnover occurs gradually, and "never through a sudden, massive, and extended injection of new blood" (Schonfeld 1981, 231). Such organizations tend to be dominated by what Downs (1967, 96–97) calls "conservers," or middle-level officials who "tend to be biased against any change in the status quo." By contrast, weakly institutionalized parties generally lack recruitment filters and bureaucratic career paths. As a result, old guard leaders may be easily removed from the hierarchy, and reformers may enter the party and rise up through its ranks with relative ease. Such leadership fluidity tends to facilitate party change (Kitschelt 1994a, 214; Roberts 1998, 47).

Second, institutionalization limits party leaders' strategic autonomy. In an institutionalized setting, established routines limit the array of options considered by party leaders, which may delay the search for appropriate responses to environmental shocks. Moreover, most institutionalized parties possess complex rules of internal accountability, such as the division of leadership into competing powers and requirements that leadership decisions be approved by lower-level bodies (Strom 1990, 577–78; Kitschelt 1994a, 223–25). By contrast, weakly institutionalized party structures yield greater strategic autonomy. The absence of established bureaucratic routines allows party leaders to consider a wider range of strategic options, and the absence of established mechanisms of accountability gives leaders greater room for maneuver in carrying out strategies (Harmel and Svasand 1993, 68).

In sum, although the absence of stable rules, routines, and hierarchies is often a source of inefficiency for parties during normal times, it may facilitate adaptation during periods of environmental crisis or change. Although there is no guarantee that weakly institutionalized parties will adopt appropriate strategies in response to external crises, their loosely structured organizations create a greater opportunity for adaptation than exists in highly institutionalized parties.

THE PJ AS A WEAKLY INSTITUTIONALIZED MASS PARTY

Peronism is characterized by a distinctive combination of organizational strength and institutional weakness. On the one hand, the PJ is a well-organized mass party with deep roots in working- and lower-class society. Like many European labor-based parties, it possesses an extensive grassroots organization, a large membership and activist base, and a stable electoral base rooted in strong party identities. Yet unlike most European parties, the PJ's mass organization is strikingly fluid. Peronism lacks even a minimal bureaucratic structure, and the rules and procedures that govern its internal life are widely contested, frequently circumvented, and routinely modified in line with the short-term goals of party leaders.

The roots of Peronism's institutional fluidity lie in its charismatic origins.[2] The original Peronist party was largely a personalistic vehicle for

2. On Peronism's charismatic origins, see Ciria 1983, Tcach 1990 and 1991, Torre 1990, and McGuire 1997.

Juan Perón. During the first Perón government (1946–55), the party was repeatedly reorganized from above, and its hierarchy, organizational structure, and internal rules and procedures were subject to the whims of its founder. Institutional weakness persisted after Perón's overthrow. Unlike other banned working-class parties such as the French and Chilean communists and the German social democrats, which survived periods of repression by creating disciplined, hierarchical organizations, Peronism fell into a decentralized, anarchic state after 1955 (Levitsky 2003, 42–47). Attempts by union and provincial bosses to build an institutionalized party were derailed by the exiled Perón (McGuire 1997), and consequently, Peronist unions, paramilitary groups, and provincial "neo-Peronist" parties coexisted (and competed) for years without an overarching authority structure or binding internal rules. No single organizational order encompassed Peronist subgroups, and no mechanism existed to coordinate or discipline them. Formal leadership bodies were rarely operative, and when they were, they were often ignored.

In the years following Perón's death, no Peronist leader or faction was able to impose an organizational structure or binding rules of the game. As late as 1984, three different leadership bodies—the PJ's (formal) National Council, a "Superior Council" created by Perón's widow, Isabel, and a "Federal Council" led by Peronist governors—competed for authority over the movement. Although the 1987–89 Renovation process brought a degree of institutional order to the PJ, the Renovators failed to create a functioning hierarchy or effective leadership organs capable of imposing discipline or enforcing the party statutes. As a result, Peronists entered the 1990s bound together by a powerful subculture and identity, but without a functioning party bureaucracy or binding internal "rules of the game."

The contemporary PJ thus remains weakly institutionalized. There is little correspondence between the PJ's statutes and actual behavior within the party. As PJ leaders themselves recognize, the rules and procedures outlined in the party statutes are "openly violated all the time."[3] As one activist put it, "We use the party statutes when they are useful. When they are not useful, we don't use them."[4] Party leaders also routinely modify existing rules and procedures in the pursuit of short-term goals. Thus, the PJ "governs itself by constantly changing the party statutes, or by making

3. Author's interviews with Raúl Roa, former treasurer of the PJ Federal Capital branch, May 12, 1997, Buenos Aires, and PJ legislator Eduardo Rollano, June 24, 1997, Buenos Aires.
4. Author's interview with Daniel Checker, adviser to Senator José Figueroa, September 9, 1997, Buenos Aires.

exceptions."⁵ As a result, the statutes are little more than "a product of the momentary balance of power at any given time."⁶

Three Areas of Institutional Weakness

The weakly institutionalized nature of the PJ organization can be observed in three critical areas: (1) the party's leadership bodies; (2) the party hierarchy; and (3) the party-union linkage.

WEAK LEADERSHIP BODIES

According to party statutes, the National Council is the PJ's supreme day-to-day authority. In practice, however, Peronists have rarely viewed the National Council as an arena for decision-making or a source of binding authority. During Perón's lifetime, "real" authority was vested in the founding leader (even when he did not hold a formal leadership post), and formal leadership bodies were generally viewed as irrelevant. Although the contemporary National Council is formally endowed with substantial decision-making and disciplinary power, this power is rarely exercised in practice.⁷ Indeed, the party's national authorities are routinely ignored, both by lower-level branches and by office-holding party leaders. When the PJ is in power at the local, provincial, or national level, authority in the party tends to concentrate in the executive branch. Party organs "cease to function," and "the government runs the party."⁸ When these organs are controlled by someone other than the sitting executive, they are generally ignored. When the PJ is out of office, power tends to be dispersed among de facto power holders, such as governors and (decreasingly) unions. Decision-making tends to be done informally, at the margins of the National Council.

A FLUID PARTY HIERARCHY

The PJ hierarchy is strikingly fluid. Because Peronism lacks effective external filters, stable career paths, or tenure security in leadership posts, politi-

---

5. Author's interview with Ricardo Morato, former legal representative of the PJ Federal Capital branch, September 26, 1997, Buenos Aires.

6. Author's interview with Deputy Lorenzo Domínguez, September 25, 1997, Buenos Aires.

7. In a 1997 survey of thirty-one National Council members, only three claimed that the National Council "functions as the party statutes say it should," whereas twenty-eight said that it did not (Levitsky 2003, 78).

8. Author's interviews with PJ senator Omar Vaquir, September 24, 1997, Buenos Aires, and Hurlingham mayor Juan José Álvarez, July 18, 1997, Hurlingham, Province of Buenos Aires.

cians may enter the PJ with ease and rise quickly through its ranks. According to one party activist, "One of the great things about Peronism is that . . . any new member can reach the highest level if the opportunity is right. . . . You don't have to go through a long process. In other parties, you have to go through a kind of hierarchical structure. . . . With us, if you are an Argentine citizen, you can be a Peronist leader or candidate."[9]

Indeed, throughout Peronism's history, politicians without any career in the party have "parachuted" into leadership positions. For example, Juan Manuel Abal Medina (1972), Isabel Perón (1974), and José Maria Vernet (1984) ascended to top leadership posts without ever having held a formal position in the party. During the 1990s, outsiders such as automobile racer Carlos Reutemann and pop singer Ramon "Palito" Ortega gained leadership positions only months after joining the party. At the same time, the absence of tenure security in the party hierarchy allows for the rapid removal of old guard leaders. Thus, although party statutes prescribe four-year terms in the National Council, these mandates are rarely respected. Indeed, the PJ's first four acting presidents elected after 1983—Lorenzo Miguel, José María Vernet, Vicente Saadi, and Antonio Cafiero—were removed before the end of the their mandates.

Although the post-1987 Peronist Renovation partially democratized the leadership and candidate-selection process through the introduction of direct primaries, in practice, this process remains weakly institutionalized. In many provinces, internal elections are routinely circumvented by means of "unity lists" that are negotiated or imposed by party bosses (De Luca, Jones, and Tula 2002). In some cases, local party congresses cancel primaries and simply "proclaim" candidates; in others, candidates are imposed by the national leadership.[10] At the national level, although a system of direct elections for the party leadership has been in place since 1987, no such election has ever been held. The first National Council selected after the 1987 reform was "proclaimed" into existence by the party congress, and in 1991 and 1995, the National Council was drawn up by top government officials and later proclaimed by the party congress. Indeed, thirty years after Perón's death and fifteen years after the Peronist Renovation, the PJ leadership has yet to change hands by institutionalized means.

A LOOSELY STRUCTURED PARTY-UNION LINKAGE

Finally, the Peronist party-union linkage is weakly institutionalized. Most established labor-based parties are characterized by a relatively stable and

9. Author's interview, March 4, 1997, Buenos Aires.
10. This was the case in Catamarca, Corrientes, Santa Fe, Tierra del Fuego, and Tucumán in 1991; Corrientes and Tucumán in 1993; Córdoba, Santiago del Estero, and Tucumán in 1994; and Córdoba and San Juan in 1995.

taken-for-granted set of rules and procedures governing trade union participation. Party-union linkages may take the form of formal ancillary organizations, representative bodies within the party leadership (such as the
Labor Bureau in Venezuela's Democratic Action), or rules guaranteeing
the unions a bloc vote in the party congress (as in the British Labour Party).
The PJ-union linkage is strikingly different. Although unions were historically important members of the Peronist coalition, the party-union linkage
was never institutionalized (McGuire 1997; Levitsky 2003). Efforts to institutionalize this linkage, such as those of the Labor Party in the 1940s and
Augusto Vandor in the 1960s, were derailed by Perón (McGuire 1997).

Traditionally, the party-union linkage was based on two informal mechanisms: the "62 Organizations" (or "62") and the *tercio* system. The "62"
functioned as the PJ's "labor branch," representing unions within the
party leadership and nominating unionists for party candidacies and leadership posts. Yet the "62" was a thoroughly informal structure. It was
never mentioned in party statutes, held no formal position in the party
leadership, and lacked an office, a budget, and basic internal rules and
operating procedures (McGuire 1997, 98–99). Similarly, the *tercio* tradition, in which unions were granted a third of party candidacies and leadership posts, was never written into party statutes. Most PJ leaders consider
it a "retrospectively created myth" that is "more folklore than reality."[11]
Although the *tercio* was employed by many PJ branches as late as the mid-
1980s, the system was never rigorously enforced and its rule-like status
was always contested within the party.

The Effects of Weak Institutionalization

The PJ's weak institutionalization is a source of both debilitating crises
and extraordinary flexibility. On the one hand, the PJ's internal fluidity is
costly in terms of organizational cohesion and efficiency. In the absence
of functioning party organs, formal leaderships have great difficulty imposing internal discipline. Orders issued by the National Council are often
ignored by lower-level branches, and although party members who disobey
the leadership are occasionally expelled, these expulsions are rarely enforced.[12] The PJ also suffers low levels of internal trust and cooperation.
Intraparty agreements are routinely broken, alliances are highly unstable,

---

11. Author's interviews with congressional deputies Juan Carlos Maqueda, September 11,
1997, Buenos Aires, and Lorenzo Domínguez, September 25, 1997, Buenos Aires.

12. For example, Perón "expelled" the Montonero guerrillas in 1974, but most Montonero networks never left the party. As Montonero leader Dardo Cabo declared, "No one has
the right to throw us out. No one can fire us!" (De Riz 1981, 153–54).

and "betrayals" are commonplace. Consequently, Peronists must constantly monitor others' behavior and repeatedly renegotiate internal agreements, and party leaders must devote a substantial amount of time and energy to mediating internal conflicts and creating ad hoc rules and procedures to resolve them. During the 1980s and 1990s, this entailed dozens of costly "interventions" (national takeovers) of provincial party branches, occasional court battles when party authorities failed to resolve conflicts, and frequent frenzied, last-minute negotiations so that "normal" institutional processes—such as party congresses and primaries—could take place.

Finally, the absence of stable mechanisms of dispute resolution leaves the PJ vulnerable to severe institutional crises. The PJ suffered contested party congresses every year between 1983 and 1987, was formally split between December 1984 and July 1985, and remained divided, de facto, through November 1987. Schisms are even more frequent at the provincial level. Two or more Peronist parties existed in most provinces throughout the 1960s (Arias and García Heras 1993). In 1973, the party fractured in more than a third of Argentina's provinces, and during the mid-1980s, dissident factions in several major provinces—including Buenos Aires and Córdoba—abandoned the party and competed against it. Overall, nearly half of the PJ's provincial branches divided for at least one election during the 1980s, and nearly a third suffered a schism during the 1990s (Levitsky 2003, 84). In some districts (e.g., Federal Capital, San Juan, Santiago del Estero), two or more Peronist parties competed for several years. These internal conflicts have at times spilled over into the larger polity, often with devastating consequences for democratic institutions. During the early and mid-1970s, for example, violent conflict among Peronist leftists, unions, and right-wing paramilitary organizations overwhelmed the country's fragile political institutions and helped pave the way for a military coup.

Yet weak institutionalization also provides the PJ with a degree of flexibility and innovative capacity that is rarely seen in established mass parties. Whereas highly institutionalized parties tend to be resistant to rapid change, the PJ organization is highly malleable, in that it may be changed quickly in line with the short-term goals of dominant party actors. Change in the party's leadership, strategy, program, and organizational structure may be rapid and thorough, for it tends not to be slowed down by entrenched bureaucracies, routines, decision-rules, or norms of accountability.

Two aspects of the PJ organization are critical to its adaptive capacity. The first is the fluidity of its hierarchy. The absence of a bureaucratic hierarchy permits rapid and thorough leadership change. Peripheral leaders and even outsiders may "parachute" directly into top posts. At the same time, old guard leaders are easily removed. Indeed, PJ leadership changes are often virtual "housecleanings," in which the entire preexisting leadership is replaced. Thus, 80 percent of the National Council Executive Board was replaced in 1985, and 90 percent of the Executive Board was replaced in 1987. Between 1983 and 1987, turnover in the Executive Board was 100 percent. As important as housecleaning is the *threat* of housecleaning. Because old guard leaders lack tenure security in the party hierarchy, maintaining those positions requires that they remain in the good graces of those with "real" power in the party—generally those who hold public office. Thus, the PJ often experiences a "bandwagoning" phenomenon, in which members of defeated factions defect to the winning faction in an effort to avoid losing their positions in the leadership.[13] Because bandwagoning is a safer strategy than holding out, there are few "entrenched bureaucrats" in the PJ. Rather than "conservers," PJ officials become converts.

Second, Peronist officeholders enjoy substantial autonomy from the party hierarchy. Because the PJ's formal leadership bodies lack taken-for-granted authority, and because the party bureaucracy lacks both the resources politicians need to advance their careers and the stable career paths and tenure security needed to preserve them, party leadership bodies tend to be very weak vis-à-vis PJ officeholders. Thus, "control of the state means control of the party."[14] This weakness is reinforced by the absence of any established rules, procedures, or norms of executive accountability to the party. This means that office-holding party leaders such as governors and presidents enjoy substantial room to maneuver as they devise and implement adaptive strategies.

In sum, the PJ exhibits a distinctive combination of organizational strength and institutional fluidity. Whereas bureaucratic mass parties tend to be "sticky," PJ leaders may easily and quickly modify both the party's organization and program in response to environmental challenges. When party rules or organizational forms are perceived to hinder the pursuit of short-term party goals, they can be modified or dismantled without extensive debate. When the composition of formal leadership bodies does not correspond to the underlying distribution of power in the party, they may be quickly recomposed. And when the party program is perceived as un-

13. This dynamic is comparable to the pattern of "strategic defection" identified by Helmke (this volume) in her analysis of the Argentine Supreme Court.

14. Author's interview with former congressional deputy Jorge Arguello, May 19, 1997, Buenos Aires.

dermining its ability to govern or win elections, PJ leaders are relatively unconstrained by entrenched decision rules or norms of accountability when they seek to modify or abandon them. Although a fluid internal structure does not guarantee that PJ leaders will choose appropriate adaptive strategies, it clearly facilitates the search for and implementation of such strategies.

PERONISM'S DUAL TRANSFORMATION IN THE 1980s AND 1990s

The PJ's organizational flexibility was critical to its adaptation and survival during the post-1983 period. Like other labor-based parties in Latin America,[15] the PJ confronted severe coalitional and programmatic challenges during the 1980s and 1990s. On the one hand, its traditional industrial working-class base had eroded. Trade liberalization and economic crisis had decimated the manufacturing sector, which weakened industrial unions, fragmented the working class, and accelerated the growth of the tertiary and informal sectors (Palomino 1987). In this context, Peronism's close ties to the General Labor Confederation (CGT) threatened to bind it to an increasingly narrow social base. Indeed, the PJ's failure to appeal to independent and middle-class voters was a major cause of its unprecedented defeat at the hands of the Radical Civic Union (UCR) in the 1983 presidential election (Cantón 1986, 48–49, 164; Catterberg 1991, 81–82). In the programmatic realm, the debt crisis and the exhaustion of Argentina's inward-oriented economic model raised the costs of the statist and protectionist policies to which most Peronists adhered. The Alfonsín government's failure to resolve the country's mounting economic problems during the 1980s, which culminated in the 1989 hyperinflationary crisis, imposed severe constraints on the Menem government when it took office.

The PJ adapted to these challenges with striking success. The party redefined its relationship with organized labor, dismantling traditional mechanisms of union participation and replacing its union-based linkages with clientelist linkages. By the early 1990s, it had transformed itself from a labor-based party into a machine party in which unions played a relatively minor role. In the programmatic realm, the Menem government underwent a dramatic about-face, abandoning Peronism's traditional program in favor of a radical market-oriented reform program. As the following sections argue, the speed and extent of these changes were facilitated by the PJ's weakly institutionalized party structure.

15. See Roberts 1998, Burgess 1999, and Burgess and Levitsky 2003.

Coalitional Transformation: The De-Unionization of Urban Peronism

The PJ reconfigured its support base beginning in 1983, transforming it-self, in less than a decade, from a de facto labor party into a patronage-based machine. Trade unions dominated the PJ when it emerged from military rule in the early 1980s. In 1983, union bosses imposed the PJ's platform and presidential ticket (Cordeu, Mercado, and Sosa 1985, 27–30) and secured the acting party presidency, leadership of the legislative bloc, and more than a quarter of the party's legislative seats. Yet labor participation was not institutionalized. Rather, it was a product of party leaders' dependence on union resources. Thus, although traditional mechanisms of union participation such as the *tercio* were largely complied with in 1983, they were not formalized in the party statues or widely taken for granted. Indeed, they were often imposed on party leaders by powerful union bosses (Levitsky 2003, 113–14). As a result, they were vulnerable to changes in the distribution of power and preferences in the party.

Such a change occurred after the 1983 election, as politicians who had previously depended on union resources gained access to public office. Despite losing the presidency in 1983, the PJ won twelve governorships, hundreds of mayoralties, and thousands of city council seats. As Peronists established themselves in public office, they substituted state resources for union resources, building independent patronage networks at the margins of the unions. These networks provided the organizational bases for an emerging Renovation faction, which challenged labor's privileged position in the party.

This shift in the distribution of resources translated quickly into organizational change. Peronism's informal mechanisms of labor participation—the 62 Organizations and the *tercio*—collapsed in the face of the Renovation challenge. Rather than accept the "62's" as the PJ's "labor branch," the Renovators dismissed it as "a historical artifact."[16] Renovation-led party branches treated the "Group of 25" union faction as an alternative labor branch, granting the "25," rather than the "62," the right to nominate unionists for PJ legislative candidate lists. Soon other Peronist labor organizations, such as the Menem for President Labor Roundtable and the Mesa de Enlace Sindical, emerged at the margins of the "62," transforming the "62" into an "empty name"[17] that "no one pays any attention to."[18] Renovation-led party branches also openly disobeyed orders

16. *Clarín*, June 19, 1986, p. 12.

17. Author's interview with Lorenzo Minichielo, general secretary of the Quilmes section of the autoworkers' union, 15 May, 1997, Quilmes, Province of Buenos Aires.

18. Author's interview with former CGT general secretary Oscar Lescano, October 27, 1997, Buenos Aires.

from the National Council to employ the *tercio* system (Levitsky 2003, 115), and when the Renovators gained control of the national party, they definitively buried it. In late 1987, a Renovation-dominated party congress replaced the informal *tercio* with a formal system of direct primaries to select party leaders and candidates. No new mechanisms were created to represent labor within the party leadership or guarantee unions a role in the candidate and leadership selection process.[19]

The Renovation process facilitated the urban PJ's transformation from a union-based party into patronage-based machine party. The substitution of primaries for the *tercio* shifted power from the unions to neighborhood brokers (*punteros*) and local party bosses who could deliver votes. PJ politicians organized *punteros* into patronage networks, and these networks eventually replaced the unions as the party's primary linkage to its urban base. As patronage networks proliferated in urban poverty zones, rank-and-file Peronists who had once depended on unions for resources turned increasingly to *punteros*. By the mid-1990s, local patronage organizations had consolidated into municipal and provincial machines that concentrated power in the hands of mayors and governors. These changes effectively removed labor from the leadership and candidate selection process. As former CGT general secretary Saúl Ubaldini put it, "We participate only if the governors say we can participate. . . . The '62' disappeared. The *tercio* disappeared. And logically, with their disappearance, no one is going to come looking for us."[20]

The consolidation of machine politics triggered a precipitous decline in union influence in the PJ. As Table 8.1 shows, the number of union members in the PJ's legislative bloc fell steadily during the 1980s and 1990s, from a high of twenty-nine in 1983 to just three in 2001. And whereas the unions controlled the party presidency in 1983 and held at least a vice presidency through the early 1990s, it was shut out of the party leadership after 1995. Union influence over party strategy declined as well. By the early 1990s, union leaders found that "no one listened" to them in National Council meetings.[21] Although some of the larger unions were able to defend key organizational interests through direct negotiations with the Menem government (Etchemendy and Palermo 1998; Murillo 2001; Et-

19. Although the new statutes reserved 17 of 110 National Council seats for labor, they did not specify who would choose the union representatives or how they would be chosen. In the absence of any (formal or informal) institution to represent labor, the selection of union representatives fell into the hands of the political bosses who drew up the party lists.

20. Author's interview, October 3, 1997, Buenos Aires.

21. Author's interview with the leader of the pharmacy employees' union and National Council member José Azcurra, October 20, 1997, Buenos Aires.

Table 8.1 The erosion of Peronist union representation in the Chamber of Deputies, 1983–2001

	1983	1985	1987	1989	1991	1993	1995	1997	1999	2001
Number of union members in PJ bloc	29	28	22	24	18	10	6	5	4	3
Overall size of PJ bloc	111	101	105	120	120	128	130	119	99	118
Percentage of PJ bloc belonging to union	26.1	27.7	21.0	20.0	15.0	7.8	4.6	4.2	4.0	2.5

SOURCE: Gutierrez 1998, 41–44; author's calculations.

chemendy this volume), their influence over the Peronist leadership and candidate selection, the PJ platform, and party strategy in general, was minimal.

In less than a decade, then, the PJ transformed itself from a de facto labor party into a machine party. This process of de-unionization benefited the party in several ways. In the electoral realm, it enabled the PJ to adapt to an increasingly "postindustrial" electorate by allowing it both to appeal to a new constituency (independent middle-class voters) and find a new basis with which to maintain its old constituency (the urban poor) (Gibson 1997). On the one hand, the erosion of union influence enhanced the autonomy of PJ leaders, which allowed them to broaden the party's electoral appeal. Beginning in 1987, the Renovation-led PJ distanced itself from old guard unions, played down traditional Peronist language and symbols, developed a more professionalized and democratic image, and made unprecedented use of the mass media, professional pollsters, and other modern campaign technologies in an effort to reach independent voters. This outward-oriented strategy was successful. The PJ won the 1987 midterm elections, raising its share of the vote from 35 percent to 43 percent, and two years later, Menem captured the presidency with 49 percent of the vote. Critical to this success was the PJ's improved performance among middle-class voters. Survey data suggest that whereas the UCR defeated the PJ by a two-to-one margin among white-collar employees and a nearly three-to-one margin among students in 1983, the PJ split the white-collar vote and nearly split the student vote in 1989 (Catterberg and Braun 1989, 372).

At the same time, the consolidation of clientelist linkages created new bases upon which the PJ could sustain its ties to the urban working and lower classes. Clientelist organizations are better suited than unions to appeal to the heterogeneous strata of urban unemployed, self-employed, and informal sector workers generated by de-industrialization. In urban zones characterized by high structural unemployment, unions tend to be marginal or nonexistent, and corporate channels of representation are therefore ineffective. A territorial organization, and especially one based on the distribution of particularistic benefits, can be far more effective in such a context. Although the electoral impact of clientelist linkages is difficult to measure, there is some evidence that they helped the PJ retain its traditional vote (Gibson and Calvo 2000).

The PJ's coalitional transformation also enhanced its capacity to undertake market-oriented reforms. First, de-unionization weakened a potential source of intraparty opposition to the Menem program. Peronist union leaders were more critical of market-oriented reforms than were nonunion party leaders. A 1997 survey of Peronist National Council members and union leaders found that whereas 70 percent of Peronist union leaders either partially or fully opposed the Menem government's economic reforms, only 32 percent of nonunion leaders did so (Levitsky 2003, 140–42). Hence, although several large unions remained influential enough to exchange their cooperation for substantial side payments (Etchemendy, this volume), the PJ largely ceased to be a vehicle for channeling union demands. There is little question, then, that labor's virtual disappearance from the PJ hierarchy facilitated the party's shift to the right.

Second, clientelist linkages helped defuse popular sector protest in a context of economic crisis and neoliberal reform. They did so in several ways. First, in low-income areas, PJ clientelist networks distributed a variety of material goods and services and provided channels of access to the state. Local PJ organizations served as "problem-solving networks," obtaining food, medical supplies, disability pensions, and odd jobs—as well as neighborhood services such as street lights and road pavement—for residents of low-income neighborhoods (Auyero 2000; Levitsky 2001). Clientelist networks also provided a degree of social control in urban poverty zones. During periods of crisis, such as the 1989–90 hyperinflation, neighborhood brokers used a combination of persuasion and intimidation to defuse potential protests or riots. The efforts had an important effect. In contrast to the Radical governments that preceded and followed it, the Menem administration never confronted widespread urban rioting or looting.

The PJ's increased reliance on clientelism also generated electoral costs. During the 1990s wealthier and better-educated voters came to asociate Peronism with corruption and inefficiency. This left the PJ vulnerable to reformist challenges, particularly in districts with large middle-class electorates, such as the Federal Capital. Thus, the PJ vote in the capital fell from 32 percent in 1993 to an unprecedented 9 percent in 1999. More ominously, widespread perceptions of corruption—particularly among the middle and upper middle classes—contributed to a dramatic rise in public hostility toward the political elite, which was manifested in the massive protests that shook the country in December 2001. Through 2003, however, Peronism's decline in metropolitan centers was sufficiently offset by its success in peripheral provinces and urban poverty zones for it to remain Argentina's leading political force (Gibson 1997; Gibson and Calvo 2000).

Programmatic Adaptation: Menemism and the PJ's Neoliberal Turn

Weak institutionalization also facilitated the PJ's programmatic shift to the right during the 1990s. After being elected on a populist platform, the

Menem government responded to the 1989 hyperinflationary crisis by launching a radical market-oriented reform program. It eliminated a variety of regulations, price controls, and restrictions on foreign investment, lowered tariff barriers, and privatized nearly all of the country's state enterprises. It also abandoned Peronism's nationalist orientation for a pro-U.S. foreign policy. Rather than downplaying these programmatic reversals, Menem forcefully embraced them, often making dramatic public gestures to highlight his conversion. Thus, the government aligned with traditional Peronist adversaries such as the multinational Bunge y Born and the right-wing Center Democratic Union, chose Peronist Loyalty Day to issue a decree restricting public sector unions' right to strike, and sent troops to support the 1991 U.S.-led war against Iraq.

Although Menem's neoliberal strategy helped to close the government's "credibility gap" with foreign lenders and investors (Gerchunoff and Torre 1996, 736), it was not widely embraced within the PJ. Most Peronist leaders, including party president Antonio Cafiero, sought a more moderate approach (Levitsky 2003, 148–52). Nevertheless, Menem met little intra-party resistance during the 1990s. The PJ leadership made no serious effort to slow down or modify the Menem program, and all internal challenges—such as the Group of Eight in 1990 and José Octavio Bordón in 1993—failed.

Menem's capacity to undertake a radical neoliberal turn was enhanced by two features of the PJ organization: (1) the absence of tenure security in the party hierarchy, which permitted a rapid restructuring of the party leadership and encouraged large-scale bandwagoning to Menemism; and (2) the weakness of party leadership bodies, which allowed Menem to circumvent and even ignore formal mechanisms of accountability.

BANDWAGONING AND THE COLLAPSE OF THE RENOVATION

Menem's initial position vis-à-vis the PJ was strengthened by a process of bandwagoning in 1988 and 1989. In mid-1988, two-thirds of the National Council and the PJ legislative bloc belonged to the center-left Renovation faction. Yet many Renovation leaders—including PJ vice presidents José María Vernet and Roberto García, legislative bloc leader José Luis Manzano, Federal Capital mayor Carlos Grosso, and Córdoba leader José Manuel De la Sota—depended on Menem's support to retain their posts. Immediately after Menem's nomination, Renovation leaders found their positions threatened by Menem loyalists who called for a wholesale housecleaning of the party hierarchy. Because there existed a clear precedent for removing party authorities before the end of their mandates, these calls posed a credible threat. This threat, together with the fact that the Menem administration, not the party hierarchy, controlled access to top public appointments, led most Renovators to conclude that an alliance with Menem was the best means of assuring their political survival.

Menem's victory thus triggered widespread bandwagoning, as scores of Renovators joined the ranks of Menemism. Many ex-Renovators were given top positions in the government.[22] Others became the core of the new dominant faction in the legislature.[23] Although De la Sota attempted to maintain the Renovation as an internal faction, his allies quickly abandoned him. According to Cafiero, "Experience told me that such a faction would be devoured by power. If we won the 1989 election, then surely all the Renovators, or a large number of them, were going to emigrate to Menem's side. . . . I wasn't going to be able to stop this process. . . . Although we had an ideological project, it wasn't strong enough to resist the temptation of power. And power had passed into Menem's hands."[24]

The defection of the "Neo-Menemists" brought about a critical realignment within the PJ, transforming Menemism from a minority faction into a new dominant coalition.

PARTY WEAKNESS AND PRESIDENTIAL AUTONOMY

Menem's strategic autonomy was enhanced by the weakness of the PJ's formal leadership bodies, which limited the capacity of internal critics to question or slow down the reforms. The National Council, which remained in the hands of Menem critics like Cafiero (president) and Vernet (vice president) during the 1989–90 period, did not embrace Menem's neoliberal strategy. Yet because the party leadership lacked institutional means to hold the president accountable, Menem was able to ignore it. The new president never consulted the PJ leadership as he developed his initial economic program, and neither the program nor cabinet appointments were approved by the National Council. Indeed, Cafiero opposed the appointment of a Bunge y Born director as minister of the economy but was ignored.[25] Whenever the National Council held a position that diverged from the government's, Menem bypassed it. For example, he pardoned top military officers jailed for human rights violations despite the National Council's public opposition to the measure,[26] and he pushed legislation through Congress that expanded the size of the Supreme Court

22. These included Carlos Corach, Rodolfo Diaz, Guido Di Tella, and in 1991, José Luis Manzano.

23. These included majority leader José Luis Manzano, Jorge Matzkin (who succeeded Manzano as majority leader in 1991), Oscar Lamberto, and Miguel Angel Toma.

24. Author's interview with former PJ president Antonio Cafiero, October 3, 1997, Buenos Aires.

25. Author's interview with Antonio Cafiero, October 3, 1997, Buenos Aires.

26. *Clarín*, December 27, 1989, p. 12.

from five to nine even though Cafiero had negotiated a more moderate reform with the UCR.[27] In retrospect, Cafiero recognized that the National Council had "no role" in policymaking in 1989 and 1990: "We met weekly, and we kept minutes and other records. . . . But influence over the government? No. . . . I was producing reports and documents that contradicted what the government was doing. So we were ignored. . . . Menem just took off on his own. He didn't consult with anyone. . . . There was no way to make him see the existence of another authority at his side."[28]

In August 1990, Cafiero and Vernet resigned their leadership posts—a year and a half before their terms expired—and were replaced by Menem and his brother Eduardo. The "Menemization" of the National Council closed the gap between the formal party leadership and the real balance of power in the PJ. Although leaves of absence by Carlos and Eduardo Menem left the PJ presidency in the hands of ex-Renovator García between 1990 and 1993, the National Council was largely run by top cabinet officials such as Manzano and Eduardo Bauza. Thus, Bauza, Manzano, and Eduardo Menem developed the party's strategies for the 1991 midterm elections, and when the National Council's mandate expired in 1991, Bauza and Manzano drew up the new party leadership list in the presidential palace.[29] The García-led National Council largely "ratified decisions that had already been made by the executive branch."[30] In the few cases in which it took a position at odds with the executive branch, such as when the body opposed the government's decision to withdraw from the Non-Aligned Movement,[31] it was ignored. García later claimed that there were "three phases in my presidency. In the first phase, I drew up the party communiqués and got them approved by the government before signing them. In the second phase, the government sent me the communiqués, and I revised them and signed them. In the third phase, I read about the party communiqués in the newspapers."[32]

After García's departure in 1993, all top party leaders were either national government officials or governors. Party and government positions became indistinguishable. For example, following Menem's reelection in 1995, the National Council offered rubber stamp support for the execu-

27. *Clarín*, April 8, 1990, p. 13.
28. Author's interview, October 3, 1997, Buenos Aires.
29. Author's interviews with José Luis Manzano, December 5, 1997, Buenos Aires, and Roberto García, June 23, 1997, Buenos Aires.
30. Author's interview with former National Council member Juan José Zanola, October 22, 1997, Buenos Aires.
31. *Clarín*, May 2, 1991, p. 13.
32. Author's interview, June 23, 1997, Buenos Aires.

tive's entire postelection legislative agenda.[33] As one PJ legislator put it, "The National Council doesn't function. There is no debate. There aren't even any meetings. . . . The party is run by the government."[34]

The PJ's programmatic about-face was critical to its political success during the 1990s. The Menem government's stabilization of the economy contributed in an important—and probably decisive—way to the PJ's victories in the 1991 and 1993 midterm elections, as well as to Menem's overwhelming reelection in 1995. The reforms helped the PJ capture independent or conservative-leaning middle-class and upper middle-class voters who had traditionally opposed Peronism (Gervasoni 1998b). These "tactical Menemist" voters provided the PJ's margin of victory in 1991, 1993, and 1995 (Gervasoni 1998b). The Menem reforms also helped the PJ retain its traditional working- and lower-class electorate, albeit for different reasons. Many traditional Peronists were critical of the Menem economic program (Gervasoni 1998b, 32–33; Ostiguy 1998, 165, 464–66) and continued to back the PJ because of a mix of partisan loyalties (Ostiguy 1998) and clientelist benefits (Gibson and Calvo 2000). Yet if Menem had failed to end hyperinflation and restore economic growth, the PJ would have risked suffering an electoral collapse along the lines of APRA in Peru and the AD in Venezuela.

THE CRISIS AND TRANSFORMATION OF POST-MENEMIST PERONISM (1999–2003)

After PJ candidate Eduardo Duhalde was defeated by Fernando De la Rúa of the opposition Alianza in the 1999 presidential election, the PJ fell into a state of fragmentation and disorder. Although Menem remained party president, he and the Menemist-controlled National Council were quickly marginalized, as power passed into the hands of Peronist governors, particularly those of large provinces such as Buenos Aires (Carlos Ruckauf), Córdoba, (José Manuel De la Sota), and Santa Fe (Carlos Reutemann). As in past periods in opposition, no single leader or body could speak authoritatively for the party or impose discipline on provincial bosses. The PJ's disorganized response to the political-economic crisis that hit Argentina in 2001 revealed the costs of this semi-anarchic structure. Lacking a central bureaucracy or a unifying authority figure, Peronism descended into a prolonged internal conflict that eventually spilled over into the larger

33. *Clarín*, December 3, 1995, p. 22.
34. Author's interview with congressional deputy José López, May 15, 1997, Buenos Aires.

polity, further debilitating Argentina's democratic institutions. Yet it also allowed the PJ to once again renovate its leadership and program, which helped the party retain the presidency in 2003.

The Descent into Chaos

Because the vice presidency lay vacant when President De la Rúa resigned in December 2001,[35] it fell to the Peronist-controlled Congress to select an interim president. The PJ was ill-equipped to respond to the crisis. Since 1999, the party had been a loose confederation of ambitious provincial bosses who could neither trust nor impose discipline upon one another. The uncertainty triggered by De la Rúa's resignation narrowed these leaders' time horizons, and in the absence of effective mechanisms to make binding decisions, Peronism descended into a state of near-anarchy. The Peronist-led Congress called new presidential elections for March 2002. Because top PJ bosses did not trust one another in the interim presidency, they selected a relatively peripheral governor, Adolfo Rodríguez Saá of San Luis, to fill the post, with the understanding that he would not participate in the election. Almost immediately, however, Rodríguez Saá abandoned his commitment to leave office in March and began to explore ways of either participating in or postponing the election. This "betrayal" reinforced the distrust among PJ leaders, and when another round of mass protests weakened the new president, Peronist bosses abandoned him. On December 31, he resigned.

Rodríguez Saá's resignation—the second presidential resignation in ten days—threw Argentina into a deep institutional crisis. Once again, the political rules of the game were thrown up for grabs. On January 1 2002, Congress canceled the March 2002 election and appointed Eduardo Duhalde to serve out De la Rúa's term. Duhalde assumed the presidency in a context of heightened political uncertainty. Although elections were scheduled for September 2003, most PJ leaders expected a much earlier election, and some—including Menem, Rodríguez Saá, and José Manuel De la Sota—openly pursued such an outcome. In this context, Duhalde suffered an extreme form of lame duck syndrome in which Peronist bosses, expecting that the interim government would not survive, refused to commit to it.[36] Ultimately, the governors' expectations of early elections proved to be

35. Vice President Carlos "Chacho" Álvarez resigned in October 2000, and the post was never filled.

36. Virtually all of the party's most influential leaders turned down offers to join the government, forcing Duhalde to fill his cabinet with allies from his own province of Buenos Aires (*Clarín*, January 3, 2002).

a self-fulfilling prophecy. In the aftermath of the June 2002 police killing of two protesters in Buenos Aires, a weakened Duhalde moved the election forward by six months.

Although economic recovery and improved governability strengthened Duhalde's position during the second half of 2002, the political rules of the game remained in a state of flux. Peronism, which was widely expected to win the 2003 election, divided over the question of when and how to select its presidential candidate. Menem and Duhalde had been locked in a power struggle since the late 1990s, when Menem fiercely resisted Duhalde's effort to succeed him as party leader. Because Duhalde lacked a viable candidate to compete against Menem in the primary elections prescribed by party statutes, the government sought repeatedly to postpone or cancel the primaries.[37] Two other candidates, Rodríguez Saá and Santa Cruz governor Nestor Kirchner, made it clear that they would not participate in *any* primary and would instead run outside the party. The PJ lacked the means to impose a collective solution to this problem. The party's National Council and Electoral Junta, which were formally responsible for scheduling and overseeing the primaries, had been dormant for years.[38] Moreover, both bodies were controlled by Menemists. As a result, they were ignored.

Lacking an effective authority structure or binding internal rules, the PJ fell into a state of near chaos in which Menemists and Duhaldists repeatedly manipulated existing rules and procedures in pursuit of short-term advantage. Although the Menem-led National Council scheduled primaries for December 2002, Duhalde organized a party congress that not only postponed the primaries but also created a parallel Political Action Committee—to "de facto replace" the National Council as the leadership.[39] Denounced by Menem as an "institutional coup,"[40] the party congress left with the PJ with dual authority structures and competing primary dates.

By late 2002, the PJ stood at the brink of rupture. The PJ's legislative faction had split into three blocs, and both Rodríguez Saá and Kirchner appeared likely to run outside the party. Although primaries were required by party statutes, it was clear that Duhalde and his allies had no intention of allowing such a vote as long as Menem stood a chance of winning it. Unable to choose a candidate, the PJ was forced to adopt a strategy in

---

37. As one government official put it, "As long as we don't have a presidential candidate, there will be no primary" (*Clarín*, November 7, 2002).

38. In fact, the mandate of the Electoral Junta had expired in mid-2002, and its members had been reelected or rejected (*Página/12*, October 17, 2002).

39. *Clarín*, December 6, 2002.

40. Ibid., November 6, 2002.

which it endorsed no candidate and allowed all Peronist presidential contenders to run outside the party. Thus, in January 2003, the PJ congress canceled the primaries and modified the statutes—"for this time only"—to allow Kirchner, Menem, and Rodríguez Saá to run under three different "fronts." As PJ leaders recognized, the party congress had "formalized a schism."[41]

Multiple rounds of institutional manipulation and countermanipulation generated substantial costs, both for the PJ and for Argentine democracy. Prolonged institutional chaos had brought the PJ to the point of rupture and forced Peronists to adopt a conflict-limiting mechanism—multiple candidates—that seriously undermined their own electoral prospects. Peronist candidates had to divide the PJ's state campaign funds in thirds, and no candidate was able to use the PJ label and symbols. Most important, the Peronist vote was divided into three parts, which dramatically reduced the vote of any single PJ ticket and thus put at risk an election that the party had been overwhelmingly favored to win.

The PJ's institutional crisis also imposed severe costs on the larger polity. For one, the prolonged crisis induced government officials, major governors, and legislative leaders to devote an extraordinary amount of time and energy to intraparty politics at a time when Argentina was suffering the worst economic crisis in its history. More than a year of severe intraparty conflict exacerbated the crisis and further eroded Argentina's credibility among international lenders and investors. It also limited the government's capacity to address either the extraordinary social crisis triggered by the economic collapse or the political demands of disenchanted middle sector voters. Finally, the PJ's internal conflict also damaged Argentina's already fragile democratic institutions. Notwithstanding the fixed electoral terms mandated by Argentina's presidential system, the electoral calendar remained up in the air throughout 2002. Moreover, repeated institutional manipulation reinforced the already low levels of public trust in politicians and political institutions. Indeed, the credibility of Argentina's electoral institutions eroded to the point where opposition candidates warned of fraud and called for international observers for the 2003 election.[42]

Out of Chaos, Another Renovation?

Yet the PJ's internal fluidity may also have enhanced its ability to adapt and survive the 2001–2 crisis. As under Menem a decade earlier, the weak-

41. Ibid., January 25, 2003, January 28, 2003.
42. Ibid., February 8, 2003.

ness of the PJ's formal leadership bodies enhanced President Duhalde's strategic flexibility in the face of a deep economic crisis. In 2001–2, the PJ's formal leadership bodies were controlled by Menem, who continued to defend convertibility and back IMF demands for fiscal austerity and debt payment, and who responded to the 2001 crisis by calling for dollarization, or the replacement of the peso with the U.S. dollar. However, the Duhalde government ignored the formal party leadership and moved in a sharply different direction: it ended convertibility, adopted a more independent position vis-à-vis the IMF, and pursued more expansionary fiscal and monetary policies. These programmatic changes, which helped revive the economy in late 2002, could not have taken place had Duhalde been held even minimally accountable to the National Council.

The PJ's internal fluidity also enhanced its capacity to adapt to a changing electoral environment. Because most Argentines associated the 2001 crisis with the market-oriented policies undertaken by the Menem and De la Rúa administrations, public support for such policies declined sharply after 2001. Surveys carried out in the initial months of 2003 found that a growing majority of Argentines adhered to "neostatist" positions.[43] Given that a Peronist government had been responsible for the bulk of Argentina's neoliberal reforms, this shift could be expected to pose a problem for the PJ. Yet as in the past, the PJ's internal fluidity permitted the rise of leaders and candidates with markedly different electoral and programmatic profiles. Although Menem maintained a right-of-center profile during the 2003 electoral campaign, the PJ's other two presidential candidates, Rodríguez Saá and Kirchner, adopted anti-neoliberal platforms. Rodríguez Saá campaigned as a traditional populist, striking alliances with militant union leaders, railing against the IMF, and openly questioning the privatizations of the 1990s.[44] Kirchner positioned himself on the progressive center-left, identifying his candidacy with the election of leftist president Luiz Ignacio (Lula) da Silva in Brazil.[45]

Kirchner's victory in the 2003 presidential election pushed the PJ in a left-of-center direction. Much like Menem in 1989, Kirchner quickly concentrated power in the party as scores of erstwhile Menemists—some of whom had backed neoliberal policies throughout the 1990s—flocked to the pro-government camp. Menem and his allies were pushed to the margins of the party, and many left-of-center Peronists who had been marginal players during the Menem period quickly gained influence.

43. *La Nación*, February 9, 2003.
44. Ibid., February 8, 2003.
45. *Página/12*, January 12, 2003; *La Nación*, January 11, 2003.

With the National Council dormant and the party presidency effectively vacant, Kirchner enjoyed substantial autonomy during his initial months in office. Like Menem in 1989, he used that autonomy to undertake a major programmatic shift. Whereas Menem had aligned the PJ with conservative and economic elites, Kirchner aligned with left-of-center politicians, progressive intellectuals, and human rights groups. He distanced his government from the neoliberal policies of the 1990s, elevated anticorruption to the top of the agenda, and pushed vigorously for the prosecution of military officers involved in past human rights violations. These moves earned the Kirchner government substantial public support during 2003 and 2004—including that of many progressive middle-class voters who had opposed the Menem-led PJ for more than a decade. This infusion of public support contributed to the PJ's overwhelming victory in the fall 2003 legislative and gubernatorial elections.

As it had a decade earlier, then, the PJ's fluid internal structure allowed it to adapt to changing economic and political circumstances by renovating its leadership and undertaking a rapid and far-reaching programmatic change. Although the longer-term policy and electoral consequences of these changes remain uncertain, they were critical to the PJ's capacity to survive the 2001–2 crisis and regain control of the presidency and the legislature in 2003.

CONCLUSION

Peronism has long been characterized by a distinctive combination of organizational strength and institutional weakness. Its internal fluidity has often been a source of inefficiency and disorder, and it has frequently resulted in debilitating institutional crises and schisms. Yet it has also enhanced the party's flexibility, which has at times been critical to Peronism's survival. This chapter explored both sides of the PJ's flexibility. During the 1980s and 1990s, the PJ's fluid internal structure facilitated its adaptation to the challenges of working-class decline and the crisis of import substitution industrialization, which enabled the party to survive—and even thrive—in the neoliberal era. In 2001–2, as in the 1970s, it permitted a descent into internal chaos that badly weakened democratic institutions and diverted the attention of much of the country's political leadership from a profound socioeconomic crisis. In 2003, it appears to have helped the party renovate itself yet again in the wake of the post-Menemist crisis.

The PJ's future direction is uncertain. In the programmatic realm, it is clear that the market-oriented shift of the 1990s was a short-term adaptation, rather than a long-term transformation. Indeed, the Kirchner government's shift to the left suggests that Peronism's programmatic orientation remains very much up for grabs. Peronism's coalitional changes appear to be more permanent. Although the PJ continues to draw the bulk of its support from low-income voters, its working- and lower-class linkages have been thoroughly transformed. In urban areas, union-based linkages have eroded and been replaced by clientelistic linkages. Given the long-term decline of industrial unionism, these changes are unlikely to be reversed. Hence, although the PJ remains Argentina's "party of the poor," its days as a labor-based party are probably over.

A New Iron Law of Argentine Politics? Partisanship, Clientelism, and Governability in Contemporary Argentina

Ernesto Calvo and María Victoria Murillo

As Argentina fell once again into economic recession and political crisis in December 2001, President Fernando De la Rúa fled the Presidential Palace in a private helicopter. Food riots, protests, and severe repression resulted in half a dozen deaths, an unknown number of injured, and the burning of some of the National Congress's quarters. Harassed in restaurants, theaters, and even while walking in the streets, politicians escaped from public view while citizens banged pots and pans, shouting, "Throw everyone out!" This demand united the middle class, who wanted access to their frozen bank accounts, with the unemployed *piqueteros*, who were demanding food and jobs from the state. As a result, for the second time in twenty years, economic crisis and political turmoil led to the resignation of a Radical president in Argentina.

Between 1983 and 2001, Peronists (Justicialist Party, or PJ) and Radicals (Radical Civic Union, or UCR) won two presidential races each, breaking the old "iron law" of Argentine politics: "Only Peronists can win in free and open elections." However, the resignation of both Radical presidents before the ends of their mandates hinted at a new rule: non-Peronist candi-

We are thankful for the comments of Javier Corrales, Jorge Domínguez, Tulia Faletti, Anna Gryzmala-Busse, Frances Hagopian, John Huber, Steve Levitsky, James McGuire, David Samuels, Andrew Schrank, Susan Stokes, and the participants in the conference "Rethinking Dual Transitions: Argentine Politics in the 1990s in Comparative Perspective" at Harvard University.

dates could win the presidency, but they could not govern effectively enough to hold onto it. As a result, the 2001–2 political crisis did not bring about a collapse of the party system as in Venezuela and Peru in the early 1990s, but of the non-Peronist forces (Torre, this volume). Indeed, although the PJ was divided into three presidential "fronts," each with its own candidate, it won the presidency and two-thirds of the votes in the 2003 presidential election. In contrast, the Radical presidential candidate gained less than 3 percent of votes, with two former Radicals taking the rest.

In this chapter, we explain the mechanisms that provide the Peronists with a comparative advantage in governing when they control the national executive, and in sustaining a competitive party machine when they are the opposition. We also show the difficulties faced by non-Peronist executives, who usually lack congressional majorities and hold only a minority of provincial governments. We explain the Peronists' advantage by focusing on the stability of their subnational electoral coalitions and their broader capacity to access and use public resources for electoral gain. That is, Peronists are more effective in using patronage than Radicals are. Along with an electoral system that overrepresents provinces where the PJ vote is concentrated, this comparative advantage in accessing and using public resources consolidates the Peronists' control over a majority of provinces and municipalities even when non-Peronists control the presidency. As a result, non-Peronist presidents are more likely to face policy gridlock and weak support coalitions. When this is combined with Peronists' higher capacity to control social mobilization, it explains why non-Peronist presidents do not finish their mandates.

The chapter is divided into five sections. First, we describe the competitive electoral market established since 1983, to show the Peronist advantages in winning and *retaining* provincial and local governments that provide leverage to Peronist presidents. We explain this advantage by focusing in the second section on Peronism's better access to fiscal resources, and in the third section on the better electoral returns Peronism obtains from investing in public jobs. In the fourth section, we discuss the implications of our findings for democratic governance in Argentina and we conclude in the last section with our contribution to the comparative study of patronage.

THE ARGENTINE ELECTORAL MARKET

Argentina ratified a constitution in 1853 which established a federal system governed by a president and a bicameral legislature. This constitutional design worked with relative stability until the first military coup in 1930. The coup began a fifty-year period of political instability, which eroded the state's capacity to generate stable social expectations. From the time that universal suffrage for males was established in 1912 until President De la Rúa's resignation in December 2001, Argentina had six elected presidents and another six military presidents ousted by military coups. Only four presidents were elected by popular vote in free and fair elections and finished their mandates: Radicals HipólitoYrigoyen (1916–22) and Marcelo T. de Alvear (1922–28), and Peronists Juan D. Perón (1946–52) and Carlos Menem (1989–95 and 1995–99).

During the second half of the twentieth century, Argentine political instability has been associated with the "iron law of Argentine elections" (only the Peronists can win competitive elections) and a lack of partisan alternation of power except through military coups. In this period, the Argentine party system was based on two loosely organized political coalitions: those supporting the Peronist movement and those opposing it. The Peronist movement emerged in the 1940s from a coalition of urban working classes in the most developed areas of the country and local bosses in the most rural provinces.[1] The main opposition to Peronism throughout this period was the UCR, a centrist party that emerged from the urban vote in the early twenty century, and which traditionally represented the middle classes in the most developed and urbanized provinces.[2] From its emergence in 1945 until 1983, the Peronist party won all national elections in which it was allowed to run. This "iron law" of Peronist electoral victories has been used to explain Argentina's recurring military coups in 1955, 1962, 1966, and 1976 (Cavarozzi 1987; O'Donnell 1973).

The return to democracy in 1983 marked the beginning of a period of democratic stability, with competitive elections and effective power alternation in the national executive. Two presidential elections were won by the PJ, and two by Radical candidates. Raúl Alfonsín (UCR) was the first presidential candidate to break the "iron law" when he defeated Peronist Italo Luder in 1983. That electoral defeat drove Peronism into a process of internal restructuring that allowed it to win in 1989 and 1995. In 1999,

---

1. Mora y Araujo (1980a), Smith (1980), and Llorente (1980a) discuss electoral support for Peronism in the 1946 election when Perón was first elected president, showing the support of urban workers in the most developed provinces and an alliance with greater class diversity in the less developed provinces. Mora y Araujo (1980b) and Llorente (1980b) discuss the evolution of this dual coalition after Perón became president until he was reelected in 1973. They show the persistence of this dual support and Peronism's increasing gains in the less developed provinces.

2. The studies mentioned in note 1 compare the electoral coalitions of both parties. David Rock (1975) discusses the origins and evolution of the UCR.

Table 9.1   President's party and congressional control

	Party of the president	Peronist deputies	Alianza deputies	PJ senators	UCR-Alianza senators
1983–1985	UCR	111	129	21	18
		43.7%	50.6%	45.6%	39.1%
1985–1987	UCR	98	129	21	20
		38.4%	50.6%	45.6%	43.5%
1987–1989	UCR	99	114	21	20
		38.4%	44.7%	45.6%	43.5%
1989–1991	PJ	120	90	28	12
		47.1%	35.3%	61.2%	26.1%
1991–1993	PJ	124	84	28	10
		48.6%	32.9%	61.2%	21.7%
1993–1995*	PJ	127	84	28	10
		49.8%	32.9%	61.2%	21.7%
1995–1997*	PJ	131	90	39	20
		51.4%	35.3%	55.7%	28.6%
1997–1999*	PJ	119	106	39	20
		46.6%	41.6%	55.7%	28.6%
1999–2001*	UCR-FREPASO	99	120	39	20
		38.8%	47.0%	55.7%	28.6%

SOURCES: Dirección Nacional Electoral, Ministerio del Interior; Molinelli, Palanza & Sin (1999); Fuertes & Micozzi (2002).

*The number of senators increased from forty-eight to seventy-two.

Fernando De la Rúa, a Radical running as the candidate of a broader alliance, defeated Peronist Eduardo Duhalde. This reinforced the image of a competitive electoral market in Argentina. However, the resignation of both Alfonsín and De la Rúa before the ends of their terms signaled a "new iron law" in which non-Peronist candidates could win the presidency, but not hold it.

Peronism's Electoral Stability at the Subnational Level

To explain partisan differences in governability, we focus on the subnational electoral coalitions that generate the different conditions affecting policy gridlock and the stability of national electoral coalitions for the Peronists and the Radicals. Since the return of democracy in 1983, Peronists have controlled both houses of Congress during Peronist presidential administrations (1989–99 and 2003–) and have controlled the Senate even when they lost the presidency. By contrast, non-Peronist presidents (1983–89 and 1991–2001) won national electoral majorities, but never controlled the Senate and only briefly held a plurality of seats in the lower house (Table 9.1).

Second, Peronist politicians were more able than Radicals to win and retain control of provincial governments (Table 9.2). Since the return of democracy, between two and seven Radicals have won in a given year's gubernatorial elections, whereas between twelve and seventeen Peronists have won. Moreover, whereas the UCR has only maintained control over the governorship of one province—Rio Negro—in the four elections since 1983, the PJ has kept the governorships of eight provinces, thereby enhancing the stability of subnational electoral coalitions.

Finally, the predominance of Peronists at the local level was so great that even in 1999, when they lost the presidency, they won almost half the municipalities, whereas the Alianza, a UCR-FREPASO electoral coalition, won only a third—despite its presidential victory. Additionally, different patterns emerge in comparing the richer and more populated metropolitan provinces in the center of the country, with the poorer and less populated ones of the periphery (Gibson and Calvo 2000). In 1999 the Peronists obtained 50 percent of municipalities in the metropolitan provinces and the Alianza 41 percent, whereas in the periphery the Peronists won 40 percent of municipalities and the Alianza 22 percent. This difference hints at the importance of electoral geography, which will be discussed later.

In short, Peronism's subnational dominance made political and legislative gridlock more likely to emerge under non-Peronist presidents, thereby contributing to the new "iron law" of governance in Argentina. As Jones and Hwang (2005) have shown, the party that controls both chambers is almost never defeated in a congressional vote. However, both of the post-1983 Radical presidents, Alfonsín and De la Rúa, lacked control of the Senate and consequently suffered important political setbacks when trying to pass labor legislation. In 1984, Alfonsín sent a bill to Congress to reform the corporatist trade union law that was defeated in the Senate. The failed reform prompted the reunification of the Peronist labor movement, which organized thirteen general strikes over the next four years, undermining the Alfonsín's government's economic policies. Similarly, De la Rúa sent a bill to reform labor legislation in 2000 and surprisingly obtained its approval from the PJ-controlled Senate. Soon afterward, however, allegations that the Radicals had used bribery to achieve this goal led to the resignation of Vice President Carlos Álvarez and the subsequent dissolution of the governing coalition. In addition to the legislative effect of Peronist majorities, Peronist control of most governorships also affected the capacity of Radical presidents to achieve fiscal restraint (see Eaton, this volume).

Peronist subnational coalitions and their legislative effects in generat-

Table 9.2 Parties winning gubernatorial elections (1983 to 1999)

Province	1983	1987	1991	1995	1999
Buenos Aires	UCR	PJ	PJ	PJ**ntPJ	PJ
Catamarca	PJ	PJ	Frente Cívico y Social (UCR)*	Frente Cívico y Social (UCR)	Frente Cívico y Social (UCR)
Córdoba	UCR	UCR	UCR	UCR	PJ
Corrientes	Autonomista Liberal	Autonomista Liberal	(federal intervention)	PAL/Partido Nuevo**	PJ
Chaco	PJ	PJ	Acción Chaquena	UCR	UCR
Chubut	UCR	PJ	UCR	UCR	Alianza
Entre Ríos	UCR	PJ	PJ	PJ	Alianza
Formosa	PJ	PJ	PJ	PJ	PJ
Jujuy	PJ	PJ	PJ	PJ	PJ
La Pampa	PJ	PJ	PJ	PJ	PJ
La Rioja	PJ	PJ	PJ	PJ	PJ
Mendoza	UCR	PJ	PJ	PJ	Alianza
Misiones	UCR	PJ	PJ	PJ	PJ
Neuquen	MPN	MPN	MPN	MPN	MPN
Río Negro	UCR	UCR	UCR	UCR	UCR
Salta	PJ	PJ	Pdo. Ren. Salteno	PJ	PJ
San Juan	Pto. Bloquista	Pto. Bloquista	PJ	PJ	Alianza
San Luis	PJ	PJ	PJ	PJ	PJ
Santa Cruz	PJ	PJ	PJ	PJ	PJ
Santa Fe	PJ	PJ	PJ	PJ	PJ
Santiago del Estero	PJ	PJ	PJ	PJ	PJ
Tierra del Fuego	***	***	Mopof	Mopof	PJ
Tucumán	PJ	PJ	PJ	Fuerza Repub.	PJ
Total PJ	12	17	14	14	15
Total UCR/ Alianza	7	2	4	5	7

SOURCES: Ministry of the Interior.

*1991 Intervention before the election.

**PAL from 1993 to 1995 and Partido Nuevo from 1995 to 1997.

***Tierra del Fuego was not a province.

ing divided governments has thus often limited presidential power in Argentina, which is critical to explaining democratic governance (or the lack of it) since the 1983 democratic transition. In the following sections, we explain the subnational dominance of Peronism by exploring the comparative electoral advantage of patronage spending.

ACCESS TO PATRONAGE IN ARGENTINA: ELECTORAL AND FISCAL INSTITUTIONS

Two different mechanisms worked to provide Peronism with an electoral advantage in controlling Congress and provincial governorships after 1983: (1) electoral rules, which overrepresented the sparsely populated provinces and restricted the entrance of third parties in those provinces, and (2) the geographic concentration of the Peronist vote in these provinces. These two factors enhanced the party's access to fiscal resources so that it could maintain and expand its subnational dominance. Together, they explain Peronism's greater electoral stability, as well as its better access to public resources.

Electoral Institutions and Geographic Overrepresentation

Argentina's electoral rules, established by military decree during the 1983 transition, benefit the less populated provinces. Twenty-four provinces serve as electoral districts for the 257 members of the Chamber of Deputies and the 72 members of the Senate (three per province). Each province is represented in the Chamber of Deputies in proportion to its population, provided that no district receives fewer than five deputies or fewer legislators than its share during the 1973–76 democratic period. As a result, the provinces in the least populous quartile (Catamarca, La Rioja, San Luis, La Pampa, Santa Cruz, and Tierra del Fuego) have 3.9 percent of the population and 11.7 percent of the seats in the Chamber of Deputies (and 25 percent in the Senate). In contrast, the province of Buenos Aires, which has 39 percent of the national population, has 27 percent of the deputies and three senators.[3] Hence, a third of the population in the smaller provinces elects almost half the seats.[4]

3. Prior to 1991, Tierra del Fuego was not a province, and the City of Buenos Aires was a federal district. Prior to the 1994 constitutional reform, there were two instead of three senators per province and the president was elected by an electoral college whose members doubled the number of senators and deputies of every province.

4. According to Samuels and Snyder (2001, 661–62), Argentina ranks twelfth in the world in lower-chamber malapportionment and first in terms of upper-chamber malapportionment. Cabrera (1996) and Gibson, Calvo, and Falleti (2001) analyze the impact of electoral overrepresentation in legislative elections.

Moreover, as a result of the closed party ballot with proportional representation system used for legislative elections, as well as population differences among provinces, the number of political parties with legislative representation ranges from more than six in the city of Buenos Aires to close to one in small provinces such as La Rioja and Santiago del Estero. Whereas the province of Buenos Aires elects thirty-five deputies in midterm legislative elections, the other fourteen provinces elect only two or three. As a result, the party that wins 50 percent of the vote gets around 56 percent of seats in the large provinces, and 72 percent in the less populated provinces. The number of effective legislative parties decreases when provinces elect fewer legislators, because there are fewer seats to distribute. Therefore, a small number of parties in the least populated (and most overrepresented) provinces receive more seats per vote than a greater number of parties competing in the larger (and underrepresented) provinces.

In short, the electoral system benefits the PJ because of the geographic distribution of its constituencies. It allows the PJ to win more seats per vote than the UCR and helps explain both the PJ's electoral advantage (in winning provincial governorships and Senate seats regardless of the outcome of presidential elections) and its more stable lower-house coalitions.

Fiscal Institutions, Access to Public Funds, and Peronist Bias

Electoral institutions and the geography of the Peronist vote give the PJ a partisan advantage over the UCR. This advantage grants the PJ greater access to patronage resources, which in turn foster subnational electoral stability. Peronists are better able than Radicals to extract and thereby utilize fiscal resources for electoral gain. This advantage hinges on the distributive nature of Argentina's federal institutions and its provinces' territorially based income inequalities. That is, thanks to fiscal federal institutions, Peronist control of Congress provides the party with more resources for political spending, which provincial and local executives can use to maintain their incumbency.

Argentina's fiscal federal institutions have evolved since 1934, when the provinces agreed in Congress to delegate the authority for levying and collecting taxes to the federal government. Using a revenue-sharing formula determined by Congress, centrally collected resources are divided between the federal and provincial governments (see Eaton, this volume). As Eaton explains, during the democratic period, the share of GDP controlled by provinces grew while that controlled by the federal government declined, even discounting public debt for both levels of government. The fact that the provinces control a larger share of the fiscal pie underscores the importance of provincial governorships for getting access to public monies; however, the Peronist advantage in obtaining fiscal resources is based not only on its broader electoral success at the provincial level, but also on the fact that the distribution of fiscal monies is biased in a way that favors Peronist-controlled provinces.

We show the existence of a pro-Peronist bias in the allocation of resources to the provinces using a pooled cross-sectional data set of economic and political provincial indicators. Our analysis shows that Peronist-controlled provinces are able to extract greater federal resources than their UCR counterparts, even when controlling for differences in income, population, and overrepresentation generated by the electoral system.

The data set includes cross-sections of the twenty-four provinces and the city of Buenos Aires for the years 1987, 1990, 1995, and 2000. Two years were under UCR presidents (1987 and 2000) and the other two were under Peronist presidents (1990 and 1995).[5] In order to test for the existence of a partisan bias in the allocation of fiscal resources, we analyze the impact of the Peronist and UCR vote on (1) the *share of provincial expenditures* financed by the federal government, and (2) the *relative share of fiscal resources* (revenue-sharing) received by each province. The measurements of federal government financing and relative revenue-sharing ratio are similar to those used by Gibson and Calvo (2000), Remmer and Wibbels (2000), and Saiegh and Tommasi (1999a).

> *Share of expenditures financed by the federal government:* describes the percent of province *i*'s total expenditures financed by both revenue sharing and other special transfers from the federal government.
>
> *The relative revenue-sharing ratio:* Measures province *i*'s share of the total federal resources over its population share.

We then entered the PJ vote share and the UCR-Alianza vote share with the usual controls for income, population, and overrepresentation.

The independent variables in the model include the UCR and Peronist vote for province *i* and the usual controls for explaining revenue sharing and federal financing: population share, income, and voting power of province *i*. Because the revenue-sharing formula in Argentine has population and income components, we introduce variables measuring the median voter's income and the population of every province. To capture the elec-

---

5. Although it would be preferable to also use 1985, a year in which the UCR held as many governorships as in 2000, data limitations lead us to use 1987. Given that a significant departure from previous revenue-sharing strategies takes place in 1988, we think that the sample remains adequate.

Table 9.3   Revenue sharing, federally financed expenditures, and the Peronist vote

	Percentage of provincial spending financed by the federal government (ln)	Relative revenue-sharing ratio
PJ vote share (ln)	0.28**	0.39***
	(0.11)	(0.11)
Alianza vote share (ln)	−0.04	−0.02
	(0.08)	(.07)
Median income (ln)	−1.03***	−0.67***
	(0.17)	(0.17)
Overrepresentation (Dip)	0.03	0.07**
	(0.03)	(0.034)
Population (ln)	−0.20***	−0.44***
	(0.04)	(0.04)
1990	1.14***	0.44**
	(0.22)	(0.22)
1995	−0.02	0.45***
	(0.09)	(.094)
2000	−0.04	0.68***
	(0.09)	(0.09)
Constant	7.89***	7.77***
	(1.29)	(1.25)
R^2	0.63	0.869
N	87	87

NOTE: OLS estimates with standard errors in parenthesis. *Significant at the 0.1 level, **Significant at the 0.05 level, ***Significant at the 0.01 level. PJ vote describes the share of Peronist vote in Province i. Alianza vote describes the share of the Alianza vote in Province i. Median-income describes the median income of the economically active population (EPH, INDEC). Overrepresentation describes the share of representatives of province i over the share of population of province i. Natural logs allow quantities to be interpreted as relative change, % of change in the dependent variable per 1% change in the independent variables (elasticities).

toral power of different provinces, we introduce a variable measuring the degree of electoral overrepresentation of every province i voter. The measure of overrepresentation is the share of legislators in province i over the share of population of province i, with larger values representing larger voting power. To render the results more readily interpretable, natural logarithms were used for both the dependent and independent variables.

Table 9.3 shows both positive and significant effects from the Peronist vote on both the amount of federally financed expenditures and on revenue sharing. In fact, a 1 percent increase in the Peronist provincial vote leads to a 0.28 percent increase in the percent of expenditures financed by the federal government and a 0.39 percent increase in revenue sharing. As expected, the analyses show a strong, negative relationship between the median voter's income and both dependent variables: the share of expendi-

tures financed by the federal government and the amount of revenue sharing received by the province. A 1 percent decline in median income also
leads to a 1.03 percent increase in federal financing and a 0.67 percent
increase in revenue sharing. Moreover, overrepresentation has a positive
effect on the relative revenue-sharing ratio, thereby explaining why the
four most populous provinces, which account for 67.4 percent of the population and 71.1 percent of the provincial share of the gross provincial product, only received 44 percent of federal revenue transfers.

To summarize, Table 9.3 shows that, regardless of who controls the
presidency,[6] and even controlling for overrepresentation, Peronist-controlled provinces received higher levels of federal funding for their local
expenditures and a larger share of revenue-shared resources than those
controlled by representatives of the UCR-FREPASO Alianza.[7] By contrast,
larger Alianza vote contingents have little impact on federal financing and
the relative revenue-sharing ratio. Hence, the impact of electoral overrepresentation and the geography of PJ voters favor Peronist access to fiscal
resources. As a result, the combination of the geographic distribution of
Peronist voters and federal institutions give Peronist incumbents an advantage over Radical ones. Peronists gain access to 70 percent of all provincial expenditures and 69 percent of all provincial employment—equivalent
to 945,000 public employees in 2001—and are thereby able to organize
patronage to maintain their electoral predominance.

COMPARATIVE ADVANTAGES OF PATRONAGE IN ELECTORAL
RETURNS

While the previous section establishes the PJ's advantage in accessing public resources for patronage, this section shows that not only do Peronists
have broader access to public resources; they also use them more effectively to get reelected. In other words, Peronist local incumbents get
greater electoral returns from the same resources invested in patronage
and are thereby more likely to keep their voters than are Alianza local
incumbents. We explain the greater electoral efficiency of the Peronists'
use of patronage by focusing on its constituencies' greater dependency on

6. The year dummies already reflect two Peronist administrations (1990, 1995) and two
UCR administrations (the 1987 baseline, and 2000). The models presented were robust to
different specifications, and Hausman tests conducted using a PJ president dummy and
interacting with the PJ and Alianza vote share were not statistically significant.

7. The dependent variables are UCR votes for the 1987 and 1990 elections, the sum
of UCR and FREPASO votes for the 1995 election, and their coalition's votes for the 1999
election.

public monies, as well as on a partisan effect resulting from historical ties between Peronism and its low-income constituencies.

Efficiency Advantages in Using Patronage at the Provincial Level

Using the same cross-sectional provincial data set summarized in Table 9.3, we now turn our attention to explaining the impact of patronage on the PJ and UCR vote at the national level. As before, we pooled the votes for the UCR and FREPASO for the 1995 election. We also included dummies to estimate the effect of incumbency—for both incumbent governors and president—and introduce indicators of income, public employment, and changes in the effective number of competing parties.

The dependent variables shown in Table 9.4 are the *percent of congressional votes* obtained by Peronism (models 1 and 2) and UCR-Alianza (models 3 and 4) in every province *i* and year *j*. The explanatory variables are (1) incumbent governor, a dummy variable indicating whether the governor is Peronist or not (models 1 and 2) or UCR-Alianza or not (models 3 and 4); (2) incumbent president, a dummy variable indicating whether the president is Peronist or not (models 1 and 2) or UCR-Alianza or not (models 3 and 4); (3) median voter income, describing the median provincial worker's income, as reported by the Argentine Census Bureau (INDEC) in province *i* and year *j*; (4) public employment, describing the number of provincial public employees per thousand inhabitants of province *i* in year *j*; and (5) public expenditures per capita, describing the gross provincial expenditure per capita in Argentine pesos for province *i* and year *j*. Finally, we use (6) the Laakso and Taagapera index of the effective number of competing parties to control for the change in votes expected in more competitive party systems.[8]

The OLS results in Table 9.4 show that changes in public employment and public spending are positively associated with Peronist vote gains and with UCR-Alianza losses. At the same time, both benefit from incumbency; an incumbent governor results in approximately 7 percent more votes for Peronists and approximately 9 percent for the UCR-Alianza. If we control for incumbency, though, patronage benefits the Peronists more than the Radicals. Public employment per thousand inhabitants has a positive and significant effect for Peronists. A 1 percent increase in provincial public employment leads to a 0.066 percent increase in the Peronist vote. Hence, doubling the number of provincial public employees, from 5 percent of

8. $ENCP = \dfrac{1}{\sum v_{(j)}}$, where $v_{(j)}$ is the share of votes for every party I.

Table 9.4 Impact of income and employment on the Peronist and UCR-Alianza vote

	PJ vote	PJ vote	UCR-Alianza vote	UCR-Alianza vote
Incumbent governor	7.08***	6.88***	9.29***	9.06***
	(1.75)	(1.74)	(2.28)	(2.26)
Incumbent president	7.77*	13.82***	8.88*	12.45**
	(4.25)	(4.78)	(4.27)	(5.14)
Median voter income (ln)	−5.47*	−9.07***	4.93	7.23*
	(3.2)	(3.52)	(3.46)	(3.8)
Public employment per 1000 (ln)	6.65***	—	−2.20	—
	(1.89)		(2.06)	
Public expenditures per capita (ln)	—	6.58***	—	−3.35*
		(1.79)		(1.94)
Effective number of competing parties	−23.97***	24.11***	−17.94***	18.06***
	(2.45)	(2.43)	(2.54)	(2.51)
1995	5.69	−14.83***	5.36	10.49**
	(4.03)	(5.06)	(4.32)	(5.47)
2000	5.25*	8.74***	2.82	4.60*
	(2.08)	(2.25)	(2.30)	(2.49)
Constant	78.66*	103.39***	28.73	14.69
	(19.99)	(19.96)	(24.62)	(25.16)
R^2	0.72	0.73	0.57	0.58
N	83	83	83	83

NOTE: Incumbent governor is a dummy variable that indicates a Peronist governor in the PJ equations and an UCR-Alianza governor in the Alianza equation. Incumbent president is a dummy variable that indicates a Peronist president in the PJ equation and a UCR-Alianza president in the Alianza equation. Public employment is a variable describing the natural log of the total number of provincial public employees per 1000 citizens for 1987, 1990, 1995, and 2000. Public expenditures indicates describes the natural log of the total expenditures in pesos for every province i in every year of the sample. Effective number of competing parties is a reduced version of the Laakso and Taagepera formula including only major parties. * $p<0.2$, ** $p<0.1$, *** $p<0.01$.

the economically active population (Buenos Aires) to 11 percent of the economically active population (Salta), should led to approximately 6 percent more votes for Peronism. By contrast, public employment is not statistically significant in explaining the UCR-Alianza vote, and public expenditures are negatively associated with the UCR-Alianza vote. Thus, at the provincial level, higher spending in public employment does not give Radicals an electoral advantage.

Public expenditures per capita also have a substantial and statistically significant effect on the Peronist vote. Increasing public expenditures per capita by 1 percent leads to a 0.07 percent growth in the Peronist vote, showing a similar effect to that of public employment. This is not surprising, given that most provincial resources in the Argentine provinces are used to pay salaries. The effect, though, is not statistically significant for the UCR-Alianza vote. Therefore, once we control for incumbency benefits, investing in public employment provides the PJ with substantial electoral returns, but does not serve the UCR-Alianza as well.

In sum, we have shown that there is a different electoral return for investing in public employment and expenditures for Peronist as opposed to Radical incumbents. That is, the Peronists receive not only a larger share of fiscal resources, but also larger returns for every peso spent at the local level. The demographic characteristics and partisan linkages of Peronist voters explain the electoral differences generated by patronage for both parties.

The Demographic and Partisan Linkages of Peronist Voters

Although both PJ and UCR incumbents reap electoral returns from increasing public employment paid with those public funds, PJ incumbents also get more votes-per-buck than their contenders. The explanation for these differentials is related to the geographic distribution, demographic characteristics, and partisanship of Peronist voters.

Whereas their geographic distribution in poorer and less populated provinces benefits Peronists with larger access to fiscal monies, their demographic characteristics make them more dependent on public resources and employment. The provincial data in Table 9.4 show the lower-income voters' higher propensity to vote for Peronism, and higher-income voters' tendency to vote for the UCR-Alianza. However, Table 9.4 also shows that greater public employment and public expenditures increase electoral returns for Peronism more than for Radicals, even when controlling for the economic dependence (income) of voters and the electoral bias introduced by geographic overrepresentation (effective number of competing parties). Hence, there is a partisan effect that cannot be accounted for by income and geographic overrepresentation, which we attribute to the partisan linkages between the PJ and its constituencies. That is, even controlling for socioeconomic status, Peronist voters rely more on public monies.

The partisan effect we find results from historical allegiances of electoral constituencies that cannot simply be accounted for by patronage. After social constituencies have established partisan allegiances with political parties—based on the distribution of public, club, or private goods—they generate social linkages beyond their dependence on public largesse. These allegiances, in turn, generate long-term expectations regarding the distributive consequences of incumbency in public, club, and private goods, thereby reinforcing partisan loyalties. In Argentina, income and education have been predictors of alignment with Peronism because partisan identities have been rooted in deep sociopolitical and cultural cleavages since the 1940s (Ostiguy 1998; Mora y Araujo 1980b). Historically, Peronism has contained a dense network of local activists that maintained partisan loyalties even when the party was proscribed (James 1988). In the 1990s, although President Menem's market reforms won him the support of many high-income voters, Peronism's traditional constituencies did not abandon it. As a result, the PJ vote remained associated with low socioeconomic status in terms of income, occupation, and educational level (Gervasoni 1998c). Levitsky (2003, this volume) explains this phenomenon by pointing to Peronism's transformation from a party based on linkages to labor to one based on clientelistic machine politics.[9] In contrast, electoral loyalty to the UCR in the late 1990s was still associated with high socioeconomic status.[10]

These socioeconomic links between parties and their constituencies were further reinforced by the use of patronage. Both the PJ and the UCR used public employment to sustain these ties during the 1983–2001 period, but they benefited different constituencies with patronage. Auyero (2000) shows how Peronist informal networks and local subcultures reinforced partisan identities even in the context of market reforms, thus buttressing partisan expectations for the distribution of private goods. Calvo and Murillo (2004) show that in Peronist-controlled provinces average public wages were lower, but their level was still higher than the alternative private wages for workers with low educational attainment in non-Peronist provinces. As a result, less educated workers were favored by public sector employment to a larger degree in Peronist than in non-Peronist provinces. Additionally, lower average public wages in Peronist-controlled provinces allowed governors to hire more public employees with the same budget constraints, thereby maximizing returns from patronage. Hence, socioeconomic linkages increase Peronist returns from public jobs, while patronage served to reinforce the traditional linkages between the party and its constituencies.

9. Whereas McGuire (1997) provides a compelling description of Peronist social linkages based on public and club goods (such as social policy or benefits derived from union membership) in the 1940s and 1950s, Levitsky (2003) shows their evolution toward private good distribution through clientelistic ties based on party machines in the 1990s.

10. For the 1983, 1985, and 1987 elections, Catterberg (1989) shows that the Peronist vote was associated with lower socioeconomic status. For both the 1989 and the 1995 elections, Gervasoni (1998a) finds that support for Peronism was associated with lower material wealth and education. Cantón and Jorrat (2002) show the importance of party identification in explaining the vote in the 1999 presidential election in the metropolitan area of Buenos Aires.

DEMOCRATIC GOVERNANCE IN ARGENTINA

We have shown Peronism's comparative advantage regarding access to fiscal resources and the electoral returns derived from investing in public jobs. The combination of electoral and fiscal federal institutions along with the geographic distribution of its voters provided the PJ with more public resources than the UCR to invest in patronage. The combination of the previously defined partisan linkages and demographic characteristics of Peronist voters—which increase their dependence on public funds—explains why it gets better electoral returns from its investment in public employment. In contrast, the UCR's social composition of relatively wealthier constituencies, and its voters' geographic concentration in the most populated provinces, reduces its access to public monies and guarantees smaller electoral returns for engaging in patronage.

These two elements—better access to funds and better electoral returns from investing in patronage—explain why Peronists and Radicals are bound to reap such different benefits from public employment at the subnational level. It also explains why Peronist incumbents are more stable than Radicals. However, the positive effect of patronage for incumbents at the local level makes clear that Radicals are still a patronage-prone party, despite their comparative disadvantage.

The greater political stability of Peronist incumbents at the subnational level allows them to keep their legislative and provincial predominance even when they lose presidential elections. Therefore, we attribute the Peronists' comparative advantage in governability to the stability of their subnational coalition, which is based on both their greater access to patronage and their more effective electoral use of it. Electoral rules, fiscal federal institutions, and geographic overrepresentation explain the PJ advantage in access to patronage. The characteristics of Peronist constituencies and their social linkages with the party explain the PJ's greater electoral effectiveness in using patronage.

The PJ's comparative electoral advantage at the subnational level makes legislative gridlock and policy stalemate more likely for non-Peronist presidents. Indeed, Peronist control of Congress after the 2001 midterm elections, together with the resignation of Alianza vice president Carlos Álvarez in October 2000, explains why, after De la Rúa abandoned the presidency, Congress selected Peronists Adolfo Rodríguez Saá (who lasted a week) and Eduardo Duhalde as interim presidents.

As the events of 2000–2001 show, executive crises are not limited to policy gridlock and its consequences; they may be triggered by extensive social mobilization. Both Alfonsín and De la Rúa suffered urban riots that contributed in an important way to their resignations. Social unrest declined dramatically under their Peronist successors. The conditions of the crisis were established at the subnational level, but the crisis was triggered on the streets.

The Peronists' advantage in terms of social mobilization—the capacity to take and control the streets—is based on the historical role of labor in the original Peronist coalition (Torre 1990).[11] Although economic liberalization during the 1990s reduced formal sector employment and weakened the labor movement, the PJ largely maintained its capacity to take the streets by converting labor ties into clientelistic networks, which could also be mobilized or used to control social unrest (Levitsky, this volume; Auyero, this volume). This adaptation allowed the PJ to maintain its strategic advantage in controlling popular mobilization, as became apparent in its ability to control the massive riots that erupted in the last few days of Alfonsín's and De la Rúa's presidencies.

The 2003 elections provided a new puzzle: why did the non-Peronist parties collapse, leaving their voters orphaned, while the Peronists survived the 2001–2 crisis? (Torre, this volume). Although the PJ fragmented into three presidential candidacies in 2003 (in part because of the high value attached to its partisan label), its three factions gathered 60 percent of the vote in the first electoral round, and no political outsider arose from the ashes of political parties as in Venezuela or Peru. In contrast, the UCR collapsed at the national level, thus relying on local incumbents—and patronage—to survive at the subnational level.[12] Meanwhile non-Peronist voters were left looking for new alternatives, such as the two new coalitions led by former Radical politicians: ARI on the center-left and the MFR on the center-right.

We think that the same conditions affecting the stability of Peronist subnational electoral coalitions explain Peronism's higher electoral resilience and the difficulties for outsiders to succeed based on charismatic appeals (as Hugo Chávez did in Venezuela). That is, the combination of federalism and the use of patronage and clientelistic networks to reinforce partisan linkages enhanced both the PJ's resilience and the resistance of the Argentine political system to neopopulism. Constituencies receiving either public or private goods from parties with whom they have estab-

11. Gaudio and Thompson (1990) and Murillo (2001) discuss Peronist ties with labor unions and their effects on labor unrest.

12. In May 2003, when its presidential candidate won less than 3 percent of the vote, the UCR still had 656 mayors, 7 governors, 62 deputies, and 22 senators, whereas the two coalitions led by former Radical politicians (ARI and the MFR) had only 3 mayors, 38 deputies, and 3 senators, *combined*.

lished linkages are less likely to be attracted by outsiders denouncing the political system. At the same time, federalism heightened the influence of subnational coalitions in preserving or undermining governability at the national level. This combination of factors also helps to explain why neo-populism has been less prevalent in Latin American countries with federal structures and extensive patronage use, such as Brazil and Mexico.

In Argentina, subnational governance explains the strength of Peronist provincial governors, as well as why the three Peronist candidates in 2003, including former president Menem, were former or current governors. The importance of subnational politics—including both formal institutions and patronage—makes it difficult for political outsiders to overcome the obstacles posed by federalism in a national election, or to centralize presidential power outside Peronism. The new "iron law" of Peronism is thus shaping the expectations of the electorate, as well as party machines.

CONCLUSIONS

Our findings inform our understanding of the distributive effects of patronage and its implications for democratic governance in comparative perspective. The literature on patronage has generally dismissed this partisan component because it associates the success of clientelism with contextual conditions, but does not focus on subnational variation related to prior political allegiances and political institutions.

Public jobs are private goods that can be distributed to partisan constituencies in the absence of civil service rules. Patronage can serve to reward loyal supporters and their dependents through publicly provided income, whereas it also provides access to further resources that loyal supporters can distribute through clientelistic networks.[13] Hence, patronage distribution contributes to the stability of electoral coalitions by shaping expectations about future distribution of public jobs.[14] However, the electoral efficiency of patronage distribution hinges on the ability of political parties

13. In describing clientelistic networks in Argentina, Auyero (2000, 165–66) discusses the case of a client whose husband received a public job as garbage collector and whose daughter was appointed as a municipal employee thanks to the recommendation of the patron who also held a position in the local administration. The networks of clientelism and public sector recruitment are enmeshed because there are no formal mechanisms of recruitment for public jobs.

14. Cox and McCubbins (1986) show that patronage can serve to distribute resources to core rather than swing voters to maintain stable coalitions for risk-averse politicians. Kitschelt (2000) distinguishes between partisan coalitions based on programmatic and those based on clientelistic appeals. However, Diaz-Cayeros, Estevez, and Magaloni (2001) argue that politicians combine a portfolio that includes both public and private goods.

to access public jobs at different levels of government, and their constituencies' dependence on those jobs. As we show, these two elements can be unequally distributed among political parties within the same country. Partisanship provides national networks for differential access to resources that influence the ability of incumbents to distribute jobs, depending on the country's fiscal institutions. It also generates expectations among groups of voters about the future distribution of public resources, regardless of their dependence on those resources.

Patronage-based subnational electoral coalitions appeal to voters who are more dependent on public jobs and who are risk-averse in terms of changing their expectation about future patrons.[15] These voters expect that redistribution will continue to be spread among local supporters of the party that has represented them in the past. That is, they attach their loyalty to political parties based on prior redistribution either in the form of public, club, or private goods and lasting expectations of continued redistribution, even if the portfolio of goods changes. Indeed, private goods such as patronage can be used to sustain these distributive expectations.

Therefore, depending on the institutional structure and historical legacies of core supporters, pork-prone political parties have different (1) access to public resources, which depend not just on incumbency but also on fiscal institutions, and (2) constituencies, with different income expectations and labor market alternatives, based on the prior expectations of redistribution generated by the political party. Political parties with more dependent constituencies and greater access to public jobs have higher returns from patronage, which helps them sustain their partisan linkages. We show that that parties' differences regarding patronage are not simply related to an original choice between programmatic and clientelistic linkages depending on their historical origin (Shefter 1994). Even among pork-prone parties, there may be differences in terms of the electoral returns obtained from their investment in public jobs.

Our subnational analysis allows us to demonstrate the importance of partisanship in explaining variation in the electoral effectiveness of patronage within a country. By focusing on the subnational level, we can hold constant the fiscal and federal institutions as well as partisan linkages defined at the national level. This focus also allows us to explain the competi-

15. The moral economy arguments explain the reasons for higher risk aversion in lower-income individuals based on a minimum threshold of income rather than maximization of income (Scott 1976). Following Stokes and Medina (forthcoming), the logic of patronage as a risk-minimizing instrument for politicians (Cox and McCubbins 1986) can be extended to clients who prefer (or expect to receive) short-term private goods rather than public goods that may benefit them in the long run.

tive electoral advantage of parties that do not control the national government, but maintain stable electoral coalitions. It also allows us to show the result of partisanship on electoral effectiveness of patronage within the same pork-prone political systems, by emphasizing the variation in the demographic characteristics of constituencies (demand side) and access to patronage and networks to carry it out (supply side).

 Our argument implies that in countries where patronage is distributed at the subnational level, formal institutions that define the share of resources available to subnational incumbents, as well as income, education, and private sector alternatives for constituents, influence the electoral effectiveness of patronage. To test these effects, the ideal case study should have subnational electoral districts and previously defined partisan linkages and fiscal and electoral institutions. Argentina provides an ideal case to test these effects because it is a federal country with subnational electoral districts and whose fiscal and electoral institutions were defined in periods previous to the one we study (the 1930s in the former, and the 1976–83 military regime in the latter). Moreover, Argentine partisan linkages are deeply rooted and were defined primarily by the distribution of both public and club goods (and reinforced by cultural identities), rather than private goods. As a result, Peronists could take advantage of these prior partisan linkages, along with the demographics and geographic distribution of Peronist constituencies, when distributing private goods like patronage.

We began this chapter with the puzzle of why non-Peronists are able to win presidential elections but are unable to govern until the end of their terms in office, a pattern that we call the new "iron law" of Argentine politics. We explained this new "iron law" of Argentine politics based on the Peronist comparative advantage in terms of achieving subnational electoral stability. In turn, we linked the Peronists' ability to achieve subnational electoral stability to their capacity to obtain higher returns—in vote counts—from patronage than their rivals. Subnational access to public jobs and constituencies' dependence on these jobs provide a partisan advantage regarding patronage that explains why non-Peronists have greater difficulty achieving democratic governance than Peronists.

Emerging Patterns of Civic Organization and Protest

10

Demanding Accountable Government: Citizens, Politicians, and the Perils of Representative Democracy in Argentina

Enrique Peruzzotti

The link between Argentine politicians and their constituents has seriously eroded, as witnessed by the events of December 2001. Mass mobilizations took place in major urban metropolitan areas, reflecting a withdrawal of social trust in political elites. In this dramatic political moment, the wave of angry public protests against politicians swept aside the most challenging task of the democratization process: the consolidation of strong representative institutions. The following pages trace the genealogy of this crisis of representation. I argue that the 2001–2 crisis of representation is not an isolated or circumstantial event, or just the product of failed socioeconomic policies. Rather, it is the latest stage in the conflict between civil and political society over what constitutes representative government and can be traced back to the 1983 transition to democracy.

A new kind of relationship between citizens and politicians distinguishes contemporary (post-1983) Argentine democracy from previous democratic experiences. Perhaps the most striking novelty of the past twenty years has been the emergence of a more sophisticated and demanding citizenry that is determined to redefine preexisting ideals of democratic

A previous version of this chapter was presented for the conference "Rethinking Dual Transitions: Argentine Politics in the 1990s in Comparative Perspective," March 20–22, 2003, Harvard University. The author is grateful for the valuable comments from those who participated in the meeting. I also wish to thank Steve Levitsky and Vicky Murillo whose sharp remarks helped improve the earlier draft.

representation, to create a civic concern for governmental accountability. The dramatic experience of state terrorism under military dictatorship from 1976 to 1983 gave rise to the human rights movement. This actor played a crucial educational role in Argentine society. The movement's rights-oriented politics and discourse and its systematic condemnation of the horrors of state terrorism brought about a much-needed public concern for civil rights and the rule of law. Society's new awareness of public officials' violations of the law resulted in the rise of politics aimed at increasing government accountability.

Throughout the 1990s, the politics of "social accountability" triggered unprecedented civic and media-based protests and exposés of illegal governmental behavior. Carlos Menem's administration's disregard of demands for greater accountability fed public anger and frustration against his government. The emergence of an electoral coalition in the 1999 presidential elections organized around a call for honest government unleashed great hopes in the middle-class electorate. Unfortunately, those hopes proved short-lived, when a major corruption scandal shocked the administration. The Senate scandal extinguished popular expectations for institutional and political reform and convinced many middle-class Argentines that the problem of corruption was not limited to a particular administration, but extended to political leaders as a whole. In 2001–2, public anger and frustration triggered a shift from accountability politics toward forms of protest that often rejected representative institutions altogether. The first part of this chapter analyzes the cultural and political innovation that took place between 1983 and 2000, and how it redefined the links between citizens and the political system. The second part focuses on the development of the crisis of representation that shook the stability of Argentina's democratic system in December 2001.

POLITICAL INNOVATION AND THE REDEFINITION OF REPRESENTATION: THE EMERGENCE OF A CIVIC CRY FOR ACCOUNTABLE GOVERNMENT

Redefining Representation

To understand the current crisis of representation, it is necessary to examine cultural innovation during democratization, and how this altered established populist notions of democratic representation. The most distinctive phenomenon of the current democratic period is the emergence of a political culture that stands in clear rupture with the "authorization" view of representation of the populist democratic tradition and its replacement by an "accountability" model of representation (Pitkin 1972, 38).

Historically in Argentina, populism's model of authorization has shaped democratic representation. The two most significant democratizing movements in twentieth-century Argentina—Yrigoyenism and Peronism—shared a highly majoritarian understanding of democracy, to the detriment of constitutional safeguards or "horizontal" forms of accountability. In this view of the representative contract, elections granted the populist leader the right to act as the people's trustee. Elections were understood to be the decisive moment of the representative contract; they were momentous decisional acts that foreclosed any further challenge or deliberation (Peruzzotti 1996). The electorate abdicated all political agency and subordinated itself to the leader's will until the next election.

The shift from an "authorization" to an "accountability" model of representation introduced new questions of legal and political accountability. The notion of accountability refers to making public officials answerable for their behavior, in the sense of being forced to justify and report their decisions, and of eventually being sanctioned for those decisions. Thus, the "accountability model" complements the process of electoral authorization of political power with a set of institutional mechanisms geared toward ensuring the authorized agents' responsiveness and accountability. As accountability theorists argue, insofar as representative democracy implies the existence of a fundamental gap between political representatives and citizens, it requires institutional mechanisms to ensure that such separation does not result in unresponsive or illegal governments. The central question that "accountability" addresses is precisely how to regulate and reduce the gap between representatives and constituents, while preserving the division of labor between political authorities and citizenry that characterizes the relations of representation.

What prompted such a significant cultural and political transformation? I have argued elsewhere that the emergence of a human rights movement represented a cultural turning point in Argentine society (Peruzzotti 2002a 83). The movement was made up of a series of organizations that were either formed or achieved public notoriety during the most recent dictatorship. In 1976, a military junta took power, establishing a system of state terrorism that led to the clandestine abduction, detention, torture, and murder of thousands of Argentine citizens. It is in this context that the human rights movement arose. The movement consisted of a heterogeneous convergence of family-based groups, religious organizations, and civil libertarian associations. Neither the church nor the unions, political parties, or lawyers' associations provided significant support to the human rights cause. The Catholic hierarchy's refusal to endorse the movement's activities eliminated the possibility of having the church as a protective umbrella organization, as in Chile and Brazil. Thus, it was only after the regime began to liberalize that the movement's politics began to exert some influence on Argentine society. By the end of the dictatorship, the human rights movement had managed to generate widespread popular support for its cause. The issue of human rights occupied a central place in the agenda of most political parties and became a pivotal concern of Raúl Alfonsín's presidency, when the military junta's historic trial took place.[1]

The significance of the movement's struggle goes beyond their demands for justice and retribution. Its discourse and practices acted as a catalyst for political learning, triggering a profound renewal of the country's democratic tradition. The human rights movement inaugurated a new form of politics that introduced a healthy concern for rights and constitutionalism in Argentine political culture. By questioning all forms of state authoritarianism, whether military or civilian, the rights-based politics and discourse of the movement transformed Argentine democratic traditions. It reunited two elements that the populist political culture that had shaped previous processes of democratization had kept apart: democracy and the rule of law (Peruzzotti 2002a, 83). Such a cultural shift transformed preconceived populist notions about the nature of representative government. In effect, the appreciation of rights and constitutional guarantees redefined the representative contract from an authorization to an accountability view. Constitutional mechanisms and guarantees were no longer perceived as "obstacles" or "formalities" that delay or prevent the fulfillment of popular aspirations; rather, they were now seen as indispensable protective institutional barriers against state despotism.

The "accountability" model breaks with the "blank check" attitude of political delegation and introduces a combination of institutional and noninstitutional mechanisms to assure that representatives are held accountable throughout their period in office. Institutionally, the elected official is monitored and controlled by what Guillermo O'Donnell has termed "vertical and horizontal mechanisms of accountability," that is, by the vote and

---

1. Upon taking office, Raúl Alfonsín signed a decree ordering the trials of both the military juntas and the leadership of the terrorist organizations. The trial of the nine commanders started on April 22, 1985, and lasted five months. The members of the three juntas were individually charged with specific crimes such as abduction, torture, and murder. The court gave its verdict on December 9, 1985: Jorge Rafael Videla and Emilio Massera, the former Army and Navy commanders during the worst years of the repression, were given life sentences. For an interesting analysis of the trial and of the human rights policies under Alfonsín's administration, see Nino 1996b.

by the system of separation of powers, checks and balances, and due process (1999b).[2] Citizens and civic organizations in the public sphere can contest decisions and condemn the unlawful actions of public officials (Peruzzotti and Smulovitz 2002, 23–52; Cohen 1999, 216). Both institutional and extra-institutional mechanisms are crucial for institutionalizing and strengthening mechanisms of political distrust that can help reduce the inherent risks involved in the act of political delegation.[3] The "accountability" model of representation therefore presupposes a redefinition of the representative relationship: the former is no longer based on a basic trust in the personal qualities of those in power; rather trust is transferred to a set of impersonal safeguards that protect the citizenry against eventual breaches of trust by authorities. There is no longer a direct relationship of trust between constituents and representatives, but the generation of political trust is now institutionally mediated. It is the existence of working safeguards against unresponsive or irresponsible behavior on the part of officials that generates social trust in representative institutions.

These changes in the political culture translate into a more critical civic and electoral attitude of voters toward both representatives and representative institutions: the represented no longer stand as passive subjects but assume an active monitoring role. Such an attitudinal change should not be misinterpreted as a sign of political cynicism or disbelief in politics. Actually, it is the result of both the leveling-off of high expectations for elected representatives and public officials and an enhanced trust in institutions.

The emergence of a more sophisticated and vigilant citizenry and electorate resulted into two fundamental political developments that address the two dimensions (political and legal) of the concept of accountability: (1) the so-called electoralization of politics (Miranda 2002), and (2) the politics of societal accountability. The first development illustrates the introduction of a concern for political accountability into electoral politics (Peruzzotti and Smulovitz 2002, 25–30).[4] Many voters are no longer linked to parties by strong and unreflective bonds of loyalty, but assume a discriminating attitude at the ballot box and are willing to change parties

2. The concept of horizontal accountability refers to the operation of an intrastate system of checks and balances to control or punish actions or omissions by agents or agencies of the state that might be considered unlawful. Vertical accountability refers mainly (although not exclusively) to elections as a mechanism of political control.

3. For the notion of institutionalized mechanisms of distrust, see O'Donnell 2003b, Sztompka 1999, and Rose-Ackerman 2001, 543.

4. The concept of political accountability refers to the responsiveness of government policies to the preferences of the electorate. It is usually assumed that free competitive elections are the central institution for this type of control.

and candidates if the representatives do not meet their expectations. The second development refers instead to a concern for legal accountability:[5] citizens are eager to protect themselves from the hazards of electoral delegation by developing a social and institutional setting that can lower those risks. That entails addressing the institutional deficits and malfunctioning of horizontal mechanisms of accountability.

The Politics of Electoral Accountability

The erosion of populist allegiances created conditions conducive to the emergence of an independent electorate (Peruzzotti 2001). In the past, populist identities conspired against the development of competitive electoral politics. The refusal by populist movements to complete the transition from social movement to political party prevented the institutionalization of an expanded party system.[6] Perceiving themselves as privileged interpreters of the popular will, populist movements refused to pigeonhole themselves into a mere party identity. The political culture and dynamics that resulted from *movimentista* forms of self-understanding made it impossible to form a civil society with sufficient autonomy from political society, leading instead to the fragmentation of society into two irreconcilable camps: Peronism and anti-Peronism.

In electoral terms, polarization was evidenced by the existence of two strong and mutually exclusive political subcultures in the electorate. The division of the electorate into two rigid and loyal camps made electoral competition predictable and noncompetitive. Under normal conditions— the absence of proscriptions and fraud—the Peronist party would systematically carry the election. After winning the nomination as Peronism's presidential candidate in 1982, Italo Argentino Luder stated that "to be the Peronist candidate is to have the certainty of being president" (quoted in Waisbord 1995, 30). This reflected the prevailing state of mind in Argentine society. In Argentina, which lacked a large and independent electorate and where rigid political camps predominated, electoral dynamics moved along predictable tracks.[7] The electoral certainty about Peronism's victory

5. The notion of legal accountability refers to a set of institutional mechanisms aimed at ensuring that the actions of public officials are legally and constitutionally framed.

6. Botana (1983), Cavarozzi (1989), De Riz (1986), and Peruzzotti (1999) have all stressed the "movementist" features of Argentine populist movements and their negative impact on the party system.

7. The belief that the PJ reflected the majority of the electorate and that it was therefore not necessary to court independent voters was a major flaw in the losing 1983 Peronist campaign. As Waisbord argues, "The absolute conviction of the electoral victory (of Peronism) steered all efforts to the party activists and adherents . . . the objective (of the campaign) was to reinforce loyalties and to satisfy specific requests of local party bosses rather than listening to the needs of the electorate" (Waisbord 1995, 31). In contrast, Alfonsín's campaign

in the minds of both the electorate and representatives precluded the electorate's use of the vote as a mechanism of political accountability. This is because it is precisely electoral *uncertainty* that disciplines political representatives, turning the vote into an ultimate "weapon" of popular control over political representatives. When the electorate is split into two immobile groups, this disciplinary function of elections disappears.

The unexpected victory of Radical Civic Union (UCR) candidate Raúl Alfonsín over Peronist candidate Italo Luder—by a striking 12 percentage points—in 1983 was the first sign of the breakdown of past allegiances and the inauguration of a new era of electoral politics in Argentina. This new era was marked by the end of a central aspect of the previous period: the existence of two rigid and polarized electorates. The partial dissolution of "captive electorates" has given way to more fluid and unpredictable electoral behavior.[8] Many electoral analysts have emphasized the emergence of a considerable sector of free-floating independent voters (mainly in the large metropolitan areas) who have produced important realignments both at the level of the electorate and of electoral coalitions. The period has not only witnessed the alternation of power between the Radical and the Peronist parties, but also the significant growth (and decline) of other party organizations and electoral coalitions.

The "electoralization of party politics" is a direct consequence of the previously described transition from an "authorization" to an "accountability" notion of representation. It indicates the emergence of more autonomous and discriminating sectors within the Argentine electorate whose vote is determined not by partisan loyalties but by specific issues and governmental performance. In contrast with delegation to a leader or movement, there is now an "accountability" dimension in the vote of a considerable sector of the electorate, particularly educated, urban middle-class voters. That is, there is an expectation that elected officials are politically accountable to the electorate, irrespective of party labels and loyalties. It is policy outcomes, governmental performance, and openness to issues

---

was directed at the independent electorate from the start, to bring the Radicals new votes (24).

8. The dissolution of captive electorates does not affect all parties or regions of the country equally. The PJ has been able to retain a significant percentage of loyal voters and still maintains the political control of a significant number of provinces. Through the skillful use of patronage resources, the PJ was able to preserve a substantial electoral base among working- and lower-class sectors. It is also the dominant political force in peripheral provinces like Santiago del Estero, San Luis, Jujuy, La Rioja, and Formosa. In the aftermath of the crisis of representation, it has emerged as the only significant national political structure and consolidated its territorial dominance with the control of sixteen out of twenty-four provinces. On this subject, see the contributions of Torre, Levitsky, Calvo and Murillo, and Auyero in this volume.

and demands raised by the media, social movements, and civic publics in the public arena that will affect the fate of a government or of specific politicians.

The Politics of Social Accountability

Parallel to the concern for political accountability expressed by the "electoralization of politics," Argentine society witnessed the emergence of numerous civic campaigns demanding more transparent and accountable government. Those initiatives ranged from case-based social movements, such as those spawned by a handful of politically linked murders that generated public outrage, to professional NGOS that developed programs to control and monitor governmental agencies. Investigative journalism provided a crucial ally to this form of politicization and helped expose innumerable cases of governmental corruption or wrongdoing.

The legal dimension of governmental accountability brings together these heterogeneous actors and initiatives. It involves a diverse set of activities whose goals are (1) to monitor the behavior of public officials and agencies to make sure they abide by the law; (2) to expose cases of governmental wrongdoing; and in many cases, (3) to fuel the operation of horizontal agencies, such as the judiciary or legislative investigation commissions, that otherwise would be biased or not initiated. The emergence of a politics of societal accountability is directly linked to the previously mentioned changes in the public's attitudes toward the exercise of representative government. Its ultimate objective is to guarantee the operation of *horizontal mechanisms of accountability* within the state, to assure both the effectiveness of rights and the proper functioning of representative institutions.

In the politics of societal accountability in Argentina, there are three leading actors:

1. NGOS *and advocacy organizations.* The post–human rights movement stage has been characterized by the consolidation of a specialized group of NGOS and civic associations that show a common concern for increasing the transparency and accountability of representative government. In recent years, these associations—such as Poder Ciudadano (Citizen Power), Fundación para el Ambiente y los Recursos Naturales (Foundation for the Environment and Natural Resources, FARN), Conciencia (Conscience), Coordinadora contra la Represión Policial e Institutional (Council Against Police and Institutional Repression, CORREPI), Coordinadora de Familiares de Víctimas Inocentes (Council of Relatives of Innocent Victims, CO-

FAVI), Asociación por los Derechos Civiles (Association for Civil Rights), and the Centro de Estudios Legales y Sociales (Center for Legal and Social Studies, CELS)—have launched a variety of initiatives to make the exercise of political power more transparent and to increase citizens' monitoring of state agencies or officials. The initiatives range from campaigns to demand public disclosure of the assets of senators and deputies to the surveillance of police behavior and reporting of police abuses.

2. *Social movements that emerged as the result of specific cases of wrongdoing by public authorities.* Throughout the 1990s there were numerous movements and drives that demanded truth and justice in specific cases of human rights violations. Several of these initiatives galvanized large numbers of people, thousands of whom marched to support the movements' demands for independent justice. Perhaps the most famous cases of wrongdoing that gave rise to such outcry were the murder of schoolgirl María Soledad Morales in the northwestern province of Catamarca,[9] the death of Army private Omar Carrasco in an isolated garrison of the Patagonian province of Neuquén,[10] and the assassination of news photographer José Luis Cabezas in the summer resort of Pinamar.[11] These three highly publicized deaths sparked extensive mass mobilizations. The public demanded guarantees from the authorities for proper police investigations and judicial procedures, since there were strong indications that authorities had been involved in covering up or deliberately mishandling the initial investigations. In other words, citizens pressed for the unbiased performance of accountability agencies.

3. *Watchdog journalism.* The appearance of a more inquisitive type of watchdog journalism in the 1990s resulted in the exposure of numerous instances of government corruption and wrongdoing (Waisbord 2002, 289–325). It was under the Menem administration that investigative journalism gained national notoriety by disclosing countless episodes of offi-

---

9. The María Soledad case refers to the demand for justice in the rape and murder of a high school student in the province of Catamarca. For an analysis of the case, see Smulovitz and Peruzzotti 2003.

10. The Carrasco case refers to the mistreatment and murder of conscript Omar Carrasco by military officers while doing the then-mandatory military service in a remote barrack in the province of Neuquén. As a result of the scandal that followed, Menem's government ended compulsory military service. See Behrend, forthcoming.

11. The case refers to the murder of press photographer José Luis Cabezas in January 1997. From early on, his murder was linked to his photographs of a businessman Alfredo Yabran, the head of a vast business empire that always attempted to avoid public exposure. For a detailed analysis of the case, see Behrend, forthcoming.

cial corruption. One of the first scandals surfaced in 1991 when the newspaper *Página 12* revealed that the U.S. ambassador to Argentina had sent a letter to the government, accusing high-ranking officials of soliciting bribes from the U.S.-based Swift Corporation to allow machinery to be imported. Only months later, the president's sister-in-law, Amira Yoma, was implicated in a drug money laundering scandal. Shortly afterwards, two of Menem's close aides were involved in the sale of spoiled milk to a federal nutrition program for poor children. Another prominent member of the administration, the head of the national agency of social services for senior citizens (PAMI), had to step down when he was accused of receiving bribes from favored providers. Yet another exposé questioned the building of an oversized airstrip near Menem's private summer residence in Anillaco. In 1995, a major scandal broke out when the newspaper *Clarín* revealed that Argentine weapons had been sold to Ecuador. Argentina was one of the guarantors of the 1942 peace treaty between Ecuador and Peru. Months later, the media revealed a new and much more important sale of weapons to Croatia in 1991 that violated the United Nations embargo.[12] Political scandals were not unique to the Menem administration. In fact, the most significant scandal would take place under Fernando De la Rúa's administration. As I will show later, this Senate scandal provides important clues for understanding the anger against political representatives, which has propelled the most recent wave of public protest and mobilization in Argentina.

The politics of societal accountability represent an important subinstitutional complement to the institutionalized mechanisms of accountability. Social accountability has helped schematize and limit different forms of state abuse of power. Its contribution to the agenda of legal accountability is threefold. First, it plays a crucial *signaling function*. The reporting of specific cases of wrongdoing provides a vivid illustration of certain shortcomings in the performance of horizontal agencies or representative institutions. Media attention is crucial for making a demand heard by the public as well as political authorities. Watchdog journalism is essential here, as independent journalists help uncover cases of governmental corruption or give voice to mobilized social actors. Social mobilizations and media exposés signal an accountability deficit, transforming it into a more general issue on the public agenda. The mobilizations and media exposure in cases like Carrasco and Bulacio[13] served not only to highlight a specific

---

12. For an analysis of watchdog journalism in Argentina, see Waisbord 2002.

13. The Bulacio case was the result of police violence that ended with the death of teenager Walter Bulacio. The murder gave rise to social mobilizations that demanded justice and an end to police violence against youth.

and extreme instance of abuse of power or wrongdoing by state agencies, but also to bring public attention to the persistence of questionable yet long-established institutional practices of police violence against youth in poorer neighborhoods, or of military mistreatment and violence against conscripts. The mobilizations and the social reaction that both cases generated were decisive for putting institutional misconduct into the spotlight and simultaneously transforming the social appreciation of the issue.

The impact that those cases had on public opinion helped to create a new social sensitivity to ingrained (and largely ignored or socially tolerated) institutional behavior and contributed to the transformation of the social perception of the problem, which encouraged the organization of other protest movements against police or military violence and enabled them to frame the issue in the new discourse of rights and accountability. For instance, an immediate reaction of the families whose sons were receiving military training in Carrasco's unit was to refuse to send them back to the barracks after their leaves of absence were over. The fear that this reaction could be extended nationwide forced a rapid response from Army chief Martín Balza, who flew to Zapala to meet with the parents and to assume personal responsibility for the conscripts' safety (Behrend, forthcoming).

Second, through pressure and symbolic sanctions, social initiatives can *activate an otherwise reluctant network of horizontal agencies of accountability.* In many cases, societal mechanisms go beyond the signaling function and directly affect the workings of horizontal agencies or the careers of those officials under suspicion. They do so by exerting symbolic sanctions on those agencies or officials that social mobilizations or the media's accusations have placed in the spotlight. The high political costs of public mobilizations, *escraches*,[14] and press exposés may force reluctant agencies or officials to minimize them by making or reversing decisions in order to appear to be addressing institutional failures. For example, an agency might initiate lawsuits or form parliamentary investigation commissions, or ask officials under suspicion to resign. The notoriety of the Carrasco case, and the military's interest in trying to change its public image after massive human rights violations of the past, forced the Army chief to face

---

14. The term *escraches* refers to a form of symbolic punishment of individuals suspected of corruption or human rights violations but who either have been given amnesty or have not been punished through the courts. Human rights organizations first used this tactic against human rights violators who had been absolved by an amnesty decree or by the Law of Due Obedience. *Escraches* were mass rallies of public condemnation held outside the alleged perpetrator's residence. This strategy of public shaming was later adopted by other organizations.

up to the crime and end any cover-up. As a result, the military officials who were directly responsible for the death of Army private Omar Carrasco were tried and sentenced to prison (Behrend, forthcoming).

Third, social accountability politics can lead to the *establishment of permanent societal watchdog organizations* that monitor the performance of specific public agencies. For example, a group of social movements that were created in the face of police brutality and violence created two organizations for the supervision of the police forces (CORREPI and COFAVI). Those organizations not only provide legal assistance to the families of the victims, they also actively monitor police behavior, acting as external "fire alarms" (McCubbins and Schwartz 1984) that are set off by new violations of human rights by police officers. Furthermore, they are forcing legislators to review the legal framework that regulates the police. Some of these social watchdogs provide important support to case-based social movements. For example, the initial complaint filed by Carrasco's father was covered in the local newspaper, which alerted local human rights organizations. The organizations not only provided the family with legal defense on the local judicial level, but also brought the case to the attention of the Defense Ministry and the National Congress (Behrend, forthcoming).

As previously argued, the emergence of these three forms of politicization is directly linked to the consolidation of a new representative ideal that places great trust in democratic institutions. The politics of social accountability serve to test whether the actions of political representatives and nonelected officials abide by the normative principles embedded in liberal representative democracies. As Offe (2001) argues, those practices function "to authenticate the core assumptions that turn out to be capable of withstanding and disconfirming trust." "Trust," Offe states, "is the residue that remains after the propensity to distrust has turned out to be unfounded" (2001, 76). It is by strengthening mechanisms of institutionalized distrust and sanctioning breaches of trust by specific public officials that the politics of social accountability contributes to building and generalizing social trust in political representatives.

There are, however, two possible dangers arising from such politics. The first regards the failure of institutional mechanisms and political society to adequately address public demands. If officials systematically disregard claims for greater transparency, a democracy might witness a sharp decline in citizens' confidence in political representatives. As Sztompka argues, "If failure is widely perceived, generalized trust is replaced by pervasive distrust" (1999, 145). The second danger is with respect to the number of disclosures of illegal behavior by representatives. For generalized trust to pervade, institutional mechanisms of distrust must be activated relatively infrequently. If there is a proliferation of accusations and scandals, and institutions of control are hyperactive, this signals to the average citizen that breaches of trust are pervasive, feeding a culture of public distrust (Sztompka 1999, 145).

Both scenarios have occurred in Argentina. On the one hand, there was a generalized public view that on many occasions, agencies of distrust were reluctant to fulfill their controlling role or would easily yield to political pressure. This was especially so in cases involving accusations against high-ranking members of the administration. On the other hand, throughout the 1990s, Argentines were bombarded by allegations of illegal or corrupt behavior by public officials. The frequency and extent of media revelations during Menem's decade as president contributed to the public's perception of corruption as widespread.

THE BUILD-UP TO THE DECEMBER 2001 CRISIS AND THE LIMITS OF SOCIAL AND ELECTORAL ACCOUNTABILITY POLITICS

The emergence of the center-left Front for a Country in Solidarity (FREP-ASO) and later, the Alianza (a FREPASO-UCR electoral coalition) brought a breath of fresh air into Argentine politics and a promise to restore political representatives' lost credibility. The FREPASO and later the Alianza's platform was closely tied to the public's concern for greater governmental accountability. The Alianza's electoral victory not only meant a change of political figures but, more fundamentally, the introduction of a new style of politics. Central to the coalition's discourse was the need to put an end to Menemism's pompous, corrupt, and behind-the-scenes style, replacing it with a more austere, honest, and transparent way of doing politics. The Alianza promised to renew the ties between civil society and representative institutions. These ties had been seriously eroded in the last Menem administration by the abundance of corruption scandals, which created a gap between citizens and politicians that widened with each new media exposé of governmental wrongdoing.

The Senate Scandal

The expectation of political and institutional renewal promised by the Alianza's 1999 electoral victory was short-lived. A major scandal shook the administration very early on, generating not only a crisis for the governing coalition but an end of public hopes for political and institutional reform. The Senate scandal was triggered by a newspaper editorial written by prestigious political journalist Joaquín Morales Solá, who suggested that a group of Peronist senators had received substantial bribes in exchange for their support of a labor reform law proposed by the then minister of labor. The scandal set off an earthquake within the administration. Vice President Carlos "Chacho" Álvarez (FREPASO) firmly condemned the actions of those accused of wrongdoing, which he saw as a crucial test for the governing alliance's electoral promise to bring more transparency and accountability to the political system. Instead, President Fernando De la Rúa (UCR) stated on several occasions that he believed the accusations were unfounded. These two differing positions among the government's heads generated a tense political climate. The Radical party closed ranks around the government and the Senate, while Álvarez publicly demanded the resignation of those senators and cabinet members who were suspected of taking part in the political scheme. Not only were Álvarez's pleas ignored: in a mid-August cabinet change, De la Rúa promoted the labor minister in question to the position of General Secretary of the Presidency. The vice president responded immediately. On the very day that the new cabinet members were sworn in, he resigned.[15]

Among all the political scandals of the 1990s, why focus on this one? Many analysts and political commentators have made extensive references to the number of corruption scandals that marked Menem's terms. The public was subjected to almost daily exposés and claims about illegal or corrupt governmental activities. The glut of scandals led some authors to wonder whether the citizenry was reaching a state of scandal fatigue that would spread skepticism and political apathy (Waisbord 1995, 315–20).[16] Undoubtedly, the extent and frequency of media revelations helped nourish a feeling of skepticism about the workings of representative institutions and the mechanisms of institutional distrust in large sectors of the public. The politics of social accountability helped expose and condemn official wrongdoing and ostracized several prominent Menemist figures.

15. Over time, the scandal gradually faded out from the public eye, but it was rekindled in December 2004 with the self-incriminating testimony of a former member of the legislature. For a detailed analysis of the scandal, see Peruzzotti, forthcoming.

16. The upsurge of civic mobilizations since December 2001 seems to question this diagnosis. Actually, Waisbord himself tempers the scandal fatigue diagnosis by pointing out the existence of many cases that contradict the fatigue hypothesis, like the civic mobilizations that took place nationwide in the María Soledad, Jose Luis Cabezas, and Omar Carrasco cases, or as a result of the terrorist bombing of the Israeli Embassy and Argentina's leading Jewish community center (AMIA). Those scandals not only generated public outrage and massive mobilizations demanding truth and justice, but in some cases succeeded in bringing the culprits to the authorities. In Waisbord's view, wrongdoings that represent a clear affront to civil society, like those involving human rights violations, are the ones that are going to elicit a strong civic response (1995, 320–23).

At the same time, it challenged a government that was hostile to the very idea of legal accountability. The cry for accountability was thus channeled into electoral politics, and there were great expectations for the Alianza government after their victory in the polls. Supporters believed that the De la Rúa administration would not only address the calls for change in economic and social policies, but also address the demands for greater transparency and legal accountability that had been raised under Menem. The Alianza's anticorruption discourse and the promise of political renewal only served to reaffirm such convictions.

What made the Senate scandal distinctive was that it revealed the limits of the two innovative forms of politicization described in the previous section. In the first place, the scandal cast serious doubts on the effectiveness of the electoral road to political and legal accountability. The scandal involved an administration that had made anticorruption one of its prominent banners. The De la Rúa administration's disappointing reaction, followed by the resignation of the vice president and the rupture of the governing coalition, confirmed to a large part of the public that the problem of the absence of legal accountability was not limited to the Menem government, but affected all of political society.

Second, the very nature of the scandal—the accusation that the laws passed by Congress were attained through bribes—went to the very heart of the country's representative institutions. If there is a generalized belief in society that political representatives respond not to the electorate but to the highest bidder, elections lose all meaning as a mechanism for political accountability. This was not simply another corruption case, but an event that cast serious doubts on the operation of Argentina's system of representation. In contrast to many of the previously mentioned corruption exposés, the Senate scandal affected the credibility and reputation not of just some isolated officials, but that of political society as a whole.

Third, political society's reaction to the accusations only serves to strengthen the public's worst suspicions. The attitude assumed by a country's institutions and representatives in any scandal shows their receptiveness to demands from those they claim to represent. The way that Argentine political society came together in defense of its prerogatives and corporate interests, and the fact that with the sole exceptions of Carlos Álvarez and Antonio Cafiero, there were no major political figures who acted promptly to dissociate themselves from those who were later shown to have crossed the line, further confirmed to many citizens that the representative institutions had detached themselves from the wishes and hopes of the people.

At the same time, the scandal illustrated some limitations of the politics of social accountability and made the malfunctioning of the horizontal mechanisms of accountability in Argentina sadly visible.[17] First, the scandal showed the inability of the media and of its supporting civic actors to go beyond making unsupported allegations, or *denuncismo*.[18] Second, it highlighted how institutional safeguards had been distorted and expropriated by unscrupulous officials who had mastered the art of "surviving accountability." The fact that the scandal brought together the key players in the intrastate system of checks and balances (the executive power, the legislative, the judiciary, the anticorruption office, and so on) made the picture more pitiful.

It is the combination of these factors that made the Senate scandal a poignant turning point in Argentina's contemporary system of representation. The symbolic costs that the scandal imposed on the political system helps us understand the current anger and resentment toward political representatives in important parts of the electorate and civil society. This anger and frustration has brought about important changes in both electoral and civic dynamics: in electoral terms, there has been a transition from swing votes to protest votes, while at the societal level the institutional concern that guides the politics of social accountability has been displaced by a wave of mobilizations that, in many instances, turn their back on institutional politics.

The 2001 Legislative Elections and the Rise of Electoral Protest

The outcome of the legislative election that took place in October 2001 was an early sign of the dissolution of the link between the electorate and political society. The election's novelty was the impressive jump in electoral absenteeism and the so-called protest vote: more than 40 percent of the Argentine electorate either abstained from voting or cast null or blank

17. Judge Liporaci, who was handling the case of "bribes in the Senate," added to the generalized feeling of suspicion toward the Senate when he claimed that, in his view, there were firm indications that seemed to confirm the accusation. Judge Liporaci was himself accused of illegal personal enrichment because he could not justify his purchase of a mansion worth U.S.$1.5 million. Consequently, the Consejo de la Magistratura (the Council of Magistrates) started investigating Liporaci. Two months latter, Liporaci declared the "lack of merit" of the eleven senators charged with bribery. In January, the prosecutors appealed the judge's ruling, and by February, the Council of Magistrates suspended Liporaci from his post and initiated the judicial process to remove him on corruption charges. To avoid the trial, Liporaci resigned in March, resulting in the case being passed into the hands of two more judges.

18. *Denuncismo* refers to the proliferation of civic or media disclosures of alleged wrongdoing that are not based on independent investigations but on rumors or "off the record" leaks.

votes. This amounted to almost 4.7 million lost votes, compared to the previous 1999 election results (see Torre, this volume). In this sense, it represented a major break with past electoral patterns. Whereas the *electoralization* of politics entailed a game where a significant proportion of players shifted party preferences from election to election, in this case, the swing vote became the "protest vote" or electoral abstention, with an important part of the electorate rejecting the existing political offers.

Abstentions, blank suffrages and null votes are different ways of expressing public disappointment with the political class. The protest vote—that is, going to the polls to cast a null or blank vote—represents a *voice* strategy that is still channeled within the mechanisms provided by representative institutions. Abstentions, however, represent an *exit* strategy. The choice signals a termination of the representative contract by the represented and their abdication from the electoral game. The fact that some voters chose this way to express their anger with representative institutions was a powerful indicator of the degree of decay of the links between the citizenry and their political representatives. Yet the message was largely ignored. It would take the traumatic events of December 2001 and January 2002 for representatives to realize an abyss had opened between them and their constituents.

The December 2001 Crisis: The Rise of Civic Mobilizations Against Political Representatives

The state of affairs that the October 2001 electoral results hinted at became vividly and tragically palpable less than two months later, when thousands of Argentines took to the streets and plazas of the country, demanding the resignation of all of the country's political representatives. On December 19 and 20, without any previous planning or coordination, crowds of citizens expressed their disappointment with the governing administration by banging pots and pans in their homes and streets of the major urban centers. The protest was sparked by a nationally televised presidential address on December 19, in which De la Rúa announced that he had decreed the existence of a state of siege—and the consequent restriction of constitutional guarantees—in response to a series of food riots in parts of Greater Buenos Aires. The public responded immediatly: spontaneously, thousands of Argentines took the streets and plazas to demand the resignation of the president and his cabinet. In Buenos Aires, a massive and spontaneous outpouring of people in Plaza de Mayo met with the use of violent force by the police, taking the lives of several protesters. Far from discouraging protest, the next day there was a second massive nationwide *cacerolazo* (banging of casserole pots and pans) that forced De la Rúa to step down halfway through his four-year term.

While the Peronist leadership secretly commended the pot-banging protests that paved the way for their early return to power, they would soon realize that the protests were not aimed just at De la Rúa's administration but at the whole political class. Even under newly appointed authorities, mass mobilizations and protests grew in breadth and anger, resulting in political turmoil. Interim president Adolfo Rodríguez Saá resigned on December 31, only seven days after being named by the National Congress. Likewise, in the next interim president Eduardo Duhalde's first months in power, the menace of the *cacerolazos* represented a latent threat to the stability and continuity of his administration.[19]

The epicenters of the public unrest were the city and the province of Buenos Aires, where 859 *cacerolazos* and mobilizations took place between December and March. Other major cities, including Rosario, Córdoba, and Mendoza, also witnessed a considerable number of protests. Yet after an initial period of proliferation of *cacerolazos* and the attempt to made them a weekly event, this form of protest gradually vanished from the public scene. The end of the *cacerolazos* did not imply, however, the end of social protest. The climate of protests initiated in December sparked a heterogeneous multitude of vocal groups (such as savings account holders, debtors, and protesters against the Supreme Court) and mass mobilizations (like *llaverazos*, or crowds rattling keys at banks, and *escraches*, public shaming of officials at their homes). It also led to the establishment of popular assemblies in some of the country's main cities. Finally, it fueled a remarkable increase in activism among organizations of the unemployed.[20]

Part of the social energy unleashed by the *cacerolazos* was subsequently channeled through a multitude of groups and organizations that were more focused. On the one hand, the Duhalde administration's economic measures launched a wave of mobilizations of those who were directly affected by them, mainly depositors and debtors. On the other hand, there

19. As the number and intensity of the *cacerolazos* declined with the passing of time, the Duhalde administration's concern shifted to the problem posed by the increasing mobilizations and demands of the unemployed movement (*piqueteros*).

20. The number of roadblocks substantially increased in 2002, reaching a record number of 2,336 or an average of 194 roadblocks a month. The killing of two protesters during a demonstration in April sent a dramatic warning to the government about the political damage that mobilizations could do to the Duhalde administration. The government response was to dramatically increase the number of social funds for the unemployed, distributed funds not directly to the beneficiaries but to the different *piquetero* organizations. From May to October, the total number of social subsidies jumped from 1,100,000 to 2,050,000. The strategy paid off: during the same six-month period, the number of roadblocks decreased from 514 to 86.

were numerous social initiatives and mobilizations directed toward certain institutions or political figures. Most notably, there were mobilizations that demanded the removal of the Supreme Court justices and numerous public shamings and attacks organized against specific political figures.

Most of those initiatives can still be framed within the concept of social accountability. For example, organizations of savers whose bank accounts were frozen and forcibly converted into pesos, mortgage-holders who rattled their keys in front of banks and financial institutions in outrage over policies that threatened their ownership rights, and debtors who had taken out loans in dollars, turned to legal and social mobilization to protect their rights against what they considered a breach of private contracts and a violation of constitutional guarantees by the authorities. Citizens and civic organizations have also extensively used the courts to claim deposits or settle debts. This points to a central strategy of the politics of social accountability for defending rights claims: legal mobilization. The *escraches* and mobilizations against the Court justices and politicians can also be seen as an outgrowth of the politics of social accountability. The mobilizations of these groups of protesters entailed a severe (and many times violent) condemnation of the actual workings of horizontal institutions and a strong demand to change their members.

The most striking development of the post-*cacerolazo* period, however, was the proliferation of popular *asambleas* (assemblies) throughout the city of Buenos Aires and in other large urban centers, like Rosario and Mar del Plata. The establishment of neighborhood-based popular assemblies took place in January and February 2002, while the public continued with the *cacerolazos*. The assemblies were in a way an outgrowth of the latter, since they were a result of neighbors meeting in the streets to protest. As with the *cacerolazos*, these associational forms developed spontaneously and from *below* without the intervention of any organized social or political group. Since a central aspect of the movement, like the *cacerolazos*, was a radical critique of political parties and representative institutions, the assemblies adopted a loose horizontal, participatory and deliberative type of structure to avoid the "dangers" of delegation.

Initially, the assemblies were loose groupings of neighbors who met to express their anger with the current social and political situation and to demand the resignation of all political representatives. But the assemblies grew in size, and the meetings adopted a regular schedule and an organizational form. By the end of February and early March, many assemblies had established different commissions to deal with specific issues that affected the neighbors in the locality (soup kitchens, press and communication, health, unemployment, exchange of goods and services, and so on).

The attempts to establish an overreaching umbrella organization resulted in the establishment of two major cross-neighborhood meetings (the Inter-barrial of Centenario Park, and the so-called Colombres). The cross-neighborhood organizations' goal was to provide a forum that would allow the exchange of opinions and the coordination of activities among the different neighborhood assemblies of the city of Buenos Aires.

As previously occurred with the *cacerolazos*, the wave of civic effervescence that fed the assemblies gradually faded. Participation in the weekly meetings drastically dropped in numbers over the course of 2002. By 2003, only a reduced core of people actively participated in the assemblies' meetings and commissions. The experience shows the limitations of a discourse that emphasizes horizontality and direct forms of democracy and that is highly suspicious of anything "representative." The significant burdens of active participation took their toll on assemblies, leaving only a nucleus of neighborhood members and leftist party activists. The attempt to recapture delegated power through grassroots organizations, to establish a fully participatory and consensual process of decision-making, proved not only burdensome for ordinary citizens but also generated innumerable internal conflicts and, eventually, fragmentation and demobilization.

CONCLUSIONS

The accountability model of representation is inextricably tied to the legitimacy of the new Argentine democracy. Finding ways to assure governmental responsiveness and responsibility has been one of the central concerns of a citizenry that, after the horrors of authoritarianism, has placed great trust in institutional safeguards against unresponsive or irresponsible government. Political society's failure to adequately respond to the public's demands generated what is perhaps the most severe crisis of the democratic period since 1983. The perception that the mechanisms of institutionalized distrust were notoriously deficient, and that political representatives are not seriously interested in addressing such a deficit, resulted in a massive withdrawal of public trust in political society.

The distinctiveness of the 2001–2 crisis in relation to past democratic experiences is that this time, removal of trust in the existing political parties and leaders did not imply removal of trust in representative institutions. The common denominator of the politics of electoral and social accountability is public concern for the quality and performance of democratic institutions. The politics of social accountability represent a form of public intervention that is guided by an institutional concern: that of protecting and strengthening the institutional logic of democratic institutions and condemning their capture by unscrupulous public officials or politicians. In this sense, there is a common denominator between the wave of public mobilization that rocked the country in the summer of 2001–2 and the previous forms of politicization that have emerged within Argentine civil society since 1983. What connects the politics of rights, the politics of social accountability, the *cacerolazos*, and the assemblies is a shared concern for improving the quality of the new democracy's institutional arrangements. However, there is also an important difference: the latest wave of public mobilization was triggered by the spread of social frustration toward what was perceived as a political system that was deaf to public cries for greater accountability. Whether such frustration will eventually turn social energies into an antipolitical or anti-institutional movement remains an open question. There is certainly something double-edged in the last wave of civic engagement that was absent in the previous forms of civic politics. This is why it is essential that political representatives restore their public credibility by addressing social demands for greater transparency and accountability. Any other shortcuts to building trust would not only be disappointing, but would risk reversing the learning process that has provided the current democratic structure with a solid foundation.

Protest and Politics in Contemporary Argentina

Javier Auyero

CONTENTIOUS VIGNETTES

Argentina, December 2001: Close to three hundred stores were attacked or looted in eleven provinces during the week of December 14 to 21, 2001. Approximately twenty people died, all of them under thirty-five, killed either by the police or by store owners. Hundreds were seriously injured, and thousands arrested. The provinces of Entre Rios and Mendoza were the first to witness hundreds of persons blockading roads and gathering in front of supermarkets demanding food and, when refused, entering the stores and taking away the merchandise. Soon, the wave extended to Santa Fe, Corrientes, Córdoba, Neuquén, Tucumán, Santiago del Estero, Chubut, Rio Negro, and Buenos Aires. After a week of looting, thousands of hungry, desperate, and exhausted people gathered in front of municipal buildings in the north, center, and south of the country to demand food from those they blamed for its absence—officials and politicians.

Northeast, 1999: Between June 7 and December 17, hundreds of tents dotted the main square in the city of Corrientes. *Los placeros*, as the teach-

For his editorial assistance I am grateful to Tyson Smith. For critical comments on an earlier draft, I am deeply thankful to Vicky Murillo and Steve Levitsky. This research was funded by a fellowship from the John Simon Guggenheim Memorial Foundation and by the American Sociological Association's Fund for the Advancement of the Discipline Award supported by the American Sociological Association and the National Science Foundation. Parts of this chapter were adapted from my *Contentious Lives: Two Argentine Women, Two Protests, and the Quest for Recognition* (Duke University Press, 2003).

ers, lawyers, public servants, and courthouse employees camping in the plaza called themselves, demanded back wages (in arrears of two to five months), complained of recent layoffs in the public sector, and protested the generalized custom of public nepotism. Demonstrators ate and slept in the square, while organizing dozens of marches, demonstrations, and street and bridge blockades that, by mid-December, isolated Corrientes from the rest of the country. By the end of the year, virtually no school classes had been held, most public employees and the police were on strike, and regular provision of social services was suspended. These six contentious months came to be known as *el correntinazo;* no other protest in contemporary democratic Argentina had lasted as long.

South, 1996: Between June 20 and June 26, thousands of residents of Cutral-Co and Plaza Huincul, two oil towns in the southern province of Neuquén, blocked all the access roads to the area, effectively halting the movement of people and goods for seven days and six nights. *Los piqueteros,* as the protesters in the barricades named themselves, demanded, "genuine sources of employment," rejected the intervention of their elected representatives and other local politicians (accusing them of dishonesty and of conducting "obscure dealings"), and demanded to speak to the governor in person. The sheer number of protesters, twenty thousand according to most sources, intimidated the soldiers of the Gendarmería Nacional, who had been sent by the federal government to clear the national road. On June 26, the day after the Gendarmería had left, Governor Sapag acceded to most of their demands in a written agreement he signed with a representative of the newly formed picketers' commission. *La pueblada,* as this episode came to be known, was another extraordinary event in contemporary democratic Argentina: It is unusual these days to see troops retreating in defeat and authorities conceding to popular demands.

Northwest, 1993: On December 16, the city of Santiago del Estero witnessed what the *New York Times* (December 18, 1993, p. 3) called "the worst social upheaval in years." Thousands of public servants and city residents, demanding their unpaid salaries and pensions (in arrears of three months), invaded, looted, and burned three public buildings (the government house, the courthouse, and the legislature) and nearly a dozen local officials' and politicians' private residences. Described by the main Argentine newspapers as "hungry and angry people," these disgruntled citizens voiced their discontent with widespread governmental corruption. This episode, known as *el santiagazo,* was the most violent protest in contemporary democratic Argentina, and a unique event in modern Latin America: it was an uprising that converged on the residences of wrongdoers and the symbols of public power, without human fatalities and during which (almost) no store was looted.

CONTINUITIES

It is hardly news by now that the last decade witnessed the emergence of new and unconventional forms of popular contention and collective violence in Argentina. Sieges of (and attacks on) public buildings (government offices, legislatures, courthouses), barricades on national and provincial roads, camps in central plazas, lootings, and (more recently) rallies including demands of food from supermarkets became widespread in the south (the provinces of Neuquén, Rio Negro, Santa Cruz, Tierra del Fuego), center (Córdoba, Buenos Aires), and north (Jujuy, Salta, Santiago del Estero, Corrientes, Chaco, to name just a few) of the country. El santiagazo, la pueblada, el correntinazo, and the recent wave of lootings are analyzed as crucial events in the current cycle of protest in the country (Laufer and Spiguel 1999; Cafassi 2002; Fradkin 2002), main examples of the resistance to the implementation and outcomes of neoliberal adjustment programs (Carrera 1999; Klachko 1999), key cases that illustrate a changing repertoire of contention (Auyero 2001; Farinetti 1999; Villalón 2002), or as episodes that encapsulate the emerging modalities and meanings of protest (Scribano and Schuster 2001; Svampa and Pereyra 2003).

Estallidos, saqueos, road blockades, country-wide rallies, and massive occupations of central plazas are approached as variations of the same theme, namely, as part of a wave, cycle, or repertoire of contention that, having its roots in the consequences of structural adjustment policies (Tenti 2000; Oviedo 2001), represents a rupture with traditional political practices (clientelism being the most cited one; for the effects of this form of political arrangement, see Calvo and Murillo in this volume) and a novel form of popular politics (Dinerstein 2001; Svampa and Pereyra 2003; for the middle class's "politics of accountability," see Peruzzotti in this volume). In many ways, scholarly accounts echo protesters' discourse: many of the leaders and participants of insurgent organizations also mention el santiagazo, la pueblada, and el correntinazo as founding episodes (true "events" in the strict sense of the term) of their struggle: the 1993 rebellion being the one that inaugurated the resistance against menemismo, the 1996 insurgency being the birthing place of the piqueteros, the 1999 corren-

tinazo as the first massive collective action during the De la Rúa administration (Kohan 2002; Cafassi 2002; see Svampa and Pereyra 2003).

True, it would be hard to think of episodes other than these to better
account for the nature of Argentine popular contention. However, the brief
opening narratives attest to an undeniable fact: there are significant *differences* among the collective actions of protesters, picketers, and looters.
There are also important differences in their perceptions and identities
during episodes that have been taken as paradigmatic examples of the
same cycle, wave, or repertoire. In all these episodes, however, we can de-
tect crucial *continuities* between popular contention and routine politics.
These continuities are overlooked by the emphasis, shared by most scholars of protest in Argentina, on the *rupture that popular contention establishes
with everyday forms of doing politics*. Dinerstein (2001) states that the road
blockades "reinvent the forms of (doing) politics." Scribano and Schuster
(2001), in turn, affirm that the "unaffiliated" are the main actors in this
wave of social protest, which constitutes "a mode of rupture with regular
social order" (2001, 21). Svampa and Pereyra (2003, 93), to take the most
recent example, assert that picketers' organizations represent a "first concrete challenge against *punteros* (political brokers)." In what follows, rather
than attempt to explain the aforementioned episodes in full, I will focus on
the continuities between contentious and routine politics paying particular
attention to (a) the workings of clientelist networks, which I consider central to understanding the origins and unfolding of the *santiagazo* and some
of the 2001 lootings; and (b) elite factionalism and party politics, which
I consider crucial to the understanding of the 1996 *pueblada* and 1999
correntinazo.

THE CLIENTS' REVOLT

Understood as the distribution (or promise) of resources by political officeholders or political candidates in exchange for political support (see
Calvo and Murillo in this volume), clientelism has been traditionally understood as the opposite of collective action; as a form of atomization and
fragmentation of the electorate or the "popular sector" (Rock 1975; O'Donnell 1994), and as a way of inhibiting collective organization and discouraging real political participation. Most academics and journalists concur
that the dominance of this type of political arrangement frustrates contention.[1] Yet if we take the trouble to look at specific episodes of protest in

---

1. Scott and Kerkvliet's (1977) analysis of both clientelist networks and popular struggle
and Burgwald's (1996) study of a case of "collective clientelism" are the main exceptions.

Argentina we see that clientelist networks are deeply imbricated with the course of contention.

On December 16, 1993, high school and university students, retired elderly, informal sector workers, and unemployed youth joined municipal and provincial government workers in the rally in front of the Government House of Santiago del Estero. Angry protesters threw bricks, sticks, bottles, and flat paving stones at the Government House while trying to enter the building. The police fired tear gas and rubber bullets at the crowd, who then backed off toward the middle of Santiago's main square. Soon, the police seemed to have run out of ammunition and abandoned the scene. The final sacking of the Government House began. Forty minutes later, the courthouse, just two blocks away, became the target of hundreds of protesters. They broke its windows and entered the building, where they took computers, typewriters, and court case files, and burned desks and chairs. The police report on the "riot" reads: "[Around 1 p.m., a] group arrived at the Congress and, making use of the same methods used in the previous two buildings, they entered, destroyed and burned different pieces of furniture and documentation, and looted different objects." Here's how a protester describes to me what he calls "the procession" through downtown on the day of the "explosion":

> When we were in the Government House, the public employees were clapping at the fire. It seemed natural to move on to the Congress. And, while we were going there, the feeling was that it had to be the same. It was at the Congress where the most anger had accumulated because legislators voted in favor of the *Ley Omnibus*.[2] . . . So it seemed natural to them that, having already settled the differences with the Government House and the Courthouse, the Congress was next.

Another protester talked about this "natural" character of the crowd's actions in terms of "necessity." "It was as if it was understood that it was necessary to go to the Congress, because there was still the anger caused by the repression that happened the day that they approved the *Ley Omnibus*." After being in the Congress building, some protesters returned to their homes or to the main square, but "a very dynamic group began to

---

2. Ley Omnibus is the name given to the local adjustment law that the parliament passed on November 12, 1993, and that implied the layoff of hundreds of temporary workers, the reduction of public administration wages, and the privatization of most public services. In a province where close to half of wage earners are public employees such a law was destined to provoked massive protests.

move around by mopeds and bicycles," another protester recounted. This "very dynamic group" arrived at a politician's home and was joined by neighbors in the burning and sacking. As the police report continues: "[After attacking the Congress building] groups, in estimated numbers of four to five hundred people, moved around the streets of the city, and later on they entered the private residences of officials and ex-officials. . . . Groups . . . were moving in a state of excitation through different parts of the city."

The residences that protesters attacked, sacked, and burned on December 16 have been, in a way, defined as targets in the previous months. The "precision" with which the crowd moved from one home to another (a precision that officials and some of the press used as evidence of the presence of activists) does in fact illustrate the previous process of reconfiguration of the city's geography in terms of the localization of the sources of corruption and suffering, sources who, in the words of another participant, "deserved to be burned down." "How do you decide where to go?" I ask Marilú, a public employee. "Here, in Santiago, everybody knows each other and we know where people live. . . . Someone says, 'let's go there because he has also been stealing from us.' Because that's how it is here in Santiago, we all know each other." Although the great majority of the local political elite is considered corrupt in protesters' views, not everybody's house is looted. Some attacks are negotiated on the spot. When hundreds of protesters reach the home of Deputy Washerberg, "The guy is freaking out with his sons in the back part of the house. His wife comes out of the house to defend him, 'Please, don't do it . . .' She is crying, kneeling in front of us. In any case, Washerberg opposed the *Ley Omnibus*, and he voted against it. . . . So, after his wife cries so much, five gallons of tears, they don't enter his house" (Mariano).

Others, whose homes "deserve to be burned down," are spared for logistical reasons: "The next target" Mariano added, "was the home of Corvalán, a union leader close to the government. They don't burn his house because he lives in a housing compound; they fear that his neighbors' houses will also be reached by the fire." And others, are (partially) saved from attack because of the scattered police action: "We are trying to break into Lobo's house when the cops come," Raúl recalled, and Mario added, pointing at the interaction between the size of the town and the intermittent repression in the making of the protesters' itinerary:

> Santiago is a small town. Everyone knows each other, everyone knows who's who. We leave Congress and go to the governor's house. . . . From there we take another street and go to [govern-

ment official] Cramaro's house. It is very nice house, with a lot of wood and many nice things inside. They enter and trash it. Some cops come in and take us out, running. We then take the Avenue . . . and the groups go to [former governor] Juarez's house either by foot or by bike . . . [former governor] Iturre's house is a spectacular house, with a swimming pool. . . . They also loot and burn it. After that, someone says we should go to [Deputy] Granda's house. . . . He is inside, alone. They go into the house and don't even touch him. But, again, they loot and burn it. They start to take things out, silver trays and tea pots. . . . *It is a moment of joy. It is like stealing from the fellows that have abused power for so many years.* (My emphasis)

Through mutual signaling (signaling that comprised negotiation, logistics, and protection from potential repressive action) protesters moved from one place to another. In this mutual signaling, local radio programs played a very important role by broadcasting the crowd's actions "as if it were a soccer match." The places that protesters attacked have, indeed, different histories and meanings (while the plaza and the government house have long been centers of political life and thus of protest, the home of local politicians became sites of contention only during 1993). On December 16, however, claims against corruption and wage demands get concretized in all of them, public buildings and private homes provide concrete representations to protesters' rage.

Routine politics was deeply imbricated in the itinerary of the crowd; after all, the protestors' route included the homes of the political bosses, the best-known political patrons, and homes that many protesters used to visit quite frequently. As Carlos told me, in one single comment that encapsulated the continuities between personalized political networks and contention:

Here, in Santiago, there are gangs that serve many, many purposes. These gangs are formed by marginal youngsters. The Radical party or the Peronist party invite these youth for a barbecue, taking them for party rallies in exchange for food or money. . . . These youngsters know every single mechanism to get what they want from politicians, ministers, or members of the parliament. They are not Peronists or Radicals, they just go with everybody. They know the politicos' houses. They've been there, because the corrupt politician invites them to their residences, and they begin to figure out how politics work. These are the youngsters who attack the politicos' houses on December 16. They knew perfectly where they lived.

The rootedness of contention in local context gives protest its power and meaning. The *santiagazo*, the deeds and beliefs of the crowd, the emphasis protesters placed on their "honesty" vis-à-vis the corrupt political class and on the personalized character of the punishment they were administering have to be understood in a context such as the Santiago of the 1990s in which widespread public nepotism and patronage politics were the prevailing way of conducting government affairs. Local sociologists refer to the "modelo juarista" (in reference to the five-time governor Carlos Juarez) as a system of power based on the distribution of jobs in the public sector (46 percent of wage earners in the province are public employees) and public housing[3] carried out through well-oiled clientelist networks (Tasso 1999). In a context in which politics take such a personalized character it should not come as a surprise that collective insurgency takes the form it took on December 16. Prevailing political routines gave the *santiagazo* its character; they also provided the crowd with a set of beliefs about right and wrong in politics and who is to be (personally) blamed for their plight.

LA PUEBLADA, LOS PIQUETEROS, AND THE LOCAL POLITICOS

Early on June 20, 1996, one of the main radio stations of Cutral-Co, Radio Victoria, aired the bad news: The provincial government called off a deal with Agrium, a Canadian company, to build a fertilizer plant in the region. The radio station then "open[ed] its microphones to listen to the people's reaction. . . . A neighbor called saying that the people should show its discontent . . . [another one] said that we should get together in the road," Mario Fernández, director and owner of the radio station, recalls.[4] All my interviewees mention those radio messages as central in their recollections, not only in terms of how the radio called on people but also in terms of how the local radio framed the cancellation of the fertilizer plant project. On Radio Victoria, the former mayor Grittini and his political ally, the radio station owner and director Fernández, depicted the cancellation of the deal with Agrium as a "final blow to both communities," as the "last hope gone," and as an "utterly arbitrary decision of the provincial government." Daniel remembers that "there was a lot of anger . . . the radio said

---

3. See *Informe El Liberal 2.*
4. Quoted in Sanchez 1997, 9.

that we should go out and demonstrate, they were saying that it was the time to be courageous." "I learned about the blockade on the radio . . . they were talking about the social situation," Zulma says. Daniel, Zulma, and the rest point toward both the same framing articulator and its similar functions. The radio both made sense of the "social situation" and persuaded people to take to the streets.

As the radio broadcast "the ire that we felt," as Daniel explained to me, and called people to the Torre Uno (the site memorializes the discovery of oil in the region) on Route 22, cabs brought people there free of charge. Was this a sudden eruption of indignation? Were radio reporters and taxi drivers merely the first to spontaneously react? Hardly so. Factionalism within the governing party, the Movimiento Popular Neuquino (MPN), and particularly, the actions of the former mayor Grittini, who had been waging his own personal fight against Mayor Martinasso and Governor Sapag,[5] were at the root of both the "injustice framing" and the mobilization of resources.[6] In an interview that he preferred I not tape, "because the truth cannot be told to a tape recorder," Martinasso told me, "Grittini backed the protest during the first couple of days. How? Well, in the first place [by] buying a couple of local radio stations so that they would call people to the route." "Is it that easy to buy a radio station?" I innocently asked him. "I myself purchased Radio Victoria so that they would broadcast nice things about my administration. The radio's reception area was built with the money I paid to the owner . . . that's how politics work in Cutral-Co." Grittini and his associates' efforts (Radio Victoria's owner Fernández being a key figure at this stage) did not end there. Although there is no conclusive evidence, many sources (journalists, politicians, and protesters) indicate that he also sent the trucks that brought hundreds of tires to the different pickets and some of the bulldozers to block the traffic. He has also been behind the free distribution of food, gasoline, firewood, and cigarettes in the barricades. Some even say that Grittini paid $50 per night to hundreds of young picketers and that his associates provide them with wine and drugs. Below are some excerpts of my interviews with former picketers that point to the crucial role played by party politics in the origins of this contentious episode:

DANIEL: In the first picket, the one on the curve before the Torre Uno,

5. Months before, in the party primaries current governor Sosbich allied with Cutral-Co former mayor Grittini against then governor Sapag. Sapag won the primaries, and Mayor Martinasso, who initially sided with Sosbisch-Grittini, switched factions and joined Sapag's group.
6. For classic statement on resource mobilization theory, see McCarthy and Zald 1973 and 1977 and Jenkins 1983.

we were around thirty persons. Mattresses, food, coffee, and milk were brought to us . . .

JAVIER: And who brought you all these things?

DANIEL: Well, maybe . . . politics had something to do with it . . .

JAVIER: Tell me a little bit about the first organization? Who decided where to place a barricade?

MARY: I think that everything was coming from the top, it was all prepared. Because it was a big coincidence that everything took place around the Torre Uno. But I have no idea who organized it or who spread the first warning. But we saw (especially the first couple of days) a lot of politicians . . . even so, I stayed there out of curiosity.

JAVIER: How was it all organized?

CECILIA: I really don't recall but . . . I might be wrong, but I think politicians began [it]. I went to the Torre Uno because my brother invited me, that's all. But I know that politicians were the first to begin. At that time, I didn't care because it was a just cause, it was for the people who were in need. I didn't care whether politicians were around or not.

JAVIER: So, you, the picketers, were not the ones who decided to blockade the road . . .

JOTE: No, no, no. . . . This was encouraged by one of the factions of the MPN. There was a radio that promoted the whole thing. It was like calling for a rally.

Thus, while the radio aired its angry messages (telling people that "something has to be done" and calling them to go to the Torre Uno), cabs drove people there and to the other barricades for free, tires were brought to the pickets, food, cigarettes, and other essentials were distributed free of charge ("We even got diapers for the babies!" many women protesters recalled). This mobilization of resources and a framing process did not, however, operate in a vacuum but rather, as we just saw, via well-established political networks through which the distribution of resources and the spread of information took place. The mobilization and the framing also took place under background conditions that were ripe for a large-scale protest, namely, the skyrocketing of unemployment in the area and the ensuing rapid process of collective inmiseration (see Auyero 2003; Costallat 1999; Favaro, Bucciarelli, and Luomo 1997; and Favaro and Bucciarelli 1994).

LOS PLACEROS AND THE ELITES

If the *pueblada* illustrates how elite factionalism is linked with the mobilization of resources that sparked the initial protest, the case of the *correntinazo* shows how elite infighting opens up the opportunity for mobilization. During the *correntinazo* protesters demanded unpaid wages (in arrears of five months), protested against layoffs in the public sector, and called for "punishment of those responsible for the situation"—that is, protested against widespread public nepotism.

Since March 1999, protests had been escalating in frequency and size. Much like in Santiago del Estero, as school classes were scheduled to begin, teachers were the first to take to the streets demanding their unpaid December (1998) salary bonuses. In April the teachers' union also led massive rallies demanding unpaid wages; on May 11, they joined other public employees and blockaded the General Belgrano Bridge (the bridge that connects Corrientes with the neighboring city of Resistencia, in the province of Chaco, across the Paraná River) for the first time that year. Following this, there was a generalization of protest with large marches and demonstrations, strikes by public employees, teachers, and the police.

Amid increasing factionalism among ruling elites, demonstrators redoubled their intensity, and the demonstrations expanded to include more and more public employees, unemployed, and students. Following the month of April, two governors were deposed in rapid succession and the mayor (and local strongman) of Corrientes removed and arrested under charges of embezzlement of payroll funds. A coalition of opposition parties (Peronist, Radicals, Autonomistas Liberales) ousted the two governors and the mayor (the three of them from the PANU) on charges of mismanagement of government funds and incompetence. A few weeks later, the local chamber of deputies decided to intervene in the municipality of Corrientes to remove the mayor (Corrientes's foremost *caudillo* and former governor from 1993 to 1997), "Tato" Romero Feris, on charges of corruption.

The new government of Corrientes, headed by Hugo Rubén Perié, confronted an extremely difficult situation. The provincial debt that the former government had contracted had bankrupted the local administration. The new coalition government faced three different although interrelated challenges: one came from the ousted PANU; the other came from the national government, which was threatening to intervene; the third came from the thousands of public employees who, since June 7, had been camping in the main square in front of the local congress, which they had renamed La Plaza del Aguante y la Dignidad (Plaza of Endurance and Dignity).

The PANU did not leave the provincial and municipal governments peacefully. As the disputes between the governing party and the opposi-tional coalition increased, clashes between activists on both sides grew in frequency and violence. On June 11, days before the removal of the PANU governor, two party activists were shot and injured. That day, followers of PANU occupied the local legislature for forty-eight hours protesting Brail-lard's removal. Perié took office on July 3, amid attacks on the offices of the coalition parties, presumably by members of the deposed PANU. The office of the Radical Party was burned to the ground, and the offices of the Peronist and the Partido Autonomista Liberal were also attacked. A few days later, a councilman from the Partido Liberal (an active participant in the protest against the PANU) was attacked in front of his house (again, the perpetrators were said to be members of the PANU). On July 7, un-known culprits attempted to set the house of the president of the chamber of deputies (from the Radical Party) on fire. Supporters of the PANU were also victims of attacks. Three hundred protesters assaulted the radio sta-tion and the mansion of a local commentator who was a loyal supporter of Mayor "Tato" Romero Feris, denouncing him as a "mercenary of the air." His bodyguards responded with a volley of bullets from his house. The leader of the PANU, former mayor Feris repeatedly threatened to mobilize his followers against the new government saying that he could not "hold (his) people back." A few days after being deposed, he told reporters that "members of my party tried to resist our removal from the municipal building. They tried to keep it under our control. . . . I opposed this resis-tance but if this keeps going on a time will come when . . . this will end up in an explosion, we are on the verge of an explosion. . . . If we light the fuse, this will end up in an armed confrontation among our brothers."

Beginning in early June, approximately two hundred tents dotted the square in front of the Congress building. Teachers erected the first tents (modeling their protest on the *carpa blanca* [white tent] erected in Buenos Aires by teachers two years before); a week later workers from the interior of the province occupied the remaining space in the plaza. Lawyers, school transport workers, municipal workers, kindergarten teachers, courthouse employees, health workers, even relatives of police agents, and many oth-ers had their own tents, not all of them represented by their unions (dissi-dent factions of large unions joined the protest as "autoconvocados" [self-convened]). The square became the spatial representation of the brokerage efforts of different unions and factions. It was in the square where the dozens of marches, demonstrations, and the street and bridge blockades were planned. On June 7, right before moving into the Plaza 25 de Mayo and renaming it Plaza del Aguante, nearly twenty-five thousand people manned a roadblock at the General Belgrano Bridge.

Protesters were demanding not only their back wages but also a dialogue with the authorities, "defending our right to be heard," as a leaflet distributed in the square read. As a teacher put in on July 4, "They haven't paid us for three months. We don't have anything for our basic needs. We organized marches, asked for meetings, but no one attended to us." They were also asking for "justice," namely, the prosecution of the "corrupt and thieves," as another leaflet read. The best summary I was able to find about these demands came from the title of one of the leaflets distributed in the square (*Aguanta. Hoja del Pueblo Correntino Autoconvocado*). The title page reads: "Salaries or Justice?" At the bottom of the page it says: "Salaries and Justice." In short, demands changed in the course of the protest. After the PANU officials were deposed, and probably strengthened by their victory, the leaders of the plaza began to call for "the real and effective democratization of all the offices of the state, popular administration of public resources, provincial control of public services . . . and no layoffs in the public administration."

Contrary to what might be expected, the new government did not condemn the actions of protesters. Members of the coalition which ousted the governing PANU repeatedly acknowledged the importance of the *placeros* (who followed the events inside the legislature since the sessions in the Chamber of Deputies were broadcast in the square) in the removal of first the governor and then the mayor. As a member of the coalition put it, "The people in the square gave us the strength (to displace the governor)." That same day, the new governor admitted that they needed to obtain some funds from the federal government "because the Plaza del Aguante y la Dignidad will not give us a lot of time to find a solution. . . . If we do not find a solution the people's support will last only a few hours." In another interview, the new governor acknowledged the relevance of the protest: "In Corrientes there has never been such an important popular protest. It was able to depose 'Tato' Romero Feris . . . we cannot betray their trust . . . the people in the plaza know that I am not a magician. And if they had so much patience with 'Tato,' they should have some patience with me." When a delegation from the Plaza marched to Buenos Aires with the intention of camping in the Plaza de Mayo (Buenos Aires's main square facing the Government House), Governor Perié identified with them saying, "The Correntinos are fed up . . . if we do not receive a solution (namely, funds to pay the overdue salaries), the people of Corrientes will know what to do." As the new governor obtained some funds, his minister of government and justice went to the General Belgrano Bridge, told protesters about the news, and led them from their barricades to the main square where the archbishop celebrated a mass. This episode encapsulated the validation of the *aguante* not only by government officials but also by another powerful player in local politics: the Catholic Church. Repeatedly, church authorities recognized the legitimacy of the protesters' demands and of their "struggle."

THE LOOTERS AND THE *PUNTEROS*

"You are invited to destroy the Kin supermarket this coming Wednesday at 11:30 a.m., the Valencia supermarket at 1:30 p.m., and the Chivo supermarket at 5 p.m."[7] This and similar flyers circulated throughout poor neighborhoods in Greater Buenos Aires inviting residents to join the crowds that looted several dozen supermarkets and grocery stores during December 2001. Many investigative journalists' reports agree that the flyers were distributed by members of the Peronist party, some of them local officials, others well-known grassroots leaders (Young 2002; Bonasso 2002). In 67 of the 128 cases where there is detailed reporting (out of a total number of 289 looting episodes), party brokers were present among the looters; in many cases they were seen directing the crowds to and from their targets (for anecdotal evidence, see Bonasso 2002). In many others (either lootings, attempted attacks, or claims for food in supermarkets), firsthand observers' reports point to the presence of union leaders and grassroots organizers and picketers' organizations.

The flyers in particular betray a connection that analysts of the recent wave of violent contention in Argentina have consistently overlooked: the obscure (and obscured) links that looters maintained with political entrepreneurs and, through them, with established power holders. The flyers, furthermore, point to a dimension that scholars of collective violence throughout the world have only recently begun to give due attention: the role of political entrepreneurs in the promotion, inhibition, and/or channeling of physical damage to objects and persons.

The peak of collective violence during 2001 has been the subject of many scholarly (Cafassi 2002; Fradkin 2002; Lewkowicz 2002), journalistic (Bonasso 2002; Martinez 2002; Camarasa 2002), and insiders' accounts (Kohan 2002; Colectivo Situaciones 2002). The lootings, however,

---

7. This section is based on current research.

remain an uncharted terrain for social scientists. The few existing studies and journalistic reports on the recent "food riots" are single-actor accounts dominated by what sociologist Charles Tilly (2003) calls the steam boiler analogy or what historian E. P. Thompson (1993) labels a "spasmodic view" of popular revolt. The main actors of the lootings (*saqueos* in Spanish) were said to be the poor and unemployed who, responding to a rapid reduction in the standard of living by visible government (in)action (namely, the suspension of many food distribution programs) and the skyrocketing level of joblessness (in December unemployment rates reached 21 percent of the economically active population), suddenly exploded in anger and plundered stores and supermarkets (Fradkin 2002). Poverty and unemployment, together with state inaction, prevailing analyses assert, created an insurmountable pressure that built up during 2001 until everything exploded—tellingly, the title of a widely read book on the 2001 events (Cafassi 2002) is *Olla a Presión*—Pressure Cooker.

Existing studies cannot account for what even a superficial observation of the recent lootings would note: attacks on supermarkets and stores occurred in areas with similar unemployment rates and poverty levels; in towns or districts that were suffering from the same official indifference. In addition, the various lootings had different degrees of mass participation and registered different degrees of violence—in some cases, the premises were completely destroyed, looters killed or wounded, on other occasions, the merchandise was taken away with no damage to property or people whatsoever.

The bulk of the looting occurred in municipalities with high poverty and unemployment levels. However, not every municipality with high levels of poverty and unemployment had lootings. Some municipalities (like La Matanza in Buenos Aires and Rosario in Santa Fe) had high looting activity, while others with similar levels of poverty and unemployment (like Florencio Varela in Buenos Aires, and La Banda in Santiago del Estero) had none. Noting these geographic variations in looting activity, in attendance, and in the level of violence involved, some investigative journalists (Amato 2002; Young 2002; Guagnini 2002) call our attention to the presence of organizers and political brokers among the looters. Although rightly highlighting the importance of the presence of organizers as a key element in the lootings, journalistic accounts fall into simplistic recitals of the ways in which their actions proceeded. Organizers, most reports agree, "manipulated" the crowd, while law enforcement officers "conspired" to let the crowd act. The multitude, in these accounts, is seen as a "passive instrument of outside agents," as George Rudé (1964) would put it.

Contrary to single-actor accounts that see the poor and the unemployed exploding in rage, somewhat chaotically, after a mounting period of collective suffering, the presence of brokers and other organizers among many of the looting crowds points to the existence of previously connected actors. Evidence that grassroots activists, union leaders, and party brokers were in attendance thus gives *prima facie* plausibility to the theoretical arguments made about the existing linkages among participants in joint action, destructive or otherwise. Recent research on contentious politics (McAdam, Tarrow, and Tilly 2001) and on collective violence (Tilly 2003) highlights precisely this aspect of episodes that authorities call "riots": "In practice," writes Charles Tilly (2003, 32), "constituents' units of claim-making actors often consist not of living, breathing whole individuals but of groups, organizations, bundles of social relations, and social sites such as occupations and neighborhoods."

The presence of these organizers, however, tells us little about how and why they created an opportunity for others to act and less about how and why thousands of people took advantage of that opportunity. To understand and explain organizers' and looters' actions we need to examine the operation of the their networks in the everyday life of poor neighborhoods (*barrios* located within municipalities) in the period immediately *before* the lootings, and reconstruct the concrete steps through which these networks became mobilizing structures *during* the lootings. In-depth investigation of both issues will serve to challenge the pernicious, but widespread, premise that sees "crowd manipulation" at the center of the December lootings.

A *punteros'* looting? Previous research (Auyero 2001; Levitsky 2003; Torres 2002) shows that in poor working-class neighborhoods, shantytowns, and squatter settlements throughout Argentina one of the increasingly relevant ways in which the poor and the unemployed solve the pressing problems of everyday life (access to food and medicine, for example) is through patronage networks in which brokers of the Peronist party are key actors. Depending to a great extent on the (not always legal, not always overt) support of the local and federal states, these problem-solving networks work as webs of material and symbolic resource distribution and of protection against the risks of everyday life. Within these networks, Peronist brokers channel the flow of goods and services from their political patrons to their clients and the flow of political support (in the form of attendance at rallies, participation in party activities, and sometimes votes) from their clients to their patrons. Punteros provide food in state-funded soup kitchens, broker access to state subsidies for the unemployed or to public hospitals, distribute food or food vouchers to mothers, children, and the elderly, and occasionally give out toys (manufactured by workfare recipients) to parents who cannot afford any.[8] As Goldberg (2003) writes: "The main source for all these most basic necessities [food, clothes, and medicine] among impoverished Argentines is the Peronist neighborhood broker, or *puntero*" (for a detailed description of brokers' practices, see Auyero 2001 and Levitsky 2003). Other basic needs aside, the procurement of food is, according to our own ethnographic observations and those of other analysts (Torres 2002; Levitsky 2003) the main task of brokers of the Peronist party.

Some classic works (notably Scott and Kerkvliet 1977 and Scott 1977) have shown that an interruption in the flow of resources that routinely circulate within these networks providing for the survival of large numbers of people can actually trigger collective, often violent, action. Newspaper reports (see, for example, *Clarín*, December 19, 2002) suggest that this was precisely the case during the months prior to the lootings: Many of the social assistance programs that fed the operation of patronage networks were severely curtailed during 2001, causing a major disruption in the working of clientelist politics and, thus, creating the condition for an upsurge of popular violence.

During the week-long looting brokers of the Peronist party were quite active, as usual, in search of food for their clients. During this violent week, however, brokers sought out food neither in the usual places nor through their usual means. Given that the traditional sources of food for their clients (state-funded programs at municipal, provincial, and federal levels) were not responding, brokers turned their attention to local supermarkets. Demanding food from supermarkets was hardly an original joint practice. Far from creating a new form of collective violence, brokers were drawing upon past looting experiences (massive ones in 1989) and more recent collective claims for food in big supermarkets that had organizations of the unemployed (locally known as *piqueteros*) as their central actors. Either following the explicit orders of their patrons or—as is more likely given the decentralized character of the Peronist party[9]—acting on their own (but with the tacit approval of their leaders), they searched for food *for and with* their clients by means other than the usual ones: they

8. In a survey of 112 UBs (Unidades Básicas, grassroots offices of the Peronist party) in La Matanza, Quilmes, and the Federal Capital, Levitsky (2003, 188) shows that more than two-thirds of them engage in direct distribution of food or medicine. Nearly a quarter of them regularly provide jobs for their constituents. Sixty percent of the UBs of Greater Buenos Aires surveyed by this author participate in the implementation of at least one government social program.

9. On the decentralized character of the Peronist party, see Levitsky's (2003) insightful analysis.

looted. Although flyers inviting people to attack supermarkets did indeed circulate, the sequence seems to have been more subtle. Although there are reports that say that brokers "took" prospective looters to the sites, the process seems to be less straightforward. Through their networks, brokers publicized information (or rumors) concerning the upcoming distribution of food in local supermarkets. Given their reputation as food-providers, residents of poverty enclaves acted on this information broadcasted by brokers and began gathering in front of these stores. With hundreds (and sometimes thousands) of desperate people believing in the imminent giving out of food gathered in front of unguarded stores, minor contingencies then determined the unfolding (or the absence thereof) of collective violence.

TASKS AHEAD

Contentious and routine politics are, this chapter argues, mutually imbricated. Here I focused on four cases of mass collective action to show that an understanding of the everyday operation of clientelist politics is key to grasping the origins and unfolding of two extraordinary episodes, the 1993 *santiagazo* and some of the 2001 lootings, and an understanding of the factionalism of the elites and of the usual way of doing politics are crucial to comprehending the course of both the 1996 *pueblada* and the 1999 *correntinazo*.

So, where does this (admittedly uneven) journey through various contentious episodes leave us? When writing about subaltern groups—even more so when seeking to understand subaltern's joint actions—we are always navigating between two equally pernicious traps: miserabilistic and populist interpretations. Under the spell of the first, we are inclined to see protest as the self-defeating acts of the victims of an all-powerful system. Under the influence of the second (undoubtedly more pervasive among social scientists), we are disposed to see every act of protest as an act of heroic resistance of a people untouched by domination, a people without the deep marks left by sustained misery and destitution, a people without ties to the elites, without personal commitments or loyalties to local power holders. In order to understand and explain the course of popular contention in the country, we have to avoid falling into these traps, looking closely not only at episodes of collective action but also at the continuities that they establish with the everyday political life of those who during days, weeks, or months expressed their frustrations and grievances in the streets, roads, and plazas. It is there, in the back and forth between the *barrio,* the *unidad básica,* and the *piquete*—namely, in the mutual imbrication that exists (whether progressively minded academics like it or not) between mobilizing structures, routine politics, and clientelist networks—where we will find the answers to the questions we still have about popular contention in Argentina.

Conclusion:
Theorizing About Weak Institutions:
Lessons from the Argentine Case

Steven Levitsky and María Victoria Murillo

This concluding chapter examines some theoretical lessons of the Argentine case. Specifically, it draws on the previous chapters to probe further into the causes and consequences of institutional weakness. As noted in the introduction, institutionalist approaches have become increasingly dominant in the field of comparative politics over the last two decades. The institutionalist turn was given a boost by the end of the Cold War, which led to the widespread adoption of formal democratic and market institutions. The proliferation of new constitutions, legislatures, judicial systems, central banks, and electoral systems in the developing and postcommunist worlds created an unprecedented opportunity to apply existing institutionalist theories to new cases.

Yet scholars have also pointed to important limitations inherent in the (direct) application of U.S.-based institutionalist theories to Latin American democracies (O'Donnell 1996, 2003a; Weylanda 2002; Helmke and Levitsky 2004; Munck 2004). Of particular concern is the literature's narrow focus on formal rules. In much of Latin America, formal rules—indeed, the rule of law in general—are unevenly enforced. In some cases, they are evaded altogether (O'Donnell 1993, 1999a; Weyland 2002a, 66–68). Institutions—and even regimes—also remain far less stable than in the advanced industrialized countries. Rather than fixed or "taken for granted" constraints, then, many remain highly contested (Munck 2004).

Finally, many of the "rules of the game" that structure political life in Latin America are informal (O'Donnell 1996; Helmke and Levitsky 2004).

Drawing on the Argentine case, this chapter reevaluates some of the assumptions underlying much of the recent literature on political institutions. Rather than take the enforcement and stability of formal rules for granted, we treat them as dimensions along which cases vary. In this way, we seek to refine existing institutionalist approaches in order to enhance their utility in contexts—including, but not limited to, much of Latin America—in which stable and effective formal institutions are the exception, not the rule.

The chapter is organized into four sections. The first section provides a conceptual discussion of weak institutions and their relevance for the study of Argentina and Latin America. The second section discusses the implications of this conceptual distinction for theory building in comparative politics. The third and fourth section present hypotheses, derived from the chapters in this volume, about the consequences and causes of weak institutions.

THE CONCEPT OF INSTITUTIONAL WEAKNESS

In the introduction, we defined strong institutions as those that are stable and enforced. A major concern regarding the export of the U.S.-based theories of institutions to Latin America is that many of these theories take these dimensions for granted. In both its rational choice and historical institutionalist variants, the new institutionalism in political science has focused mainly on formal institutions (Hall and Taylor 1996; Carey 2000). Studies in these traditions tend to equate institution with parchment rules, assuming—at least implicitly—that the rules on paper either reflect or generate shared expectations about how others will behave. Such a conceptualization thus takes for granted that the formal rules are (1) *enforced* with sufficient rigor that they are routinely complied with and (2) sufficiently *stable* for actors to develop shared expectations based on past behavior. In other words, formal institutions are assumed to be *strong* institutions. These assumptions hold relatively well in the United States and other advanced industrialized democracies. In these countries, core political institutions are highly stable. The U.S. Constitution and Britain's parliamentary regime have remained intact for centuries. Although secondary rules may change in these countries, the underlying rule-making processes are effectively fixed. Moreover, because these countries have considerable state capacity and an institutionalized rule of law, formal rules and procedures are systematically enforced and widely complied with.

Assumptions of institutional strength do not travel as well to Latin America. In much of the region, formal rules are neither stable nor effectively enforced. Rather than take root and generate shared behavioral expectations, rules—and in many cases, rule-making processes—change repeatedly, and rules that exist on paper are, in practice, unevenly or sporadically enforced. Institutional instability has long characterized much of Latin America. During the nineteenth century, because of prolonged civil wars and frequent military coups, constitutions were routinely ignored, suspended, discarded, and rewritten. For example, Bolivia's first constitution, written in 1826, was "never fully implemented" (Loveman 1993, 238) and was abolished within three years. Successor constitutions in 1831 and 1834 were also quickly discarded, and new constitutions were promulgated in 1839, 1843, 1851, 1861, 1868, 1871, 1878, and 1880 (Loveman 1993, 239–60). Bolivia was hardly an exception. Venezuela and Ecuador experimented with nine and eleven constitutions, respectively, during the nineteenth century, and the Dominican Republic went through fifteen different constitutions between 1844 and 1896 (Loveman 1993, 141–56, 183–203, 370).

Lack of effective enforcement is also widespread in Latin America. Enforcement may be particularistic, uneven across territory, social classes, or ethnic groups, or simply so infrequent that the rules are routinely violated (O'Donnell 1993, 1999a). For example, Argentina's constitutional guarantee of lifetime tenure for Supreme Court justices, which has formally been in effect since 1853, was routinely violated during the second half of the twentieth century. Virtually every incoming government that took power after 1945—both civilian and military—stacked the Supreme Court with impunity (Helmke, this volume).

Although political institutions in Latin America are not uniformly weak (just as U.S. institutions are not uniformly strong), these examples highlight an important point: institutional stability and enforcement cannot be taken for granted. Rather, they should be treated as dimensions along which cases vary. In other words, institutions may be characterized by varying degrees of both enforcement and stability.

Figure C.1 puts the dimensions of enforcement and stability together to produce four distinct types. The upper left corner of the figure corresponds to strong institutions, or those that are both stable and enforced.[1] These

---

1. In the language of rational choice institutionalism, strong institutions are in equilibrium because most actors comply with them and have no incentives to modify them.

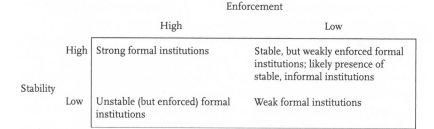

Figure C.1   Two dimensions of institutional strength

"pure" cases of institutional strength—characterized by a tight coupling between formal rules and actual behavior—predominate in the literature. Many political institutions in the United States, most notably the U.S. Constitution, fall into this category. Though less widespread, strong institutions may also be found in Argentina. For example, the country's core democratic institutions, including regular free elections, have been stable and enforced since 1983. So, too, have key aspects of the electoral system, including the provincial list–based, proportional representation system, in which provincial party branches nominate lists of candidates for the Chamber of Deputies.[2] These electoral rules, which allow provincial bosses to exert enormous influence over Congress (Jones and Hwang, this volume), have been stably enforced since 1983, even in the face of significant political opposition. Another example is the rules delegating responsibility for revenue collection from the provinces to the central government, which have endured since their establishment in the 1930s (Eaton, this volume).

The lower left quadrant corresponds to institutions that are enforced but unstable. In such cases, the rules on the books are generally complied with, but these rules are modified repeatedly. As a result, no particular rules of the game take root, and actors are unable to develop shared expectations based on past behavior. Unstable institutions abound in Argentina. An example is the rules governing presidential elections. During the latter half of the twentieth century, the country shifted from a plurality system with an electoral college (1958, 1963) to a two-round presidential run-off system (1973), back to a plurality system (1983), and then to a modified run-off system in which a second-round vote was held if no presidential candidate won 40 percent of the vote (post-1994).[3] Similar instability exists at the provincial level, where the rules for how governors are elected—and

2. In Argentina, this system is known as the *lista sabana*.
3. The threshold shifts to 45 percent if the margin of difference between the top two finishers is below 10 percentage points.

how many terms they may remain in office—are routinely modified (Calvo et al. 2001). Likewise, the specific rules and procedures governing the distribution of revenue from the federal government to the provinces have been repeatedly renegotiated since the 1930s (Eaton, this volume).

The upper right corner of Table C.1 corresponds to formal institutions that are stable but not enforced. In other words, rules remain on the books for long periods of time but are routinely ignored. Because state actors are unable or unwilling to enforce them, they serve, in effect, as "window-dressing" institutions. In such cases, political actors often play by informal rules of the game. An example is postrevolutionary Mexico, where many aspects of the 1917 constitution—including those prescribing fair elections and strict limits on presidential authority—were ignored for decades. Although the political rules of the game in Mexico were relatively stable after the 1930s, these rules—including the well-known *dedazo,* in which presidents single-handedly selected their successors—were largely informal (Weldon 1997; Langston 2003). An Argentine example is the constitutional norm of judicial tenure security, which, though enshrined in the 1853 constitution, has been violated by nearly every civilian and military administration since the 1940s. As Helmke's chapter shows, Argentine elites adhere to an informal norm in which incoming governments are widely expected to stack the Supreme Court. Another example is primary elections in the Peronist party. Although internal elections for presidential candidates and national party leaders were enshrined in the PJ statutes in 1987 and have remained on the books ever since, no such election was held for the national leadership between 1987 and 2005, and only once (in 1988) was a competitive presidential primary held.

Finally, the lower right quadrant of Table C.1 corresponds to institutions that are neither stable nor regularly enforced. In this "pure" form of institutional weakness, the coupling between formal rules and actual behavior is very loose: rules exist on parchment, but in practice, they do little to constrain actors or shape their expectations. Many nineteenth-century Latin American constitutions fall into this category. In stark contrast to the U.S. Constitution, many Latin American constitutions were routinely circumvented (hence, the widespread use of "states of exception") *and* frequently replaced. Many Argentine institutions also combine instability and low enforcement. An example is the rules governing presidential mandates. Between 1928 and the 2003, the constitutional provision that elected presidents serve a single six-year term (later reduced to four years) was never once complied with in full. In 1930, 1962, 1966, 1976, 1989, and 2001, elected presidents were removed before the end of their mandates. Two presidents—Perón and Menem—completed their terms but modified the constitution to allow for a second term. Another example is the tax system. Argentine tax laws are routinely ignored, and as a result, virtually every administration in modern Argentine history has modified them with the goal of improving enforcement.

It should be noted that even these "pure" cases of institutional weakness differ from the *absence* of an institution. Because they exist on paper, even unstable or weakly enforced institutions may softly guide actors' expectations by providing at least some cues about others' behavior. Even when parchment rules are unlikely to be enforced or complied with, actors must at least take them into account as they develop strategies—in part, because other actors may comply with or attempt to enforce them. Indeed, rules that are widely subverted may nevertheless serve as a point of reference—even a kind of focal point in the menu of available options—for actors. In the "state of nature" associated with the absence of rules, such "soft" guidance or reference points do not exist.

Institutions thus vary not only in their design but also in their level of stability and enforcement. Each of these institutional patterns can be found in both Latin America and in the United States and established democracies, although the particular mix of institutional types varies considerably across cases. Moreover, contrary to the assumptions of much of the literature, which tends to view only strong formal institutions as stable or "equilibrium" outcomes, all four of these patterns may be enduring. For example, institutionalists often assume that a lack of enforcement will undermine institutional stability. In other words, if rules are not stably enforced (i.e., in equilibrium), they will fail to generate shared expectations and will consequently collapse.[4] Yet some formal rules endure *precisely because they are not enforced.* Take electoral rules in postrevolutionary Mexico. Had these rules been rigorously enforced, such that elections were free of fraud and other abuses, they would likely have generated intense political conflict that could have threatened the stability of the regime. In other words, the extraordinary stability of the post-1917 Mexican regime rested, in part, on the systematic failure to comply with core elements of the 1917 constitution. Argentina offers a contrasting case. After a similar period of electoral fraud between 1930 and 1943, Argentine electoral rules were largely complied with, in that there was little in the way of fraud or manipulation of the vote-counting process. One consequence of this rule enforcement, however, was sustained *instability,* as powerful actors who

4. According to this logic, as actors perceive that a failure to comply has a high probability of going unpunished, they become less likely to follow the rules over time, which erodes the behavioral expectations generated by institutions. See Greif and Laitin 2004 for a related interpretation applied to endogenous institutional change.

disliked particular electoral results (usually Peronist victories) opted to do away with elections entirely.

THEORETICAL IMPLICATIONS

Variation in formal institutional strength has important implications for our understanding of how institutions work. Whether institutions are strong or weak has a dramatic effect on actors' expectations and behavior. In a context of strong institutions, actors can assume that (1) others will play by the rules and (2) the rules will endure into the foreseeable future. When institutional change occurs, it generally does so in predictable ways and through clearly defined (namely, legal or constitutional) procedures. In such a context, actors' short-term discretion is relatively low: the menu of behavioral options is limited to those prescribed or permitted by the formal rules. These constraints reduce actors' uncertainty. Because actors believe that others are similarly constrained by the rules, and that the rules will endure, they develop stable expectations about how others will behave, which lengthens their time horizons and facilitates cooperation (O'Donnell 1994). Moreover, where institutions are expected to persist (and be enforced) into the foreseeable future, actors are likely to take them seriously. Consequently, they will invest time and energy into questions of institutional design, and once institutions are in place, they will invest in the skills and organizations necessary to achieve their goals through those institutions (North 1990b, 364–65; Pierson 2000b).

Institutional weakness creates markedly different patterns of expectations and behavior. Where institutions are weak, actors cannot assume that others will comply with the rules, or that the rules will persist into the foreseeable future. Rules (and rule-making processes) may change unexpectedly and dramatically, and through irregular means. In such a context, actor discretion vis-à-vis the rules is much greater. Actors may select strategies that are prescribed by the rules, but they may also choose among various extra-institutional options. The result is greater uncertainty.[5] In the absence of stable and binding rules of the game, actors cannot develop

5. Uncertainty may be greatest at medium-to-low levels of institutional strength. At the lowest levels of formal institutional strength, where *no one* expects them to be enforced, nonenforcement is a stable and predictable outcome. In other words, actors operate with a shared understanding that no one is playing by the formal rules. At medium-to-low levels of institutional strength, by contrast, the level of predictability is lower. Because the formal rules are at least intermittently enforced, and because at least some actors play by them, actors remain uncertain which—if any—rules will prevail in a given instance. We thank Kurt Weyland for suggesting this point.

expectations based on past behavior. Such uncertainty generally results in lower levels of trust and cooperation, and in shorter time horizons (O'Donnell 1994, 59). Finally, where institutions are weak, actors will take them less seriously. If politicians do not expect the rules of the game to endure or be enforced, they will be unlikely to invest in them.

These differences in actor expectations have important implications for theories of political institutions. Comparative studies of political institutions, which focus largely on differences in formal institutional design, often take for granted a tight coupling between formal rules and actor expectations and behavior. In other words, they assume that formal constraints can be mapped more or less directly onto strategic action. Where parchment rules are not systematically enforced or complied with, however, the assumption that formal institutions shape actors' incentives and behavior—and consequently, that institutional design has a significant effect on political outcomes—becomes more problematic.

The existence of variation of institutional strength poses challenges for several different areas of comparative research. For example, cross-national comparisons of institutions must contend with the fact that two formal rules that are identical on paper may function differently in practice. Debates over constitutional arrangements and their effects—such as the literature on presidentialism versus parliamentatism—rarely examine differences in institutional strength. Yet as studies of presidentialism in Latin America have shown, constitutional checks on executive power are in many cases weakly enforced, and consequently, presidents' real authority may far exceed their constitutional prerogatives (Hartlyn 1994; O'Donnell 1994; Weldon 1997). Such cases of "hyperpresidentialism" (Nino 1996a) cannot be attributed strictly to constitutional design: they are also a product of institutional weakness.

Variation in institutional strength also has important implications for research on institutional diffusion. Much of this literature assumes that formal institutional arrangements will have uniform effects across cases.[6] Yet several recent studies have shown that parchment rules function quite differently as they diffuse across countries, in part because of variation in the degree to which the rules are actually enforced (Kopstein and Reilly 2000; Mukand and Rodrik 2002). Indeed, elites may import formal institutions without any intention of enforcing them.[7]

Variation in institutional strength is also critical to research on institu-

6. See, for example, Lora's (2001) liberalization index measuring the spread of market reform in Latin America.

7. According to Weyland (2004), policymakers sometimes adopt formal institutions simply to demonstrate their "modernity."

tional design. Theories of institutional design often assume that actors operate with long time horizons. In other words, they assume that actors expect the rules they create to both endure and constrain future behavior (Moe 1990; Geddes 1994, 1996). Based on these assumptions, scholars have shown that political competition may induce politicians to create self-binding institutions in an effort to constrain their rivals—and prevent them from reversing certain policies—when they are in power (Moe 1990).[8] For example, the Pinochet government in Chile created a new constitution, an autonomous central bank, and other self-binding institutions with a clear eye toward binding its democratic successors (Boylan 2001). However, politicians who do not expect institutions to endure are likely to behave in a very different manner. Thus, the Argentine military, which was almost certainly less confident in the durability of its own institutions, did not invest heavily in designing rules for the post-transition period. It never created a new constitution or self-binding economic institutions. Instead, it sought to negotiate an informal pact with its expected successors, the Peronists, which would ensure its protection after it left power. Only when this pact began to unravel did the military government issue an amnesty decree to protect it from future prosecution (Munck 1998, 155–56), and (as the military might have expected) this law was immediately repealed by the Alfonsín government.

Similarly, scholars who treat institutions as "credible commitment" mechanisms (North and Weingast 1989; Shepsle 1991) argue that actors create institutions to bind themselves over the short term in order realize mutually beneficial long-term gains. Thus, executives may delegate authority to parliaments and courts as a means of establishing a credible commitment not to expropriate private sector profits in order to improve their longer-term creditworthiness and access to revenue (North and Weingast 1989). Such theories of executive self-restraint take for granted the existence of a stable institutional context in which actors expect the rules they create to endure and be enforced. However, if politicians' time horizons are short and they do not expect the institutions they create to endure, they may be less likely to design them with an eye toward establishing credibility—and more likely to maximize their short-term discretion and power. This dynamic can be seen in nineteenth-century Bolivia. Between 1825 and 1899, "every Bolivian president faced uprisings and coup attempts; several were assassinated in office, . . . and almost all failed to complete their terms" (Loveman 1993, 235). In this context of extreme

8. For applications to Latin America, see Geddes 1994, Boylan 2001, Schamis 2001, and Bill Chavez 2003.

instability, presidents had little interest in establishing mechanisms of credible commitment, preferring instead to maximize their short-term power resources. Thus, although General José Miguel Velasco designed a liberal constitution in 1839 that limited executive and military power, he "was unable to implement the . . . Constitution or to consolidate his government" before he was toppled in an armed uprising. His successor, José Ballivián, wrote a new constitution that created an "all-powerful presidency," provided the executive with vast patronage resources, and extended the presidential term to eight years (Loveman 1993, 242–45). Uninterested in creating mechanisms of long-term credible commitment, Ballivián designed a constitution that maximized his short-term access to power resources.

Finally, institutional weakness also has important implications for theories of institutional development. Recent research on the role of path dependence has shown that political institutions are often prone to "increasing returns" (Pierson 2000b). According to Pierson, institutions "encourage individuals and organizations to invest in specialized skills, deepen relationships with other individuals and organizations, and develop particular political and social identities. These activities increase the attractiveness of existing institutional arrangements relative to hypothetical alternatives. As social actors make commitments based on existing institutions and policies, their cost of exit from established arrangements rises dramatically" (2000a, 259). As these asset-specific commitments accumulate and other investments are forgone, actors develop a strong vested interest in the existing institutional arrangements—as well as the skills and resources needed to defend them (North 1990b, 364–65). Consequently, it becomes increasingly costly to reverse course. Such feedback mechanisms explain the persistence of institutional legacies and the relative stability of many institutions.

However, if actors do not expect institutions to endure or be enforced, they will be less likely to invest in skills or organizations appropriate to those institutions, and thus less likely to develop a stake in them. In such cases, it may be relatively easy to reverse earlier institutional choices. An example may be drawn from Levitsky's chapter on the Peronist party organization. During both his presidency and his exile, Perón repeatedly reorganized the Peronist party from above. Between Peronism's foundation in 1945 and Perón's death in 1974, no single party structure remained in place for more than a few years. Given that the party organization could be dissolved and re-created from scratch at virtually any moment, Peronists learned not to invest in it, but instead to invest in personal relationships with Perón. As a result, few vested interests grew attached to the party bureaucracy. No "lock in" effect occurred, and throughout the second half of the twentieth century, the cost of reversing course and radically reorganizing the party remained low.

Variation in stability and enforcement thus has far-reaching implications for how institutions shape actors' expectations and behavior. Given that most polities in the developing world more closely resemble Argentina (with its abundance of weak institutions) than the United States (where many political institutions are exceptionally strong), it is essential that scholars begin to refine existing theories of institutions so that they may be usefully applied in a broader range of cases. The sections that follow take an initial step in that direction, using the Argentine case to develop hypotheses about the consequences and causes of weak institutions.

THE CONSEQUENCES OF INSTITUTIONAL WEAKNESS

Several of the chapters in this volume focused on the effects of institutional weakness, examining, for example, how a case in which the rules are either unstable or not enforced may generate political behavior and outcomes that diverge from those expected from the formal rules. Building on these analyses, this section outlines four initial hypotheses about the effects of institutional weakness.

Problems of Coordination

First, the chapters provide support for the argument—made by scholars such as Nino (1992) and O'Donnell (1993, 1994)—that institutional weakness creates severe problems of coordination among political and economic actors. The absence of stable and binding rules of the game heightens actors' uncertainty about others' behavior. Because actors cannot be certain that existing rules will endure into the future, their time horizons will be shorter. They may have an incentive to defect in anticipation of new rules rather than be left as "suckers" playing by the old ones. And because the rules are not systematically enforced, actors develop expectations that others will not always comply with them. In a dynamic that resembles a reverse tit-for-tat (Axelrod 1984), actors who encounter unsanctioned defection will become more likely to defect in the future, making cooperation progressively more difficult to sustain (Nino 1992).

As the Argentine case illustrates, the coordination problems caused by the absence of stable and binding rules may have a range of deleterious effects, both political and economic. The political costs of coordination failure are seen clearly in Peronism's response to the 2001–2 crisis. The PJ has long lacked binding rules to ensure internal cooperation and discipline, and amid the uncertainty generated by De la Rúa's resignation, internal distrust and unmediated conflict threw the party into turmoil. A near-total lack of cooperation and discipline among party bosses contributed to the collapse of Adolfo Rodríguez Saá's interim presidency (after barely a week) in 2001 and brought Peronism to the brink of a costly schism in 2002. With the party in a state of virtual anarchy, conflict between Duhalde and Menem in anticipation of the 2003 presidential election spilled beyond institutional channels. Party leaders first ignored, and later discarded, the PJ's formal candidate-selection system (primary elections). Because they lacked mechanisms to establish nomination rules that would gain widespread compliance (several candidates threatened to defect and run outside the party), PJ leaders were forced to abandon the nomination process entirely and allow three different Peronists to run in the general election. Because this solution divided the Peronist vote among three candidates, the PJ's inability to resolve internal conflicts put an assured victory at risk.

Coordination problems have also had severe consequences for public policy. As Spiller and Tommasi (this volume) argue, continuous institutional instability in Argentina has hindered the forging of intertemporal agreements, which has limited cooperation—and fostered distrust—among key political actors, such as presidents, legislators, governors, and interest groups. As a result, political and economic actors operate with extremely short time horizons and generally do not seek to establish durable policy arrangements. Because formal rules are not sufficiently credible to ensure intertemporal agreements, political actors tend to change policies in pursuit of short-term goals when given the opportunity. The result has been repeated—and often far-reaching—policy swings, which, according to Spiller and Tommasi, is a major cause of Argentina's poor economic performance during much of the twentieth century.

The Search for Rigid Policy Solutions

A second—and related—hypothesis is that institutional weakness creates incentives for actors to adopt highly rigid policy arrangements in an effort to overcome the credibility problems generated by past institutional failures. Where previous governments have repeatedly abandoned rules that they or their predecessors have set up, new governments will have an especially difficult time convincing political and economic actors that they intend to play by the rules this time. To achieve credibility in such a context, governments may seek to create rigid rules and procedures that tightly bind them in their policymaking discretion and which are extremely difficult to "unbind." In other words, to ensure political or economic actors that they will not be burned by policymaking discretion, governments create procedures that lock in certain outcomes and are very costly to overturn. Although such rigid policy arrangements tend to create negative externalities in other areas, the government's willingness to pay those costs is often essential to the credibility of the arrangements. Hence, "hypercommitment" mechanisms may generate short-term credibility, but they frequently do so at the cost of reducing policymakers' capacity to adapt to changing political or economic conditions.

The Convertibility Law provides an example of such a "hypercommitment" (Tommasi and Spiller, this volume). Convertibility was designed to address a severe credibility gap vis-à-vis investors, creditors, and Argentine citizens after years of macroeconomic policy instability. The law tied the government's hands in monetary and exchange rate policy, rigidly fixing a desired outcome—exchange rate parity with the dollar—to gain the trust of skeptical actors. The system was extremely difficult to overturn. Because (public) legislative action was required to end convertibility, the system could not be altered without risking a run on the currency (with possible hyperinflationary consequences) (Starr 1997). Convertibility generated substantial negative externalities in other policy areas, particularly trade competitiveness, which the government used to signal its "hypercommitment" to sustain it. Convertibility's rigidities helped restore investor and creditor confidence in the short term. However, it left Argentine governments without the macroeconomic tools to respond to the post-1998 economic downturn—with devastating consequences (Galiani, Heymann, and Tommasi 2003).

Institutional Fluidity and the Capacity for Rapid Change

A third hypothesis is that institutional instability can facilitate change. Stable institutions tend to inhibit rapid or far-reaching change (Huntington 1968; Zucker 1977; Schedler 1995). They narrow actors' choice sets, stabilize expectations, and routinize behavior in ways that reinforce existing patterns and take radical alternatives off the table. Because asset-specific investments give actors both a stake in established institutions and a greater capacity to defend them, proposals for radical change tend to face widespread and effective resistance. Strong institutions thus tend to be "sticky," in that they do not change as quickly as underlying preferences and power distributions. At best, change tends to be slow and incremental.

By contrast, weaker institutions are more open to rapid or far-reaching change. Where the rules are not systematically enforced, actors' choices are not confined to a set of stable and narrowly defined options; rather, they have a wider menu of strategic options available to them. They may choose among alternatives prescribed by the formal rules (say, A, B, and C), but they may also choose options that violate the rules (say, D and E), or they may seek to change the rules in order to create new options. In addition, few rules are buttressed by powerful vested interests. Hence, weak institutions tend to be highly fluid. Rather than slow and incremental, change is often rapid and extensive.

Although institutional fluidity creates uncertainty and disorder, it is also a source of flexibility and innovation. Such flexibility may enhance the capacity of an organization or regime to adapt during crises. Stable and effective rules of the game limit the speed with—and often the extent to—which organizations can adapt to external shocks. In a highly stable institutional setting, decision makers tend to consider a narrower range of strategic alternatives (Nelson and Winter 1982, 74–83), none of which may be appropriate in a context of crisis. Even when leaders do come up with viable adaptive strategies, established routines and decision rules may limit their capacity to implement them. By contrast, unstable institutions provide actors with greater room for maneuver in searching for and carrying out adaptive strategies. Such rapid adaptation was seen in Peronism's transformation during the 1990s. As Levitsky's chapter argues, the flexibility generated by Peronism's weakly institutionalized party structure facilitated its transformation, during the late 1980s and early 1990s, from a labor-based populist party into a vehicle for implementing radical market-oriented reforms. These rapid and far-reaching programmatic changes helped the PJ survive as a major political force during the neoliberal era. The PJ's internal fluidity also helped it adapt quickly to the political-economic crisis of 2001–2, as the party shed its Menemist program and leadership for the more progressive orientation of Nestor Kirchner.

Informal Responses to Formal Institutional Weakness

Finally, institutional weakness creates incentives for political actors to pursue goals through informal channels. In some cases, actors' informal strategies adhere to (or evolve into) alternative rules and procedures that, though unwritten, are widely known, accepted, and complied with. Such informal institutions often serve as guidelines for how to behave in a context in which the formal rules are not enforced (Helmke and Levitsky 2004).[9] Helmke's chapter on the Supreme Court provides a useful example. Argentina's constitutional guarantee of lifetime tenure was routinely violated beginning in the 1940s: most civilian and military governments removed unfriendly justices and replaced them with allies. Court stacking so frequently accompanied changes of government that it became widely expected—and virtually taken for granted—among Supreme Court justices. These expectations generated a distinct, informal pattern of behavior. Thus, Helmke finds a pattern of "strategic defection," in which justices support the executive while its hold on power is firm, but when the government is perceived to be on its way out, justices tend to defect and issue rulings in line with its expected successor.

Another example may be drawn from Peruzzotti's chapter on citizen protest during and after the 1990s. According to Peruzzotti, much of this protest can be seen as a "societal" response to the state's failure to enforce the law. Thus, the repeated failure of the Argentine judiciary and other formal democratic institutions to check state abuses (or hold state officials accountable for those abuses) created an incentive for civic and media organizations to mobilize in pursuit of those ends. As citizens learned that they could effectively punish abusive state officials through protest and media exposure, a semi-institutionalized pattern of "societal accountability" took hold.[10] Whether civic protest can substitute for formal institutions of horizontal accountability—or help strengthen those institutions— remain questions for further investigation.

THE ORIGINS OF INSTITUTIONAL WEAKNESS

The issue of how to explain institutional strength has received relatively little scholarly attention, in large part because much of the literature takes it for granted. As this book has made clear, however, the degree to which parchment institutions are stable and enforced varies considerably. Such variation requires explanation. In this final section, we use the Argentine case to develop some initial propositions about the causes of institutional strength and weakness. We focus on (1) institutional origins, particularly actors' intentions and the presence or absence of an initial equilibrium,

9. For example, the lack of enforcement of traffic rules in Argentina has given rise to a widely shared informal norm in which no one ever halts at stop signs. Thus, when foreign drivers halt at a stop sign, they may cause a traffic accident because drivers do not expect such formal rule-abiding behavior.

10. See also Smulovitz and Peruzzotti 2003.

and (2) the role of time in creating expectations of stability and, consequently, encouraging investment in institutions.

The Creation of Weak Institutions

As noted, much of the institutionalist literature in political science conflates the creation of formal institutions with the emergence of *stable and effective institutions*. That is, actors with the will and capacity to create formal rules are presumed to be both willing and able to enforce them. And once they make it into parchment, rules are assumed to be in equilibrium, and are thus either accepted by all actors powerful enough to seriously contest them or successfully imposed by one set of actors upon another.[11]

Yet formal institutions may also be "born weak." Such an outcome may occur, intentionally or unintentionally, for a variety of reasons. For one, actors may not intend to create strong institutions.[12] As the literature on institutional isomorphism has shown, actors may create formal rules because they are viewed as publicly or internationally appropriate (Meyer and Rowan 1991), not because they seek to employ them. Indeed, many of these institutions are little more than "window dressing," created by state elites who have no intention of actually enforcing them (Weyland 2004).[13] Such institutions may be in equilibrium, but it is often an equilibrium based on the shared expectation that the rules will *not* be enforced.

Actors may also create formal rules that they do not expect to endure. For example, actors may create formal rules only as a short-term means of demonstrating strength or weakening opponents during a period of political conflict. Although they may initially be enforced, such rules often have little utility—even to their creators—beyond their initial task. For example, Peronist leaders routinely employ statutory reforms as short-term weapons in intraparty power struggles, often inserting clauses stipulating that the

11. Although scholars differ over the nature of the underlying equilibrium, with some emphasizing cooperative or contractual foundations (Shepsle 1986) and others emphasizing the role of power and coercion (Knight 1992; Thelen and Steinmo 1992), they converge around the assumption that such an equilibrium exists. Neither theoretical approach allows for the possibility that formal institutions may be designed on parchment but fail to stick or be effectively enforced. See Jones-Luong and Weinthal 2004 for an insightful discussion of both views of institutional origins.

12. We thank Pauline Jones-Luong for highlighting this point.

13. For example, President Menem responded to corruption allegations during his second term by creating a National Office of Public Ethics. However, the office was almost certainly intended to be "window dressing." Not only did it fail to investigate major corruption allegations raised in the media, but it also refused—in direct violation of its own rules—to make public President Menem's declaration of wealth. See *Clarín*, September 1, 1998.

new rule be applied "this time only." Thus, in their effort to weaken Carlos Menem—who held the PJ presidency—in 2002, allies of Eduardo Duhalde enacted "temporary" reforms to the PJ statutes that canceled the party's presidential primary (which Menem was likely to win) and created a parallel "political action committee" that usurped power from the Menem-led National Council.

Alternatively, actors may create formal institutions that they intend to be strong, but nevertheless fail to enforce or sustain them. Newly created rules may fail to achieve equilibrium, in the sense that they are accepted by, or successfully imposed upon, all actors powerful enough to seriously contest them. For example, formal rules may be created by actors who temporarily control rule-making bodies (particularly the executive branch or the legislature) but lack the power to make those rules binding on all actors. In other words, institutional designers are able to write the rules, but their authority is either too limited or too tenuous to systematically enforce them or to ensure that they endure long enough to shape actors' expectations. Such a situation may occur, for example, when elected civilian governments take office but "real" power is held by military or religious authorities (as in Guatemala in the 1980s or postrevolutionary Iran). Thus, it may be the case that institutional designers neither include powerful actors in the rule-making consensus nor definitively defeat them. In such cases, excluded groups are likely to subvert (and when possible, overturn) the rules—via a coup or behind the scenes pressure—as soon as they have the capacity to do so. In such a context, actors will immediately assign a lower probability to their expectations about others' complying with and sustaining the new rules, which may encourage them to defect and to try to change the status quo.

Argentina is a case of repeated failure to achieve an institutional equilibrium, via either consensus or imposition. Throughout much of the twentieth century, civilian and military governments attempted, but failed, to impose rules and regimes that excluded powerful actors. For example, the first Perón government imposed a new constitution in 1949 without incorporating Radicals, conservatives, and other political forces. This lack of consensus eroded its legitimacy, which made alternative institutions both imaginable and desirable for excluded actors. Hence, although Perón was able to win electoral majorities, his opponents—many of whom retained substantial power resources—never accepted the new rules of the game, and when Perón was overthrown in 1955, the 1949 constitution was quickly and easily discarded.[14] The decades that followed Perón's ouster

14. By contrast, the 1853 and 1994 constitutions were more stable, even if they were not always fully enforced. The 1853 constitution was imposed upon all provinces after a military

were characterized by a stalemate in which no single group could achieve a definitive victory and major political actors repeatedly failed to converge around core institutional arrangements. Efforts to impose both electoral (1957–66) and military (1966–72) regimes that excluded Peronism failed because Peronism and labor used their considerable electoral and mobilizational power to make such regimes unsustainable (O'Donnell 1973, 1988; Cavarozzi 1987; McGuire 1997). For several decades, then, governments created formal rules without either forging a consensus behind them or compelling other powerful actors to play by them. As a result, many of these rules failed to endure beyond the administration that created them.

Time, Actor Expectations, and Asset-Specific Investments

Variation in institutional strength is also affected by time.[15] When institutional arrangements persist (and are enforced) over time, surviving repeated crises and changes of government, actors develop expectations of stability. These expectations induce them to invest in assets specific to those institutions. Thus, actors who expect institutions to endure will develop skills, technologies, and organizations that are appropriate to those institutions (North 1990a, 1990b; Pierson 2000b). As these asset-specific investments accumulate over time, the existing arrangements became increasingly attractive relative to their alternatives, thereby raising the cost of institutional change. In other words, actors develop a vested interest in institutional continuity. These "increasing returns" create a path-dependent dynamic: an initial period of institutional persistence creates expectations of stability, which induces actors to invest in those institutions. Asset-specific investments further enhance institutional resilience by increasing the cost of change, which further reinforces expectations of stability. The result is thus a virtuous cycle in which expectations of stability reinforce existing institutional arrangements.

Such virtuous cycles are not inevitable, however. Where formal institutions are repeatedly overturned or rendered ineffective, the path-dependent effect just outlined is less likely to take hold. Rather, actors will develop expectations of institutional weakness. Consequently, they will be less likely to invest in those institutions or develop skills and technologies appropriate to them. In the absence of increasing returns, the cost of over-

---

victory, and the 1994 constitution was achieved through consensus, after a negotiated agreement between the leaders of the PJ and the UCR (Acuña 1994).

15. On the role of time in institutional development, see especially Pierson 2004.

turning the rules will remain low. Because actors know that new institutions are unlikely to endure, they will have less vested in them. And because they know that new rules are unlikely to be enforced, they have less to fear from them. The result is a vicious cycle in which actors continually expect—and therefore contribute to—institutional demise.

Patterns of institutional weakness may be reinforced by the fact that actors invest in the skills and technologies appropriate to an unstable institutional environment or to alternative informal rules of the game. In a context of persistent regime instability, for example, actors may choose not to invest in political parties and legislative skills—which are only useful under democratic institutions—and instead develop skills (insurrectionary capacity), resources (clandestine networks and other nonparty organizations), and relationships (to the church, the military, or foreign powers) that enhance their capacity to operate in multiple regime settings. These investments may give actors a stake in noninstitutional politics, which will only reinforce existing patterns of institutional weakness.

Thus, institutional fluidity can be as self-reinforcing as institutional stability. If actors develop expectations that formal institutions will not endure or be effective, they will not invest in them. As a result, the cost of subverting or replacing existing institutions will remain low, which increases the likelihood of further rounds of change—and reinforces expectations of institutional weakness. Although such initial periods of institutional failure may be the product of historically contingent circumstances (including sheer bad luck), they may help to lock a polity into a long-term path of institutional weakness.

Argentina followed a path of institutional instability in the aftermath of the Great Depression and the political incorporation of the working classes. Decades of regime instability, in which not only rules but also rule-making processes were repeatedly overturned, had a powerful effect on actor expectations. Because of the frequent collapse, suspension, or purging of institutions as important as the Constitution, the Congress, and the Supreme Court, Argentines failed to develop stable expectations around many of the country's political rules of the game. Instead, they developed expectations of instability. Betting that institutions would be replaced or purged with each change of government or regime, political and economic actors failed to take them seriously or invest in them. As a result, few developed a stake in any particular institutional arrangement. In fact, many powerful actors—including Peronist unions, economic elites, and conservative politicians—invested little in electoral, legislative, and other democratic institutions and instead developed skills, organizations, and relationships (particularly with the military) that helped them survive in context of regime instability.[16] Consequently, for a wide array of institutions, the cost of changing the rules remained low.

There are at least some signs that this pattern of institutional weakness may be changing in post-1983 Argentina. Although earlier patterns of institutional instability have clearly persisted into the contemporary period, one important change has nevertheless occurred: the overarching rulemaking process—the democratic regime—has stabilized. The 1983 election ushered in a period of competitive elections in which the neither the PJ nor the UCR was able to launch a hegemonic project or was threatened with permanent exclusion. Moreover, the political actor that had posed the greatest threat to democratic regimes, the military, was decisively defeated following the ill-fated 1982 war with Great Britain. Several other factors increased the cost of overturning the post-1983 regime, particularly the brutality and colossal failure of the last military dictatorship, which created unprecedented public support for democratic institutions, and the regional spread of democratic norms in the post–Cold War era. The survival of democracy constituted a major change in actor expectations, and it appears to have encouraged greater investment in democratic institutions. As the chapters by Peruzzotti and Torre argue, much of the civic mobilization that took place during the 1990s was aimed at making democratic institutions more accountable, not replacing them. Whether—and how quickly—this regime stability will strengthen other institutions remains uncertain.

CONCLUSION

We opened this book with the claim that an analysis of late twentieth-century Argentine democracy was useful for understanding many of the political and economic processes taking place elsewhere in Latin America. Because of shared historical, cultural, and socioeconomic characteristics, as well as broadly similar economic and political challenges, theories generated by research on Argentina should be of some utility in understanding political and economic processes in other Latin American cases.

In this concluding chapter, we adopted a different comparative focus: the United States and other advanced capitalist countries. The new institutionalism in political science is based largely on studies of these countries, and we use Argentina, a contrasting case, to refine that literature. U.S.-based institutionalist theories tend to assume that formal institutions are

---

16. On Peronist unions' failure to invest in democratic institutions, see McGuire 1997.

stable and systematically enforced. Our study of Argentine politics makes it clear that these assumptions do not always hold. Argentine political institutions vary considerably in terms of their strength: whereas some rules are robust and routinely complied with, many others are fluid and widely subverted. If the new institutionalism in political science is to generate theories that are truly comprehensive, in that they are applicable not only to advanced capitalist countries but also to developing ones, then the strength of formal institutions cannot be taken for granted. Rather, institutional strength should be treated as a dimension along which particular institutions vary. We have used the Argentine experience to explore some of the consequences of weak institutions and develop some initial hypotheses about their origins. Argentina is hardly an exceptional case, however. Similar patterns are likely to be found in other countries—in Latin America and elsewhere—with historically weak political institutions.

The export of U.S.-based institutionalist theories to Latin America has, in many respects, been fruitful. Yet theory building in comparative politics should not be a one-way street. As this book has suggested, comparative institutionalism would benefit enormously from an exchange in which Latin American and other developing countries are used to both refine existing theories and generate and test new ones (O'Donnell 2003a). Such cross-fertilization would greatly enrich our understanding of comparative politics. Indeed, it is only through such a dialogue that comparative politics will become truly global in scope.

REFERENCES

Abós, Alvaro. 1986. *El posperonismo*. Buenos Aires: Editorial Legasa.

Acuña, Carlos H. 1991. La relativa ausencia de exportaciones industriales en la Argentina. Determinantes políticos y sus consecuencias sobre la estabilidad y el tipo de democracia esperables. *Realidad Económica*, no. 100 (June): 6–38.

———. 1994. Politics and economics in the Argentina of the nineties (or, why the future no longer is what it used to be). In *Democracy, markets and structural reform in Latin America*, ed. William Smith, Carlos Acuña, and Eduardo Gamarra. New Brunswick, N.J.: Transaction Publishers.

———. 1995. Algunas notas sobre los juegos, las gallinas y la lógica política de los pactos constitucionales (Reflexiones a partir del pacto constitutional en la Argentina). In *La nueva matriz política argentina*, ed. Carlos Acuña. Buenos Aires: Nueva Visión.

Adelman, Jeremy. 1994. *Frontier development: Land, labour, and capital on the wheatlands of Argentina and Canada, 1890–1914*. Oxford: Oxford University Press.

Adrogué, Gerardo. 1995. El nuevo sistema partidario argentino. In *La nueva matriz política argentina*, ed. Carlos H. Acuña. Buenos Aires: Nueva Visión.

Adrogué, Gerardo, and Melchor Armesto. 2001. Aún con vida: Los partidos políticos en la década del noventa. *Desarrollo Económico* 40, no. 160:619–52.

Alcántara, Manuel. 2004. *Proyecto de elites latinoamericanas (PELA)*. Salamanca: Universidad de Salamanca.

Aldrich, John H., Mark M. Berger, and David W. Rohde. 2002. The historical variability in conditional party government, 1877–1994. In *Party, process, and political change in Congress: New perspectives on the history of Congress*, ed. David W. Brady and Mathew D. McCubbins. Stanford: Stanford University Press.

Alemán, Eduardo. 2003. Gatekeeping in Latin American legislatures. Paper presented at the XXIV International Congress of the Latin American Studies Association, Dallas, March.

Alemán, Eduardo, and Sebastián M. Saiegh. 2004. Legislative preferences, political parties, and coalition unity in the Chilean Chamber of Deputies. Paper presented at the Annual Convention of the American Political Science Association, Chicago, September.

Alesina, Alberto, and Allan Drazen. 1991. Why are stabilizations delayed? *American Economic Review* 81 (December): 1170–89.

Amato, Alberto. 2002. *La trama política de los saqueos. Clarín Digital*, December 19.

Ames, Barry. 2002. *The deadlock of democracy in Brazil*. Ann Arbor: University of Michigan Press.

Arceo, Enrique, and Eduardo Basualdo. 2002. Las privatizaciones y la consolidación del capital en la economía argentina. In *Privatizaciones y poder económico*, ed. D. Azpiazu. Buenos Aires: Flacso-Universidad Nacional de Quilmes.

Arias, Maria Fernanda, and Raúl García Heras. 1993. Carisma disperso y rebelión: Los partidos neoperonistas. In *Perón: del exilio al poder*, ed. Samuel Amaral and Mariano Ben Plotkin. Buenos Aires: Cántaro Editores.

Auyero, Javier. 2000. *Poor people's politics: Peronist survival networks and the legacy of Evita*. Durham: Duke University Press.

————. 2001. Glocal riots. *International Sociology* 16, no. 1:33–53.

————. 2003. *Contentious lives: Two women, two protests, and the quest for recognition*. Durham: Duke University Press.

Axelrod, Robert. 1984. *The evolution of cooperation*. New York: Basic Books.

Azpiazu, Daniel, ed. 2002. *Privatizaciones y poder económico*. Buenos Aires: FLACSO / Universidad Nacional de Quilmes.

Azpiazu, Daniel, and Hugo Notcheff. 1994. *El desarrollo ausente*. Buenos Aires: FLACSO.

Baldrich, Jorge. 2003. The political economy of short run fiscal policy. Some evidence from Argentina, 1994–2001. Manuscript. Universidad de San Andrés.

Baglini, Raúl, Andrés D'Ambrosio, and Hipólito Orlandi. 1993. Juicio a la corte. Manuscript. Buenos Aires.

Bambaci, Juliana, Pablo T. Spiller, and Mariano Tommasi. 2001. Bureaucracy and public policy in Argentina. Manuscript. Buenos Aires: Center of Studies for Institutional Development (CEDI), Fundación Gobierno y Sociedad.

Basualdo, Eduardo. 2000. *Concentración y centralización del capital en la Argentina durante la década del noventa*. Buenos Aires: FLACSO / Universidad Nacional de Quilmes.

Behrend, Jacqueline. Forthcoming. Mobilization and accountability: A study of societal control in the Cabezas case in Argentina. In *Enforcing the rule of law: The politics of social accountability in Latin America*, ed. Enrique Peruzzotti and Catalina Smulovitz. Pittsburgh: Pittsburgh University Press.

Benton, Allyson Lucinda. 2002. Presidentes fuertes, provincias poderosas: La economía política de la construcción de partidos en el sistema federal argentino. *Política y Gobierno* 10, no. 1:103–37.

Bertea, Aníbal, and Teresa Iturre. 2000. Argentina: Descentralización en un país federal. In *Línea de referencia: El proceso de descentralización en Argentina, Brasil, Bolivia, Chile y Peru*. Quito: Sociedad Alemana de Cooperación Técnica.

Bill Chavez, Rebecca. 2003. The construction of the rule of law in Argentina: A tale of two provinces. *Comparative Politics* 35, no. 4 (July): 417–37.

Bisang, Roberto. 1996. Perfil tecno-productivo de los grupos económicos en la industria Argentina. In *Estabilización macroeconómica, reforma estructural y comportamiento industrial*, ed. J. Katz. Buenos Aires: CEPAL-Alianza.

Bisang, Roberto, and Martina Chidiak. 1995. Apertura económica reestructuración y medio ambiente. La siderurgia argentina en los 90. Working Paper 19. CENIT, Buenos Aires.

Bonasso, Miguel. 2002. *El palacio y la calle*. Buenos Aires: Planeta.

Botana, Natalio. 1979. *El orden conservador. La política argentina entre 1880 y 1916*. Buenos Aires: Editorial Sudamericana.

————. 1983. Tradiciones e institutiones en la democracia Argentina. In *La nueva democracia Argentina, 1983–1986*, ed. Garzon Valdes et al. Buenos Aires: Sudamericana.

Boylan, Delia. 2001. *Defusing democracy: Central bank autonomy and the transition from authoritarian rule*. Ann Arbor: University of Michigan Press.

Brusco, Valeria, Marcelo Nazareno, and Susan C. Stokes. 2004. Vote buying in Argentina. *Latin American Research Review* 39, no. 2:66–88.

Burgess, Katrina. 1999. Loyalty dilemmas and market reform: Party-union alliances under stress in Mexico, Spain, and Venezuela. *World Politics* 52, no. 1 (October): 105–34.

Burgess, Katrina, and Steven Levitsky. 2003. Explaining populist party adaptation in Latin America: Environmental and organizational determinants of party change in Argentina, Mexico, Peru, and Venezuela. *Comparative Political Studies* 36, no. 8 (October): 859–80.

Burgwald, Gerrit. 1996. *Struggle of the poor: Neighborhood organization and clientelist practice in a Quito squatter settlement*. Amsterdam: CEDLA.

Cabrera, Ernesto. 1996. Multiparty politics in Argentina: Electoral rules and changing patterns. *Electoral Studies* 15, no. 4 (November): 477–95.

Cafassi, Emilio. 2002. *Olla a presión. Cacerolazos, piquetes y asambleas, sobre fuego Argentino*. Buenos Aires: Libros del Rojas.

Calvo, Ernesto, and Juan Manuel Abal Medina, eds. 2001. *El federalismo electoral Argentino: Sobrerepresentación, reforma política y gobierno dividido en Argentina*. Buenos Aires: Eudeba.

Calvo, Ernesto, and Maria Victoria Murillo. 2004. Who delivers? Partisan clients in the Argentine electoral market? *American Journal of Political Science* 48, no. 4 (October): 742–57.

Calvo, Ernesto, Mariela Szwarcberg, Juan Pablo Micozzi, and Juan Facundo Labanca. 2001. Las fuentes institucionales del gobierno dividido en la Argentina. In *El federalismo electoral Argentino, reforma politica y gobierno dividido en Argentina*, ed. Ernesto Calvo and Juan Manuel Abal Medina. Buenos Aires: Eudeba.

Camarasa, Jorge. 2002. *Días de furia*. Buenos Aires: Sudamericana.

Cantón, Dario. 1986. *El pueblo legislador: Las elecciones de 1983*. Buenos Aires. Centro Editor de América Latina.

Cantón, Darío, and Jorge R. Jorrat. 2002. Economic evaluations, partisanship, and social bases of presidential voting in Argentina, 1995 and 1999. *International Journal of Public Opinion Research* 14, no. 4 (August): 413–27.

Carey, John M. 2000. Parchment, equilibria, and institutions. *Comparative Political Studies* 33, nos. 6–7 (August–September): 735–61.

Carey, John M., and Matthew Soberg Shugart. 1995. Incentives to cultivate a personal vote: A rank ordering of electoral systems. *Electoral Studies* 14, no. 4:417–39.

————, eds. 1998. *Executive decree authority*. New York: Cambridge University Press.

Carrera, Iñigo Nicolas. 1999. Fisonomia de las huelgas generales de la decada de 1990. PIMSA, 155–73.

Carrió, Alejandro. 1996. *La Corte Suprema y su independencia*. Buenos Aires: Abeledo-Perrot.

Carrió, Alejandro, and Alberto F. Garay. 1991. *La jurisdicción "Per Saltum" de la Corte Suprema: Su estudio a partir del caso Aerolíneas Argentinas.* Buenos Aires: Abeldo Perrot.

Catterberg, Edgardo. 1989. *Los argentinos frente a la política. Cultura política y opinión pública en la transición argentina a la democracia.* Buenos Aires: Editorial Planeta.

————. 1991. *Argentina confronts politics: Political culture and public opinion in the Argentine transition to democracy.* Boulder, Colo.: Lynne Rienner.

Catterberg, Edgardo, and Maria Braun. 1989. Las elecciones presidenciales Argentinas del 14 de Mayo de 1989: La ruta a la normalidad. *Desarrollo Económico,* no. 115 (October-December): 361–74.

Cavallo, Domingo. 2002. What will happen when the Supreme Court decides in favor of savers. http://www.cavallo.com.ar/Weeklyopinion/court.html.

Cavarozzi, Marcelo. 1986. Political cycles in Argentina since 1955. In *Transitions from authoritarian rule: Latin America,* ed. Guillermo O'Donnell, Philippe C. Schmitter, and Laurence Whitehead. Baltimore: Johns Hopkins University Press: 19–45.

————. 1987. *Autoritarismo y democracia (1955–1983).* Buenos Aires: Centro Editor de América Latina.

————. 1989. El esquema partidario Argentino: Partidos viejos, sistema débil. In *Muerte y Resurrección,* ed. M. Cavarozzi and M. A. Garretón. Santiago: FLACSO.

————. 1994. Politics: A key for the long term in South America. In *Democracy, markets and structural reform in Latin America,* ed. William Smith, Carlos Acuña, and Eduardo Gamarra. New Brunswick, N.J.: Transaction Publishers.

Cavarozzi, Marcelo, and Juan Manuel Abal Medina, eds. 2003. *El asedio a la política. Los partidos latinoamericanos en la era neoliberal.* Buenos Aires: Homo Sapiens Ediciones.

CEPAL. *See* Comisión Económica para América Latina y el Caribe.

Cetrángolo, Oscar, and Juan P. Jiménez. 1996. El conflicto en torno a las relaciones financieras entre la nación y las provincias. Segunda parte: desde la Ley 23.548 hasta la Actualidad. *Centro de Estudios para el Cambio Estructural, Serie de Estudios,* no. 10 (February).

CGE. *See* Confederación General Económica.

Chalmers, Douglas A., Scott B. Martin, and Kerianne Piester. 1997. Associative networks: New structures of representation for the popular sectors? In *The new politics of inequality in Latin America: Rethinking participation and representation,* ed. Douglas A. Chalmers et al. Oxford: Oxford University Press: 543–82.

Cheresky, Isidoro. 2003. Las elecciones nacionales de 1999 y 2001: Fluctuación del voto, debilitamiento de la cohesión partidaria y crisis de representación. In *De la ilusión reformista al descontento ciudadano: Las elecciones en Argentina, 1999 y 2000,* ed. I. Cheresky and J. M. Blanquer. Rosario, Argentina: Homo Sapiens.

Chudnovsky Daniel, and Andrés López. 1997. *Auge y ocaso del capitalismo asistido: La industria petroquímica latinoamericana.* Buenos Aires: CEPAL-Alianza.

Ciria, Alberto. 1983. *Política y cultura popular: La Argentina peronista, 1946–55.* Buenos Aires: Ediciones de la Flor.

Clinton, Joshua, Simon Jackman, and Douglas Rivers. 2004. The statistical analysis of roll call data. *American Political Science Review* 98:355–70.

Cohen, Jean. 1999. Trust, voluntary association and workable democracy. In *Democracy and trust*, ed. Mark Warren. Cambridge: Cambridge University Press.

Colectivo Situaciones. 2002. *19 y 20 Apuntes para el nuevo protagonismo social*. Buenos Aires: Ediciones de Mano en Mano.

Collier, Ruth Berins, and David Collier. 1979. Inducements versus constraints: Disaggregating "corporatism." *American Political Science Review* 73, no. 4 (December): 967–86.

———. 1991. *Shaping the political arena*. Princeton: Princeton University Press.

Comisión Económica para América Latina y el Caribe (CEPAL). 1999. *Panorama económico de America Latina*. Santiago: CEPAL.

Confederación General Económica (CGE). 1993. *El libro azul de las provincias: Las economías regionales en la transformación económicas en la transformación económica de la República Argentina*. Buenos Aires: Instituto de Investigaciones Económicas y Financieras de la Confederación General Económica.

Cordeu, Mora, Silvia Mercado, and Nancy Sosa, eds. 1985. *Peronismo: La mayoría perdida*. Buenos Aires: Sudamericana-Planeta.

Corrales, Javier. 1998. Coalitions and corporate choices in Argentina, 1976–1994: The recent private sector support for privatizations. *Studies in Comparative International Development* 32, no. 4 (winter): 24–51.

———. 2001. Strong societies, weak parties: Regime change in Cuba and Venezuela in the 1950s and today. *Latin American Politics and Society* 43, no. 2:81–114.

———. 2002. *Presidents without parties*. University Park: Pennsylvania State University Press.

Costallat, Karina. 1999. Efectos de las privatizaciones y la relación estado-sociedad en la instancia provincial y local: El Caso Cutral Co–Plaza Huincul. Manuscript. Buenos Aires: INAP.

Cox, Gary, and Mathew D. McCubbins. 1986. Electoral politics as a redistributive game. *Journal of Politics* 48, no. 2 (May): 370–89.

———. 1993. *Legislative leviathan: Party government in the House*. Berkeley and Los Angeles: University of California Press.

Dahl, Robert. 1957. Decision-making in a democracy: The Supreme Court as a national policymaker. *Journal of Public Law* 6:279–95.

Dakolias, Maria. 1996. A strategy for judicial reform: The experience in Latin America. *Virginia Journal of International Law* 36, no. 1:168–231.

Danesi, Silvina. 2003. A 18 años de democracia, la gestión en la H. Cámara de Diputados de la Nación. Manuscript. Universidad de San Andrés.

Delamata, Gabriela. 2003. De los estallidos provinciales a la generalización de las protestas. Perspectiva y contexto en la significación de las nuevas protestas. *Revista de Ciencias Sociales* (Universidad de Quilmes), no. 14.

De Luca, Miguel, Mark Jones, and María Inés Tula. 2002. Back rooms or ballot boxes? Candidate nomination in Argentina. *Comparative Political Studies* 35, no. 4 (May): 413–36.

De Riz, Liliana. 1981. *Retorno y derrumbe. El ultimo gobierno peronista*. Mexico: Folios Ediciones.

———. 1986. Política y partidos. Ejercicio de análisis comparado. *Desarrollo Económico* 25, no. 100:659–82.

———. 1996. Argentina: Democracy in turmoil. In *Constructing democratic governance: South America in the 1990s*, ed. Jorge Domínguez. Baltimore: Johns Hopkins University Press.

———. 1998. From Menem to Menem: Elections and political parties in Argentina. In *Argentina: The challenges of modernization*, ed. Joseph S. Tulchin and Allison M. Garland.Wilmington, Del.: Scholarly Resources Books.

De Riz, Liliana, and Gerardo Adrogué. 1991. Democracia y elecciones en la Argentina: 1983–1989. In *Reforma institucional y cambio político*, ed. Dieter Nohlen and Liliana De Riz. Buenos Aires: Legasa.

Díaz Alejandro, Carlos. 1970. *Essays on the economic history of the Argentine republic.* New Haven: Yale University Press.

Diaz-Cayeros, Alberto, Federico Estevez, and Beatriz Magaloni. 2001. Private versus public goods as electoral investments: A portfolio diversification model of policy choice. Paper prepared for the workshop "Citizen-Politician Linkages in Democratic Politics," Duke University, March 30–April 1.

Dinerstein, Ana. 2001. El poder de lo irrealizado. El corte de ruta en Argentina y el potencial subversivo de la mundialización. OSAL, September.

Di Tella, Torcuato. 1968. Stalemate or coexistence in Argentina. In *Latin America: Reform or Revolution*, ed. James Petras and Maurice Zeitlin. Greenwich, Conn.: Fawcett Publishers.

Domínguez, Jorge I. 1998. Free politics and free markets in Latin America. *Journal of Democracy* 9, no. 4 (October): 70–84.

Downs, Anthony. 1967. *Inside bureaucracy.* Boston: Little, Brown.

Doyon, Louise. 1988. La organización del movimiento sindical peronista (1946–1955). In *La formación del sindicalismo peronista*, ed. Juan Carlos Torre. Buenos Aires: Legasa.

Duarte, Marisa. 2002. Privatización y crisis laboral en la Argentina de los años 90. *Estudios del Trabajo*, no. 23:33–60.

Eaton, Kent. 2001. Decentralisation, democratisation and liberalisation: The history of revenue sharing in Argentina, 1934–1999. *Journal of Latin American Studies* 33, no. 1:1–28.

———. 2002. *Politicians and economic reform in new democracies: Argentina and the Philippines in the 1990s.* University Park: Pennsylvania State University Press.

———. 2004. *Politics beyond the capital: The design of subnational institutions in South America.* Stanford: Stanford University Press.

Eckstein, Harry. 1975. Case study and theory in political science. In *Handbook of political science*, vol. 7, *Strategies of inquiry*, ed. F. Greenstein and N. Polsby. Reading, Mass.: Addison-Wesley.

Economist Intelligence Unit. 1999. *Country report: Argentina.* December.

———. 2001. *Country report: Argentina.* September.

Entel, Alicia. 1997. *La ciudad bajo sospecha. Comunicación y protesta urbana.* Buenos Aires: Paidos.

EIU. *See* Economist Intelligence Unit.

Epstein, Lee, and Jack Knight. 1996. On the struggle for judicial supremacy. *Law and Society Review* 30, no. 1:87–120.

————. 1998. *The choices justices make.* Washington, D.C.: Congressional Quarterly Press.

Escolar, Marcelo, and Ernesto Calvo. 2002. *Transferencia electoral y reestructuración partidaria en la elección federal argentina 2001: Categoría diputados nacionales.* Buenos Aires: UNDP Political Reform Program Report.

Escolar, Marcelo, Ernesto Calvo, Natalia Calcagno, and Sandra Minvielle. 2002. Últimas imágenes antes del naufragio: Las elecciones de 2001 en Argentina. *Desarrollo Económico* 42, no. 165 (April-June): 25–44.

Etchegaray, Fabian, and Carlos Elordi. 2001. Public opinion, presidential popularity, and economic reforms in Argentina, 1989–1996. In *Public support for market reforms in new democracies,* ed. Susan Stokes. New York: Cambridge University Press.

Etchemendy, Sebastián. 2001. Constructing reform coalitions: The politics of compensations in Argentina's economic liberalization. *Latin American Politics and Society* 43, no. 3 (fall): 1–35.

————. 2004. Repression, exclusion and inclusion: Government-union relations and patterns of labor reform in liberalizing economies. *Comparative Politics* 36, no. 3:273–90.

Etchemendy, Sebastián, and Vicente Palermo. 1998. Conflicto y concertación: Gobierno, Congreso y organizaciones de interés en la reforma laboral del primer gobierno de Menem. *Desarollo Económico* 37, no. 148 (January-March): 559–90.

Faletti, Tulia. 2003. Governing governors: Coalitions and sequences of decentralization in Argentina, Colombia, and Mexico. Ph.D. diss., Department of Political Science, Northwestern University.

Farinetti, Marina. 1999. ¿Qué queda del "Movimiento Obrero"? Las formas del reclamo laboral en la nueva democracia Argentina. *Trabajo y Sociedad* 1 (July-September): http://habitantes.elsitio.com/proit/zmarina.htm.

————. 2000. El estallido: la forma de la protesta. Manuscript. Buenos Aires.

————. 2002. Los significados de un estallido social: Santiago del Estero en 1993. Master's thesis, School of Social Sciences, University of Buenos Aires.

Favaro, Orietta, and Mario Bucciarelli. 1994. Efectos de la privatización de YPF: La desagregación territorial del espacio neuquino. *Realidad Económica* 127:88–99.

Favaro, Orietta, Mario Bucciarelli, and Graciela Luomo. 1997. La conflictividad social en neuquén. El movimiento cutralquense y los nuevos sujetos sociales. *Realidad Económica* 148:13–27.

Ferejohn, John A., and Barry Weingast. 1992. A positive theory of statutory interpretation. *International Review of Law and Economics* 12.

Fernández, Raquel, and Dani Rodrik. 1991. Resistance to reform: Status quo bias in the presence of individual-specific uncertainty. *American Economic Review* 81, no. 5 (December): 1146–55.

Ferreira Rubio, Delia, and Matteo Goretti. 1998. When the president governs alone: The *decretazo* in Argentina, 1989–93. In *Executive decree authority,* ed. John M. Carey and Matthew Soberg Shugart. New York: Cambridge University Press.

————. 2000. Executive-legislative relationship in Argentina: From Menem's *Decretazo* to a new style? Paper presented at the conference "Argentina 2000:

Politics, economy, society and international relations," Oxford University, May 15–17.

FIEL. *See* Fundación de Investigaciones Económicas Latinoamericanas.

Finocchiaro, Charles J., and David W. Rohde. 2002. War for the floor: Agenda control and the relationship between conditional party government and cartel theory. Manuscript. Michigan State University.

Floria, Carlos, and Cesar García Belsunce. 1992. *Historia de los argentinos.* Buenos Aires: Larousse.

Fox, Jonathan. 1994. The difficult transition from clientelism to citizenship: Lessons from México. *World Politics* 46, no. 2 (January): 151–84.

Fradkin, Raúl. 2002. *Cosecharás tu siembra.* Buenos Aires: Prometeo Libros.

Fraga, Rosendo. 1995. *Argentina en las Urnas, 1916–1994.* Buenos Aires: Editorial Centro de Estudios Unión para la Nueva Mayoria.

Frieden, Jeffrey. 1991a. *Debt, development and democracy.* Princeton: Princeton University Press.

———. 1991b. Invested interests: The politics of national economic policies in a world of global finance. *International Organization* 41, no. 2:425–51.

Fundación CECE. *See* Fundación Centro de Estudios para el Cambio Estructural.

Fundación Centro de Estudios para el Cambio Estructural (CECE). 1997. *Federalismo fiscal en Argentina.* Buenos Aires: Fundación CECE.

Fundación de Investigaciones Económicas Latinoamericanas (FIEL). 1993. *Hacia una nueva organización del federalismo fiscal en la Argentina.* Buenos Aires: Ediciones Latinomericanas.

Gadano, Nicolás, and Federico Sturzenegger. 1998. La privatización de las reservas en el sector hidrocarburífero. El caso de Argentina. *Revista de Análisis Económico* 13, no. 1:75–115.

Galiani, Sebastián, Daniel Heymann, and Mariano Tommasi. 2003. Great expectations and hard times: The Argentine convertibility plan. *Economia: Journal of the Latin American and Caribbean Economic Association* 3, no. 2 (spring): 109–60.

Galmarini, Sebastián. 2004. *Sistema de partidos en la Argentina.* Buenos Aires: Bitácora Global.

Garay, Candelaria. 2003. Origins of the unemployed movement in Argentina: Government policy initiatives as a trigger for contention. Manuscript. Department of Political Science, University of California, Berkeley.

Garman, Christopher, Stephan Haggard, and Eliza Willis. 2001. Fiscal descentralization: A political theory with Latin American cases. *World Politics* 53, no. 2 (January): 205–36.

Gaudio, Ricardo, and Andrés Thompson. 1990. *Sindicalismo peronista/gobierno radical. Los años de Alfonsín.* Buenos Aires: Fundación Frederich Ebert and Folio Ediciones.

Geddes, Barbara. 1994. *Politicians' dilemma.* Berkeley and Los Angeles: University of California Press.

———. 1996. Initiation of new democratic institutions in Eastern Europe and Latin America. In *Institutional design in new democracies,* ed. Arend Lijphart and Carlos H. Waisman. Boulder, Colo.: Westview Press.

George, Alexander L., and Andrew Bennett. 2004. *Case studies and theory development in the social sciences.* Cambridge: MIT Press.

Gerchunoff, Pablo, and Juan Carlos Torre. 1996. Argentina: La política de liberalización económica bajo un gobierno de base popular. *Desarrollo Económico*, no. 36 (October-December): 733–68.

Gerchunoff, P., C. Bozzalla, and J. Sanguinetti. 1994. *Privatización, apertura y concentración. El caso del sector siderúrgico Argentino*. Series Reforma Política Pública. Santiago de Chile: CEPAL.

Gervasoni, Carlos. 1997. La sustentabilidad electoral de los programas de estabilización y reforma estructural: Los casos de Argentina y Perú. Paper prepared for delivery at the Twentieth International Congress of the Latin American Studies Association, Guadalajara, Mexico, April 17–19.

———. 1998a. El impacto de las reformas económicas en la coalición justicialista. *Boletín SAAP* 4, no. 6:67–101.

———. 1998b. Estructura y evolución de las coaliciones electorales en la Argentina: 1989 y 1995. Manuscript. Facultad de Derecho y Ciencias Sociales, Universidad Católica, Argentina.

———. 1998c. Del distribucionismo al neoliberalismo: Los cambios en la coalición electoral Peronista durante el gobierno de Menem. Paper prepared for delivery at the 1998 meeting of the Latin American Studies Association, Chicago, September 24–26.

Giarraca, Norma, et al. 2002. *La protesta social en la Argentina*. Buenos Aires: Alianza.

Gibson. Edward L. 1996. *Class and conservative parties: Argentina in comparative perspective*. Baltimore: Johns Hopkins University Press.

———. 1997. The populist road to market reform: Policy and electoral coalitions in Mexico and Argentina. *World Politics* 49, no. 3 (April): 339–70.

———, ed. 2004. *Federalism and democracy in Latin America*. Baltimore: Johns Hopkins University Press.

Gibson, Edward, and Ernesto Calvo. 2000. Federalism and low-maintenance constituencies: Territorial dimensions of economic reform in Argentina. *Studies in Comparative International Development* 35, no. 3 (fall): 32–55.

Gibson, Edward, Ernesto Calvo, and Tulia Falleti. 2001. Federalismo redistributivo: Sobrerrepresentación territorial y transferencia de ingresos en el hemisferio occidental. *Política y Gobierno* 6, no. 1:15–44.

———. 2004. Reallocative federalism: Territorial overrrepresentation and public spending in the Western Hemisphere. In *Federalism and Democracy in Latin America*, ed. Edward Gibson. Baltimore: Johns Hopkins University Press.

Gibson, Edward, and Tulia Falleti. 2003. Unity by the stick: Regional conflict and the origins of Argentine federalism. In *Representing regions: Federalism in Latin America in comparative perspective*, ed. Edward Gibson. Baltimore: Johns Hopkins University Press.

Godio, Julio, Héctor Palomino, and Achim Wachendorfer. 1988. *El movimiento sindical Argentino (1880–1987)*. Buenos Aires: Puntosur.

Goldberg, Jonathan. 2003. Campaign conscripts. How to fill a stadium with Argentina's poor (and other ways to win the presidency). *The American Prospect* (online edition), April 2003.

Gourevitch, Peter. 1989. *Politics in hard times: Comparative responses to international economic crises*. Ithaca: Cornell University Press.

Greif, Avner, and David Laitin. 2004. A theory of endogenous institutional change. *American Political Science Review* 98, no. 4 (November): 633–52.

Guagnini, Lucas. 2002. La trama política de los saqueos. *Clarín Digital,* December 19.

Guido, Pablo. 2002. En el 2014 todos seremos empleados públicos. Manuscript. Fundación Atlas.

Guido, Pablo, and Gustavo Lazzari. 2001. Tasa de desempleo encubierto en las provincias. Manuscript. Fundación Atlas.

Gutierrez, Ricardo. 1998. Desindicalización y cambio organizativo del peronismo argentino, 1982–1995. Paper presented at the Twenty-first International Congress of the Latin American Studies Association, Chicago, September 24–26.

Gwartney, James, Robert Lawson, and Walter Block. 1996. *Economic freedom of the world, 1975–1995.* Vancouver, B.C.: The Fraser Institute.

Haggard, Stephan, and Robert Kaufman. 1995. *The political economy of democratic transitions.* Princeton: Princeton University Press.

———, eds. 1992. *The politics of economic adjustment.* Princeton: Princeton University Press.

Hall, Peter, and Rosemary Taylor. 1996. Political science and the three new institutionalisms. *Political Studies* 44, no. 5:936–57.

Harmel, Robert, and Kenneth Janda. 1994. An integrated theory of party goals and party change. *Journal of Theoretical Politics* 6, no. 3:259–87.

Harmel, Robert, and Lars Svasand. 1993. Party leadership and party institutionalization: Three phases of development. *West European Politics* 16, no. 2 (April): 67–88.

Hartlyn, Jonathan. 1994. Crisis-ridden elections (again) in the Dominican Republic: Neopatrimonialism, presidentialism, and weak electoral oversight. *Journal of Interamerican Studies and World Affairs* 36, no. 4 (winter): 91–144.

Hellman, Joel. 1998. Winners take all: The politics of partial reform in postcommunist transitions. *World Politics* 50:203–34.

Helmke, Gretchen. 2002. The logic of strategic defection: court-executive relations in Argentina under dictatorship and democracy. *American Political Science Review* 96:291–303.

———. 2003. Checks and balances by other means: The Argentine Supreme Court in the 1990s. *Comparative Politics* 35, no. 2:213–30.

———. 2004. *Courts under constraints: Judges, generals and presidents in Argentina.* New York: Cambridge University Press.

Helmke, Gretchen, and Steven Levitsky. 2004. Informal institutions and comparative politics: A research agenda. *Perspectives on Politics* 2, no. 4 (December): 725–40.

Hopenhayn, Hugo, and Pablo A. Neumeyer. 2003. The Argentine great depression, 1975–1990. Manuscript. Universidad Torcuato Di Tella, Buenos Aires.

Huntington, Samuel P. 1968. *Political order in changing societies.* New Haven: Yale University Press.

Iaryczower, Matías, Pablo Spiller, and Mariano Tommasi. 2002. Judicial decision-making in unstable environments: The Argentine Supreme Court, 1936–1998. *American Journal of Political Science* 46, no. 4 (October): 699–716.

———. Forthcoming. The Supreme Court. Chap. 8, in *The institutional foundations of public policy: A transactions approach and an application to Argentina,* ed. Pablo Spiller and Mariano Tommasi. New York: Cambridge University Press.

IDB. See Inter-American Development Bank.

Inter-American Development Bank (IDB). 1997. *Latin America after a decade of reforms: Economic and social progress*. Washington, D.C.: IDB.

International Standard Industrial Classification of Economic Activities (ISIC). 2004. Department of Economic and Social Affairs, Statistics Division. Revision 3.1. New York: United Nations.

James, Daniel. 1988. *Resistance and integration: Peronism and the Argentine working class, 1946–1976*. New York: Cambridge University Press.

Jenkins, Craig. 1983. Resource mobilization theory. *Annual Review of Sociology* 9.

Jepperson, Ronald. 1991. Institutions, institutional effects, and institutionalism. In *The new institutionalism in organizational analysis*, ed. Walter W. Powell and Paul J. DiMaggio. Chicago: University of Chicago Press.

Jones, Mark P. 1997a. Federalism and the number of parties in Argentine congressional elections. *Journal of Politics* 59, no. 2:538–49.

———. 1997b. Evaluating Argentina's presidential democracy: 1983–1995. In *Presidentialism and democracy in Latin America*, ed. Scott Mainwaring and Matthew Soberg Shugart. New York: Cambridge University Press.

———. 2001. Political institutions and public policy in Argentina: An overview of the formation and execution of the national budget. In *Presidents, parliaments, and policy*, ed. Stephan Haggard and Mathew McCubbins. New York: Cambridge University Press.

———. 2002. Explaining the high level of party discipline in the Argentine congress. In *Legislative politics in Latin America*, ed. Scott Morgenstern and Benito Nacif. New York: Cambridge University Press.

Jones, Mark P., and Wonjae Hwang. 2004. Government and opposition in Argentina, 1989–2004: Understanding inter-party dynamics through roll call vote analysis. Manuscript. Rice University.

———. 2005. Party government in presidential democracies: Extending cartel theory beyond the U.S. Congress. *American Journal of Political Science* 49, no. 2:267–82.

Jones, Mark, Sebastián Saiegh, Pablo Spiller, and Mariano Tommasi. 2001. Keeping a seat in Congress: Provincial party bosses and the survival of Argentine legislators. Paper presented at the annual meeting of the American Political Science Association, San Francisco, August 20–September 2.

———. 2002. Amateur legislators–professional politicians: The consequences of party-centered electoral rules in a federal system. *American Journal of Political Science* 46, no. 3 (July): 356–69.

———. Forthcoming. Congress and career paths of Argentine politicians. In *The institutional foundations of public policy: A transactions approach and an application to Argentina*, ed. Pablo T. Spiller and Mariano Tommasi. New York: Cambridge University Press.

Jones, Mark, Pablo Sanguinetti, and Mariano Tommasi. 2000. Politics, institutions and fiscal performance in a federal system: An analysis of the Argentine provinces. *Journal of Development Economics* 61, no. 2:305–33.

———. 2002. Voters as fiscal liberals. Manuscript. Michigan State University.

Jones-Luong, Pauline, and Erika Weinthal. 2004. Contra coercion: Russian tax reform, exogenous shocks, and negotiated institutional change. *American Political Science Review* 98, no. 1 (February): 139–52.

Kay, Stephen. 2003. State capacity and pensions. Paper prepared for the Latin American Studies Association Twenty-fourth International Congress in Dallas, Texas, March 27–29.

Kessler, Timothy. 1998. Political capital: Mexican financial policy under Salinas. *World Politics* 51:36–66.

King, Gary, and Robert X. Browning. 1987. Democratic representation and partisan bias in congressional elections. *American Political Science Review* 81, no. 4:1251–73.

King, Gary, Robert Keohane, and Sidney Verba. 1994. *Designing social enquiry.* Princeton: Princeton University Press.

Kitschelt, Herbert. 1994a. *The transformation of European social democracy.* Cambridge: Cambridge University Press.

———. 1994b. Austrian and Swedish social democrats in crisis: Party strategy and organization in corporatist regimes. *Comparative Political Studies* 24, no. 1:3–35.

———. 2000. Linkages between citizens and politicians in democratic polities. *Comparative Political Studies* 33, no 6/7 (August/September): 845–79.

Klachko, Paula. 1999. Cutral-Co y Plaza Huincul. El primer corte de ruta. PIMSA, 121–54.

Knight, Jack. 1992. *Institutions and social conflict.* New York: Cambridge University Press.

Kohan, Aníbal. 2002. *A las calles! Una historia de los Movimientos Piqueteros y Caceroleros de los '90 al 2002.* Buenos Aires: Ediciones Colihue.

Kollman, Raúl. 2002. Un aparato sin chapas. *Página/12*, March 29.

Kopstein, Jeffrey S., and David A. Reilly. 2000. Geographic diffusion and the transformation of the postcommunist world. *World Politics* 53, no. 1 (October): 1–37.

Kosacoff, Bernardo. 1993. La industrial Argentina: Un processo de restructuración desarticulada. In *El desafío de la competitividad,* ed. Kosacoff. Buenos Aires: Alianza-CEPAL.

Krehbiel, Keith. 1991. *Information and legislative organization.* Ann Arbor: University of Michigan Press.

Krueger, Anne. 1993. *Political economy of policy reform in developing countries.* Cambridge: MIT Press.

Krugman, Paul. 2001. Reckonings: A Latin tragedy. *New York Times,* 21 July.

Kurtz, Marcus. 2001. State developmentalism without a developmental state: The public foundations of the free market miracle in Chile. *Latin American Politics and Society* 43 (summer): 1–26.

Langston, Joy. 2003. The formal bases of informal power: Mexico's PRI. Paper prepared for the conference "Informal Institutions and Politics in Latin America," Helen Kellogg Institute for International Studies, University of Notre Dame, April 24–25.

Larkins, Christopher. 1998. The judiciary and delegative democracy in Argentina. *Comparative Politics* 30, no. 4:423–42.

Laufer, Rubén, and Claudio Spiguel. 1999. Las "Puebladas" Argentinas a partir del "Santiaguenazo" de 1993. Tradición, histórica y nuevas formas de lucha. In *Lucha popular, democracia, neoliberalismo: Protesta popular en América Latina en los años del ajuste,* ed. Margarita López Maya. Caracas: Nueva Sociedad.

Levitsky, Steven. 2001. An organized disorganization: Informal organization and the persistence of local party structures in Argentine Peronism. *Journal of Latin American Studies* 33, no. 1 (February): 29–66.

———. 2003. *Transforming labor-based parties in Latin America: Argentine Peronism in comparative perspective.* New York: Cambridge University Press.

Levitsky, Steven, and Maxwell Cameron. 2003. Democracy without parties? Political parties and regime change in Fujimori's Peru. *Latin American Politics and Society* 45, no. 3 (fall): 1–33.

Levitsky, Steven, and Maria Victoria Murillo. 2003. Argentina weathers the storm. *Journal of Democracy* 13, no. 4 (October): 152–66.

Levitsky, Steven, and Lucan A.Way. 1998. Between a shock and a hard place: The dynamics of labor-backed adjustment in Argentina and Poland. *Comparative Politics* 30, no. 2 (January): 171–92.

Lewkowics, Ignacio. 2002. *Sucesos Argentinos.* Buenos Aires: Paidos.

Lindemboin, Javier, Leandro Serino, and Mariana González. 2000. La precariedad como forma de exclusion. In *Crisis y metamorfosis del mercado de trabajo,* ed. Javier Lindemboin. Buenos Aires: Cuadernos del Ceped.

Linz, Juan J., and Arturo Valenzuela, eds. 1994. *The failure of presidential democracy.* Baltimore: Johns Hopkins University Press.

Llanos, Mariana. 1998. Privatization and democracy: A study of the legislative process for state reform in Argentina (1983–1997). Ph.D. diss., Oxford University, April.

———. 2001. Understanding presidential power in Argentina: A study of the policy of privatization in the 1990s. *Journal of Latin American Studies* 33, no. 1 (February): 67–99.

———. 2002. *Privatization and democracy in Latin America: An analysis of president-Congress relations.* New York: Palgrave.

Llorente, Ignacio. 1980a. Alianzas politicas en el surgimiento del peronismo: El caso de la provincia de Buenos Aires. In *El voto Peronista. Ensayos de sociología electoral Argentina,* ed. M. Mora y Araujo and I. Llorente. Buenos Aires: Editorial Sudamericana.

———. 1980b. La composición social del movimento Peronista hacia 1954. In *El voto Peronista. Ensayos de sociología electoral Argentina,* ed. M. Mora y Araujo and I. Llorente. Buenos Aires: Editorial Sudamericana.

Locke, Richard. 1995. *Remaking the Italian economy.* Ithaca: Cornell University Press.

Lodola, Germán. 2003. Popular protest and policy outcomes: The case of Argentine unemployed workers' organizations. Manuscript. Department Of Political Science, University of Pittsburgh.

Londregan, John B. 2000. *Legislative institutions and ideology in Chile.* New York: Cambridge University Press.

López Echagüe, Hernán. 2002. *La política está en otra parte.* Buenos Aires: Norma.

López, Ernesto, and David Pion-Berlin. 1996. Entre la confrontación y la adaptación: Los militares y la política gubernamental en la Argentina democrática. In Ernesto López and David Pion-Berlin, *Democracia y cuestión militar.* Buenos Aires: Universidad Nacional de Quilmes.

López Maya, Margarita, ed. 1999. *Lucha popular, democracia, neoliberalismo: Protesta popular en America Latina en los años del ajuste.* Caracas: Nueva Sociedad.

Lora, Eduardo. 2001. *Structural reforms in Latin America: What has been reformed and how to measure it?* Inter-American Development Bank Research Department Working Paper, 466. Washington, D.C.

Loveman, Brian. 1993. *The constitution of tyranny.* Pittsburgh: University of Pittsburgh Press.

Lozano, Claudio. 1992. La privatización de SOMISA. Working Paper 22. Instituto de Estado y Participación (IDEP), Buenos Aires.

Lucangeli, Jorge. 2001. La competitividad de la industria manufacturera durante los 90. *Boletín Informativo Techint* 307 (July-September).

M&S Consulting. 2002. Hacia una política comercial competitiva: El caso del complejo metalúrgico. Unpublished report.

Macón, Jorge. 1985. *Las finanzas públicas Argentinas.* Buenos Aires: Ediciones Macchi.

Magar, Eric. 2001a. Illusions of congressional effacement: Decrees, statutes, and veto incidence in Argentina, 1983–1994. Ph.D. diss., Department of Political Science, University of California at San Diego.

———. 2001b. The elusive authority of Argentina's Congress: Decrees, statutes, and veto incidence. Paper presented at the annual meeting of the American Political Science Association, San Francisco, August/September.

Mahoney, James. 2000. Path dependence in historical sociology. *Theory and Society* 29, no 4:507–48.

Mainwaring, Scott. 1999. *Rethinking party systems in the third wave democratization: The case of Brazil.* Stanford: Stanford University Press.

Mainwaring, Scott, and Timothy R. Scully, eds. 1995. *Building democratic institutions: Party systems in Latin America.* Stanford: Stanford University Press.

Mainwaring, Scott, and Matthew Soberg Shugart, eds. 1997. *Presidentialism and democracy in Latin America.* New York: Cambridge University Press.

Mallon, Richard, and Juan Sourrouille. 1975. *Economic policymaking in a conflict society: The Argentine case.* Cambridge: Harvard University Press.

March, James G., and Johan P. Olsen. 1984. The new institutionalism: Organizational factors in political life. *American Political Science Review* 78:734–49.

———. 1989. *Rediscovering institutions: The organizational basis of politics.* New York: The Free Press.

Martínez, Tomás. 2002. *Episodios Argentinos.* Buenos Aires: Aguilar.

Martucelli, Danilo, and Maristella Svampa. 1997. *La plaza vacia.* Buenos Aires: Losada.

Matsushita, Iroshi. 1988. *El movimiento obrero argentino, 1930–1945.* Buenos Aires: Ediciones Siglo XX.

Maxfield, Sylvia. 1997. *Gatekeepers of growth: The international political economy of central banking in developing countries.* Princeton: Princeton University Press.

McAdam, Doug, Sidney Tarrow, and Charles Tilly. 2001. *Dynamics of contention.* New York: Cambridge University Press.

McCarthy, John, and Mayer Zald. 1973. *The trend of social movements in America.* Morristown, N.J: General Learning Press.

———. 1977. Resource mobilization and social movements. *American Journal of Sociology* 82:1212–41.

McCubbins, Matthew, and Thomas Schwartz. 1984. Congressional oversight overlooked: Police patrols versus fire alarms. *American Journal of Political Science* 28, no. 1 (February): 165–79.

McGuire, James W. 1995. Political parties and democracy in Argentina. In *Building Democratic Institutions: Party Systems in Latin America*, ed. Scott Mainwaring and Timothy R. Scully. Stanford: Stanford University Press.

———. 1997. *Peronism without Peron: Unions, parties, and democracy in Argentina*. Stanford: Stanford University Press.

Meyer, John, and Brian Rowan. 1991. Institutionalized organizations: Formal structure as myth and ceremony. In *The institutionalism in organizational analysis*, ed. Walter W. Powell and Paul J. DiMaggio. Chicago: University of Chicago Press.

Miller, Jonathan. 1997. Judicial review and constitutional stability: A sociology of the U.S. model and its collapse in Argentina. *Hastings International and Comparative Law Review* 231 (fall): 151–62.

Ministry of Labor and Social Security. 2000. Personal comprendido en convenios o acuerdos de empresa. Manuscript. Collective Bargaining Management Office. Buenos Aires.

———. 2002. Personal comprendido en convenios o acuerdos de empresa. Manuscript. Collective Bargaining Office. Buenos Aires.

Miranda, Diego. 2002. Crisis de representación política en Argentina. *Revista* SAAP (Buenos Aires) 1, no. 1:63–111.

Moe, Terry. 1990. The politics of structural choice: Toward a theory of public bureaucracy. In *Organization theory: From Chester Barnard to the present and beyond*, ed. Oliver Williamson. New York: Oxford University Press.

Molinelli, N. Guillermo, María Valeria Palanza, and Gisela Sin. 1999. *Congreso, presidencia y justicia en Argentina: Materiales para su estudio*. Buenos Aires: Fundación Gobierno y Sociedad, Editorial Temas.

Mora y Araujo, Manuel. 1980a. Introducción: La sociología electoral y la comprensión del peronismo. In *El voto Peronista. Ensayos de sociología electoral argentina*, ed. M. Mora y Araujo and I. Llorente. Buenos Aires: Editorial Sudamericana.

———. 1980b. Las bases estructurales del peronismo. In *El voto Peronista. Ensayos de sociología electoral argentina*, ed. M. Mora y Araujo and I. Llorente. Buenos Aires: Editorial Sudamericana.

———. 1991. El cuadro político y electoral argentino. In *Reforma institucional y cambio político*, ed. Dieter Nohlen and Liliana De Riz. Buenos Aires: Legasa.

Mora y Araujo, Manuel, and Ignacio Llorente eds. 1980. *El voto peronista*. Buenos Aires: Editorial Sudamericana.

Morgenstern, Scott. 2002. Towards a model of Latin American legislatures. In *Legislative politics in Latin America*, ed. Scott Morgenstern and Benito Nacif. New York: Cambridge University Press.

Morgenstern, Scott, and Benito Nacif, eds. 2002. *Legislative politics in Latin America*. New York: Cambridge University Press.

Mukand, Sharun, and Dani Rodrik. 2002. In search of the Holy Grail: Policy convergence, experimentation, and economic performance. Discussion Paper no. 3525. London: Centre for Economic Policy Research.

Munck, Gerardo. 1998. *Authoritarianism and democratization: Soldiers and workers in Argentina, 1976–1983*. University Park: Pennsylvania State University Press.

———. 2004. Democratic politics in Latin America: New debates and research frontiers. *Annual Review of Political Science* 7:437–62.

Murillo, María Victoria. 1997. Union politics, market-oriented reforms and the reshaping of Argentine corporatism. In *The new politics of inequality in Latin America: Rethinking participation and representation*, ed. Douglas Chalmers et al. New York: Oxford University Press.

———. 1999. Recovering political dynamics: Teachers' unions and the decentralization of education in Argentina and Mexico. *Journal of Latin American Studies* 41 no. 1:31–57.

———. 2001. *Labor unions, partisan coalitions and market reforms in Latin America*. New York: Cambridge University Press.

———. 2002. Political bias in policy convergence: Privatization choices in Latin America. *World Politics* 54, no. 4 (July): 462–93.

Murillo, María Victoria, and Lucas Ronconi. 2004. Teachers' strikes in Argentina: Partisan alignments and public sector labor relations. *Studies in Comparative International Development* 39, no. 1:77–98.

Murillo, María Victoria, and Andrew Schrank. 2005. With a little help from my friends: External and domestic allies and labor rights in Latin America. *Comparative Political Studies* 38, no. 8 (October): 971–99.

Murmis, Miguel, and Juan Carlos Portantiero. 1971. *Estudio sobre los orígenes del peronismo*. Buenos Aires: Editorial Siglo XXI.

Mustapic, Ana Maria. 2001. Oscillating relations: President and Congress in Argentina. In *Legislative politics in Latin America*, ed. Scott Morgenstern and Benito Nacif. New York: Cambridge University Press.

———. 2002. Del Partido Peronista al Partido Justicialista: Las transformaciones de un partido carismático. In *El asedio a la política: Los partidos latinoamericanos en la era neoliberal*, ed. Marcelo Cavarozzi and Juan M. Abal Medina. Buenos Aires: Gedisa.

Myers, David J., and Henry Dietz, eds. 2002. *Capital city politics in Latin America: Democratization and empowerment*. Boulder, Colo.: Lynne Rienner.

Navarro, Marisa. 2002. Evita. In *Los años peronistas (1945–55)*, ed. Juan Carlos Torre. Buenos Aires: Sudamericana.

Negretto, Gabriel L. 2001. Government capacities and policy making by decree in Latin America: The cases of Brazil and Argentina. Paper presented at the annual meeting of the American Political Science Association, San Francisco, August/September.

Nelson, Richard R., and Sidney G. Winter. 1982. *An evolutionary theory of economic change*. Cambridge: Harvard University Press.

Nino, Carlos. 1992. *Un país al margen de la ley*. Buenos Aires: Emecé.

———. 1996a. Hyper-presidentialism and constitutional reform in Argentina. In *Institutional design in new democracies*, ed. Arend Lijphart and Carlos H. Waisman. Boulder, Colo.: Westview Press.

———. 1996b. *Radical evil on trial*. New Haven: Yale University Press.

Norden, Deborah L. 1996. *Military rebellion in Argentina: Between coups and consolidation*. Lincoln: University of Nebraska Press.

North, Douglass C. 1990a. *Institutions, institutional change, and economic performance*. New York: Cambridge University Press.

———. 1990b. A transaction cost theory of politics. *Journal of Theoretical Politics* 2, no. 4:355–67.

North, Douglass, and Barry Weingast. 1989. Constitutions and commitment: The evolution of institutions governing public choice in seventeeth-century England. *Journal of Economic History* 49, no.4 (December): 803–32.

Novaro, Marcos, ed. 2002. *El derrumbe político en el ocaso de la convertibilidad.* Buenos Aires: Grupo Editorial Norma.

Nun, José. 1967. The middle-class military coup. In *The politics of conformity in Latin America,* ed. Claudio Veliz. New York: Oxford University Press.

Nuñez Miñana, Horacio, and Alberto Porto. 1982. Coparticipación federal de impuestos: Distribución primaria. *Jornadas de Finanzas Públicas* 15:1–73.

———. 1983. Coparticipación federal de impuestos: Distribución secundaria. *Jornadas de Finanzas Públicas* 16:1–60.

Octavio de Jesus, Marcelo, and Alejandra Ruscelli. 1998. The lasting transition in the judiciaries in South America: A country study. Paper presented at the Twenty-first International Congress of the Latin American Studies Association, Chicago.

O'Donnell, Guillermo. 1973. *Modernization and bureaucratic-authoritarianism: Studies in South American politics.* Berkeley: Institute of International Studies, University of California.

———. 1978. State and alliances in Argentina, 1956–76. *Journal of Development Studies* 15, no. 1 (October): 3–33.

———. 1988. *Bureaucratic authoritarianism: Argentina, 1966–1973, in comparative perspective.* Berkeley and Los Angeles: University of California Press.

———. 1993. On the state, democratization, and some conceptual problems: A Latin American view with some postcommunist countries. *World Development* 21, no. 8 (August): 1355–69.

———. 1994. Delegative democracy? *Journal of Democracy* 5, no. 1 (January): 55–69.

———. 1996. Illusions about consolidation. *Journal of Democracy* 7, no. 2:34–51.

———. 1998a. Horizontal accountability and new polyarchies. Working Paper no. 253. The Helen Kellogg Institute for International Studies, University of Notre Dame.

———. 1998b. Polyarchies and the (un)rule of law in Latin America. Working Paper no. 254. The Helen Kellogg Institute for International Studies, University of Notre Dame.

———. 1999a. Polyarchies and the (un)rule of law in Latin America: A partial conclusion. In *The (Un)rule of Law and the Underprivileged in Latin America,* ed. Juan Mendez, Guillermo O'Donnell, and Paulo Sergio Pinheiro. Notre Dame: University of Notre Dame Press.

———. 1999b. Horizontal accountability in new democracies. In *The self-restraining state: Power and accountability in new democracies,* ed. Andreas Schedler, L. Diamond, and M. F. Plattner. Boulder, Colo.: Lynne Rienner.

———. 2003a. Ciencias sociales en America Latina. Mirando hacia el pasado y atisbando hacia el futuro. *Latin American Studies Association Forum* 34, no. 1 (spring).

———. 2003b. Horizontal accountability: The legal institutionalization of mistrust. In *Democratic Accountability in Latin America,* ed. Scott Mainwaring and Christopher Welna. Oxford: Oxford University Press.

O'Donnell, Guillermo, and Phillipe C. Schmitter. 1986. *Transitions from authoritarian rule: Tentative conclusions about uncertain democracies.* Baltimore: Johns Hopkins University Press.

Offe, Claus. 2001. How can we trust our fellow citizens? In *Democracry and trust*, ed. Mark Warren. Cambridge: Cambridge University Press.

O'Neill, Kathleen. 2003. Decentralization as an electoral strategy. *Comparative Political Studies* 36, no. 9 (November): 1031–67.

Orlanski, Dora. 1994. Crisis y transformación del estado en Argentina (1960–1993). *Ciclos en la Historia, la Economia y la Sociedad* 4, no. 7.

Orren, Karen, and Stephen Skowronek. 2002. The study of American political development. In *Political science: The state of the discipline*, ed. Ira Katznelson and Helen Milner. New York: Norton.

Ostiguy, Pierre. 1998. Peronism and anti-Peronism: Class-cultural cleavages and political identity in Argentina. Ph.D diss., Department of Political Science, University of California at Berkeley.

Oviedo, Luis. 2001. *Una historia del Movimiento Piquetero.* Buenos Aires: Ediciones Rumbos.

Oxhorn, Philip D. 1998. Is the century of corporatism over? Neoliberalism and the rise of neopluralism. In *What kind of democracy? What kind of market? Latin America in the age of neoliberalism*, ed. Philip D. Oxhorn and Graciela Ducatenzeiler. University Park: Pennsylvania State University Press.

Oxhorn, Philip D., and Graciela Ducatenzeiler. 1998. What kind of democracy? What kind of market? In *What kind of democracy? What kind of market? Latin America in the age of neoliberalism*, ed. Philip D. Oxhorn and Graciela Ducatenzeiler. University Park: Pennsylvania State University Press.

Palanza, M. Valeria, and Gisela Sin. 1997. Partidos provinciales y gobierno nacional en el congreso (1983–1995). *Boletín SAAP* 3, no. 5:46–94.

Palermo, Vicente. 1997. Moderate populism: A political approach to Argentina's 1991 convertibility plan. *Latin American Perspectives* 25:36–62.

Palermo, Vicente, and Marcos Novaro. 1996. *Política y poder en el gobierno de Menem.* Buenos Aires: Grupo Editorial Norma.

Palermo, Vicente, and Juan Carlos Torre. 1992. A la sombra de la hiperinflación. La política de reformas estructurales en la Argentina. Manuscript. CEPAL, Buenos Aires.

Palomino, Hector. 1987. *Cambios ocupacionales y sociales en Argentina, 1947–1985.* Buenos Aires: CISEA.

Panebianco, Angelo. 1988. *Political parties: Organization and power.* Cambridge: Cambridge University Press.

Pastor, Manuel, and Carol Wise. 1999. Stabilization and its discontents: Argentina's economic restructuring in the 1990s. *World Development* 27, no. 3.

————. 2001. From poster child to basket case. *Foreign Affairs* 80:60–72.

Penfold, Michael. 1999. Institutional electoral incentives and decentralization outcomes: Comparing Colombia and Venezuela. Ph.D. diss., Department of Political Science, Columbia University.

Peralta-Ramos, Mónica. 1978. *Acumulación del capital y crisis política en la Argentina (1930–1974).* Mexico City: Siglo XXI.

Perelli, Carina. 1995. La personalización de la politica: Nuevos caudillos, outsiders, politica mediatica y politica informal. In *Partidos y clase politica en America Latina en los 90*, ed. Carina Perelli, Sonia Picado, and Daniel Zoviatto. San Jose: Instituto Interamericano de Derechos Humanos.

Peruzzotti, Enrique. 1996. Civil society and constitutionalism in Latin America:

The Argentine experience. Ph.D. diss., Department of Sociology, The Graduate Faculty, The New School for Social Research.

———. 1999. Constitucionalismo, populismo y sociedad civil. Lecciones del caso argentino. *Revista Mexicana de Sociología* 61, no. 4:149–72.

———. 2001. The nature of the new Argentine democracy: The delegative democracy revisited. Part 1. *Journal of Latin American Studies* 33 (February): 140–41.

———. 2002a. Towards a new politics: Citizenship and rights in contemporary Argentina. *Citizenship Studies* 6, no. 1:77–93.

———. 2002b. Civic engagement in Argentina: From the human rights movement to the cacerolazos. Manuscript. Buenos Aires.

———. Forthcoming. Media scandals and social accountability: Assessing the role of the Senate scandal in Argentina. In *Enforcing the rule of law*, ed. Enrique Peruzzotti and Catalina Smulovitz.

Peruzzotti, Enrique, and Catalina Smulovitz. 2002. Accountability social: La otra cara del control. In *Controlando la política. Ciudadanos y medios en las nuevas democracias latinoamericanas*, ed. Enrique Peruzzotti and Catalina Smulovitz. Buenos Aires: Editorial Temas.

Pierson, Paul. 2000a. The limits of institutional design: Explaining institutional origins and change. *Governance* 13, no. 4 (October): 475–99.

———. 2000b. Increasing returns, path dependence, and the study of politics. *American Political Science Review* 94, no. 2:251–67.

———. 2004. *Politics in time: History, institutions, and social analysis.* Princeton: Princeton University Press.

Piffano, Horacio. 1998. La asignación de potestades fiscales en el federalismo argentino. Document no. 4. Buenos Aires: Center of Studies for Institutional Development (CEDI).

Pion-Berlin, David. 1997. *Through corridors of power: Institutions and civic-military relations in Argentina.* University Park: Pennsylvania State University Press.

Pírez, Pedro. 1986. *Coparticipación federal y descentralización del estado.* Buenos Aires: Centro Editor de América Latina.

Pitkin, Hanna Fenichel. 1972. *The concept of representation.* Berkeley and Los Angeles: University of California Press.

Poder Ciudadano. 1997. *Quien es quien en el poder judicial.* Buenos Aires: Perfil Libros.

Poole, Keith T., and Howard Rosenthal. 1997. *Congress: A political-economic history of roll call voting.* New York: Oxford University Press.

———. 2001. D-nominate after 10 years: A comparative update to Congress: A political-economic history of roll-call voting. *Legislative Studies Quarterly* 26:5–29.

Porto, Alberto. 1990. *Federalismo fiscal: El caso argentino.* Buenos Aires: Editorial Tesis.

Pozzi, Pablo. 2000. Popular upheaval and capitalist transformation in Argentina. *Latin American Perspectives* 27, no. 114:63–87.

Przeworski, Adam. 1991. *Democracy and the market: Political and economic reforms in Eastern Europe and Latin America.* New York: Cambridge University Press.

Przeworski, Adam, and Fernando Limongi. 1997. Modernization: Theories and facts. *World Politics* 49 (January): 155–83.

Randall, Laura. 1978. *An economic history of Argentina in the 20th century.* New York: Columbia University Press.

Ranis, Peter. 1992. *Argentine workers: Peronism and contemporary class consciousness.* Pittsburgh: University of Pittsburgh Press.

Rauch, James E., and Peter B. Evans. 1999. Bureaucratic structure and bureaucratic performance in less developed countries. Discussion Paper no. 99–06. Department of Economics, University of California at San Diego.

Remmer, Karen, and Eric Wibbels. 2000. The subnational politics of economic adjustment: Provincial politics and fiscal performance in Argentina. *Comparative Political Studies* 33, no 4:419–51.

República Argentina. Various dates. *Diario de sesiones de la Cámara de Diputados de la Nación.*

Roberts, Kenneth. 1995. Neoliberalism and the transformation of populism in Latin America. *World Politics* 48, no. 1:82–116.

———. 1998. *Deepening democracy? The modern left and social movements in Chile and Peru.* Stanford: Stanford University Press.

———. 2002. Social inequalities without class inequalities in Latin America's neoliberal era. *Studies in Comparative International Development* 36, no. 4 (winter): 3–33.

Rock, David. 1975. *Politics in Argentina, 1890–1930: The rise and fall of radicalism.* Cambridge: Cambridge University Press.

Rodden, Jonathan, and Erik Wibbels. 2002. Beyond the fiction of federalism: Macroeconomic management in multitiered systems. *World Politics* 54, no. 4 (July): 494–531.

Rogers, William D., and Paolo Wright-Carozza. 1995. *La Corte Suprema de Justicia y la seguridad jurídica.* Buenos Aires: Editorial Abaco de Rodolfo Depalma.

Rohde, David W. 1991. *Parties and leaders in the postreform House.* Chicago: University of Chicago Press.

Rose-Ackerman, Susan. 2001. Trust, honesty and corruption: Reflection on the state-building process. *European Journal of Sociology* 42:27–71.

Rudé, George. 1964. *The crowd in history.* New York: John Wiley & Sons.

Ruíz Moreno, Isidoro J., ed. 1980. *La federalización de Buenos Aires: Debates y documentos.* Buenos Aires: Emecé Editores.

Saiegh, Sebastian, and Mariano Tommasi. 1998. Argentina's fiscal federal institutions: A case-study in the transaction-cost theory of politics. Paper prepared for the Conference "Modernization and Institutional Development in Argentina," United Nations Development Programme, Buenos Aires, May.

———. 1999a. Why is Argentina's fiscal federalism so inefficient? Entering the labyrinth. *Journal of Applied Economics* 2, no. 1:169–209.

———. 1999b. The Argentine federal tax-sharing arrangement as a case study in the transaction cost theory of politics. Working Paper. Centro de Estudios para el Desarrollo Institucional (CEDI), Universidad de San Andrés, Buenos Aires.

———. 1999c. Why is Argentina's fiscal federalism so inefficient? Working Paper. Centro de Estudios para el Desarrollo Institucional (CEDI), Universidad de San Andrés, Buenos Aires.

Samuels, David, and Richard Snyder. 2001. The value of a vote: Malapportionment in comparative perspective. *British Journal of Political Science* 31, no. 4:651–72.

———. 2003. *Ambition, federalism, and legislative politics in Brazil.* New York: Cambridge University Press.

Sanchez, Pilar. 1997. *El Cutralcazo. La pueblada de Cutral Co y Plaza Huincul.* Buenos Aires: Cuadernos de Editorial Agora.

Sawers, Larry. 1996. *The other Argentina: The interior and national development.* Boulder, Colo.: Westview Press.

Schamis, Hector. 2001. *Re-forming the state: The politics of privatization in Chile and Britain.* Ann Arbor: University of Michigan Press.

Schedler, Andreas. 1995. Under- and overinstitutionalization: Some ideal-typical propositions concerning new and old party systems. Working Paper no. 213. The Helen Kellogg Institute for International Studies, University of Notre Dame.

Schonfeld, William R. 1981. Oligarchy and leadership stability: The French communist, socialist, and Gaullist parties. *American Journal of Political Science* 25, no. 2 (May): 215–40.

Schuster, Federico, et al. 2002. La trama de la crisis. Modos y formas de protesta social a partir de los Acontecimientos de Diciembre de 2001. *Informes de Coyuntura* 3. Instituto Gino Germani, University of Buenos Aires.

Schvarzer, Jorge. 1998. *Implantación de un modelo económico. La experiencia argentina entre 1975 y el 2000.* Buenos Aires: AZ Editora.

Scott, James. 1976. *The moral economy of the peasant.* New Haven: Yale University Press,

———. 1977. Patronage or exploitation? In *Patrons and clients in Mediterranean societies,* ed. Ernest Gellner and John Waterbury. London: Duckworth.

Scott, James, and Benedict J. Kerkvliet. 1977. How traditional rural patrons lose legitimacy: A theory with special reference to Southeast Asia. In *Friends, followers, and factions: A reader in political clientelism,* ed. Laura Guasti, Carl Landé, James Scott, and Steffen Schmidt. Berkeley and Los Angeles: University of California Press.

Scribano, Adrián. 1999. Argentina "Cortada": Cortes de ruta y visibilidad social en el contexto del ajuste. In *Lucha popular, democracia, neoliberalismo: Protesta popular en América Latina en los años del ajuste,* ed. Margarita López Maya. Caracas: Nueva Sociedad.

Scribano, Adrián, and Federico Schuster. 2001. Protesta social en la Argentina de 2001: Entre la normalidad y la ruptura. OSAL, September.

Segal, Jeffrey A. 1997. Separation-of-powers games in the positive theory of Congress and courts. *American Political Science Review* 91:28–44.

Shefter, Martin. 1994. *Political parties and the state.* Princeton: Princeton University Press, 1994.

Shepsle, Kenneth A. 1986. Institutional equilibrium and equilibrium institutions. In *Political science: The science of politics,* ed. Herbert F. Weisberg. New York: Agathon Press.

———. 1991. Discretion, institution and the problem of government commitment. In *Social theory for a changing society,* ed. Pierre Bourdieu and James Coleman. Boulder, Colo.: Westview Press.

Shleifer, Andrei, and Daniel Treisman. 2000. *Without a map. Political tactics and economic reform in Russia.* Cambridge: MIT Press.

Shugart, Matthew Soberg, and John M. Carey. 1992. *Presidents and assemblies: Constitutional design and electoral dynamics.* New York: Cambridge University Press.

Shugart, Matthew Soberg, and Stephan Haggard. 2001. *Presidents, parliaments, and policy.* New York: Cambridge University Press.

Sidicaro, Ricardo. 2002. *Los tres peronismos.* Buenos Aires: Siglo XXI.

Silva, Eduardo. 1996. *State and capital in Chile.* Boulder, Colo.: Westview Press.

Smith, Peter. 1980. Las elecciones de 1946 y las inferencias ecológicas. In *El voto Peronista. Ensayos de sociología electoral argentina,* ed. M. Mora y Araujo and I. Llorente. Buenos Aires: Editorial Sudamericana.

Smith, William. 1990. Democracy, distributional conflicts and macroeconomic policymaking in Argentina, 1983–1989. *Journal of Inter-American Studies and World Affairs* 32, no. 2 (summer): 1–36.

Smulovitz, Catalina. 1995. Constitución y poder judicial en al nueva democracia Argentina. La experiencia de las instituciones. In *La nueva matriz politica Argentina,* ed. Carlos Acuña. Buenos Aires: Nueva Visión.

———. 1997. Ciudadanos, derecho y política. Buenos Aires. *Agora* 7:159–87.

Smulovitz, Catalina, and Enrique Peruzzotti. 2003. Societal and horizontal controls: Two cases of a fruitful relationship. In *Democratic accountability in Latin America,* ed. Scott Mainwaring and Christopher Welna. Oxford: Oxford University Press.

Snyder, Richard. 2001a. *Politics after neoliberalism: Reregulation in Mexico.* New York: Cambridge University Press.

———. 2001b. Scaling down: The subnational comparative method. *Studies in Comparative International Development* 36, no. 1:93–110.

Spiller, Pablo T., and Rafael Gely. 1990. A rational choice theory of Supreme Court statutory decisions with applications to the *State Farm* and *Grove City* cases. *Journal of Law, Economics, and Organization* 6, no. 2: 263–300.

Spiller, Pablo T., Ernesto Stein, and Mariano Tommasi. 2003. Political institutions, policymaking processes, and policy outcomes. An intertemporal transactions framework. Manuscript. Inter-American Development Bank.

Spiller, Pablo T., and Mariano Tommasi. 2000. Los determinantes institucionales del desarollo Argentino: Una aproximación desde la nueva economia institucional. Working Paper (May). Centro de Estudios para el Desarrollo Institucional (CEDI), Universidad de San Andrés, Buenos Aires.

———. 2003. The institutional foundations of public policy: A transaction approach with application to Argentina. *Journal of Law, Economics and Organization* 19, no. 2 (October): 291–306.

———, eds. Forthcoming. *The institutional foundations of public policy: A transactions theory and an application to Argentina.* New York: Cambridge University Press.

Spiller, Pablo T., and Santiago Urbiztondo. 1994. Political appointees vs. career civil servants: A multiple principals theory of political bureaucracies. *European Journal of Political Economy* 10, no. 3:465–97.

Starr, Pamela. 1997. Government coalitions and the viability of currency boards: Argentina under the Cavallo plan. *Journal of Interamerican Studies and World Affairs* 39, no. 2 (summer): 83–133.

Stokes, Susan C. 2001. *Mandates, markets, and democracy: Neoliberalism by surprise in Latin America.* New York: Cambridge University Press.

Stokes, Susan C., and Luis Medina. Forthcoming. Monopoly and monitoring: An approach to political clientelism. In *Citizen-party linkages in democratic poli-*

tics, ed. Herbert Kistchelt and Steve Wilkinson. Cambridge: Cambridge University Press.

Strom, Kaare. 1990. A behavioral theory of competitive political parties. *American Journal of Political Science* 34, no. 2 (May): 565–98.

Svampa, Maristella, and Sebastian Pereyra. 2003. *Entre la ruta y el barrio. La experiencia de las organizaciones piqueteras*. Buenos Aires: Editorial Biblos.

Sztompka, Piotr. 1999. *Trust. A sociological theory*. Cambridge: Cambridge University Press.

Tarrow, Sidney. 1998. *Power in movement: Social movements and contentious politics*. New York: Cambridge University Press.

Tasso, A. 1999. Sistema patronal, dominación y poder en el noroeste Argentino. Manuscript. Santiago del Estero, Argentina.

Tcach, César. 1990. Una interpretación del peronismo periferico: El partido peronista de Córdoba (1945–1955). Documento CEDES, no. 54. Centro de Estudios del Estado y Sociedad, Buenos Aires.

———. 1991. *Sabattinismo y Peronismo: Partidos políticos en Córdoba, 1943–1955*. Buenos Aires: Editorial Sudamericana.

Tenti, Emilio. 2000. Exclusión social y acción colectiva en la Argentina de hoy. *Punto De Vista* 67:22–28.

Thelen, Kathleen. 1999. Historical institutionalism in comparative perspective. *Annual Review of Political Science* 2:369–404.

Thelen, Kathleen, and Sven Steimo. 1992. Historical institutionalism in comparative politics. In *Structuring politics*, ed. Sven Steimo, Kathleen Thelen, and Frank Longstreth. Cambridge: Cambridge University Press.

Thompson, E. P. 1993. *Customs in common*. New York: The New Press.

Tilly, Charles. 1978. *From mobilization to revolution*. Reading, Mass.: Addison Wesley.

———. 1986. *The contentious French*. Cambridge: Harvard University Press.

———. 2003. *The politics of collective violence*. Cambridge: Harvard University Press.

Tommasi, Mariano. 2002. Fiscal federalism in Argentina and the reforms of the 1990s. Paper prepared for the Center for Research on Economic Development and Policy Reform (Stanford University) project "Federalism in a Global Environment." May.

Tommasi, Mariano, and Pablo Spiller. 2000. *Las fuentes institucionales del desarrollo argentino*. Buenos Aires: Editorial Universidad de Buenos Aires.

Torre, Juan Carlos. 1990. *La vieja guardia sindical y los orígenes del peronismo*. Buenos Aires: Editorial Sudamericana.

———. 1998. *El proceso politico de las reformas económicas en América Latina*. Buenos Aires: Paidós.

Torres, Pablo. 2002. *Votos, chapas y fideos*. Buenos Aires: de la Campana.

Veliz, Claudio. 1980. *The centralist tradition of Latin America*. Princeton: Princeton University Press.

Verbitsky, Horacio. 1993. *Hacer la corte*. Buenos Aires: Editorial Planeta.

———. 1997. *Un mundo sin periodistas: Las tortuosas relaciones de Menem con la ley, la justicia, y la verdad*. Buenos Aires: Planeta.

Viguera, Aníbal. 2000. *La trama política de la apertura económica en la Argentina (1987–1996)*. La Plata: Ediciones al Margen / UNLP.

References

Villalón, Roberta. 2002. Piquetes, cacerolazos y asambleas vecinales: Social protests in Argentina, 1993–2002. Master's thesis, University of Texas at Austin.

Vogel, Steven K. 1996. *Freer markets, more rules.* Ithaca: Cornell University Press.

Waisbord, Silvio. 1995. *El gran desfile. Campañas electorales y medios de comunicación en la Argentina.* Buenos Aires: Editorial Sudamericana.

———. 2002. Interpretando los escándalos. Análisis de su relación con los medios y la ciudadanía en la Argentina contemporánea. In *Controlando la politica. Ciudadanos y medios en las nuevas democracias latinoamericanas,* ed. Enrique Peruzzotti and Catalina Smulovitz. Buenos Aires: Editorial Temas.

Waisman, Carlos. 1987. *Reversal of development in Argentina.* Princeton: Princeton University Press.

Weingast, Barry. 2002. Rational choice institutionalism. In *Political science: The state of the discipline,* ed. Ira Katznelson and Helen Milner. New York: Norton.

Weiss, John. 1999. Trade reform and manufacturing performance in Mexico: From import substitution to dramatic export growth. *Journal of Latin American Studies* 31:151–66.

Weldon, Jeffrey. 1997. Political sources of *presidencialismo* in Mexico. In *Presidentialism and democracy in Latin America,* ed. Scott Mainwaring and Matthew Soberg Shugart. New York: Cambridge University Press.

Weyland, Kurt. 1999. Neoliberal populism in Latin America and Eastern Europe. *Comparative Politics* 31, no. 4:379–401.

———. 2002a. Limitations of rational-choice institutionalism for the study of Latin American politics. *Studies in Comparative International Development* 37, no. 3 (spring): 57–85.

———. 2002b. *The politics of market reform in fragile democracies.* Princeton: Princeton University Press.

———. 2004. Learning from foreign models in Latin America policy reform: An introduction. In *Learning from foreign models in Latin America policy reform,* ed. Kurt Weyland. Baltimore: Johns Hopkins University Press.

Wiarda, Howard. 1973. Toward a framework for the study of political change in the Iberic-Latin tradition: The corporative model. *World Politics* 25, no. 2 (January): 250–78.

Young, Gerardo. 2002. La Trama Política de los Saqueos. *Clarín Digital,* December 19.

Zucker, Lynne G. 1977. The role of institutionalization in cultural persistence. *American Sociological Review* 42 (October): 726–43.

CONTRIBUTORS

Javier Auyero is Associate Professor of Sociology at SUNY at Stony Brook. His main areas of interest are political ethnography, collective action, and urban poverty in Latin America. He is the author of *Poor People's Politics* (Duke University Press, 2001) and *Contentious Lives: Two Argentine Women, Two Protests, and the Quest for Recognition* (Duke University Press, 2003), and currently is editor of *Qualitative Sociology*.

Ernesto Calvo is Assistant Professor of Political Science at the University of Houston. His research interests are in the area of Latin American political economy, party politics, and elections. He coordinated the Programa de Reforma Politica for the Instituto Nacional de Administracion Publica in Argentina (2000–2001). He recently published *La Nueva Politica de Partidos: Crisis Politica, Realineamientos Partidarios y Reforma Electoral* (Prometeo, 2005).

Kent Eaton is Associate Professor of National Security Affairs at the Naval Postgraduate School in Monterey. He is the author of *Politicians and Economic Reform in New Democracies: Argentina and the Philippines in the 1990s* (Penn State University Press, 2002) and *Politics Beyond the Capital: The Design of Subnational Institutions in South America* (Stanford University Press, 2004). His current research focuses on subnational police reform, decentralization in post-conflict settings, and regional separatism in Latin America.

Sebastián Etchemendy is Assistant Professor of Political Science and International Studies at the Torcuato Di Tella University in Buenos Aires. He received his Ph.D. in Political Science from the University of California at Berkeley. His main field is comparative political economy. He has published articles on economic liberalization in Argentina, Spain, and Chile in the journals *Desarrollo Económico*, *Latin American Politics and Society*, *Comparative Politics*, and *Comparative Political Studies*.

Gretchen Helmke is Assistant Professor of political science at the University of Rochester, where she specializes in comparative political institutions with a focus on Latin America. She has published articles in the *American Political Science Review, Comparative Politics, Desarrollo Económico,* and *Perspectives on Politics.* She is the author of *Courts Under Constraints: Judges, Generals, and Presidents in Argentina,* published in 2005 by Cambridge University Press.

Wonjae Hwang is a postdoctoral fellow at the Center for International Studies at University of Missouri at St. Louis. His primary areas of interest include globalization, inequality, and interstate and intrastate conflict. He also has broader interests in international institutions and the empirical evaluation of theoretical models. He recently published an article in the *American Journal of Political Science* and currently is working on a project that examines the internal politics of the United Nations.

Mark P. Jones is Associate Professor in the Department of Political Science at Rice University. His research focuses on the effect of electoral laws and other political institutions on governance, representation, and voting. He has served as a consultant on Argentine politics for the U.S. government and as a consultant/adviser for numerous government institutions and political parties and candidates at the national, provincial, and municipal levels in Argentina.

Steven Levitsky is John L. Loeb Associate Professor of the Social Sciences at Harvard University. His primary areas of research include political parties, informal institutions, and political regimes and regime change in Latin America. He is author of *Transforming Labor-Based Parties in Latin America: Argentine Peronism in Comparative Perspective* (Cambridge University Press, 2003). He is currently working on a book on the emergence and dynamics of competitive authoritarian regimes in Africa, Central Europe, Latin America, and the former Soviet Union.

María Victoria Murillo is Associate Professor of Political Science and International and Public Affairs at Columbia University. Previously she was an Associate Professor at Yale University, a Peggy Rockefeller Fellow at the David Rockefeller Center for Latin American Studies, and a postdoctoral fellow in the Harvard Academy for International and Area Studies, both at Harvard University. She is the author of *Labor Unions, Partisan Coalitions, and Market Reforms in Latin America* (Cambridge University Press, 2001). Currently she is working on the politics of policymaking in Latin America with a particular focus on the privatization and regulation of public utilities.

Enrique Peruzzotti is Associate Professor at the Department of Political Science and International Relations of the Torcuato Di Tella University in Buenos Aires. He has been visiting professor at Cornell University, FLACSO Ecuador, the American University of Paris, and the Universidad Federal de Minas Gerais, and research fellow at the Woodrow Wilson Center, the University of London, Columbia University, and the University of New Mexico. He is the editor (with C. Smulovitz) of *Enforcing the Rule of Law: Social Accountability in Latin America* (University of Pittsburgh Press, forthcoming) and *Controlando la Política:Ciudadanos y Medios en las Nuevas Democracias* (Temas, 2002).

Pablo T. Spiller is the Jeffrey A. Jacobs Distinguished Professor of Business and Technology at the Haas School of Business, University of California, Berkeley, and Research Associate, NBER. He has held academic positions at the University of Pennsylvania, Stanford University, and the University of Illinois, at Urbana-Champaign. He has published several books and more than ninety articles in the general area of political economy and industrial organization. His most recent book, with Mariano Tommasi, *The Institutional Foundations of Public Policy: The Case of Argentina,* is forthcoming from Cambridge University Press. He is the co-editor of the *Journal of Law, Economics and Organization* and associate editor of the *Journal of Applied Economics, The Regulation Magazine,* and *The Utilities Project.* He has been a Special Adviser to the Federal Trade Commission's Bureau of Economics, and was also an elected Member of the Board of Directors of the American Law and Economics Association.

Mariano Tommasi is Professor and Chairman of the Department of Economics at Universidad de San Andres, Director of the Center of Studies for Institutional Development, Argentina, and President of the Latin American and Caribbean Economic Association. While writing the chapter for this book, he was Visiting Professor at Yale University. He specializes in institutional economics, politics, and public policy. He is finishing a book on Argentine political institutions and public policies to be published by Cambridge University Press.

Juan Carlos Torre received his Ph.D from the Ecole Des Hautes Etudes en Sciences Sociales (Paris). He is currently professor at the Universidad T. Di Tella and editor of *Desarrollo Económico,* a social science journal published in Buenos Aires. He has been visiting professor in the United Kingdom, Brazil, and Spain, visiting scholar at the Institute for Advanced Studies (Princeton), and a Guggenheim Fellow. He has published several books and articles on Argentine social history, in particular, on Peronism and trade unions. He has also written on democratic transitions and the political economy of economic reform in Latin America.